Cultural Heritage Tourism

ABOUT THE SERIES
The American Association for State and Local History Book Series addresses issues critical to the field of state and local history through interpretive, intellectual, scholarly, and educational texts. To submit a proposal or manuscript to the series, please request proposal guidelines from AASLH headquarters: AASLH Editorial Board, 2021 21st Ave. South, Suite 320, Nashville, TN 37212. Telephone: (615) 320-3203. Website: www.aaslh.org.

ABOUT THE ORGANIZATION
The American Association for State and Local History (AASLH) is a national history membership association headquartered in Nashville, Tennessee. AASLH provides leadership and support for its members who preserve and interpret state and local history in order to make the past more meaningful to all Americans. AASLH members are leaders in preserving, researching, and interpreting traces of the American past to connect the people, thoughts, and events of yesterday with the creative memories and abiding concerns of people, communities, and our nation today. In addition to sponsorship of this book series, AASLH publishes *History News* magazine, a newsletter, technical leaflets and reports, and other materials; confers prizes and awards in recognition of outstanding achievement in the field; supports a broad education program and other activities designed to help members work more effectively; and advocates on behalf of the discipline of history. To join AASLH, go to www.aaslh.org or contact Membership Services, AASLH, 2021 21st Ave. South, Suite 320, Nashville, TN 37212.

Cultural Heritage Tourism

Five Steps for Success and Sustainability

Cheryl M. Hargrove

ROWMAN & LITTLEFIELD
Lanham • Boulder • New York • London

Published by Rowman & Littlefield
A wholly owned subsidiary of The Rowman & Littlefield Publishing Group, Inc.
4501 Forbes Boulevard, Suite 200, Lanham, Maryland 20706
www.rowman.com

Unit A, Whitacre Mews, 26-34 Stannary Street, London SE11 4AB

British Library Cataloguing in Publication Information Available

Library of Congress Cataloging-in-Publication Data

Names: Hargrove, Cheryl M., author.
Title: Cultural heritage tourism : Five steps for success and sustainability
   growth / Cheryl Hargrove.
Description: Lanham : Rowman & Littlefield, 2017. | Series: American
   Association for State and Local History book series | Includes
   bibliographical references and index.
Identifiers: LCCN 2016055442 (print) | LCCN 2016056734 (ebook) | ISBN
   9781442278820 (cloth) | ISBN 9781442278837 (pbk.) | ISBN 9781442278844
   (ebook)
Subjects: LCSH: Heritage tourism.
Classification: LCC G156.5.H47 H366 2017 (print) | LCC G156.5.H47 (ebook) |
   DDC 910.68/4—dc23
LC record available at https://lccn.loc.gov/2016055442

♾™ The paper used in this publication meets the minimum requirements of American National Standard for Information Sciences—Permanence of Paper for Printed Library Materials, ANSI/NISO Z39.48-1992.

Printed in the United States of America

To John and Liz, for their unwavering support.

Contents

List of Illustrations

List of Illustrations

List of Tables

Foreword

From the very beginning of our travel business in 1915, American Express has helped our customers experience the great cultural heritage destinations of the world. From the fortifications of Gibraltar to the historic treasures of the Acropolis, we've always known the importance of cultural heritage in capturing the imagination of travelers and fulfilling their greatest wanderlust. We've also seen firsthand how the promotion of cultural heritage tourism can strengthen the economies of destinations and support small businesses.

Cultural Heritage Tourism: Five Steps for Success and Sustainability is a must-read for any intrepid leader interested in leveraging local cultural heritage resources to drive tourism. Cheryl Hargrove has written the definitive guide for communities that want to preserve and share their cultural heritage with the world while managing them responsibly for future generations. Through her step-by-step methodology, she clearly defines the travel segment and provides strategies to engage stakeholders and develop authentic travel experiences as well as ideas for marketing cultural heritage resources and ensuring their sustainability.

This work is near and dear to me and American Express. For more than forty years, we have supported preservation projects both in the United States and internationally, assisted local communities in developing their tourism potential, and invested in public education campaigns that generate support for preservation. Initiatives like this do double duty: demonstrating our desire to support the communities in which we live and work as well as the places our customers love and to strengthen the travel industry overall.

The time is ripe for communities to leverage guidebooks like Cheryl's to preserve their local heritage and plant the seeds for future travel. Americans are thinking local more than ever before. Trends like the local food movement and events that American Express champions, such as like Small Business Saturday and the recent National Park Service Centennial, have placed a spotlight on the importance of citizens supporting their communities as well as the beauty, diversity, and richness of the nation's cultural and environmental resources. It's clear that communities have a unique opportunity right now to take advantage of the cultural resources within their environs and leverage them for local economic development.

I'm delighted that Cheryl has penned this action plan to assist communities in developing their destination's full tourism potential. We at American Express hope this pivotal book will be a catalyst for the creation of many new cultural heritage journeys for generations of citizens and international tourists to enjoy for years to come.

Timothy J. McClimon, President
American Express Foundation

Preface

Today's savvy traveler desires authentic experiences, and demands exceptional service. That's the premise—and sometimes the challenge—for cultural heritage tourism, one of the industry's fastest-growing segments. Its appeal and sustainability resides in authenticity and quality, cultural sensitivity, and valued experiences that set one place apart from all others. *Cultural Heritage Tourism: Five Steps for Success and Sustainability* details a comprehensive process for utilizing cultural heritage resources to create high-quality, respected visitor experiences with maximum local impact.

Based on proven steps created more than twenty-five years ago, I've expanded the cultural heritage tourism process to help organizations and agencies better plan for visitation, make smarter choices for reusing historic sites, sensitively interpret cultural resources, and ensure greater benefits for both residents and resources. Since serving as director of the first national heritage tourism program in the United States, I've worked with and researched destinations large and small to develop, market, and manage their tourism, focusing on local culture and heritage. My work with individual sites and institutions, along with input from more than a dozen industry experts, confirms that a holistic approach to cultural heritage tourism yields the best results. Whereas other books may provide a theoretical approach to cultural heritage tourism, this book offers practical instruction for a comprehensive process—from inception to delivery management—based on three decades of application and lessons learned.

Like all forms of economic development, cultural heritage tourism requires planning, prioritization, investment, and responsible management. This book details a step-by-step process to identify, assess, organize, fund, develop, market, manage, and measure cultural heritage tourism for an individual site, a small community, a region, or a metropolitan city. Other factors, such as infrastructure and tourism services—necessary to maximize the potential and sustainability of this industry sector—are widely discussed for a holistic approach to cultural heritage tourism as part of an economic or community development strategy for any size of destination.

Written for the layperson, without industry jargon or terminology to defeat or deflect from using the content provided, *Cultural Heritage Tourism: Five Steps for Success and Sustainability* offers insights into how to engage the necessary stakeholders and move projects forward. Planners, preservationists, cultural resource managers, tourism industry leaders, community activists, and public officials will find chapters filled with practical tips, sample forms, reference lists, and trending information. Lessons learned from other industry experts are integrated into this book to explain various cultural heritage tourism components—from inception to evaluation. Case studies from around the country, representing both large and small museums, historic sites, cultural districts, government agencies, and nonprofit institutions, provide relevant examples for review and consideration. Whether pondering the best use for a historic site, enhancing existing cultural and heritage tourism products, adding new events or venues to the cultural heritage mix, seeking to better manage current visitation, or identifying new markets for your cultural heritage experiences, this book will help you achieve the desired results.

Each chapter begins with a clear overview of the topic, often with background and context for orientation, followed by detailed explanation and instruction for application. Organized into five sections, the chapters group related content to help readers delve into applicable instruction with supporting materials and reference documents to further explain the intricacies described. Starting with an overview of cultural heritage tourism as a sustainable economic development strategy, chapter 1 and section I (chapters 2 to 4) present a global perspective on the industry segment and offer insights into visitor needs and expectations. This section defines what cultural heritage tourism is, profiles the cultural heritage traveler, discusses how this segment is different from other forms of tourism or economic development, and identifies important trends to watch. In this section, you also learn how to identify local culture and heritage, understand visitor needs and expectations, and determine visitor readiness. This foundational section explains how to accurately assess competitiveness, capitalize on opportunities, and minimize challenges, which may potentially impact success in cultural heritage tourism.

Section II defines specific strategies to engage community, arts, tourism, public, and preservation stakeholders in establishing a vision for sustainability. Chapters 5 to 7 outline the steps for building consensus and a framework for oversight. The opportunity for collaboration is great, and successful programs require partnerships among culture and heritage institutions as well as tourism marketing organizations, private businesses, and government agencies plus input from visitors. Even an individual project requires collaboration and aspirational goals, and this section defines the benchmarks for success. Whether focusing on education or economics, articulating specific metrics is important to measuring the impact of cultural heritage tourism. Setting policies to preserve and protect historic and cultural integrity, defining strategies to fund or direct development, and establishing systems to stay on track are just some of the planning components addressed in this section.

Section III converts planning to action, with chapters 8 to 10 providing particular instruction on developing inspiring and authentic cultural heritage attractions, investigating and telling your story, and funding your project. This section's content shares specific ways to create the desired activities, products, and services valued by visitors and residents, showcasing local history and culture. While some sites may see lagging visitation, this section helps define strategies to jump-start tired museums and infuse life—through new and time-tested interpretive techniques—to attract today's savvy cultural heritage traveler. Some of our cultural heritage requires sensitive and respectful presentation to ensure that all voices are heard. Beyond the individual site or event, the broader needs of visitors and the necessary infrastructure (parking, restrooms, and signage) required to host visitors are also addressed in this section. To realize the maximum economic impact from cultural heritage tourism, visitors must first find their site or destination and then engage in the authentic experience and locate additional places (lodging, dining, shopping, and touring) to spend money.

Marketing cultural heritage tourism requires research-based planning, effective engagement, and targeted promotions. Section IV describes how to market for positive impact. Technology plays a huge role in marketing products and places, and identifying the most successful strategies is a key instruction in this section. Chapter 11 focuses on marketing plan development, various marketing strategies, and articulating how to promote your cultural heritage tourism brand promise to visitors. This chapter also explains specific techniques for engaging residents and community leaders as local ambassadors for cultural heritage tourism.

Managing for sustainability is the ultimate goal of a successful cultural heritage tourism program. Section V, starting with chapter 12, defines strategies to maintain consistency and quality. The importance of delivering a positive brand promise is paramount, as is hosting visitors in a professional and courteous manner, as discussed in chapter 13. Affirming the role of cultural heritage and tourism managers relative to growing and managing cultural heritage tourism is also deliberated on. Chapter 14 explores how to conduct appropriate research to measure the impact of cultural heritage tourism. Recognizing that this process never ends, defining your role in cultural heritage tourism management and building collaborations for success (see chapter 15) is a key outcome of this section.

This book includes a comprehensive glossary of terms to help break down barriers to communication and also provides a list of references and resources to aid in the development, implementation, funding, marketing, and management of cultural heritage tourism. These additional sources of information provide a directory for continuous use at any phase of cultural heritage tourism.

Cultural Heritage Tourism: Five Steps for Success and Sustainability is designed to help elected officials, institutions, and industry leaders recognize the value of their cultural heritage. Cultural heritage tourism, when implemented as a principled process, not only produces a positive economic impact from visitor spending but also gives new life to old buildings and local traditions. Cultural heritage tourism protects and demonstrates a distinctive "sense of place" as something to cherish. Our history and culture set us apart from all other countries, tell our stories of hardship and resilience, showcase the people and places unique to each state and tribal nation, and help convey what is important—to current and future generations. My hope is that, after reading this book, you find new yet practical and sustainable ways to share your history and culture with visitors and residents. By following the tenets of this book, we can commemorate our cultural heritage at these special sites and share it with others.

Acknowledgments

Beyond all the arts and cultural practitioners, preservationists, historians, and tourism professionals who answered my calls, provided information, and offered insights for this book, a special team provided exhaustive hours of counsel and guidance. Thank you Becky Anderson, Julie Heizer, and Kate Miller for helping me throughout this journey.

Special appreciation goes to all the outstanding organizations and destinations cultivating exceptional cultural heritage tourism experiences across the United States. Some are profiled in this book. Your efforts are an inspiration to us all, and it is my privilege to tell your stories in this book.

Credit must be given to the National Endowment for the Arts for funding the first initiative to look at the relationship between preservation and tourism and the National Trust for Historic Preservation for leading the effort to formalize the heritage tourism movement in the United States. Many individuals and institutions laid the foundation for the industry segment as it is known today, and I was fortunate to work with exceptional thought leaders including Amy Webb, Carolyn Brackett, Barb Pahl, Peter Brink, and other professionals who acknowledged the value of sharing our history with visitors. Partners in Tourism, comprised of leaders in federal agencies and nongovernmental organizations, have also been instrumental in keeping cultural heritage tourism at the forefront of policy and programming. Thanks to Tony Tighe, Kimber Craine, Ron Anzalone, Carol Shull, Randy Cohen, and other Washington-based partners; your tireless dedication of time and resources over the past thirty years has helped sustain cultural heritage tourism efforts around the country.

Cultural heritage tourism continues to gain recognition and momentum in part due to researchers including Davidson-Peterson Associates, Mandala Research LLC, the U.S. Department of Commerce, Young Strategies, and PlaceEconomics, whose reports substantiate the impact of cultural heritage tourism to communities worldwide. While consistent and timely research is a continuing deficiency for our industry segment, appreciation is extended to all the states, cities, and individual organizations exploring the impact of cultural heritage tourism today.

I particularly want to recognize the American Association for State and Local History for the opportunity to write this book and for valuing cultural heritage tourism as an important economic development strategy for many museums, historic sites, festivals, communities, cities, states, tribes, and regions. Working together, we can continue to preserve, protect, and promote our authentic assets for the enjoyment and appreciation of local residents, current travelers, and future generations of visitors.

Chapter 1

Cultural Heritage Tourism

An Authentic Place-Based Approach to Economic Development

Tourism does not go to a city that has lost its soul.

—Arthur Frommer

The soul of a city, county, town, region, or state is often visually defined by its architecture, its landscapes, and its unique businesses and interesting attractions. A destination's soul is also found in its people and the traditions, food, music, dance, language, and other art forms that, when combined, provide a vibrancy and personality to distinguish one place from all others. History also defines the soul of a place; how a destination shares its stories of the past impacts its relevance to the present and the education of both residents and visitors. Cultural heritage tourism is defined as "traveling to experience the places, artifacts and activities that authentically represent the stories and people of the past and present. It includes cultural, historic, and natural resources."[1] The chapter-opening quote by tourism guru Arthur Frommer defines the opportunity—and challenge—for cultural heritage tourism in America.

Understanding what makes cultural heritage tourism distinct in the travel and tourism industry, describing why and how it may be a viable economic development strategy for some destinations, and defining the important foundation required for sustainable cultural heritage tourism are three areas for exploration and discussion in this chapter.

Several consumer and industry trends impact cultural heritage tourism's development and sustainability. As tourism grows and new markets begin to travel, cultural heritage tourism faces additional challenges that need to be addressed. These issues require thoughtful consideration before launching into cultural heritage tourism planning, development, and marketing.

Historical Context

People have traveled to experience different cultures and visit historic sites for centuries since before the grand tours of Europe. In the United States, some places, such as Boston, Charleston, Philadelphia, San Francisco, and Santa Fe, have attracted travelers for decades due to their distinctive architecture, historical events, arts, and unique landscapes. During the WPA era, the writers project provided jobs for historians. Early activities, such as saving Mount Vernon, Charleston, and New Orleans; enacting historic preservation ordances, and the start of historic house tours (at historic places like Natchez), launched a relationship between historic preservation and tourism. Despite this interest in visiting historic cities, the formalized cultural heritage tourism movement in the United States is relatively new. Several milestones established the foundation for the current cultural heritage tourism industry as we know it today:[2]

- The Alabama Bureau of Tourism and Travel recognized the importance of cultural heritage in 1983 by publishing and marketing one of the first guides to African American historic sites, *Alabama's Black Heritage Guide*.
- The success of the National Trust for Historic Preservation's Main Street program—where commercial revitalization of historic downtowns began attracting visitors as well as residents—led this national organization to work with the National Endowment for the Arts to formally explore the relationship between preservation and tourism in the mid-1980s.
- In 1988, the San Francisco Convention and Visitors Bureau hired its first cultural tourism director.
- At the White House Conference on Travel and Tourism in 1995, keynote presenter and author, storyteller, humorist, and radio personality Garrison Keillor (former host of *Prairie Home Companion*) famously stated, "All tourism is cultural tourism," thus providing a national platform to address issues and opportunities related to cultural heritage tourism.
- "Cows on Parade" debuted in Chicago in 1999, influenced by a similar exhibition in Zürich in 1986. The traveling exhibition went to more than fifty countries and spurred other cities and towns to consider creation of their own sculptural icons to display and auction.[3]
- In 2005, twenty-nine federal agencies and national organizations (Partners in Tourism) gathered with delegates from all states and territories for a Cultural and Heritage Tourism Summit to continue a national dialogue around issues and opportunities related to cultural heritage tourism.[4]
- A CHT Exchange brought practitioners together with representatives from federal agencies and national organizations in Washington, D.C., in 2011, 2012, and 2014 to discuss issues impacting the advancement of cultural heritage tourism.

In the past three decades, destinations of all sizes and geographic locations have in some way focused on or marketed their history and culture for visitors. The advent of National Scenic Byways and All American Roads[5] (established by the U.S. Congress in 1991), National Heritage Areas, cultural districts, heritage trails, and creative placemaking (as a design strategy) further contribute to the growth in cultural heritage tourism products and experiences available to travelers today. Placekeeping has risen as a strategy to retain cultural identity, especially in ethnic neighborhoods, to counter gentrification.

Why? In part due to homogenization. As developers of strip malls and national chains populated roadsides and thoroughfares, many of America's landscapes took on a visual "sameness" where every gateway looked the same. Seeking distinction to set one destination apart from all others, American cities and communities embraced the concept of cultural heritage tourism to showcase their unique assets and activities. Some neighborhoods need strategies for spatial justice; placekeeping retains culture and memory by respecting artistic expression and community identity—keeping local places "local."[6] Other communities and cities focus on cultural heritage tourism management to offset often negative impacts of tourism: trash and traffic.

Another reason, besides preservation, is economics. The earliest primary research conducted for the National Trust for Historic Preservation revealed that visitors to historic sites stay longer and spend more than other types of travelers. This profile of a cultural heritage traveler has been consistent for the past thirty years. New generations of travelers are being added to the market profile to further expand the size and scope of cultural heritage tourism.

Defining Cultural Heritage Tourism

There is no single definition for cultural heritage tourism in the United States. In fact, the national tourism industry did not record visits to historic sites or engagement in cultural activities until the early 1990s. The National Trust for Historic Preservation, a leading pioneer in the recognition and formalization of this industry segment, created one of the first definitions for heritage tourism. After several research studies, the National Trust expanded its heritage tourism definition to include cultural resources, in part due to the similar demographic and behavioral profile of travelers visiting both cultural and heritage activities.

> The National Trust formalized its cultural heritage tourism definition as follows:
>
> Cultural heritage tourism is traveling to experience the places, artifacts and activities that authentically represent the stories and people of the past and present. It includes cultural, historic, and natural resources.
> —National Trust for Historic Preservation (2015) http://www.preservationnation.org

Another national association, Americans for the Arts, involved in developing and marketing cultural heritage tourism states, "Cultural tourism is based on the mosaic of places, traditions, art forms, celebrations, and experiences that define this nation and its people, reflecting the diversity and character of the United States."[7]

Cultural heritage tourism utilizes existing assets—the built environment, natural landscapes, and cultural resources—delivered as experiences to tell the stories of the people who settled, live, work, and play there, past to present. The past affords an opportunity to convey the relevance of historical events to present-day issues and experiences. The unique architecture, landscapes, cuisine, traditions, celebrations, craft, and/or performing arts (dance, music, and drama) set the stage for these stories to be interpreted in distinctive programs, festivals, and tours. UNESCO (the UN Educational, Scientific, and Cultural Organization) includes the following categories of cultural heritage:

- Cultural heritage:
  - Tangible cultural heritage, including movable cultural heritage (paintings, sculptures, coins, and manuscripts), immovable cultural heritage (monuments, archaeological sites, and historic sites), and underwater cultural heritage (shipwrecks and underwater ruins and cities)
  - Intangible cultural heritage (oral traditions, performing arts, rituals, and language)
- Natural heritage: natural sites with cultural aspects, such as cultural landscapes and physical, biological, or geological formations
- Heritage in the event of armed conflict: protection of cultural property during time of war, as defined by the 1954 Hague Convention, where damage (looting, theft, or destruction) to the cultural property of any people means "damage to the cultural heritage of all mankind."[8]

There are numerous subsets of cultural heritage tourism and other niche segments that complement cultural heritage tourism. These subsets and niche segments have evolved in recent years as the result of detailed research on visitor profiles, interests, and activity engagement. Subsets of cultural heritage tourism worthy of consideration include the following:

- African American heritage tourism
- Agritourism
- Culinary tourism
- Ecotourism
- Film tourism
- Geotourism
- Historic tourism
- Indigenous tourism
- Military tourism
- Music tourism
- Nature-based tourism

Responsible tourism and sustainable tourism are two recent categories designed to counter global approaches and impacts of mass-market tourism. Both of these categories embrace the principles and tenets of cultural heritage tourism, with particular emphasis on asset-based economic development, resource stewardship, and balance of internal–external benefits. Descriptions of these niche markets and complementary tourism approaches are included for reference at the end of this chapter.

Research indicates cultural heritage travelers enjoy and engage in other types of activities, demonstrating the importance of "place" to destination branding. Looking holistically at a destination and defining its overall vision for growth and sustainability are the initial steps in determining whether cultural heritage tourism is a good fit for the community, county, city, or state. Utilizing all of these subsets or emphasizing a particular category of cultural heritage allows destinations to customize experiences for specific audiences and focus on the most sustainable strategies for development, funding, and marketing. (Creating an inventory of assets as a foundation for cultural heritage tourism is explored in chapter 2.)

Understanding the Tourism Industry

Before answering more specific questions about cultural heritage tourism, an understanding of the tourism industry and its role in economic development is essential. Whereas traditional manufacturing and industry are often the most valued forms of economic development for a community or city, tourism may be a great complement to a diversified economic development strategy. In some instances, the travel and tourism industry becomes the major generator of jobs and revenue growth when other forms of economic development are absent, not appropriate, or not available—because of either geographic location, population, workforce, or infrastructure (transportation and public services).

The UN World Tourism Organization defines the world tourism industry as "the cluster of production units in different industries that provide consumption goods and services demanded by visitors."[9] Tourism Satellite Accounts track this consumption to derive industry size and usage. Eight industry sectors serve as the foundation for the travel and tourism industry today:

1. Attractions: manufactured, historical, cultural, and natural
2. Events and conferences: conventions, fairs, festivals, exhibitions, and meetings

3. Adventure and recreation: fishing, marine, hunting, golf, tennis, and sports facilities; ski re-sorts; recreational parks; and casinos
4. Transportation: air, rail, cruise, car rental, recreational vehicles, and taxis
5. Travel trade: travel planners, tour operators, travel agencies, and meeting planners
6. Accommodation: hotels, motels, bed-and-breakfasts, lodges, campgrounds, and time-shares
7. Food and beverage: restaurants, fast food, pubs and lounges, and caterers
8. Tourism services: destination marketing organizations, government tourism offices, travel media, automobile clubs, travel insurance, and tour guides

The size of the global tourism industry has heralded it as an important economic development strategy, according to the UN World Tourism Organization:

- Global tourist arrivals reached a record 1.184 billion in 2015. This milestone also represents an increase of 52 million travelers over the previous year. This is the sixth consecutive year of growth since 2009.[10]
- North America experienced 6 percent growth in international arrivals from 2014 to 2015.
- In 2015, international tourism receipts grew 4.4 percent, with total earnings in the destinations estimated at US$1.26 trillion worldwide in 2015.
- The industry accounts for one in every eleven jobs[11] and represents 7 percent of the world's services exports, exceeding the jobs impact of automotive manufacturing, chemical manufacturing, and mining and slightly less than education, communications, and financial services.
- The one-billionth tourist was recorded on December 13, 2012, in Madrid, Spain.[12]

In the United States, travel and tourism is the single largest services export industry, accounting for 31 percent of all U.S. services exports. The industry generates a travel trade surplus of $61 billion. International visitors who stay one or more nights in the United States reached a record 77.5 million in 2015, up 3 percent from total visitors in 2014. International visitors to the United States support 1.1 million total U.S. jobs—or one new job for every sixty-eight international visitors to the United States. The top inbound markets in 2015 (in order of volume) include Canada, Mexico, the United Kingdom, Japan, and the People's Republic of China. The trajectory for future growth is positive; by 2020, 96.4 million visitors are projected to travel to the United States—an increase of 29 percent over 2014.[13]

There are a number of definitions and planning aspects unique to the travel and tourism industry. The first and most important is the definition of a "tourist" versus a "visitor." While many destinations and organizations may use these terms interchangeably, there is a difference between these two types of travelers. Typically, a tourist stays overnight, while a visitor does not. However, negative connotations about the word "tourist" lead many destinations to use the word "visitor" for all out-of-town guests engaging in local (cultural heritage) activities, whether they stay overnight or not.

Some tourism organizations further define the tourist or visitor based on the distance one travels from home, usually either fifty or one hundred miles. These factors are important considerations when planning and developing tourism to understand the target markets as well as their potential economic impact on a destination. Optimally, if lodging is available, destinations seek to attract tourists to increase the spending impact from overnight stays. An overnight often cultivates additional revenue generation from dining, shopping, and entertainment—in addition to payment of taxes (state and local) as well as specific assessments (such as lodging taxes and user fees). Day visitors, in turn, must be encouraged to spend money locally—at attractions, retail shops, gas stations, and restaurants—to ensure that these visitors are contributing to the desired economic impact. If these day visitors arrive and utilize resources without purchasing items locally, they may end up ultimately "costing" the destination in terms of infrastructure maintenance, added public safety requirements, and other potentially negative impacts ("trash and traffic"). Tourism planning and management can alleviate—or at least anticipate and identify a solution for—these impacts. Including tourism in the overall comprehensive planning process can be a proactive approach to maximizing opportunity and minimizing risk for destinations large and small.

The motivation of the tourist or visitor is another outcome for evaluation. Whether a tourist is traveling for business, for a convention or meeting, for leisure (vacation), or to visit friends and relatives, these factors can impact what type of activities are engaged in and determine the economic impact for the destination. (Other important definitions and acronyms are included in the glossary at the end of this book.)

Understanding Cultural and Historic Preservation

Preservation and protection of cultural and historic resources includes not only the physical upkeep of buildings and structures but also establishing an ethic of stewardship. Cultivating appreciation and respect for heritage and culture starts with local leaders and residents, then spills over to visitors. Without this local pride of place, the historical fabric of a community may be lost if it is not valued. Sound preservation policies and practices are essential to ensure that the foundation of the past is available for the appreciation of future generations. Local stakeholders must adopt a stewardship philosophy to safeguard and sustain the present resources to ensure that they are appropriately cared for and available to current and future visitors.

Cultural Heritage Tourism: Focus on the Unique

Most tourists don't set out on their visit to a place and say, "Today I am going to be a cultural heritage tourist." Instead, they more likely ask what is interesting and distinctive to explore—the historic, cultural, and natural attractions unique to a destination. For planners and developers, though, understanding how this industry segment is different from mass-market tourism is significant to ensuring appropriate stewardship of resources and compatible land use to attract the tourist who will stay longer and spend more because of cultural heritage assets. While man-made attractions and resorts are important industry and economic generators, destinations utilizing their own local distinctive (built, cultural, and natural) assets gain a competitive edge as the combined collection of authentic products cannot be mass-produced or replicated in other locations. Tourists, therefore, must journey to this site or destination for a firsthand authentic experience. Cultural heritage tourism can also foster additional quality-of-life benefits for residents through the subsequent generation of new programs, activities, and attractions.

Cultural Heritage Tourism: A Viable Economic Development Strategy

Existing physical assets—historic buildings and landscapes—often provide the foundation for adaptive development and are the basis for telling the distinctive story of a place. Reusing these assets for economic development can be more cost effective than constructing new buildings and also more environmentally sensitive to preserve the original footprint of a revitalized downtown or neighborhood. Preservation of historic sites is the ultimate recycling strategy.

History is a catalyst for many things, including economic growth. Visitors and potential residents alike are drawn to places that have preserved a strong sense of historical identity. It really is historical character that makes a community unique. Cultural heritage tourism can be a growth strategy for a local economy, where authentic experiences enhance destination appeal, attract visitors, and increase spending in local businesses.
—John Dichtl, president and CEO, American Association for State and Local History

Perhaps one of the most desired reasons that cultural heritage tourism is utilized as an economic development strategy is the profile of visitors motivated by or interested in engaging in cultural heritage attractions and activities. An April 2016 report by PlaceEconomics for the New York Heritage Conservancy states, "Heritage visitors to New York City account for 31.2% of day visitors and 39.7% of overnight visitors. Direct spending from domestic heritage visitors spend more than $8 billion" in the Big Apple each year, and heritage tourism jobs result in nearly $738 million in local tax revenue for New York City.[14] Another 2015 report conducted by PlaceEconomics shows an even greater impact from heritage tourism in San Antonio, Texas. The share of heritage visitors is 58.1 percent for overnight visitors and 47.3 percent for day visitors; perhaps a more important discovery is that "the per visit expenditures of heritage visitors was greater than other tourists in all five of the primary tourist expenditure sectors—lodging, transportation, food and beverage, retail and recreation."[15]

A 2013 report by Mandala Research LLC revealed that 76 percent of all U.S. leisure travelers—or 129.6 million adults annually—engage in a cultural or heritage activity, spending US$171 billion.[16] These cultural heritage travelers are frequent travelers and spend more than general U.S. leisure travelers. The Mandala Research Report identified key characteristics of the cultural heritage tourist. They are:

- Older (age forty-nine vs. forty-seven)
- More affluent
- Generally have higher education
- Likely to be married or with a partner
- Frequent travelers—taking 3.61 leisure trips in the past three years (compared with 3.4 trips for the general leisure traveler)
- Spend more on travel, an average of $1,319 per trip versus $820 by general leisure travelers
- More likely to stay in a hotel, motel, or bed-and-breakfast
- Forty-six percent of their total trip expenditures were spent on activities, dining, and shopping[17]

The 2013 Mandala Research report provided some additional insights into traveler motivations and interests, including the following:

- Seventy-two percent seek travel experiences where the destination, buildings, and surroundings have retained their historical character.
- Sixty-six percent prefer leisure travel that is educational.
- Fifty-two percent spend more money on cultural and heritage activities while on a trip (than at home).
- A majority want to engage with locals and "do" something (immersion and participation rather than spectator).
- Forty-nine percent will pay more for distinctive lodging, accommodations that relate to the culture or heritage of the place.[18]

A 2009 Mandala Research report also determined the top activities of cultural heritage travelers. In order, the top five preferred activities engaged in by the cultural heritage traveler during a leisure trip are (1) visiting historic sites (66 percent), (2) participating in historical reenactments (64 percent), (3) visiting art museums and galleries (54 percent), (4) attending an arts-and-craft fair or festival (45 percent), and (5) attending a professional dance performance (44 percent). Other important activities include visiting state and national parks (41 percent), shopping in museum stores (32 percent), and exploring urban neighborhoods (30 percent).[19]

International travelers are also interested in U.S. cultural heritage. According to the National Travel and Tourism Office of the U.S. Department of Commerce, more than 22 million overseas visitors to the United States (excluding Canada and Mexico) engage in a cultural heritage activity—or 28 percent of all international inbound visitors. This represents a 56 percent increase from 2008 to 2015, with the majority (78 percent) of these visitors on vacation or holiday.[20] Like domestic tourists, shopping continues to be the number one activity for international tourists while in the United States. However, they traditionally favor—and participate in—cultural and heritage activities during their holiday here:

- Sixty-one percent visit national parks or monuments.
- Fifty percent visit art galleries or museums.
- Forty-six percent visit historic locations (more than amusement or theme parks at 33 percent).
- Forty percent visit small towns or the countryside.
- Thirty-two percent participate in a guided tour.
- Twenty-eight percent attend a concert, play, or musical.
- Twenty-eight percent visit cultural or ethnic heritage sites.
- Nine percent visit an American Indian community.[21]

While economic impact is certainly important to sustainability, cultural heritage tourism can also have a positive impact on the preservation and conservation of resources. This emphasis on the triple bottom line—a positive balance of economic, social, and environmental impact—is essential to sustainable destination and cultural heritage tourism planning. Additional studies were completed following the Lewis and Clark Bicentennial, Civil War Sesquicentennial, and other commemorations offer solid research on the impacts of cultural heritage tourism.

Cultural heritage tourism also has the potential to rejuvenate communities and stimulate the recognition and investment in the creative economy of an area. These social benefits often transfer to greater appreciation of and support for local artists, entrepreneurs, and other creative sectors. The designation of cultural districts and revitalization of ethnic or historic neighborhoods can result in a positive social impact for local residents and businesses. Placemaking and placekeeping serve as creative strategies to retain local identity, especially for African American, immigrant populations, and other ethnic groups whose neighborhoods are often threatened by outside development or influence. Retaining ownership and influence over the cultural heritage experiences shared with visitors ensures that local residents benefit from the positive economic and social impacts of tourism. Other notable benefits of cultural heritage tourism include:

- Potential for revenue generation through spending, resulting in increased state and local taxes and increased hotel/motel or accommodation tax (if applicable)
- Elevated brand awareness due to external recognition and accolades

- Contributions to enhanced quality of life (new or enhanced activities created for or sustained by tourists are also available for the enjoyment of residents)
- Amenities and activities that contribute to the potential for relocating other types of industry and business (and attracting a dynamic workforce)

Cultural heritage tourism may also foster these additional benefits:

- Preservation and conservation of local, unique resources
- Increased property values
- Additional education and lifelong learning opportunities
- Retention of authentic character, providing a balance between community and tourism

Just as cultural heritage tourism—and tourism at large—can contribute to positive destination impacts, if uncontrolled or not managed, it can also have negative impacts on fragile resources and indigenous populations. Cultural commodification or exploitation, staged or loss of authenticity, and degradation or destruction of physical sites (due to excessive use or uncontrolled access) are a few of the negative impacts of inappropriate development or overuse that cultural heritage tourism planners must address. Trash and traffic are also negative impacts of tourism. (The cost–benefit analysis of cultural heritage tourism is explored in future chapters.)

Cultural Heritage Tourism: Five-Step Process

In 1989, the National Trust for Historic Preservation suggested a four-step process for cultural heritage tourism. That approach, initially designed to help destinations begin cultural heritage tourism programs, has been modified here to address the planning and hosting responsibilities to include oversight of implemented programs (management) and evaluation of impacts (measurement)—hence the addition of the fifth step. As destinations and individual sites mature and the visitor becomes more savvy, management and measurement are essential to sustainable growth. Cultural heritage tourism steps are described in more detail in subsequent chapters.

Step 1: Analyze the Potential

Understanding the quality and quantity of assets is fundamental to cultural heritage tourism. Yet this inventory should include more than simply a list of the cultural, historic, and natural resources that may be available or enhanced as visitor experiences. Visitor readiness, potential sites or areas for redevelopment or expansion, and carrying capacity of current cultural and heritage sites must be factored into the potential for cultural heritage tourism. Identifying and analyzing existing plans, policies, programs, and regulations is also important in determining past efforts relative to the development and growth of cultural heritage tourism.

An assessment of the destination's current leadership (elected officials and influencers in the business and civic community), receptivity to tourism as an economic development strategy, historic preservation ethic, availability of funding for investment, and understanding resident priorities must be conducted in order to determine if and how cultural heritage tourism fits into a comprehensive management plan.

The situation analysis also allows the destination or resource manager to better understand its standing among the competition; define how cultural heritage tourism can contribute to a "sense of place"; integrate with or complement current zoning, land use, and economic development principles; and achieve desired outcomes for stakeholders.

This same assessment may also be conducted for individual buildings or sites if considered in the context of larger destination goals and owner or operator priorities. Complete the self-assessment form at the end of this chapter to find out your current cultural heritage tourism readiness and sustainability score.

Step 2: Plan and Engage

A *vision* articulates the end state desired by a particular organization, agency, or destination. Aspirational in nature, the vision conveys what successful cultural heritage tourism looks like and defines specific benefits—for the place, the resource, the managing entity, the visitor, and/or the resident. A *mission* is crafted to move the plan into action and successfully achieve the desired outcomes. For cultural heritage tourism plans, destinations or individual organizations need to articulate their mission as value propositions in terms of authentic experiences, culturally rich resources, and positive impacts on places and people.

From an expressive vision and a succinct mission, the planning process sets a course of developing goals and strategies. For an individual site, the mission may already be established, but the context of how this structure contributes to the overall destination experience is important to ensure alignment. Principles or value statements can be introduced to help guide and prioritize prioritizing strategies.

An essential ingredient to the planning process is leadership and stakeholder engagement. Section II of this book outlines the key strategies to embrace and qualities required to manage effective cultural heritage tourism programs.

Step 3: Develop Authentically

For cultural heritage tourism, this step is most significant, as it safeguards the integrity of local assets that attract visitors and their spending as well as the *soul of place*. It also identifies appropriate and sustainable redevelopment opportunities for historic sites and buildings as potential contributors to the cultural heritage tourism product mix. The development of new facilities to house cultural resources (performing arts, exhibitions, and studios) needs to be factored in with respect to their viability and marketability as potential new attractions for the destination.

While previous steps may require inclusive planning strategies, this step relies on individual entities to advance the potential for cultural heritage tourism with specific preservation, restoration, development, interpretation, and/or programming strategies to attract tourists and spending. This step also considers implications on other tourism sectors and infrastructure. For example, parking and signage needs must be considered with growth in cultural heritage tourism. Transportation systems and uses also are part of the development step to ensure adequate movement of tourists around or to specific cultural heritage attractions and to link to other tourism industry segments, such as touring, shopping, dining, entertainment, and lodging.

A key consideration for cultural heritage tourism is feasibility. Realistic expectations must be set not only for developing a specific project but also for its operation and enhancement. Funding may be available to help revitalize or restore a particular structure or site for cultural heritage tourism use, but how will the site maintain or continually enhance its operations to deliver consistent quality experiences and programs? Feasibility studies and business plans can help individual site owners, resource managers, and developers determine whether cultural heritage tourism is a good (appropriate and sustainable) fit for the asset. See chapter 10 for specific funding and development strategies.

Step 4: Market for Impact

Most destinations thrive on marketing, often due to the exemplary efforts of local convention and visitors bureaus or chambers of commerce. Often funded by a percentage of lodging tax (also known as hotel/motel or occupancy tax), these destination marketing organizations set out to attract customers interested in their particular collection of attractions or activities. In contrast, cultural and heritage institutions often have the product but not always the financial and human resources to market. As the days of "build it, and they will come" are long gone (if they ever existed), marketing is an essential ongoing requirement for all cultural heritage tourism programs.

Cultural heritage tourism affords an opportunity to identify mutually beneficial marketing strategies that realize visitation goals for the cultural heritage resource and the destination—whether it be increased attendance, increased spending, or some other outcome. Determining the best marketing strategies for desired return on investment requires research, planning, controls, and evaluation. As technology has changed the marketing landscape in recent years, understanding trends in consumer behavior and the use of trip-planning tools and mobile technology as well as social media can enhance marketing performance and return on investment. Chapter 11 delves into the development of a marketing plan and suggests implementation strategies for today's savvy marketer.

Step 5: Manage for Growth and Sustainability

Like any form of economic development, cultural heritage tourism requires an ongoing investment of time and money. Crafting and enforcing the policies, procedures, legislation, regulations, zoning, and codes are important to ensure quality control and integrity of assets. Specific management procedures and systems need to be assigned to appropriate stakeholders. Identification and allocation of financial resources—through a variety of methods including incentives, dedicated sources, grants, and donations—is paramount. Adequate, consistent funding and staffing are imperative to successful and sustainable cultural heritage tourism programs. Destination leadership is also a key management function to help guide the ongoing implementation of cultural heritage tourism and to demonstrate the value to support it.

Individual sites and organizations engaged in cultural heritage tourism also have similar management responsibilities to host guests and provide outstanding experiences that result in positive economic impact and visitor satisfaction. Sound management also ensures the required ongoing maintenance of historic sites and cultural facilities so that these assets contribute to desired cultural heritage tourism outcomes. These cultural heritage tourism tenets are explored in chapter 13.

Measurement is essential, especially with regard to attribution of cultural heritage tourism to broader destination or organizational goals. The necessary controls and evaluation methods need to be included in the schedule for implementation as well as the analysis of impact against desired outcomes. Effective cultural heritage tourism plans include benchmarks for future measurement.

Strong, clearly defined principles often represent the benchmarks on which destinations base their value proposition.

Some destinations may choose to benchmark cultural heritage tourism against performance of other tourism segments (business travel, conventions, or ecotourism) or other industries. Recently, the World Travel and Tourism Council benchmarked the travel and tourism industry against multiple other sectors—education, manufacturing, financial services, and so on. The council also compared the performance of travel and tourism to other sectors in specific countries by using the Tourism Satellite Account methodology. These comparisons allow researchers and planners to better understand the role and impact of the travel and tourism industry in the world economy.

While economic benchmarks are vitally important to evaluate (overnight visitation, tax revenue generated, volume of sales, and day visitation), social and environmental impacts are particularly important to benchmark cultural heritage tourism. Some benchmarks may be tied to the quality

Figure 1.1 *Blue Ridge Music Trails of North Carolina* guidebook cover— western North Carolina. Source: Blue Ridge National Heritage Area Partnership.

and integrity of cultural heritage tourism experiences provided to visitors. Other benchmarks may be tied to the stewardship of cultural heritage resources and the enrichment of residents' quality of life. Many benchmarks will be decided based on the life cycle of the destination, the needs of cultural and heritage resources, their current value proposition, and brand. For example, the Blue Ridge Music Trails (described in the accompanying feature) culminates the National Heritage Area's tribute to its music heritage and demonstrates the importance and impact of a comprehensive planning effort.

Cultural Heritage Tourism: A Principled Approach

Five guiding principles serve as the foundation for appropriate cultural heritage tourism development and outcomes. The National Trust for Historic Preservation proposed these guiding principles as hallmarks of a sustainable cultural heritage tourism program more than 25 years ago. Today, the five principles resonate with even more relevance as an increasingly growing number of destinations focus on their asset-based economic development to attract high-spending visitors and retain distinctive characteristics of place. These principles underscore the unique needs of cultural heritage tourism versus other tourism industry segments and economic development strategies.

Principle 1: Focus on Authenticity and Quality

Certainly one of the most important considerations for cultural heritage tourism, the focus on authenticity, ensures that experiences are accurate (based on documented or oral histories) and appropriate (true to the culture and values of the destination and/or its people). The emphasis on quality guarantees a standard of excellence and integrity for the experience available to the visitor. These two characteristics serve as the hallmark for sustainable cultural heritage tourism.

Principle 2: Preserve and Protect Resources

Without preservation and protection of historic, cultural, and natural resources, cultural heritage tourism loses its foundation for development and marketing. A sign that states "here once stood" is not as powerful as the original building or structure, nor does it provide the impetus for additional economic development opportunities. Context is also important, and preserving (restoring and utilizing) the historic fabric—exhibited by both tangible and intangible resources—is imperative to cultural heritage tourism. Respectful stewardship is required for both traditional and contemporary assets that embody the destination's unique sense of "place."[24]

> Make sure cultural heritage tourism is done right and understand what it means. Authentic. Quality. Preservation. These are the foundation and ideals.—Amy Webb, senior field director, National Trust for Historic Preservation

Principle 3: Make Sites and Programs Come Alive

Visitors want compelling and engaging experiences that relate and that are relevant to their own lives. History sleuths help identify interesting or little-known facts and stories for curated content to use as a foundation for dynamic tours and programs. Technology affords great opportunities to interpret and tell the diverse stories of people and place. Focusing on themes, periods, and/ or people, sites, and attractions can create a plethora of experiences catering to different interests delivered in desirable formats for various ages and audiences. Cultural heritage sites and programs must meet or exceed expectations of guests in order to positively contribute to the destination experience and realize a destination's brand promise.

Principle 4: Find the Fit between the Community and Tourism

As tourism grows, so does the need for thoughtful—and proactive—tourism management. Hosting visitors is a responsibility. Understanding and minimizing the potentially negative impacts from tourism allows the industry to safeguard the special attributes and character of place and focus on maximizing the benefits from visitation. Defining and monitoring the carrying capacity of sites and districts is also vital to planning and implementing appropriate transportation routes and marketing strategies to help disperse visitors around a destination and away from heavily trafficked areas or residential neighborhoods or other "sacred" places. Designing and applying sensitive development policies can safeguard the balance of outcomes and benefits to residents, resources, and visitors. Regularly surveying residents and businesses also affords an opportunity for feedback and identification of potential concerns as well as measuring their attitudes and opinions on the impact of tourism and quality of life.

Principle 5: Collaborate

As the tourism industry grew globally in the past fifty years, so did the entities involved in the planning, development, marketing, and management of tourism. At every destination level— local, state, regional, national, multinational, and international—organizations and institutions began embracing one or more aspects of tourism planning, development, management, and/or marketing. Multiple entities directly or tangentially involved in cultural heritage tourism may now exist in each destination, including the following:

- Public or government agencies: responsible for cultural and/or tourism policy, infrastructure, guide certification/training, permits, and tourism management
- Nonprofit associations: representing a sector or cluster of arts, culture, heritage, and/or tourism interests
- Private businesses: lodging, restaurants, tour operators, retail stores, attractions, galleries, art studios, nightclubs, theaters, wineries, farms, tour guide companies, and so on
- Nonprofit organizations: attractions, cultural institutions, historical societies, festival event managers, performance venues, and so on

To achieve optimum sustainability and a positive return on investment, entities involved in cultural heritage tourism must work together. This collaboration often brings together partners that have never worked in tandem or for a common goal. Mutual respect and well-defined outcomes allow partnerships to form, resulting in positive impacts benefiting the destination as a whole and its customer: the tourist. Consider cultural heritage tourism as a three-legged stool with interdependent groups converging to develop and offer visitor experiences. The cooperation and participation of these three major stakeholders—the tourism industry (lodging, retail, dining, attractions, transportation, marketing businesses, and organizations), the cultural heritage community (arts, cultural, heritage, history, preservation organizations, sites, artists, historians, and

Figure 1.2 Earl Scruggs Center—Shelby, North Carolina. Source: Earl Scruggs Center and Don Gibson Theatre.

government (public agencies, policies, regulations, permitting, investment, management, oversight and elected officials)—is imperative for consistent delivery and sustainability of cultural heritage tourism. Collaboration also allows partners to leverage individual resources for a great critical mass required to achieve maximum results and positive return on investment. Guiding principles help keep efforts on track, and a number of international organizations—from ICOMOS to the Global Sustainable Tourism Council—offer recommendations for destinations and specific sites. National Geographic's Geotourism Charter also encourages public-private participation in a sustainable and holistic approach to cultural heritage tourism. These policies, protocols, and procedures are discussed in chapter 7. The Blue Ridge Music Trails, a program of the Blue Ridge National Heritage Area, provided the structure to link attractions and venues in the region like a string of pearls. The new Earl Scruggs Center and the Don Gibson Theatre play a starring role on the trail as featured attractions. Strong leadership led a deliberate process to find "best use" scenarios. Their story at the end of this chapter underscores the importance of collaboration and sustainable strategies.

Chapter Summary

Cultural heritage tourism can be a viable economic development strategy for an organization or destination if it accepts the responsibilities and ongoing requirements of hosting visitors. Not all historic sites or communities may be ready to host visitors or have the critical mass required to attract visitors—and their spending. Reviewing the planning processes and considerations for developing, marketing, managing, and evaluating cultural heritage tourism may help inform decisions as to the appropriateness of this place-based strategy for an institution or destination. Also, the desired (or required) return on investment can impact or determine the feasibility of renovating or restoring historic sites for visitor use. The next fourteen chapters should empower your decision making and identify optimum strategies to move forward.

★ ★ ★ ★ ★

Cultural Heritage Tourism and Niche Market Descriptions

African American Heritage Tourism

A number of sites, events, activities, and places are associated with African American heritage and interpreted to include or emphasize the role of or impact on African Americans relative to U.S. history and/or current events. Sites and locations interpreting achievements, inventions, education, cultural traditions, cuisine, literature, and performing and visual arts, as well as enslavement, civil rights, and displacement, are considered components of African American tourism. Several organizations are engaged in education and developing and promoting African American tourism, including Black Meetings and Tourism (http://www.blackmeetingsandtourism.com), the National Black Tourism Bureau (http://www.natlblacktourism.com), and the Historic Black Towns and Settlements Alliance (http://www.hbtsa.org).

Agritourism

The Agricultural Marketing Resource Center states, "Agritourism describes the act of visiting a working farm or any agricultural, horticultural, or agribusiness operation to enjoy, be educated or be involved in activities." Examples of agritourism include farm tours for families and school-children, working ranches, day camps, hands-on chores, self-harvesting of produce, hayrides or sleigh rides, farmers markets, farm-to-table restaurants, and overnight stays in a bed-and-breakfast on a farm property. Two organizations to tap for more information on agritourism are the Agricultural Marketing Resource Center (http://www.agmrc.org/commodities__products/agritourism) and the National Agritourism Professionals Association (http://napa-usandcanada.com).

Culinary Tourism

Also known as food tourism, the World Food Travel Association defines culinary tourism "as the pursuit and enjoyment of unique and memorable food and drink experiences, both far and near." Food tourism is inclusive and comprises the food carts and street vendors as much as the locals-only (gastro) pubs, wineries, craft breweries and distilleries, or one-of-a-kind restaurants. For more information on culinary tourism, contact the World Food Travel Association, based in Portland, Oregon (http://worldfoodtravel.org), or Slow Food USA (https://www.slowfoodusa.org).

Ecotourism

The International Ecotourism Society now defines ecotourism as "responsible travel to natural areas that conserves the environment, sustains the well-being of the local people, and involves interpretation and education."[28] Education is meant to be inclusive of both staff and guests. The society is considered the leader in providing guidelines and standards, training, research, and publications on ecotourism (https://www.ecotourism.org/what-is-ecotourism).

Film Tourism

Film tourism or film-induced tourism is the act of inspiring people to visit places featured in movies, to watch or participate in film production (as extras), or to explore destinations as part of a film journey.[29] Many states and cities have active film commissions, providing incentives or permitting for on-site film production. While no single organization exists to oversee or document the impact of film tourism, there is a site that aggregates lists of film festivals, film promotions offered by destinations, film tours, and locations where TV series are in production (http://www.filmtourism.com).

Geotourism

The National Geographic Society's Center for Sustainable Destinations coined "geotourism" to focus on and integrate a majority of place-based tourism segments, as evidenced in its definition: "tourism that sustains or enhances the geographical character of a place—its environment, culture, aesthetics, heritage, and the well-being of its residents."[30] For more information, visit the National Geographic Society's website (http://travel.nationalgeographic.com/travel/sustainable) or the new Destination Stewardship Center, extending the work of the Center for Sustainable Destinations (http://destinationcenter.org).

Indigenous Tourism

Definitions vary from country to country and culture to culture, but typically indigenous tourism refers to tourism activity in which indigenous people are directly involved either through control and/or by having their culture serve as the essence of the attraction. Aboriginal (cultural) tourism describes all tourism businesses that are owned or operated by the first peoples of a given region, incorporating an Aboriginal cultural experience that is appropriate, respectful, and true to the Aboriginal culture being presented.[31] The mission of the American Indian Alaska Native Tourism Association is to define, introduce, grow, and sustain American Indian, Alaska Native, and Native Hawaiian tourism that honors traditions and values (http://www.aianta.org).

Military Tourism

Tourists who have an interest in current or historic military sites and facilities visit forts, battlefields, cemeteries, and monuments, and engage in reenactments or seek out educational exhibits on military strategy and artifacts (weapons, uniforms, medals, and paintings) at museums and memorials. No single organization facilitates military tourism; it is often part of a specialist tour operator or group organizing special tours, such as the International Military History Institute (https://militaryhistoryinstitute.org/).

Music Tourism

Visiting a city, county, region, or town to attend a music festival, concert, live performance, or site associated with a particular artist or band is considered music tourism. Some established icons in music tourism include the "Abbey Road" crossing in London, the Sound of Music Tour in Salzburg, the New Orleans Jazz and Heritage Festival, and the Ryman Auditorium in Nashville, but cultural heritage travelers (music tourists) also enjoy impromptu street performers on Main Streets, free community concerts in local bandstands, music and dance venues in cultural districts, and vintage record shops. As evident in the case study shared at the end of this chapter, music trails are also becoming more prevalent throughout the country. No single entity exists to coordinate or oversee the growth and marketing of music tourism in the United States.

Nature-Based Tourism

Nature-based tourism spans in two directions—the more active, adventure or extreme type of recreational travel, depending on or utilizing the natural landscape (hiking, biking, hunting, fishing, paddling, and rafting), and the more passive, spectator variety of engaging in natural settings for a particular activity (bird or wildlife watching and photographic safaris). Often, cultural heritage travelers may engage in—or are motivated to visit because of—the nature-based activities available.[32] Coupling these activities can be a strategy for extending the stay (and increasing the spending) of cultural heritage visitors. The Adventure Travel Trade Association, established in 1990, offers technical assistance, training, and marketing solutions for its members (http://www.adventuretravel.biz/about).

Other Related Definitions

Responsible Tourism

Tourism that maximizes the benefits to local communities, minimizes negative environmental impacts, and helps local people conserve fragile cultures and habitats is considered responsible tourism. Guiding principles for economic responsibility, social responsibility, and environmental responsibility are provided by the Cape Town Declaration of the International Conference on Responsible Tourism in Destinations (2002) and shared through the global Responsible Tourism Partnership (http://responsibletourismpartnership.org/cape-town-declaration-on-responsible-tourism).

Sustainable Tourism

According to UNESCO, sustainable tourism is defined as "tourism that respects both local people and the traveller, cultural heritage and the environment. It seeks to provide people with an exciting and educational holiday that is also of benefit to the people of the host country." More information on sustainable tourism may be found at UNESCO (http://www.unesco.org/education/tlsf/mods/theme_c/mod16.html), the Global Sustainable Tourism Council (GSTC) (https://www.gstcouncil.org/en), and Sustainable Travel International (http://sustainabletravel.org). The GSTC Criteria for destinations, hotels, and tour operators are discussed in chapter 7.

★ ★ ★ ★ ★

Profile of Blue Ridge Music Trails: An Instrumental Strategy

http://www.blueridgemusicnc.com

Billed as the guide to the traditional music of the North Carolina mountains and foothills, the Blue Ridge Music Trails (BRMT) builds on a legacy of collaboration to create inspiring experiences for artists, visitors, and residents. One of the five significant themes of the Blue Ridge National Heritage Area Partnership (BRNHAP), music unites western North Carolina in a regional effort to preserve and protect its natural, historical, and cultural resources to keep traditions alive, enhance residents' quality of life, and grow the local economy.[22]

Figure 1.3 Waynesville, North Carolina, Street Dance. Source: Blue Ridge National Heritage Area Partnership.

In 2010, BRNHAP entered in a partnership with the North Carolina Arts Council to create and launch the Blue Ridge Music Trails of North Carolina initiative. First developed by the North Carolina Arts Council in 2003 as a two-state effort with partner organizations in Virginia, the initiative was refocused in 2010 to spotlight the music heritage of 29 counties in North Carolina. An advisory council consisting of state and local arts and tourism organizations provided guidance during the redevelopment. To get community and musician input, BRNHAP hosted 16 listening sessions across 29 counties involving more than 186 participants. Earlier the region established the first trail guidebook focusing on cultural heritage. *The Craft Heritage Trails of Western North Carolina* and companion guide *Farms, Gardens, and Countryside Trails* (produced by Handmade in America) laid the foundation for mapping asset-based economic development.

"This initiative not only provided the opportunity to document and recognize the region's distinctive musical contributions and influences, but also gets visitors to places where music is made and heard," said Angie Chandler, executive director of the Blue Ridge National Heritage Area. The region identified these significant music-related stories to share:

- Home to many of the creators and popularizers of modern banjo styles
- The Round Peak–style fiddle and banjo ensemble tradition (developed in Surry County)
- Clogging and team square dancing, first organized in Haywood County in the 1930s
- The Mountain Dance and Folk Festival, started in 1928, the oldest continuous folk festival in the United States and model for the National Folk Festival
- Madison County—home to one of the longest, unbroken ballad singing traditions in America
- Eleven recipients of the National Heritage Fellowship, the country's highest honor in the traditional arts awarded by the National Endowment for the Arts
- The Merry Go Round (WPAQ in Mount Airy), the oldest live, regional music radio show, featuring music from the Blue Ridge
- MerleFest, held every April in Wilkesboro, one of the nation's largest and most influential "Americana" music events, preserving the legacy of Doc and Merle Watson and their contribution to American music

Why showcase music? A survey of 26 traditional music festivals and events revealed that western North Carolina's traditional music contributes at least $18.6 million directly to the region's economy, along with $972,611 of indirect impacts and $1.2 million of induced impacts.[23] The same study calculated that for every 100 visitors to a traditional music event, more than $4,000 can be expected to be returned to the local community. In 2013, the North Carolina Arts Council published the *Blue Ridge Music Trails of North Carolina* guidebook (with companion CD) for distribution at partner locations and sale online. BlueRidgeMusicNC.com was also launched to provide real-time information about performance venues, events, special concerts, educational programs, artist profiles, and an online store (featuring the guidebook, BRMT T-shirts, and other selected merchandise). A paper map of the trails is also available and distributed at visitor centers and music sites across the region.

Given limited resources, marketing has been focused on earned media and social media rather than on paid advertising. In 2015 and 2016, the North Carolina Arts Council and BRNHAP pooled resources to provide social media training to partner organizations and musicians to improve proficiency and encourage collaboration in the effort to expand the audience for BRMT. A total of 61 partners received social media training in four workshops conducted in the spring of 2016. Partners participating in the training received a social media "Songbook" with strategies and tactics to promote traditional music and the BRMT initiative on such platforms as Facebook, Twitter, Instagram, and YouTube.

"A major key to the success of this second incarnation of the Blue Ridge Music Trails is the extensive collaboration between state, regional, and local partners," said Chandler. "The North Carolina Arts Council and BRNHAP also made a concerted effort to involve more tourism partners in the creation of the brand and marketing materials," she continued.

As of mid-2016, 196 music sites are participating as partners by affiliating with the BRMT brand, displaying banners and window clings, providing event listings for the BRMT website, and joining in social media outreach. BRNHAP is tracking impact by surveying partner sites and by reviewing analytics for the BRMT website and companion social media channels (Facebook, Twitter, and Instagram). Key findings of a December 2015 "end of season" survey of partnering venues and events included the following:

- Sixty-three percent reported that the BRMT effort has either significantly or somewhat helped their traditional music venue or event since its launch in 2013.
- When asked how BRMT has helped them, the three most popular responses were that the effort has provided the event or venue with greater visibility, that it has helped preserve traditional music, and that it has boosted their reputation and credibility.
- Eighty-two percent of the respondents reporting attendance said that attendance to their venue or event was up over 2014, and nearly all of them said that it was due to a greater number of out-of-area visitors. Over half of the respondents also said that the number of local residents in their audience had also increased in 2015.

Traffic to the BRMT website in 2015 consisted of nearly 84,000 sessions and over 184,000 page views. As of August 2016, BRMT had over 2,500 followers on Facebook, over 670 on Twitter, and over 460 on Instagram.

Other themes of the federally designated Blue Ridge National Heritage Area are natural heritage, Cherokee heritage, craft heritage, and agricultural heritage. BRNHAP recently created the Blue Ridge Heritage Trail to guide visitors to 65 historic sites, museums, parks, and other attractions across western North Carolina. Trail ingredients consist of a website (http://blueridgeheritagetrail.com), visitor map and brochure, interpretive signs, and kiosks at five state welcome centers.

A companion to the *Blue Ridge Music Trails of North Carolina* is the *African American Music Trails of Eastern North Carolina*. Another project of the North Carolina Arts Council and local partners, this guidebook showcases another facet of the state's rich and diverse music heritage, focusing on jazz, rhythm and blues, funk, gospel, hymns, blues, rap, marching bands, and beach music. For more information, visit http://www.africanamericanmusicnc.com.

* * * * *

Signature Attractions on the Blue Ridge Music Trail: Striking the Right Chords
Uptown Shelby, North Carolina

http://earlscruggscenter.org
www.dongibsontheatre.org

The scenario is a familiar one across America. A landmark courthouse located in the center of a town square is abandoned when the new building is built. A local history museum opens in the abandoned building, where it operates until it too is abandoned. Down the street is a small-town

Figure 1.4 Don Gibson Theatre—Shelby, North Carolina. Source: Earl Scruggs Center and Don Gibson Theatre.

historic 1939 movie theater, dark for almost thirty years. A group of community volunteers are dedicated to finding a way to breathe new life into these two historic structures.

Many communities may relate to the dilemma that Cleveland County, North Carolina, faced; few take such a bold and strategic approach to asset-based economic development. This is their story of leadership, laser focus, and great music heritage.

In 2006, community leader Brownie Plaster, at the request of the county manager, met with other community members as part of a task force to determine what to do about the more than 10,000 objects that had been abandoned in the 1907 historic courthouse building when the local history museum shut the doors in 2004. A consultant from North Carolina State University facilitated the task force discussions. He challenged them to be concerned beyond the courthouse, to broaden their sights to the larger community, as the abandonment of the courthouse was indicative of what was going on around town and throughout other small towns in the county.

Numerous ideas and discussions took place, and a core group stepped up to continue the conversation. Thus began the research to see what they, a group of community volunteers, might be able to accomplish to create a positive impact in the community. The need to identify a catalyst to achieve this goal became paramount. In 2007, the volunteer group formed Destination Cleveland County, Inc. (DCC), a public–private partnership and nonprofit organization, to begin a research-driven investigation of opportunities. Board members traveled to the state capital for meetings with arts and humanities agencies, embarked on field trips to other towns to see success models, and conducted extensive research on best practices. The question every town and expert asked was, "What do you have that nobody else has?" Others showcased barbecue, architecture, and even similar events. Considered the gateway between Asheville and Charlotte, Shelby (population 20,325) faced a lot of competition.[25]

DCC commissioned feasibility studies for a music performance theater as well as a museum, plus economic impact reports, market analysis, and other research, to inform the discovery process and determine two catalyst projects for the community. The Department of Cultural Resources served as a resource for knowledge regarding museums, heritage tourism, traditional music, and more. A restored and repurposed courthouse had the potential to become an iconic attraction if the story appealed to a broad enough audience. Looking beyond the initial capital investment required to open the facilities, DCC leadership addressed the revenue generation potential and marketability of the attractions. An equally important success criterion was the potential to serve as an economic stimulus for other downtown businesses. If concepts didn't meet these criteria, the efforts weren't worth the investment to sustain them.

Two assets gave hope to community leaders. Legendary musicians Don Gibson and Earl Scruggs hailed from Cleveland County, and the idea of a musical tribute started to take root. Gibson, renowned for writing "I Can't Stop Loving You," "Oh Lonesome Me," and "Sweet Dreams," is buried in Shelby. Earl Scruggs, famous for his renowned three-finger roll picking style, which gave a distinctive voice to the banjo, was from nearby Flint Hill. Inducted into the Country Music Hall of Fame in 1985, Scruggs died in 2012 but left a legacy of memorabilia and music.

The historic State Movie Theater reopened in 2009 as the Don Gibson Theatre, a state-of-the-art performing space attracting award-winning acts traveling between New York, Nashville, and Austin. The restored art deco movie theater affords an intimate setting for both artists and guests. Seating for 400, the theater books approximately thirty acts per year. The building was doubled in size to create additional space to host events (and generate rental income). Renovation estimates were approximately $3 million. Capital funds were raised by the DCC, with more than half of the donations from individuals. The City of Shelby still owns the theater and leases it to DCC for a nominal annual fee. An unfortunate case of bad timing slowed the development progress, as the day of the groundbreaking for the Don Gibson Theatre was the very day Wall Street crashed. The Don Gibson Theatre celebrated its grand opening in November 2009 and has brought both domestic and international visitors to events and concerts.

Community leaders persevered, and today the Earl Scruggs Center: Music and Stories from the American South occupies the restored 1907 Cleveland County Courthouse. The county helped

Figure 1.5 Japanese visitors with volunteer Grace Constant, Earl Scruggs Center—Shelby, North Carolina. Source: Earl Scruggs Center and Don Gibson Theatre.

Figure 1.6 Student group, Earl Scruggs Center—Shelby, North Carolina. Source: Earl Scruggs Center and Don Gibson Theatre.

renovate the building's infrastructure (adding the elevator; upgrading the heating, ventilating, and air-conditioning and plumbing systems; and making the building compliant with the American with Disabilities Act). The total capital required for renovations and exhibit development, fabrication, and installation was approximately $6.2 million for the 10,000-square-foot facility, which opened in January 2014. Public areas for music and storytelling were created. Administrative offices and a gift shop were installed as part of the redevelopment. The county retains ownership of the courthouse, leasing the building to DCC for a nominal annual fee.

A tribute to the life and musical genius of Earl Scruggs, the center explores his career, his connection to the local community, and his respect for tradition married with his musical innovation. Long-term exhibits are housed on the first floor and provide insights into his life and accomplishments, as presented through recent and archival footage of Scruggs with Bill Monroe and the Bluegrass Boys along with solo performances. A display of musical instruments invites guests to learn more about the various types of banjos. The interactive "Common Thread" multimedia presentation encourages guests to play virtual mandolins, banjos, guitars, and other bluegrass instruments.[26] To date, the center has hosted more than 25,000 visitors from forty-nine states and thirteen countries. Operating on an annual budget of $400,000, the staff has grown from two to six (three full-time and three part-time equivalent staff) since opening.

Each facility now has its own working board to oversee operations and administration. DCC remains the umbrella organization focusing on governance, continued capital fund-raising, and broader strategies to leverage resources and foster greater return on investment for the two projects.

The North Carolina Arts Council, along with the Blue Ridge National Heritage Area, continues to promote the Earl Scruggs Center and the Don Gibson Theatre as key venues on the *Blue Ridge Music Trails of North Carolina*. The restoration of the courthouse and the opening of the museum and the theater have been credited with sparking commercial activity on the Shelby town square, including the Newgrass Brewery and the Dragonfly Wine Market—both featuring live music and libations.[27] Other venues, including the Don Gibson Theatre and the Cleveland County Arts Center (located across the street from the Earl Scruggs Center in a historic post office), create a synergy of activity for visitors and residents alike.

Notes

1. National Trust for Historic Preservation (2015), http://www.preservationnation.org/information-center/economics-of-revitalization/heritage-tourism/?gclid=CNXVmcL3g8gCFYsYHwodiZgGVg.
2. Partners in Tourism, *Chronology: Cultural Heritage Tourism Movement in the U.S.* (2010).
3. Described in Chicago Traveler (n.d.), http://www.chicagotraveler.com/cows_on_parade.htm.
4. President's Committee on Arts and Humanities, *A Position Paper on Cultural and Heritage Tourism in the United States* (2005), http://www.pcah.gov/sites/default/files/05WhitePaperCultHeritTourism_2.pdf.
5. The most scenic byways, those including more than one nationally significant intrinsic quality, are designated as All-American Roads by the U.S. Department of Transportation, Federal Highway Administration.
6. Roberto Bedoya (September 2014), "Spactial Justice Rasquachification, Race and the City," *Creative Time Reports.*
7. Americans for the Arts, *Cultural Tourism: Attracting Visitors and Their Spending* (2014), p. 3, http://www.americansforthearts.org/sites/default/files/pdf/2014/by_program/reports_and_data/toolkits/cultural_districts/issue_briefs/Cultural-Tourism-Attracting-Visitors-and-Their-Spending.pdf.

8. UNESCO (2015), http://www.unesco.org/new/en/culture/themes/illicit-trafficking-of-cultural-property/unesco-database-of-national-cultural-heritage-laws/frequently-asked-questions/definition-of-the-cultural-heritage.

9. UNWTO, *Understanding Tourism: Basic Glossary*, http://media.unwto.org/en/content/understanding-tourism-basic-glossary.

10. UNWTO, "International Tourist Arrivals Up 4% Reach a Record 1.2 Billion in 2015" (January 2016), http://media.unwto.org/press-release/2016-01-18/international-tourist-arrivals-4-reach-record-12-billion-2015.

11. World Travel and Tourism Council as reported in UNWTO *Tourism Highlights*, 2016 Edition, p. 3, http://www.e-unwto.org/doi/pdf/10.18111/9789284418145.

12. UNWTO *Tourism Highlights*, 2015 Edition, p. 3, http://www.e-unwto.org/doi/pdf/10.18111/9789284416899.

13. "International Visitation to the United States: A Statistical Summary of U.S. Visitation" (2015), National Travel and Tourism Office, International Trade Administration, U.S. Department of Commerce (June 2016), http://tinet.ita.doc.gov/outreachpages/download_data_table/2015_Visitation_Report.pdf; TI News (June 2015), http://travel.trade.gov/view/f-2000-99-001/forecast/Forecast_Summary.pdf.

14. PlaceEconomics for the New York Landmarks Conservancy, "Historic Preservation: At the Core of a Dynamic New York City" (April 2016), pp. 30–31.

15. "Historic Preservation—Essential to the Economy and Quality of Life in San Antonio" (February 2015), prepared by PlaceEconomics for the City of San Antonio Office of Historic Preservation, p. 13, http://www.placeeconomics.com/wp-content/uploads/2011/03/ohp_2015_report_final.pdf.

16. Mandala Research LLC, *The 2013 Cultural and Heritage Traveler Report*, p. 3, http://mandalaresearch.com/images/stories/free_download_CH_2013.pdf.

17. Ibid., p. 9.

18. bid., p. 8.

19. Mandala Research LLC, *The 2009 Cultural and Heritage Traveler Study*, p. 57. http:/mandalaresearch.com/index.php/purchase-reports/view_document/1-the-cultural-a-heritage-study?tmpl-component.

20. Preliminary "2015 Sector Report: Cultural Heritage Traveler" provided by the National Travel and Tourism Office, International Trade Administration, U.S. Department of Commerce (August 2016).

21. Ibid.

22. Modified from BRNHA Purpose Statement, Blue Ridge Heritage Trails presentation by Angie Chandler at the 2014 Cultural Heritage Tourism Exchange, Washington, D.C.

23. Traditional Music Study, "Traditional Music Venues in the Blue Ridge Region of North Carolina," North Carolina Arts Council (2012), http://ncarts.org/sites/default/files/pdf/BRMJuly2012Data.pdfhttp://ncarts.org/sites/default/files/pdf/BRMJuly2012Data.pdf.

24. National Trust for Historic Preservation, Heritage Tourism Program, Five Principles (n.d.), http://www.preservationnation.org/information-center/economics-of-revitalization/heritage-tourism/?gclid=CNXVmcL3g8gCFYsYHwodiZgGVg.

25. According to the 2010 census.

26. D. Daniel, "In North Carolina, an Earl Scruggs Museum" (January 2014), in Transit, A Guide to Intelligent Travel, *New York Times* blog, http://intransit.blogs.nytimes.com/2014/01/02/in-north-carolina-an-earl-scruggs-museum.

27. T. Lehmann, "A Visit to the Scruggs Center in Shelby, North Carolina," Bluegrass Rambles (April 2016), *Journal of Roots Music: No Depression*, http://nodepression.com/article/visit-scruggs-center-shelby-north-carolina.

28. The International Ecotourism Society (2015). https://www.ecotourism.org/what-is-ecotourism.

29. Zimmerman (2003). http://www.filmtourism.com

30. National Geographic Center for Sustainable Destinations.

31. Aboriginal Tourism Association of Canada (nd). ATAC Media Kit: backgrounder. https://aboriginalcanda.ca/en

32. Jascha M. Zeitlin and Steven W. Burr, "Community Nature-Based Tourism Development" (January 2011), Utah State University Cooperative Extension, Institute for Outdoor Recreation and Tourism, http://extension.usu.edu/files/publications/factsheet/IORT_022.pdf.

Section I

Step One:
Analyze the Potential

Chapter 2

Identifying and Assessing Local Heritage and Culture

A concerted effort to preserve our heritage is a vital link to our cultural, educational, aesthetic, inspirational, and economic legacies—all of the things that quite literally make us who we are.

—Steve Berry, American author and professor[1]

Cultural heritage tourism exists only if there are attractions, activities, and experiences that people want to experience. Some may take exception to the word "asset" when considering the historic and cultural resources available in a community or destination, preferring not to label or potentially commodify their uniqueness. When considering cultural heritage tourism, though, the definition of "asset" helps quantify the potential worth to visitors, extending their significance beyond local use and appreciation. Identification is only the first step, as not all assets may have value—even if developed and marketed—for visitors. Assessing the potential return on investment is vital to determining the appropriate end use, viability, or required development into a contributor to cultural heritage tourism. This chapter addresses ways to create an asset inventory and assess the potential for cultural heritage tourism. While some destinations may already have inventories, plans, and active cultural heritage tourism programs, this chapter serves as a reminder of potential assets to enhance or grow existing efforts, or broaden relevance to new audiences.

Identifying Historic, Cultural, and Intangible Assets

Getting started always seems the most difficult task. An asset inventory is the first step in cultural heritage tourism and begins with collecting existing documentation. Comprehensive plans, master plans, historical maps, and county and city records are all sources for initial lists and information about historic and cultural assets. State and local tourism websites provide content for historic and cultural attractions and events. Historical societies and arts organizations usually have documentation of significant assets or collections. Checking with these stakeholders and reference sites is a good place to start in developing an inventory, or initial list, of assets.

What exactly constitutes an inventory? Certainly, the brick-and-mortar structures of historical significance are components, but so too are the human and natural assets that tell the stories of a destination—its people, settlements, traditions, and industry, past to present. A more comprehensive inventory can potentially identify new ways to grow cultural heritage tourism. Three categories of assets are detailed here for reference: historic, cultural, and natural. These lists are by no means exhaustive but rather are a starter lens through which a city or community may identify the types of assets that are part of its authentic collection.

Historic

The historic and archaeological resources of a community provide a physical foundation for cultural heritage tourism. The obvious categories for historic assets include the following:

- National Historic Landmarks (designated by the U.S. Department of Interior)
- Historic properties (designated by the state or the National Register of Historic Places)
- Main Streets and commercial districts comprised of historic buildings and stores (officially designated by the state or the National Main Street Center)
- Accredited museums (art, history, heritage, and living history) recognized by the American Alliance of Museums

Traditionally, sites open to the public are the primary areas of focus, as access is important. An asset inventory spans more broadly to include sites and monuments associated with significant people, significant events, and those of architectural or archaeological significance. The age of a building or structure can also deem it an asset. The eligibility requirement for the National Register of Historic Places is at least fifty years, although some more contemporary assets may be considered due to other significant factors.[2] According to the National Register, these criteria are applied to "districts, sites, buildings, structures, and objects that possess integrity of location, design, setting, materials, workmanship, feeling, and association" for qualification.

Broadly consider how the National Register criteria may be applied to a structure, site, community, or city. A heritage asset inventory may include the following:

- Public buildings: historic courthouses, depots, bridges, jails, fountains, sculptures, and lighthouses
- Military sites and events: battlefields, forts, reenactments, and monuments
- Sacred structures: churches, synagogues, temples, and cemeteries
- Educational institutions: libraries, colleges, and interpretive centers
- Agricultural-based sites: barns, farms, farmers/fish markets, ranches, farmhouses, wineries, breweries, distilleries, orchards, and commercial fishing boats
- Entertainment and recreation sites: historic theaters, cultural arts, opera houses and heritage parks
- Historic or cultural districts: arts and entertainment or cultural districts and residential neighborhoods[3]
- Other museums: county, community, thematic, and historical
- Routes: historic driving routes, canals or heritage trails, historic walking tours, and scenic driving routes and byways[4]

What should be included when listing these assets? Certainly, the location is important, as are the current owner, whether it is open to the public (and frequency), a description of its unique characteristics (consider the categories above), and any special attributes as described in table 2.1.

Table 2.1 Historical and Physical Inventory Checklist

Texas Historical Commission Heritage Tourism Guidebook	
Historical inventories should include:	*Physical inventories should describe:*
What was on the site at a particular point in time?	The geographic location of sites and activities within a community
Who owned the site and how have ownership patterns changed over the years?	The types of resources and attractions present at those individual sites
What is significant about the site or ownership during this particular point in time?	The condition of the facilities on site
Why does the site look the way it does today?	The needs to be addressed at the sites
What use limitation does the site present?	
What are the site's limitations?	

Source: Texas Historical Commission, http://www.thc.state.tx.us (February 2004), p. 11.

Figure 2.1 Skyline, Oakland Cemetery—Atlanta, Georgia. Source: Oakland Cemetery.

For example, does a local house of worship have significant art or artifacts on view? Are important persons connected to the community buried in a sacred site's cemetery? Terri Cook, author of *Sacred Havens: A Guide to Manhattan's Spiritual Places*, considers that "religious sites are an accessible way for people to learn about the history of a community or the nation."[5] Don't overlook the darker periods in the nation's past; it is important to identify and include people or places impacted by conflict. Historic and cultural information about underrepresented populations may not be as widely available or accessible via more traditional outlets but is important to investigate and include. The information you gather at this stage of the inventory can help determine the resources' current or potential contribution to cultural heritage tourism.

One of the most frequently overlooked assets is a local cemetery. With the expense of preservation and maintenance, many organizations or public agencies use cultural heritage tourism to raise funds and awareness for the perpetual care required of a community's burial grounds. Oakland Cemetery, as described in the case study at the end of this chapter feature, hosts special tours and events to keep its site alive.

Cultural

Often associated with people or peoples, cultural assets encompass all art forms. The assets may be tangible (physical) sites, structures, artifacts, or documents. UNESCO also defines and recognizes "intangible" cultural heritage as important assets to catalog—oral histories, traditions, performing arts, rituals, social practices, festivals and events, and the knowledge, skills, and practices required to produce traditional craft.[6] Additional categories of cultural assets to consider include the following:

- Literature: books written about a local dancers, or event or located in the destination
- Films: movies about a local person or event or filmed in the destination
- Cuisine: local restaurants, diners, or cafés serving traditional food or considered a local "institution"; heirloom recipes; food/harvest festivals; artisanal foods/spices; farmers markets; famous local chefs; and farm-to-market restaurants or dining experiences
- Performing artists: artists, musicians, dancers, composers, bands, and other performers born or living in the destination and statues, burial sites, and significant sites associated with these local artists
- Cultural institutions: art museums, artists galleries, artist studios, performing arts venues, and exhibitions
- Festivals and events: commemorations, celebrations, and ethnic festivals

Cultural resources can also be created to depict or interpret important events or persons. Murals are a visually compelling way to present information, and Paducah, Kentucky, was an early adopter of this art form. As told in the case study at the end of this chapter, Paducah uses murals as a visual walk through history.

Natural

Landscape and geological features set the stage and provide context to understanding settlement patterns and the development of communities. Today, these natural assets exist in the form of parks, heritage areas, cultural landscapes, wetlands, lakes, and rivers, as well as coastal regions where wildlife and recreation are abundant.

Figure 2.2 Paducah floodwall murals along Water Street—Paducah, Kentucky. Source: Paducah Visitors Bureau.

Migratory patterns also create opportunities for telling a destination's story. Whether it's the great migration of sandhill cranes in Nebraska or sheep moving to lower pastures each fall in Idaho, festivities often mark the annual events. As evident in the story of the Trailing of the Sheep Festival at the end of this chapter, this migration also serves as a history lesson and celebration commemorating a region's heritage.

Other Local Assets

Look beyond the traditional culture and heritage to identify other assets unique to a destination. As discussed previously, residents and planners often inadvertently overlook activities and assets of potential interest to visitors. Street art (e.g., graffiti), street entertainers, retail shops selling locally made goods and foods, antique stores, and other distinctive shops, traditions or annual commemorations can hook visitors in with their quirky, solemn, sentimental, or unique appeal.

Each may have a story to tell, and each is looked at in more detail in chapter 9. Record trivia, little-known facts, and other tidbits of local history to explore; this information can be a potential basis for cultural heritage tourism development.

Pulling all this information together into a usable reference document may seem overwhelming. Consider creating an Excel spreadsheet to capture information (a template is included at the end of this chapter); include GPS coordinates, if possible, for physical sites to map assets. The intent is to have a document to reference as planning proceeds, to determine where gaps exist in categories or content, and to help organize the information required to grow cultural heritage tourism. An asset inventory helps identify what currently contributes to the destination's brand and highlights potential areas for development.

> Think like a business and not like a non-profit. Figure out what your competitive advantage is. Take a strong look at your product, how you are delivering it, how that product is placed within the marketplace. Whether you consider the marketplace other historic homes, sites, forts, whatever category, [you] need to position yourself so you can think, react like a business rather than a non-profit organization always looking for fundraising opportunities.
> —Margaret Hoogstra, Texas Heritage Trails LLC

Assessing the Potential

How can an abandoned building be converted to a tourist attraction? Can a historic house operate tours to generate revenues? Is transforming an old railroad depot into a restaurant viable? Should a city, county, or community embark on cultural heritage tourism as a form of asset-based economic development? To answer these questions, a destination or planning committee must assess the potential for sustainable cultural heritage tourism. The analysis begins with the comprehensive inventory inclusive of attractions and visitor services discussed above and then filters the list according to desired outcomes defined by both the destination and the visitor. If there is a match between supply and demand, the asset has potential for cultural heritage tourism.

Four factors impact this potential for converting existing buildings into contributing cultural heritage tourism attractions: access, physical condition, capacity, and market.

Access

Location, location, location—it is a key factor in determining whether potential visitors can easily find and experience an attraction or purposefully seek out the site. Close proximity to a major interstate or along a designated scenic byway can attract the leisure traveler as well as the more motivated cultural heritage traveler. Yet a site must also have adequate parking (or walk ability; public transit; for urban areas) lighting, and directional signage for easy navigation. Perhaps most important, the site must be open to the public—when the public wants to visit. Depending on the usage, the leisure tourist's preferred hours of operation often include weekends and/or evenings.

Providing access for mobility-impaired persons and other persons with disabilities is also a consideration for potential cultural heritage attractions. Some alternative modifications to historic structures are acceptable to meet standards set forth by the Americans with Disabilities Act of 1990, providing an opportunity for creative interpretation and use of technology. The National Park Service offers a series of Preservation Briefs to address planning solutions for accessibility of both historic buildings and landscapes.

Physical Condition

Certainly, the physical condition of a historic structure will dictate whether the site can be quickly or easily renovated or adapted for reuse. A building/property condition or assessment report may be appropriate. The National Park Service recommends evaluating the building's historic character as well as assessing its architectural integrity and physical condition to determine the appropriate treatment of the site. In addition to physical condition and historic significance, the proposed use and intended interpretation (of how or if the site will be used to tell its or a broader story) are also important to consider when evaluating the asset's potential.

Following the Secretary of the Interior's standards for one of the four treatments are essential to ensuring good stewardship of the structure, maintaining its historic integrity, and optimizing the potential for reuse.

Capacity

If you have ever visited an overcrowded site or one where the number of people on a guided tour was too large for an enjoyable experience, you've witnessed excess in carrying capacity. Carrying capacity dictates the number of people who can physically visit or be located in a site at one time or over time without compromising the integrity of the experience or the site itself.

Four Approaches to the Treatment of Historic Properties

The National Park Service offers standards for four distinct, but interrelated, approaches to the treatment of historic properties:

1. *Preservation* focuses on the maintenance and repair of existing historic materials and retention of a property's form as it has evolved over time.
2. *Rehabilitation* acknowledges the need to alter or add to a historic property to meet continuing or changing uses while retaining the property's historic character.
3. *Restoration* depicts a property at a particular period of time in its history while removing evidence of other periods.
4. *Reconstruction* re-creates vanished or nonsurviving portions of a property for interpretive purposes.

Source: National Park Service, http://www.nps.gov/tps/standards/four-treatments.htm.

Overuse can damage the physical condition of the site. Too many visitors can also strain infrastructure and increase traffic congestion along with other potentially negative impacts. Initially used to limit environmental impact, carrying capacity has been broadened to reference specific sites and entire destinations. The World Tourism Organization defines carrying capacity as "the maximum number of people that may visit a tourist destination at the same time, without causing destruction of the physical, economic and socio-cultural environment and an unacceptable decrease in the quality of visitors' satisfaction."[9]

Understanding carrying capacity and determining potentially negative impacts on the broader community and nature if exceeded are important factors to consider for cultural heritage tourism. Most state departments of recreation and parks or natural resources (if they also include management of historic sites) have guidelines for optimum carrying capacity for users and minimizing site deterioration. Check with state and local agencies for these guidelines as a reference.

Market

Knowing the current or future customer for the proposed site is a critical consideration for assessing its cultural heritage tourism potential. If no one needs or wants the proposed use or the abandoned or unused building won't attract new out-of-town customers, the assessment is dim for cultural heritage tourism. Assessing the market potential is as important to sustainability as assessing the development potential. The National Trust for Historic Preservation defined four categories to help prioritize the potential development of resources for cultural heritage tourism:

1. Attractor: An attraction or destination in its own right, the actual reason or motivation for why a group or individual will travel to a place.
2. Attraction: Physical site or event included as part of an itinerary for a destination, usually determined prior to arrival.
3. Tour while there: Usually discovered once in a city or community, these attractions or events enhance the overall destination experience but were not necessarily a motivator on their own (or were not known to the visitor in advance of the trip).
4. For local consumption only: Typically, these assets—because of a lack of either significance or relevance to the visitor—are best considered as contributors to local residents' knowledge, use, and benefit.[10]

Often, applying the "so what?" qualification—especially to question an asset's relevance and significance—can yield a better determination of potential. While it may appear harsh to prioritize according to these qualifiers, realistic outcomes are better than pie-in-the-sky projections and multipliers.

Faced with the opportunity to build new cultural attractions or create new festivals, planners and other stakeholders must also consider associated costs and impacts. New festivals and events, in particular, can divert human and financial resources from more "evergreen" or year-round products and programs. Weighing external factors out of the organizer's control, such as weather, crisis, or economic downturn, and potentially negative impacts, such as traffic congestion and litter, are important considerations for planning new events and festivals, blockbuster exhibitions, or commemorations.

Building new cultural centers or attractions can be a boom for cities and communities. Analyzing the cost of land (even if donated), plus architectural and construction costs along with budgeting for ongoing operations and maintenance, is essential before putting a shovel in the ground. The typical destination marketing evaluation methodology is more "heads in beds" (thereby increasing hotel occupancy or lodging tax to the locale), and yet, as dictated by carrying capacity, some destinations prefer to increase yield—where fewer people spend more money. A question to ask is, Is it more desirable to host 500 people each paying $5.00 admission to an attraction than to charge $50 admission to fifty people? Certainly, this pricing structure depends on perceived value by the visitor, but it can also address concerns regarding carrying capacity. Stakeholders must look at the viability and value of adding new assets as contributors to the overall cultural heritage tourism goals for the community, county, city, or state. This strategic planning/visioning process is discussed in more detail in chapter 6.

Determining Tourism Viability and Return on Investment

Potential does not necessarily translate into viability. As cultural heritage tourism has gained popularity, competition, too, has grown. In addition, the tendency to convert historic sites into museums has proliferated in recent years. In May 2014, the Institute of Museum and Library Services reported that the number of museums in the United States had doubled since the 1990s, from 17,500 to 35,144.[11] As figure 2.3 shows, almost more than half of these museums are history-centric.

Competition impacts the potential for the site to attract visitors and generate revenue from attendance or other activities. While some historic sites are successful as museums, many are barely getting by with volunteer staff, deferred maintenance, and limited hours of operation.

In her keynote speech at the 2013 National Preservation Conference, Stephanie Meeks, president of the U.S. National Trust for Historic Preservation, called house museums "a 20th Century paradigm."[12] Meeks describes the "house museum as our 'go to' strategy for preservation." Citing a 2002 study indicating the average cost of hosting each visitor at $40 per person versus revenue (via admission, gift shop, or program sales) of $8 per person, Meeks claims that the current house museum model is not sustainable for many organizations, especially smaller institutions with limited attendance and operating capital.[13] Visitors will always seek out places for learning, but the location may not always be in traditional museums or formally interpreted sites. Instead, tourists may see—and desire—a more holistic educational experience of a destination as a museum without walls. Municipalities acquiring historic buildings via donations must decide the best choice for developing or operating these facilities based on current market value and visitor

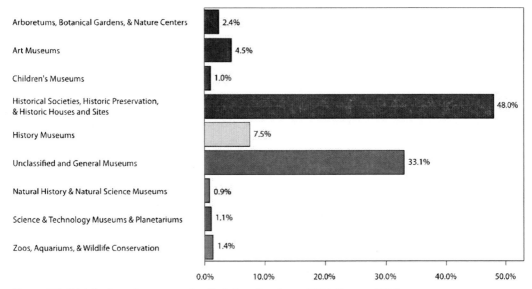

Figure 2.3 Distribution of museums by discipline, fiscal year 2014. Source: IMLS.

expectations. Another museum may not be the best or most sustainable use. Perhaps instead, a historic site is best transformed into a historic hotel, restaurant, a university classroom, low-income housing, or a community center—depending on current product gaps and the overall vision and needs of the community.

Competition from other attractions and museums is only one factor impacting viability. There are other factors to consider in determining feasibility of restoring historic sites or building new cultural attractions to enhance visitation. Development costs must be coupled with ongoing maintenance and management fees to adequately understand the price of operation. Budgeting for new exhibitions or interpretation enhancements (every five years) is also important for museums, especially to attract repeat visitors. Introducing new products and services cost time and money. Both require marketing expertise and funding to attract tourists and their spending. Adding these "once open" costs must be factored into the viability decision.

Defining sources of revenue generation, not only for the development-to-opening phase but also through the various life cycles of the attraction, is important in determining return on investment. Revenues generated from admissions and gift shop sales, as indicated above, may not be a sustainable model for house museums. Popular alternatives include diversified earned income streams—from event rental to expanded programming—to keep patrons, both local residents and out-of-town visitors, returning again and again for multiple uses.

Therefore, return on investment should be considered not only in economic terms (when or if the actual financial investment can be paid back to owners and organizers) but also in sociocultural terms. Does the advent of this new asset contribute to an increase in community pride, additional recognition for the destination, or spur other development (as in the case of an anchor attraction in a cultural district)? Does the preservation or restoration of the abandoned site foster a preservation ethic that extends to other buildings in a historic downtown or neighborhood? Does a new cultural center provide a much-needed home for a performing arts group and offer a venue for visiting artists or museums—thereby increasing the quantity and quality of cultural offerings available to residents and visitors? These benefits must be factored into the overall risk and return on investment and assessment.

Chapter Summary

As discussed, local history and culture can be found in an abandoned building, a story passed down through generations, or traditional food and craft. Cataloging these assets and activities is important in understanding what makes a destination unique, where there may be gaps in telling the authentic local stories—past to present—and identifying contributing places for visitors to eat, tour, shop, and stay. This ever-changing inventory is the basis for assessing sustainable cultural heritage tourism. Documenting and updating the inventory can seem overwhelming, but technology can aid in the process of capturing this information for use in creating cultural heritage tourism plans, programs, and experiences.

* * * * *

Profile: Tales of the Dead-Oakland Cemetery
Atlanta, Georgia

http://www.OaklandCemetery.com

The rural garden cemetery movement, started in 1831 by horticulturalists, established land-scaped settings just outside urban cities. Today, many of these historic cemeteries have become attractions thanks in part to historic preservationists and perpetual care agreements. Oakland Cemetery, just five blocks from the Georgia state capitol, features winding paths, large shade trees, and lavish sculptures of various architecture styles, including gothic to neoclassical, Egyptian, Victorian, and exotic revival. Famous residents include six governors, twenty-seven mayors, golf legend Robert T. (Bobby) Jones, and author Margaret Mitchell, plus developers, historians, and educators. Despite the significance and sacredness of the site, vandals had destroyed the gardenlike setting and many of the markers by the mid-1970s.

A group of families formed the Historic Oakland Foundation on April 28, 1976, to safeguard the future of the cemetery. Partnering with the City of Atlanta, the foundation seeks to preserve, re-store, enhance, and share the cemetery. About 70,000 people are buried at Oakland Cemetery, but only 40,000 have markers. Sections are designated for Confederate soldiers, African Americans, people of the Jewish faith, and a Potter's Field. To date, two phases of restoration work have been completed. Additional restoration and repair work is required on monuments, retaining walls, walkways, and landscaping. The foundation is undergoing a Master Planning and Comprehensive Campaign process to determine the full budget for these restoration needs and how to execute them.

To provide access to the cemetery and generate revenue, the foundation schedules a series of special events, including the Tunes from the Tombs, Arts at Oakland, the Run Like Hell 5K, Capturing the Spirit of Oakland Halloween Tours, biannual plant sales, and more than fifteen other special topic tours. The Sunday in the Park street festival invites guests to come in Victorian period costume and enjoy musical performances, storytellers, heritage craft demonstrations, a teddy bear tea party, and much more.

Private tours for schools and groups are offered year-round. The foundation also rents portions of the cemetery for special events and weddings. An online and on-site gift shop sell books (related to the cemetery and its residents), apparel, tote bags, and other gift items.

Other cemeteries across the country also generate revenue for maintenance and preservation through respectful access programs. After receiving several accolades and recognition in *Midnight in the Garden of Good and Evil*, Bonaventure Cemetery in Savannah charges fees for film or professional photography permits. Congressional Cemetery in the District of Columbia sells dog-walking memberships to cover grounds-keeping costs; there is currently a wait list.

★ ★ ★ ★ ★

Figure 2.4 Halloween Tours, Oakland Cemetery—Atlanta, Georgia. Source: Oakland Cemetery.

Figure 2.5 Jewish Ahavath Achim Section, Oakland Cemetery—Atlanta, Georgia. Source: Oakland Cemetery.

Profile: Paducah, Kentucky
From Blank Wall to City Canvas

http://www.paducahwalltowall.com

When the Ohio River crested its banks and rose over its fifty-foot earthen levee in 1937, Paducah, Kentucky, suffered its worst natural disaster in history. The U.S. Army Corps of Engineers built a fourteen-foot floodwall to protect the city. Muralist Robert Dafford used this new backdrop to portray Paducah's past (commenced in 1996 and completed in 2007). The Dafford murals team painted fifty life-size murals depicting various eras of Paducah's history—from Native American to various scenes on the rivers—to tell the stories of the city and its people. Each mural is about twenty by twelve feet, painted from detailed images researched by artists and Paducah Wall to Wall. The mural project is sponsored by the private sector and maintained by public and private funding. Taking from two to four weeks to paint (depending on weather), the cost for the murals ranges from $10,000 to $18,000, depending on size and details (including bronze interpretive panels and room and board for muralists). Repaints occur from ten to fifteen years, again depending on climate exposure. Interpretive bronze panels describe each painting.

To celebrate the twentieth anniversary of art and history in downtown Paducah, local artist Bill Ford illustrated three volumes of coloring books for sale. More than twenty local merchants sold the one-of-a-kind coloring book. Postcards, signed and numbered prints, T-shirts, and postcards of the murals are also sold, with all proceeds supporting future mural maintenance through the Floodwall Mural Advisory Board. Visitors may take a self-guided public art tour of the murals or schedule a guided tour. In 2014, TripAdvisor named the murals the top attraction in Kentucky.

* * * * *

Profile: Trailing of the Sheep Festival
Sun Valley, Ketchum, and Hailey, Idaho

http://www.trailingofthesheep.org

Long before southwestern Idaho gained an international reputation as a winter playground, the region was known for sheep. Early pioneer (and future congressman for the Idaho Territory) John Hailey brought the first sheep into the Wood River valley in the late 1860s. As mining activity declined in the region, the sheep industry became increasingly important to the local economy. In 1918, the sheep population reached 2.65 million, almost six times the state's human population—a dominance that remained until the 1970s. Sheep were exported around the world, and the area was second only to Sydney, Australia, as a sheep center. Scots, Basques, Peruvians, and other immigrants migrated here, finding jobs as sheepherders and later to start their own sheep operations.

The Great Depression and postwar development took their toll on farms, ranches, and open spaces. As the demand for recreation flourished in the 1990s, the desire to create a thirty-mile system of paved paths along Idaho's Wood River valley emerged. The Blaine County Recreation District asked ranchers to allow right-of-way on some of the sheep driveways developed in the early 1900s to connect the communities of Ketchum, Sun Valley, and Hailey. Unfortunately, bicyclists and other users of the class 1 trail system were unaware of the annual migration each spring and fall when sheep travel through the valley to spend summers grazing in the high mountains.

In 1992, local sheep ranchers Diane and John Peavey set out to help educate new residents and trail users about the history of the Wood River valley and their industry. Over coffee at a local café,

Figure 2.6 Robert Dafford painting wall-to-wall murals—Paducah, Kentucky. Source: Paducah Visitors Bureau.

the Peaveys shared local stories and then invited the gathering to walk with the sheep through the valley to experience this historic tradition firsthand. The concept for the Trailing of the Sheep Festival was born. The event afforded an opportunity to turn a potential conflict into a celebration of the valley's cultural heritage and history.

In 1996, the Peaveys garnered creative, human, and financial support from the Sun Valley/ Ketchum Chamber and Visitors Bureau and a group of volunteers to help promote and host the

Figure 2.7 Parade, Trailing of the Sheep Festival—Sun Valley, Ketchum, and Hailey, Idaho. Source: Carol Waller.

multiday event. The first Trailing of the Sheep Festival featured the Sheep Parade of 1,500 sheep down Main Street in Ketchum, the Sheep Folklife Fair, an evening of Sheep Tales (oral histories of sheep ranching), and Lamb Dine-Around, all organized with the purpose of

> preserving the stories and history of sheep ranchers and herders, celebrating the rich cultures of the past and present, and entertaining and educating children and adults about the production of local food and fiber that have sustained local economies for generations.[7]

After five years of support by the Chamber and Visitors Bureau and a host of volunteers, the Trailing of the Sheep Cultural Heritage Center, Inc., formed as a 501(c)(3) nonprofit organization to assume future development and hosting of the festival. Three part-time staff organize the event, with help from board members, an advisory council, sponsors, grantors, and more than 200 volunteers. Over the years, the festival expanded the original elements into five days of family-friendly events, including a Wool Festival, Championship Sheepdog Trials, a Sheepherder's Ball, and lamb dining experiences. The festival attracts 26,000 people annually. In 2015, visitors came from thirty-six states and eight countries, and the festival has an estimated $4.5 million impact on the Wood River valley region. This activity is particularly important to the economy, as it happens in a typically slower period: after the business summer recreation season and before the mountain is open for skiing.

"The annual Trailing of the Sheep Festival is a celebration where we gather, present and preserve the history and cultures of sheepherding in Idaho and the West," says Laura Musbach Drake, executive director of the festival. She continues, "We are proud to honor and share the stories, traditions and cultures of those who made this life what it is today."

Figure 2.8 Sheepdog at work, Trailing of Sheep Festival—Sun Valley, Ketchum, Hailey, Idaho. Source: Flaviu Grumazescu Fine & Art Photography.

The Trailing of the Sheep Cultural Heritage Center, Inc., is concluding a three-year program, Celebrating Generations, to record memories of western sheep ranching families. Year 1 honored the visionaries: the first families. Year 2 captured the oral histories of second and third generations of local sheepherding families: the survivors. Year 3 focuses on the stories of current and future generations. Documenting these oral histories is made possible through a grant from the Idaho Humanities Council, ticket sales, and general donations. The festival partners with the Western Folklife Center in Elko, Nevada, to record and archive these stories.

Key benchmarks are the following:

Late 1860s   First sheep brought to southern Idaho.

Early 1900s   Sheep driveway dedicated for trailing from southern Idaho through the valley to summer grazing in the mountains.

1980s   Ranchers allow sheep driveway to be used for trail system.

Fall 1992   Bicyclists upset with sheep droppings left on path after the fall migration. Conflict resolution: local "coffee chat" to learn about historic tradition of trailing the sheep through the valley.

1996 First Trailing of the Sheep Festival held—hosted by the Chamber and Visitors Bureau, local ranchers (the Peaveys), and volunteers.

2003 Nonprofit organization, Trailing of the Sheep Cultural Heritage Center, Inc., created to oversee growth and management of event, steward tradition.

2011 Named "Top 100 Festivals in the US"—American Business Association.

2012 Named "Top Ten Fall Festivals in the World" by msn.com travel.

2013 Recipient of the Idaho Governor's Award for Cultural Heritage and Cultural Tourism.

2013, 2014 Named "Top Ten Fall Festivals" by *USA Today*.

2015 Five-day festival attracts 26,000 visitors from thirty-six states and eight countries. Estimated economic impact is $4.5 million.[8]

2016 Five-day festival boasts more than thirty-five separate events.

Figure 2.9 Sheep herd, Trailing of the Sheep Festival—Sun Valley, Ketchum, and Hailey, Idaho. Source: Michael Edminster.

Identifying and Assessing Local Heritage and Culture

Sample Site Assessment Form

1. Name of Attraction:_____

2. Form completed by (person and organization): _____
   Phone Number: _____ E-mail: _____

3. What is authentic, unique or interesting about this site? Describe in 100 words.
   _____
   _____

4. Is this attraction privately owned and operated?
   Yes   No   Don't Know

5. If this attraction is on a designated, signed Trail or Route, please note the name(s):
   _____

6. Attraction Information (fill in as appropriate):

Address/City/State:	
County:	
Site Hours/Days of Operation:	
Site Fees:	
Contact Person:	
Phone/Fax:	
E-mail:	
Web Address (URL):	

7. Attraction Type (check or "X" as many as apply)   8. Special Programs or Events

	Museum	
	Historical/Archaeological Site	
	Performing Arts (e.g., music, dance, theater)	
	Cultural/Folk Traditional Site or Experience	
	Arts/Craft Gallery, Studio	
	Festival/Unique Holiday Celebration	
	Main Street	
	Natural Area (park, waterfall, scenic overlook)	
	Farm, Agricultural Attraction	
	Outdoor Recreation (e.g., hiking, rafting, biking)	
	Trail/Route	
	Retail Shop	
	Locally owned Restaurant, Diner, Winery, Brewery	
	Hotel/Lodge/Inn/Resort/Bed-and-Breakfast	
	Other (describe) _____	

Figure 2.10 Site assessment form. Source: Cheryl Hargrove.

Table 2.2 Physical Inventory Worksheet

Name of Site/Activity	What County Is Site/Activity Located In?
Physical Location of Site/Activity Including City	
Type of Site/Activity ☐ Historic district ☐ Historic Structure ☐ Historic/archeological site ☐ Museum/ Cultural Center ☐ Memorial/Monument ☐ Heritage Site ☐ Cultural Event/Heritage Festival ☐ Tourism Support Amenity/Service ☐ Park/Recreation Site ☐ Scenic Drive ☐ Natural Attraction ☐ Historic Landmark, National Register Property, State Archeological Landmark, Historic Site Cemetery, or Local Designation	What Is Significant About the Site/Activity?
Owner/Organization Name	Ownership ☐ City ☐ County ☐ State ☐ Private ☐ Non-profit ☐ Federal
Owner/Organization Address Owner/Organization Website Address	
Owner/Organization Phone Number	Owner/Organization Email Address
Visitorship to Site/Activity (Include method used to determine visitorship)	Marketing Efforts at Site/Activity (Attach calendar of events and other promotional material)
List Activities at site, if applicable	
Images of Sites and Activities (Please label and attach)	Hours of Operation at Site/Activity (Please list days and times open to public)

Entrance Fee Charged at Site/Activity ☐ Yes How much? _____ ☐ No	Public Restrooms Available at Site/Activity? ☐ Yes ☐ No
Accessibility of Site/Activity to Population Served ☐ Good ☐ Fair ☐ Poor	Is Site/Activity Handicap Accessible/ADA Compliant? ☐ Yes ☐ No
Routes Used to Reach Site/Activity from Nearest City	Routes Used to Reach Site/Activity from Nearest City
Name Two Features of the Site/Activity that Make it Unique from Other Sites 1. 2.	Name Two Features of the Site/Activity that Make it Unique from Other Sites 1. 2.
Improvements Most Needed to Enhance the Overall Tourist Experience at Site/Activity ☐ More staff/volunteers ☐ More/better interpretive signage ☐ More money for advertising ☐ More parking ☐ More/better directional signage ☐ Other: _____	Improvements Most Needed to Enhance the Overall Tourist Experience at Site/Activity ☐ More staff/volunteers ☐ More/better interpretive signage ☐ More money for advertising ☐ More parking ☐ More/better directional signage ☐ Other: _____

Source: Texas Historical Commission, *Heritage Tourism Guidebook*, Appendix B http://www.thc.state.tx.us/public/upload/publications/heritage-tourism-guide.pdf.

Notes

1. http://www.brainyquote.com/quotes/keywords/heritage_2.html#kh51FxzIbHt61frb.99.
2. National Register Bulletin, "How to Apply the National Register Criteria for Evaluation" (n.d.), U.S. Department of the Interior, National Park Service, http://www.nps.gov/nr/publications/bulletins/nrb15/nrb15_2.htm.
3. Modified from "Getting Started: How to Succeed in Heritage Tourism," National Trust for Historic Preservation (1993), p. 24.
4. Modified from "Cultural and Heritage Tourism—A Handbook for Community Champions" (2012), Federal Provincial Territorial Ministers of Culture and Heritage, p. 10.
5. A. Radbill and J. Chaich, "Heritage Tourism and Sacred Sites: An Introduction" (n.d.), Common Bond, p. 10.
6. "What Is Intangible Cultural Heritage?" (n.d.), UNESCO, http://www.unesco.org/culture/ich/doc/src/01851-EN.pdf.
7. Trailing of the Sheep Cultural Heritage Center, Inc., http://www.trailingofthesheep.org/history.

8. Idaho Agricultural Statistic Service.
9. E. Maggi and F. L. Fredella, "The Carrying Capacity of a Tourism Destination: The Case of a Coastal Italian City" (August 2010), citing G. McIntyre, "Sustainable Tourism Development: Guide for Local Planners" (1993), World Tourism Organization, p. 3, https://www.researchgate.net/publication/230793635_The_carrying_capacity_of_a_tourist_destination_The_case_of_a_coastal_Italian_city.
10. Modified from "Getting Started: How to Succeed in Heritage Tourism," National Trust for Historic Preservation (1993), p. 24.
11. "Government Doubles Official Estimate: There are 35,000 Active Museums in the U.S." (May 19, 2014), Institute of Museum and Library Services, https://www.imls.gov/news-events/news-releases/government-doubles-official-estimate-there-are-35000-active-museums-us.
12. S. Meeks, "House Museums: A 20th Century Paradigm," National Preservation Conference annual meeting (October 2013), National Trust for Historic Preservation.
13. Ibid.

Chapter 3

Understanding Visitor Needs and Expectations

Through travel I first became aware of the outside world; it was through travel that I found my own introspective way into becoming a part of it.

—Eudora Welty

Without people visiting, exploring, engaging, and spending time and money, the premise of cultural heritage tourism is lost. Delivering the right mix of activities and amenities is essential to net the maximum benefit from tourism. Add interesting cuisine, architecture, nature-based attractions, and shopping to the mix, and a desired cultural heritage experience takes shape. For cultural heritage tourism, the experiences must be carefully balanced with the destination's capacity, the community's character, and the residents' desires.

All tourists—and residents—desire a safe and welcoming environment. Consistently delivering the needs and meeting (or exceeding) expectations is a constant challenge. Adding to this burden is recognition that most planners, tourism industry professionals, and cultural heritage resource managers do not control all of the components of the visitor experience. Consider the impact of parking, signage, retail mix, culinary diversity, and beautification (after all, first impressions are important) on the visitor. These elements can enhance or detract from even the most dynamic cultural heritage experience. Getting everyone on board is paramount to delivering the destination's brand promise. This collaboration begins, however, with *understanding what visitors want*—and how cultural heritage tourism can deliver, if planned for, in a sustainable, market-facing approach. This research process also delves into the residents' role in defining—and delivering—visitor needs and expectations.

What Cultural Heritage Visitors Want

I am a passionate traveler, and from the time I was a child, travel formed me as much as my formal education.

—David Rockefeller

One of the first studies conducted about what motivated people to travel to cultural and historic sites in the United States cited personal enjoyment and entertainment, personal education, and education of children as the top reasons for travel.[1] While not all cultural and historic sites and attractions should "entertain," they can provide enriching, evocative learning experiences. Museums, in particular, can excel at creating surprise, awe, and delight. Providing an opportunity to deepen and broaden existing knowledge may also translate into an unexpected learning experience.[2] Connecting with the visitor through relevant stories not only generates a chance to interpret sites and places but also contributes to visitors' understanding and knowledge of place.

A study conducted by Jerry Henry and Associates in 2009 found that 80 percent of visitors like to visit places that are authentic.[3] But what is authenticity? It usually relates to the personal perception of what is real or fake, based on individual experience and understanding. Gilmore and Pine discuss how the increasing desire for authentic experiences has led companies and destinations to "actively engage customers not just individually but as a community of like-minded people, so that your offerings—and by extension your business—gain in stature as authentically constructed."[4] Gilmore and Pine recommend two standards to instruct companies and destinations: being true to your own self and being who you say you are to others.[5]

When the National Trust for Historic Preservation created its five principles for cultural heritage tourism, "focus on authenticity and quality" was first on the list.[6] At that time, the word "authenticity" was not as prolific in the global lexicon as it is today. But the intent was the same—an opportunity to present what is real, what is unique, and what sets one place apart from another. Today, as homogenization continues—both at gateways where strip malls define the entrance to many city cores and historic districts, and in the gentrification of cultural identity if the retail/restaurant mix is propagated by national chains—authenticity is a little harder to find in some destinations. And authenticity of artifacts is often debated, based on level of originality and integrity of object. Cultural and heritage resources provide the distinctive mix of architecture and artifacts, festivals and folklore, historic sites, and handmade objects that pronounce a visit to "somewhere" rather than "anywhere."

As table 3.1 shows, authenticity takes on many attributes based on the context of the asset. The PGAV Destinations study states the best examples of authenticity are places where something real happened in history, a natural place untouched by human hands, and something you could not do anywhere else.[7] Credible information is paramount to sustainability. These examples provide important criteria to review and evaluate assets to determine their potential for cultural heritage tourism.

Table 3.1 Attributes of Authenticity

Category	Attributes
Unique	Original, Artistic, Inventive, Spontaneous
Real	Historical, Natural, Landmarks
Human	Genuine, Trustworthy, Caring
Non-Commercial	Simple, Not Fake, Not Glitzy, Not "out to make a buck"
Social/Emotional	Bonding, Feeling closer to family/ friends

Source: PGAV Destinations, "Real Potential: The Power of Authenticity to Reposition Your Destination" (2009).

If an economic goal for cultural heritage tourism is to get visitors to stay longer and spend more—two characteristics proven by research over the past two decades—the availability of places to spend money is paramount to success and sustainability. Admission fees, if they are collected at cultural and heritage sites, do not generate enough revenue to cover sustainable operations, so additional sources must be tapped to part visitors from their money. Shopping, dining, and lodging are three obvious areas for sales; special events and programming are two other areas where cultural and heritage resources can capture visitor dollars.

Visitors typically want to shop at locations different from home, and locally made items become desired souvenirs. The story of Rapid City's Prairie Edge Trading Company and Galleries in the profile at the end of this chapter shares how one retail store sets them apart from the competition.

Research indicates, though, that money is not always how visitors define value. PGAV Destinations conducted a study on new motivations for travel in the postrecession era.[10] The report states that quality is defined through "affordability, quality, safety, and relaxation offered by the experience."[11]

Stress-filled lives have travelers seeking out less visited places or popular off-season destinations as a way to avoid crowds. A rising interest in opportunities that reduce stress (77 percent) or that provide personal enrichment (68 percent) are among the top motivations to splurge (spend a little extra) on a travel experience. Creating memories is still the number one motivator inspiring splurge purchases (by 80 percent), according to PGAV Destinations.[12] Meeting the aspirational goals of travelers, especially those individuals wanting to create memories, is essential to fostering repeat visits and cultivating new generations of visitors.

Trends Impacting Travel—Today and in the Future

Many consumer trends impact travel. You need only look at the annual list of trends of global research innovator JWT Intelligence[13] to see how the prediction of celebrity endorsements has become a reality or how two predictions from 2014 resonate with travelers and influence tourism development today: the desire for "immersive experiences" and the impact of technology "as a gateway to opportunity," particularly through the use of visual images and mobile devices.

Trend 1: Increased Competition

As mentioned earlier, the number of active museums has doubled in the past twenty years (from 17,500 to more than 35,000 in 2014).[14] The National Register of Historic Places has 90,540 listings, representing a total of 1.4 million individual contributing resources (including buildings, sites, structures, and objects). The United States also has designated 2,532 National Historic Landmarks, 20 World Heritage Sites, 49 National Heritage Areas, and more than 800 Preserve America communities. Add more than 2,000 Main Street communities across the country, and the supply of cultural heritage "product" is high.[15]

Competition also comes in the form of other leisure-time activities outside of travel, with multiple options now vying for a consumer's free time. Cultural heritage sites must provide dynamic and valued experiences worthy of a tourist's time and money.

Trend 2: Savvy Consumers

Consumers are better-educated, more experienced travelers and therefore have higher expectations for tour experiences than even a decade ago. In 2014, JWT Intelligence named the "age of impatience" as one of the top ten consumer trends, along with the desire for immersive experiences.[16] Places off the beaten path and destinations "new and near" are also gaining ground as consumers seek to step out of their normal environments and find little-known discoveries (events, attractions, diners, and destinations) within a day's drive.[17] Customization is key, and providing tailored experiences for each target market is essential to attracting savvy customers—especially as baby boomers age and Millennials move into the power spot for travel.

Trend 3: Impact of Technology

Perhaps the greatest technological advancement is the use of mobile devices for preplanning research, purchases, and on-site decision making. Whether it's downloading apps to provide more detailed content about exhibits and tours or finding restaurants and making reservations, smartphones help travelers locate desired information. Websites with responsive design are essential to becoming the portal for accessing information on any device—tablet, desktop, or phone.

The cultural heritage tourist is three times more likely to use a mobile device to learn about events and get recommendations and is more frequently booking dining and attractions via mobile devices (smartphones and tablets) than general travelers. Social media (Facebook, Twitter, Instagram, and Pinterest) have high usage by the cultural heritage tourist market as well: 75 percent use Facebook, and 40 percent use YouTube.[18] Destination Analysts highlights the importance of social and digital media in influencing travel decisions: 59.8 percent said that the opinions of friends and relatives impacted their interest in visiting a place. While 90 percent of word of mouth still happens via personal conversation, social media account for 35.6 percent, and e-mails, texts, postcards, and letters influence 29.4 percent of decisions regarding travel. What people of influence post, particularly friends and relatives, matters to potential travelers. Two-thirds of the respondents also hear about new technology via word of mouth.[19]

Destination Analysts[20] cites some revealing statistics regarding travel media and technology. Despite the growth in the use of mobile devices, three-quarters of travelers still prefer or strongly prefer planning on traditional devices—desktop or laptop—especially for researching activities, attractions, or events. Slightly more than one-quarter of travelers use apps in travel planning. Destination Analysts also identified profiles of technology adopters. Not unexpectedly, the innovators—the first to adopt new travel technologies—are Millennials and Gen-Xers. Innovators also travel the most and have the largest annual travel budgets. This ethnically diverse segment makes most or all their decisions regarding travel online.[21]

As technology advances rapidly into all facets of life, travel and destinations race to keep up with demand for quick access, personalization, mobile pay, and other interconnected transactions to simplify and speed up logistics.[22] The explosive growth of Instagram, Snapchat, Flickr, Pinterest, and other social media sites for image uploading and sharing demonstrates how a picture is indeed worth a thousand words. Cultural heritage sites and destinations need to consider what images resonate with visitors and how well they show on social media sites. Technology—and its impact on travel—is important to consider and integrate into all development, marketing and planning tools.

Trend 4: The Importance of Storytelling

Telling stories helps grab the attention of tourists with relevant content that connects them to the place. Engaging tourists in the conversation adds to the experience value, as dialogue helps build understanding and connection to place. Crowdsourced content turns storytelling into story involvement—a conversation with the customer and community building. TripAdvisor, Yelp, Squidoo, HubPages, blogs, and other online sites are now key trip-planning tools for consumer recommendations, ratings, and research.

Trend 5: Disruptive Business Models

The impact of the peer-to-peer movement or sharing economy has potentially favorable implications for the cultural heritage tourism segment. According to Vipin Goyal, now cofounder and partner of a start-up studio called Shipyard NYC (previously founder and chief executive officer of Side Tour, acquired by Groupon in September 2013),

> This movement is driven by an interest in supporting local communities and artisans and knowing more about the people behind the things we buy. It's a shift away from mass-market efficiency . . . that has dominated the past couple of decades. Increasingly, people want to experience the unique gems [while traveling].[23]

The sharing economy—as evidenced by the success of Airbnb and Uber—demonstrates a shift in the delivery systems for highly personal experiences and exceptional customer service. While the sharing economy is testing traditional norms, especially related to payment of hotel and motel occupancy taxes and driver registration and certification, respectively, the sharing economy is increasingly engaged in the product development, distribution systems, and hosting services of the travel and tourism industry. Social media provide insights into the desires and product development desired by new or emerging markets—particularly Millennials—to establish a new "trust economy" that satisfies a craving for authenticity and quality.

Trend 6: Desire for Immersive Experiences

An additional impact of the sharing economy is its great insight and opportunity for cultural heritage tourism development. Providing direct access for visitors to meet and interact with residents (experts and guides) opens a dialogue for locally sourced content and experiences. The social interaction with locals—or engagement in favorite local activities—also achieves a growing desire on the part of visitors (particularly cultural heritage tourists) to go beyond the superficial view of a destination that skims the surface with tours to only known attractions. Delving deeper into the character of a place allows visitors to consider life as a local and learn more about the culture—past to present.

Two travel-related stresses negatively impact the pleasure of a trip: managing details and not feeling safe. The hassle of planning logistics can be stressful, as is the concern over safety and security. To counter these concerns and to cater to the desire for immersive experiences, tour operators are increasingly adding specific opportunities for exclusive, up-close-and-personal encounters with the people and cultures that define their destinations.

In a study conducted in 2013, the Futures Company echoes this theme of immersion. According to the report, respondents defined their own success by embracing new experiences and challenges (65 percent) and always trying to learn and do new things (65 percent)—numbers

9 and 10, respectively, of the top ten contributors to success. More importantly for cultural heritage tourism, the report said that "72 percent would rather spend money on experiences than things."[24] The study continued, "Americans have established a new standard of success where pursuing passions and seeking life fulfillment now supersede the sheer accumulation of wealth." Traveling, especially to new places, topped the bucket list for Americans (88 percent) polled in the study.[25]

Figure 3.1 A view from the pulpit of the historic African Meeting House, where Frederick Douglass and other abolitionist and social activists rallied for equal rights for African Americans and women during the nineteenth and twentieth centuries. Museum of African American History—Boston, Massachusetts. Source: Courtesy of the Museum of African American History.

Millennials, who make up 32 percent of U.S. travelers, go beyond the desire for a casual meeting or local interaction in their definition of immersive experiences. The interest in cultural heritage experiences for this generation in particular is high. Destination Analysts reports a comparable desire for authentic destination products, culture, and cuisine—similar to the baby-boomer traveler.[26] According to MMGY Global, "Nearly 60 percent of Millennials would rather spend money on experiences than on material goods." Dollar-wise, that translates to the average Millennial traveler planning to spend about $5,300 per trip.[27] Millennials like to stay connected while traveling, using technology not only for on-site trip planning but also for recording experiences and sharing with others via social media.

For cultural heritage sites and destinations, providing the physical environment is only the first step to offering the desired visitor experience. Compelling content, interaction with local residents, and distinctive activities are important developments that complement architecture, historic neighborhoods, and cultural districts. Cultural heritage tourism planners, developers, marketers, and managers must consider the implications of these and other consumer trends on their own operations, business models, funding, and customer engagement. Monitoring trends helps align programs and anticipate opportunities to better meet the needs of current and future generations of travelers.

As a case in point, the Museum of African American History in Boston and Nantucket, Massachusetts, engages student interns in identifying current societal issues for discussion and deliberation. As shown in the profile at the end of this chapter, this museum is harnessing the creativity of youth to broaden its conversation and impact.

Basic Needs of Visitors

With the global proliferation of travel and access to new destinations every day, competition for visitors is fierce. The new complexity of the journey—from added airport security to cramped airplanes and congested highways—makes it even more challenging for destinations and attractions to deliver an experience that overcomes the frequent stress and hassles associated with travel today. Successful destinations and organizations realize that inviting, safe, and attractive places to visit can make the experience worth the journey.

Adequate lighting in historic neighborhoods and downtowns, pedestrian-friendly sidewalks and crosswalks, ample parking or transportation shuttles that provide convenient access to high-traffic areas, biking and walking paths, and wayfinding for both directional and informational signage are only a few infrastructure needs for tourists—and residents—to enhance livability and functionality.

One of the premier standards for rating travel destinations is the Travel and Tourism Competitiveness Index (TTCI). First compiled in 2007, the TTCI measures "the set of factors and policies that enable the sustainable development of the travel and tourism sector, which in turn, contributes to the development and competitiveness of a country."[31] The TTCI is compiled into a biannual *Travel and Tourism Competitiveness Report* and presented at the World Economic Forum in Davos, Switzerland. As shown in figure 3.2, the TTCI weighs varied factors to arrive at its measurement scores.

The United States is currently ranked fourth in the world (behind Spain, France, and Germany) for its performance. The TTCI recognized the exceptional World Heritage Sites and strong cultural, entertainment, and sport attractions of the United States, with a nod to its highly competitive business environment. Areas for improvement, though, include the quality of ground transport, safety and security, and environmental sustainability. While the TTCI measures country competitiveness, this same set of indexes translates to weighing tourism at the state and local levels. These issues have been and are becoming increasingly more important to tourism growth and sustainability. Planning for and the management of infrastructure must be considered part of the cultural heritage tourism mix. Movement of persons, a guarantee of personal safety, and environmental protection need to be on every planner's and resource manager's radar.

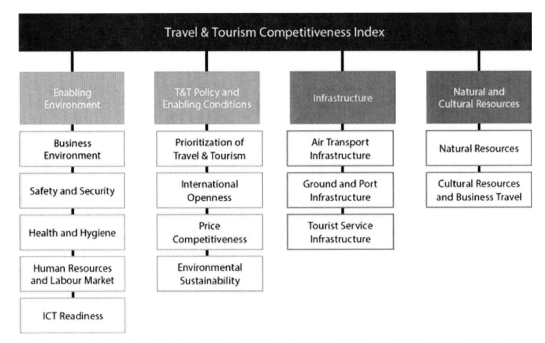

Figure 3.2 The Travel and Tourism Competitiveness Index 2015 framework. Source: World Economic Forum, *The Travel and Tourism Competitiveness Report 2015*, available at www.weforum.org/ttcr.

One indicator not included in the TTCI is hospitality. As Smith discusses, good service is the basic criterion for a positive host–guest experience.[32] She adds, "Good service is a quality of mind, an intent to please, and a genuine concern for the guest; it cannot be commoditized and bought." Educating staff at cultural, heritage, and tourism businesses is vital to ensuring that visitors feel welcome and are greeted with knowledgeable hosts. Residents also share in this important hospitality role both as local brand ambassadors and as hosts for visiting friends and relatives.

Role of Local Residents as "Visitors at Home"

Out-of-town tourists are the desired market for cultural heritage tourism for one specific reason: they bring new money to town and then leave. Often, though, the number one motivation for travelers is to visit friends and relatives. That makes local residents the chief ambassadors for a destination. And if they are unaware or uninformed about cultural heritage sites and attractions, they won't recommend these places to their friends and family. Worse, they may take these visiting guests to another county or state, resulting in "leakage" of monies that could be (and should be) spent locally. Therefore, training and teaching these local residents and hosts to be knowledge brokers and ambassadors for visiting guests can pay dividends. As residents become more proficient in the cultural heritage tourism offerings that are available to tourists, some may be tapped as local expert guides, as lecturers for group tours, or as volunteer docents for local events and programs. The importance of residents as hosts is explored more in chapter 13.

Like other forms of traditional economic development, tourism requires an investment to prepare and deliver the desired products and services to attract and host visitors. Beyond bricks and mortar, cultural heritage tourism requires investment in local residents—both frontline

Figure 3.3 Sandcastles Children's Museum—Ludington, Michigan. Source: Sandcastles Children's Museum.

employees and staff and the general population—to understand their attitudes and opinions about tourism, to gauge their knowledge of the local community (culture, heritage, area attractions, and amenities), to identify their recommendations for visiting friends and relatives, and to define the desired benefits for sharing their community with tourists. Conducting local research can help identify potential problems or issues to address (helping avoid the ambivalent mantra of "there's nothing to do here"). Often, this research can identify a gap in the supply chain. This was the case for Ludington, Michigan, and the reason to establish Sandcastle Children's Museum, which, as profiled at the end of this chapter, provided an educational alternative to outdoor recreation, especially in inclement weather.

"Ask the Customer": Engaging Visitors in the Planning Process

One way that museums and other cultural heritage sites and destinations are connecting with visitors is to engage them in the planning and development process. Asking visitors—via surveys, social media sites (Facebook in particular), and touch-screen kiosks—can yield valuable information and ideas about improving current experiences or proposing new programs and products. Visitor information centers also offer a firsthand opportunity to connect with tourists and ask opinions on a range of topics. Hotel concierges may also be a great source of information for understanding the desires of visitors. Capturing comments about customer service, the quality of restaurants or attractions, or even frequent requests for products not currently available can be beneficial to planning processes. Of course, perusing comments in the traditional guest book on entry or exit at historic house museums, sites, and cultural attractions may also provide helpful information. Beyond asking visitors for their input, collecting the data and frequently analyzing the information are what is most important. With the rapidly changing profiles of travelers, new markets constantly opening up, and diversified ways that tourists want to receive information, planners must not forget to tap current and potential customers for input.

> Research can confirm the obvious, but also reveal missed opportunities that result in a greatly improved visitor experience. Research gets us away from talking to ourselves, and listening to the customer who can say something profound.
> —Berkeley Young, president, Young Strategies, Inc.

Chapter Summary

Sustainable cultural heritage tourism begins with credible information about place (the history, culture, and assets distinctive to a destination) and learning about both current and potential customers. Researching who is visiting, understanding visitor needs and desires, and identifying trends impacting travel—today and tomorrow—along with determining resident attitudes about and knowledge of local cultural heritage make up the foundation for developing and sustaining cultural heritage tourism. Take time to get to know your customer, both local and from out of town, to inform planning decisions.

* * * * *

Profile: Prairie Edge Gallery—Principled and Purposeful Shopping
Rapid City, South Dakota

http://prairieedge.com

Outside of the Prairie Edge Gallery in downtown Rapid City stands a bronze sculpture, "Hunkayapi" (or "Tying on the Eagle Plume"), symbolizing the "wisdom of a Lakota elder and the teaching of the Lakota heritage to the next generation."[8] This respect of the Native American people and their traditions is evident throughout Prairie Edge—part museum, part gallery, and part trading company.

Ray Hillenbrand, who made his fortune in Indiana before moving to Rapid City in 1980, started Prairie Edge in the 1980s and located it in the historic Buell building. Hillenbrand established the business with two specific purposes in mind. The first is to educate the public about and to help preserve the heritage and culture of the Northern Plains Indians. The second is to provide Northern and Great Plains Indian artists and craftspeople an outlet to show and sell their finest work, reflective of their heritage and culture. The galleries feature beadwork, quillwork, paintings, drawing, cast paper, prints, photography, pottery, silverwork, jewelry, and other handcrafts by regionally and nationally acclaimed Native American artists. A book-and-music store focuses on Native American and western history, education, and culture. The Sioux Trading Post supplies crafters with furs, feathers, shells, teeth, claws, hides, buffalo parts, trade cloth, botanicals, and beads. Open daily except holidays, Prairie Edge has become one of the premier retail experiences in South Dakota, highly rated on TripAdvisor and ranked fourth of sixty things to do in Rapid City.

More than three generations of artists have had their artwork at Prairie Edge. Kevin Fast Horse, an Oglala Lakota artist, attributes his success to being one of dozens of Native American artists with backing from Prairie Edge. He says, "We will be fine as long as we have people who care about the art like the Prairie Edge owners and staff do."

"We have been around about 35 years and some of the relationships go back that far. Many of our artists have been here from day one, and their families have become engaged with the business as well," said Dan Tribby, general manager of Prairie Edge. "In these times of so much change, I think our customers can really appreciate not only the longevity of the staff, but many are purchasing artwork from the children—and in some cases the grandchildren—of artists that they first purchased from many years ago. The same goes with our staff; many have been here over twenty years. I think that is saying some about our business philosophy and how we work," Tribby continued. He added, "In these times now of the internet, we have the chance to not only reach out to people all over the world and offer the fine quality artwork that we are known for, but possibly more importantly we can play a role in the process of helping to educate the public, wherever they are, about Native American culture and history. We take that role pretty seriously."

Prairie Edge helped set in motion the redevelopment of derelict downtown and sixty-eight-car parking lot into a family-friendly Main Street Square in the heart of Rapid City. Hillenbrand and his family purchased five historic buildings (at a total cost of nearly $5 million), restored them, and then attracted a unique mix of eighteen nonfranchise boutiques, restaurants, and galleries to help transform the area. The porn shop was replaced with a British-style pub, while the Video Blue store became an independent bookstore named "Mitzi's" after Hillenbrand's sister and visionary for the family-focused district. Destination Rapid City, chaired by Hillenbrand, formed a business improvement district in 2008 to assist with funding and garner community support. Today, Main Street Square—with its public space with interactive fountains—is optimally used for arts and cultural events, festivals, live concerts, and seasonal ice skating.[9] It has become a gathering place for visitors and residents alike. It is estimated that about 400,000 guests come into downtown Rapid City now. This is for all of the events that are held at Main Street Square.

Local citizens now have a central meeting area that disappeared in the 1970s, when malls became prevalent. "Visitors go where the locals go, so with Mt. Rushmore just over 20 miles away, we have seen huge increases in visitation to the downtown area by many of those 2.5 million visitors coming to the Black Hills and Mt. Rushmore," said Tribby. He continued, "Rapid City is definitely becoming much more progressive, but we are also trying to be very smart about how we grow. It's a balancing act—keeping in mind the needs of both established business and their employees as well as looking forward to catering to the needs of Millennials. Upward and onward!"

* * * * *

Profile: Museum of African American History—Youthful Direction
Boston, Massachusetts

http://www.maah.org

Each summer, student interns for the Museum of African American History embark on a new discovery in Boston's nineteenth-century black community on Beacon Hill. As part of the John Hancock's MLK Summer Scholars program, the museum hires high school students to intern at some of the most important National Historic Landmarks in the country and learn more about how Boston shaped American history.

In 2014, seven interns set out to create a new tour for the museum. Through exhaustive research conducted over the course of seven weeks, the local MLK scholars identified sites throughout the city related to the museum's *Freedom Rising: Reading, Writing, and Publishing Black Books* exhibit on display that fall. The interns mapped the locations, wrote the script, and served as docent guides for a new "Black Books Walking Tour." Tour stops included learning about some of the area's significant people and places:

- Abiel Smith School, the oldest building in the nation, built as a public school for black children
- David Walker, an abolitionist originally from North Carolina who authored the 1829 pamphlet *Appeal . . . to the Colored Citizens of the World*, encouraging African Americans to fight for freedom and equality, an act that changed the abolition movement (Walker died in Boston in 1830)
- African Meeting House, home of the Museum of African American History
- Dr. Rebecca Crumpler, the first African American woman in the United States to earn a medical degree and the only African American woman to graduate from the New England Female Medical College, which closed in 1873[28]
- Lewis Hayden Store, an Underground Railroad station and the base for the abolitionist leader's political activism
- Robert Gould Shaw Memorial, dedicated to the Massachusetts 54th Regiment, including some of the first African Americans to fight in the Civil War

Figure 3.4 MLK summer scholar leads a tour in an Abiel Smith School exhibit gallery. Museum of African American History—Boston, Massachusetts. Courtesy of the Museum of African American History.

- Maria Stewart, writer, lecturer, and devoted activist on women's and African American rights
- Pauline Hopkins, prominent African American playwright, novelist, and columnist
- William Cooper Nell's Home, designated as a African American National Historic Site to recognize this abolitionist, who, among other activities, led the campaign to desegregate the Boston Railroad and performance halls

The MLK scholars also posted about their experience, using blogs on social media to share their insights and discoveries.

"The Museum of African American History continues to feature Black Heritage Trails® and other customized experiences to share the place-based history of the people, places and events, and the stories they represent," said L'Merchie Frazier, director of education and interpretation. "We provide a continuum of authentic history that links conversations about freedom and social issues that is not found in textbooks. We engage young audiences, including MLK Summer Scholars, in a variety of alternative lessons that help students to better understand the past and own these experiences. As Frederick Douglass said in 1855, 'It is easier to build strong children than to repair broken men.'"

John Hancock's MLK Summer Scholars program provides summer jobs for city youth where high school-age scholars learn job skills while also helping local nonprofit organizations realize their mission. The Museum of African American History received a total of $12,250 for MLK scholar positions awarded in 2016 and $9,600 in 2015. Applicants are mostly teens, ages fifteen to nineteen, and are full-time residents of the city of Boston.[29]

The Museum of African American History preserves, conserves, and interprets the contributions of African Americans. The nonprofit organization has preserved four historic sites, three of which are National Historic Landmarks, and created two Black Heritage Trails: one in Boston and one in Nantucket. These iconic structures "tell the story of the organized black communities from the Colonial Period through the 19th century."[30] The Boston museum is located in the nation's first African Meeting House, built and opened in 1806 and now the oldest existing African American church building in the nation, constructed primarily by free black artisans. The museum acquired the African Meeting House in Boston in 1972 and completed a historic restoration in 2011, returning the building to its 1855 appearance. Major grants were received from the 1772 Foundation, American Express, the Bank of America, EMC, Liberty Mutual, National Grid, the State Street Bank, Walmart, the National Trust for Historic Preservation, and the Mabel Louise Riley and Webster Foundations as well as the Mayor's Office and the Massachusetts Cultural Facilities Fund. These public-private contributions leveraged a $4 million award from the American Recovery and Reinvestment Act and the National Park Service. With these funds, almost 175 jobs will have been created during this historic restoration.

* * * * *

Profile: Sandcastles Children's Museum—A Place to Learn and Play
Ludington, Michigan

http://www.sandcastleschildrensmuseum.com

On the western shore of Lake Michigan is the small coastal town of Ludington, population 8,040. With seasonal visitation of up to 800,000 at the popular Ludington State Park, the town recognized a need to provide attractions for visitors to extend their stays—converting day visitors to overnight and expanding year-round tourism to sustain local businesses. With many nature-based,

Figure 3.5 Badger Playship, Sandcastles Children's Museum—Ludington, Michigan. Source: Sandcastles Children's Museum.

outdoor activities available, two schoolteachers identified an opportunity to offer an indoor museum for children to enjoy during inclement weather and also expand local awareness about the community. Established in October 2006 with a board of six volunteers, Sandcastles Children's Museum created its first exhibit, *Help Us Build the Museum*, in March 2007 to attract support and input from local residents, businesses, and merchants.

In 2009, following successful summer camps and sponsored activities, Sandcastles moved to a larger location on West Ludington Avenue. Official attendance for the summer season was 12,645. Programming titled *Munchkin Mondays* attracted preschoolers, while *Thrilling Thursdays* focused on programming for school-age children. A Ludington-centric theme for the museum resulted in *Our Neighborhood*, with exhibits of an ice cream shop (similar to the iconic Ludington institution "House of Flavors," operating in downtown Ludington since 1948), a post office, a sailboat, and a bubble table. Due to increased demand, the museum extended its season, staying open on Fridays and Saturdays through December 19. In 2010, two new exhibits added to the hometown feel—*Badger PlayShip*, a replica of the National Historic Landmark ferry that crosses Lake Michigan, and a bank built by Home Depot employees.

With a history of success, in November 2010, the Sandcastles Board purchased the former Elks building in downtown Ludington. The board led a capital campaign to raise $300,000 to complete the purchase and convert the landmark structure into a museum. More than 125 volunteers worked to renovate the historic building and prepare for its grand opening in May 2011.

From 2011 to 2014, the museum added new exhibits, increased attendance, and expanded hours and days of operation. In 2015, the museum renovated the second floor—previously used for storage—and added a roof deck and fire escape. Grants from the Paine Foundation, the Great Lakes Energy People Fund, and the Community Foundations for Mason and Oceana Counties; an anonymous matching grant of $50,000; and numerous individual gifts allowed the museum to conclude the renovation debt free. Upstairs featured the interactive Sandcastles Ludrock music stage and Grandpa's Farm. The roof deck became home for the Musical Playground and workshops. Attendance topped 23,000 for the year. In 2016, more renovations helped increase the footprint of the museum, including the lower-level party room and music stage for special events—even during the off-season.

"We wanted the children in our community to benefit from the learning potential of a children's museum just as the children from larger cities do. We knew that it was maybe even more important for our small town to offer a breadth of experience to our kids through hands on activities, learning workshops, and educational presentations," said Kristin Korendyke, former founding president and current executive director of Sandcastles Children's Museum. She continued, "The passion we had for our mission was motivated by our love for kids. That is what kept us going in the early years—we knew this museum would benefit their childhood experiences and in turn be good for our community as a whole."

The museum continues to depend on more than one hundred volunteers to staff the facility, build and maintain exhibits, and assist with programming and administration. Grants and fund-raisers help raise awareness and revenue for capital projects. A seven-member volunteer board governs the organization and sets long-term goals for the museum. With creativity, energy, and community engagement, it will be interesting to see what Sandcastles has in store for the next decade of experiences.

* * * * *

Notes

1. U.S. Travel Association (d.b.a. as TIA when the study was conducted in 1992).
2. Nick O'Flaherty, "What Visitors Want—The Way to Meet Museum Visitors' Expectations Is by Defying Them, *ICOMNews*, vol. 4 (2014).
3. Jerry Henry and Associates for PGAV Destinations, "Real Potential: The Power of Authenticity to Reposition Your Destination" (2009).
4. James H. Gilmore and B. Joseph Pine II, *Authenticity: What Consumers Really Want* (Cambridge, MA: Harvard Business School Press, 2007), p. 18.
5. Ibid., pp. 99, 117–28.
6. C. Strickland and C. Hargrove, "Five Principles of Heritage Tourism," Heritage Tourism Initiative, National Trust for Historic Preservation (1989).
7. PGAV Destinations, "Real Potential: The Power of Authenticity to Reposition Your Destination" (2009).
8. As reported in "Prairie Edge Replaces Controversial Statue," *Rapid City Journal*, March 19, 2008.
9. Bernie Hunhoff, "The Story behind the Square" (revised from the March/April 2013 issue of *South Dakota Magazine*), http://southdakotamagazine.com/main-street-square.
10. PGAV Destination Consulting, *The New Destination Visitor—Travel Motivations in the Post-Recession Era*, vol. 10, issue 2 (May 2013).

11. Ibid.
12. PGAV Destination Consulting, *The Splurge Traveler*, vol. 4, issue 3 (2008).
13. JWT Intelligence, https://www.jwtintelligence.com/trend-reports.
14. Institute of Museum and Library Services, "Government Doubles Official Estimate: There Are 35,000 Active Museums in the U.S. (May 2014), https://www.imls.gov/news-events/news-releases/government-doubles-official-estimate-there-are-35000-active-museums-us.
15. National Register of Historic Places, http://www.nps.gov/nr.
16. JWT Intelligence, *The Future 100—Trends and Change to Watch in 2015* (December 2014), https://www.jwtintelligence.com/trend-reports/the-future-100.
17. Robert Reid, 76-Second Travel Show, reidontravel.com (December 2014) for National Geographic *Traveler*.
18. Mandala Research LLC, "2013 Cultural Heritage Traveler Report."
19. "The State of the American Traveler," Technology Edition, vol. 20 (April 2016), produced by Destination Analysis, http://www.destinationanalysts.com/wp-content/uploads/2016/05/TheStateoftheAmericanTraveler-April2016.pdf.
20. Destination Analysts "The State of the American Traveler," vol. 18 (July 2015).
21. Destination Analysts, "The State of the American Traveler," vol. 20 (April 2016).
22. Ericsson Consumer Lab, *Orbitz Travel Trends for 2015* (December 2014).
23. JWT Intelligence, "Peer-Powered Travel Report" (2013).
24. The Futures Company, *American Express LifeTwist Study* (2014), p. 7.
25. Ibid., p. 12.
26. Destination Analysts, "Average Traveler Psychographic Intensity Index Score: Profile of Millennial Travelers in the United States (July 2015), http://www.statista.com/statistics/318096/profile-of-millennial-travelers-in-the-us.
27. As reported by P. Roesler, "Mobile Technology and Future of Travel," *Inc.com* (May 2015), http://www.inc.com/peter-roesler/mobile-technology-and-future-of-travel.html.
28. National Institute of Health, https://www.nlm.nih.gov/changingthefaceofmedicine/physicians/biography_73.html.
29. John Hancock, "MLK Summer Scholars," http://www.johnhancock.com/corporateresponsibility/signatureprograms.html.
30. Museum of African American History, http://www.maah.org/about.htm.
31. H. Al Ibrahim, R. Crotti, G. El Hassan, C. Haddad, J. Chaitan, and K. Le Quesne, Travel and Tourism Competitiveness Index, *Travel and Tourism Competitiveness Report*, World Economic Forum (2015), p. 3, http://reports.weforum.org/travel-and-tourism-competitiveness-report-2015/the-travel-tourism-competitiveness-index.
32. V. Smith, "Hosts and Guests Revisited," *The American Behavioral Scientist*, 36, no. 2 (November/December 1992): 196.

Chapter 4

Determining Visitor Readiness

> We take stock of a city like we take stock of a man. The clothes and appearance are the externals by which we judge. We next take stock of the mind, the intellect. These are the internals. The sum of both is the man or the city.
>
> —Mark Twain, *New York Times*, December 7, 1900[1]

We often forget that the aesthetics of place are our community's front window. If you walk down a street, drive through a neighborhood, or exit off the interstate, these initial images create a first impression—positive or negative. While cultural and heritage planners may initially look only at the physical attributes of structures, visitor readiness goes beyond brick-and-mortar concerns— such as hours of operation, accessibility, and amenities—to include parking, public restrooms, and signage. Informed greeters and docents are also vital to a site's visitor readiness, and the role of residents in hospitality must also be considered. This chapter looks at the components defining visitor readiness and the responsibility of hosting visitors specifically at cultural heritage sites, events, and destinations.

The Importance of Visitor Readiness

If time is the new currency for visitors and competition is the quality standard for destinations seeking tourists, visitor readiness is paramount to delivering on "brand promise." Destination marketing organizations (DMOs) (also known as convention and visitors bureaus or tourist bureaus) spend large sums of money to capture potential visitors' interest. All of the marketing in the world, however, cannot overcome disappointing experiences or—worse yet—underwhelming or not meeting expectations set forth in brochures, advertisements, and websites. With social media available to visitors 24/7, real-time evaluations or accolades are posted to record actual experiences—the good, the bad, and the ugly.

Think about the popularity of TripAdvisor not only to record comments but also as a trip planning tool. With 435 million reviews and opinions covering more than 6.8 million businesses and properties (accommodations, restaurants, and attractions) in more than 135,000 destinations,

TripAdvisor represents the world's largest travel site.[2] Consider how Instagram, Twitter, Snapchat, and Facebook now record the movements and images of travelers around the world.

"Sense of place does not begin with history or culture or nature, but as a whole place that makes it more interesting from a storytelling perspective."
—Jonathan Tourtellot, director, Destination Stewardship Center

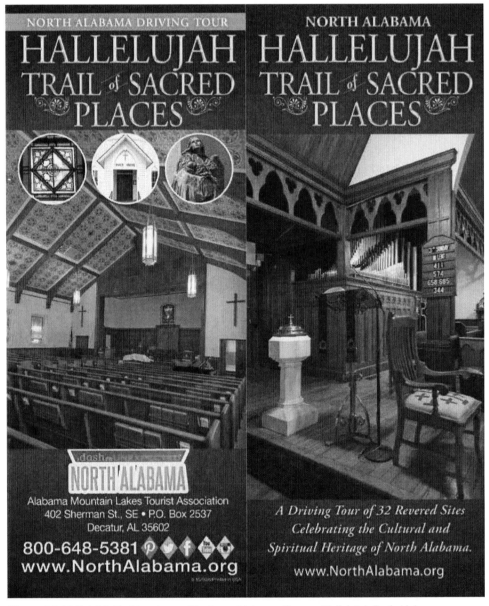

Figure 4.1 Hallelujah Trail brochure—Northern Alabama. Source: Hallelujah Trail, Alabama Mountain Lakes Tourist Association & Charles Seifried Photography.

As destination marketing organizations (DMOs) don't own the products they promote, it becomes even more important for the site manager, business owner, or tour guide to make sure the experience is exceptional. Delivering exceptional experiences begins with understanding visitor readiness. Criteria can help identify visitor ready sites. Clustering an inventory around a theme and then applying specific criteria can cull a list of qualified assets. Such was the case in developing the North Alabama Hallelujah Trail. The process of identification, selection, and marketing is told in the profile at the end of this chapter.

Defining Visitor Readiness

Visitor readiness is the consistent delivery of an experience at a site, an event, or an activity. Consistency is defined by adhering to published hours of operation, providing the experience marketed to visitors at the published price of admission (if applicable), and offering the variety of amenities and services (gift shop, tour guides, and on-site literature) to aid in the delivery of said experiences. Cleanliness and safety are expected; quality is assumed. Lancaster County, Pennsylvania, one of the first destinations to create a designation program for heritage sites, describes visitor readiness as "being prepared to welcome the public, having the ability to meet their expectations, and exhibiting high standards of appearance and operation."[4]

Criteria for Visitor Readiness

Visitor readiness should be based on industry standards set by the destination, as dictated by the profile of its tourists. For example, an urban city may have different criteria than rural communities or seasonal destinations, emphasizing weekend and evening activities. However, there are some basic overarching criteria that all attractions and businesses interested in hosting visitors should meet. These general criteria have been adapted specifically to address the cultural heritage community/assets.

Basic Operation

- Having a business license, permits, and insurance in order to operate legally
- Contact telephone number or e-mail (at minimum, for emergencies and when open)
- Prominent on-site signage
- Set schedule of operating hours
- Sufficient lighting for safety
- Well-maintained paths or roads for access

Open to the Public

- Schedule of operating hours, usually at least one weekend day and three days a week. (Some tourist boards and DMOs use criteria for set hours of operation to determine inclusion in marketing materials.)
- "By appointment only" is not recommended unless someone really is on the end of the phone number listed to contact and is ready to make an appointment at the time and day desired by the customer.
- Access provided to all people, meeting compliance with the Americans with Disabilities Act and other requirements for public use.

Staffing

- Trained volunteer or paid staff to greet visitors, provide information, and/or guide tours
- Staff on-site in case of emergency

These are the minimum criteria for visitor readiness at a business or nonprofit institution interested in hosting visitors. Certainly, the availability of a stellar gift shop and café can enhance the time spent at a site or attract locals on a more frequent basis. However, visitor readiness—especially for historic and cultural sites—must include more than just opening the door. The availability of a website is increasingly important, especially to gain awareness and assist with trip planning. Here are a few more areas to consider in determining visitor readiness, especially for cultural heritage tourism.

Exhibitions

At the heart of many museums and sites is the interpretation of a place or collection. Ensuring that proper policies and procedures are evident and adhered to is an important part of visitor readiness.

- Is there a schedule for rotating exhibits to refresh content and encourage repeat visitation?
- Are exhibitions designed to a high quality standard—well signed, attractive, and engaging?
- Is a collections policy in place and utilized to further the institution's mission?
- Are curatorial practices used to protect and preserve artifacts?

Programs

With a more market-centric shift in programming, institutions must create relevant and compelling activities for current and potential customers (members and visitors). Therefore, reviewing the type, quantity, and availability of programs is growing in importance to determine visitor readiness.

- Are multiple programs offered, or is the tour program the same for all visitors?
- Does the schedule of programs reflect the days and times that the visitors want to attend or participate?
- Is there a special or separate program for children and/or school groups?
- If a gift shop is available, does the merchandise reflect the program themes or topics (or showcase local artists or destination)?

Tour Guides and Docents

Cultural heritage tourism experiences often rely on the effectiveness of tour guides—paid or volunteer. Knowledgeable and hospitable greeters and guides may be the difference between a disappointing and an exceptional experience. Investing in the training and recognition of guides pays huge dividends in customer satisfaction and retention.

As frontline personnel, these individuals influence behavior based on their level of engagement with the customer. Visitor readiness is certainly dependent on informed personnel.

- Is there a program to recruit docents from the community?
- Do docents or guides receive training at minimum annually? Is it mandatory? Does it include information sharing as well as the development of presentation skills?

- Are tour guides encouraged to learn more about the community (participate in local familiarization tours to other attractions or restaurants) and to pass along this knowledge to visitors (in the form of recommendations or suggested places to eat, shop, or tour)?
- Are materials and tours translated into different languages for international visitors or available in Braille?
- Do guides have a staff or board member to contact in case of emergency, a conflict, or an area of concern?
- Are docents rewarded or recognized for exemplary service?

For other contributors to the cultural heritage tourism product—for example, historic hotels, retail stores, parks, and restaurants—third-party endorsements or quality ratings can be used as criteria. Here are a few rating systems or designations that may be influential in establishing or using as criteria.

Accommodations

- AAA, Mobil, or Forbes rating
- Member of Historic Hotels of America, Preferred, or Select Registry programs
- Member of state or national Bed and Breakfast Association

Corridors and Areas

- National Recreation Trail
- National Scenic Byway
- State Scenic Byway
- AAA Scenic Byway
- Civil War Trail
- National Heritage Area

Natural Lands

- National Natural Landmark
- National park
- State park
- County or city park
- Outstanding geologic area
- Centennial farm designation

Restaurants

- Health inspection rating
- Zagat rating
- Michelin rating

Retail

- Better Business Bureau
- Local chamber of commerce
- National or local Main Street association

Technology

- TripAdvisor Rating
- Yelp
- OpenTable

Applying Criteria to Evaluate Visitor Readiness

Criteria are established to evaluate each physical asset identified in your inventory. The process to evaluate visitor readiness can take many forms: conducted as "secret shopper" visits, through exit interviews with visitors, and via self-evaluation. Part of the evaluation process is to identify the method that will provide the most honest and accurate result. The outcome of the visitor readiness evaluation is important in assessing the potential of cultural heritage tourism but also to identify the optimum growth areas for development.

To help organize the inventory evaluations, consider the following categories to sort the assets:

Visitor ready: Sites meet all established criteria.
Almost visitor ready: Sites meet some criteria; need help to consistently meet or satisfy other criteria. Provide assistance to enhance quality of experience before marketing or limit marketing to what can be delivered currently.
Not ready: Sites or assets need further development to meet basic criteria or contribute to a cultural heritage visitor experience. These assets can be further subdivided into short-, mid-, and long-range potential.

A sample of how this evaluation process is recorded is provided at the end of this chapter (table 4.1). Once the asset inventory has been culled to determine levels of visitor readiness, the planning team can identify specific ways to help those sites or businesses needing assistance meet

Figure 4.2 Stone fence restored in workshop project—Native Stone Scenic Byway, Kansas. Source: Cheryl Hargrove.

the criteria. Assets meeting the visitor readiness criteria can be marketed to visitors or tapped to identify additional ways to enhance current experiences for greater engagement.

These components and others impacting quality visitor experiences are addressed in more detail in future chapters but are considerations when determining initial visitor readiness or at least recognizing areas to explore or improve. When open for business, it is particularly important for contributing assets to adhere to criteria and maintain a standard of excellence. The Native Stone Byway in Kansas hosts biannual workshops to ensure that they sustain their namesakes. Learn more about this development and maintenance program in the byway profile at the end of this chapter.

Ongoing Assessment of Visitor Readiness

If Mark Twain's quote is true, a destination must broaden the scope of visitor readiness beyond individual sites and buildings to include all aspects of hospitality and access. While many DMOs provide programs to address visitor readiness and hospitality training, cultural and heritage institutions as well as planners need to understand the holistic approach to tourism. Visitors do not isolate experiences as to who owns or operates a site or manages infrastructure; instead, they want to navigate a destination with ease and confidence, seeking out desired experiences without hassle.

Breaking down barriers—such as poor or no signage, inconvenient or insufficient parking, and limited sources for on-site information—is particularly important to creating a desirable environment for visitors (and residents) to move about a city or community. Offering public or multimodal transportation options—such as bicycle paths, pedestrian-friendly areas, and trolley routes—contributes to perceived easy access. Working in collaboration, planners, tourism industry leaders, and the cultural heritage community can create a visitor-friendly environment conducive to attracting and hosting tourists while balancing the needs of residents and industry.

Lancaster, Pennsylvania, is the model of a comprehensive designation program. Read the county profile at the end of this chapter to learn how the local planning commission created, embraced, and utilized a designation system to recognize contributing assets.

Chapter Summary

Visitor readiness begins with established criteria to define expectations and benchmark performance. Visitor readiness reaches beyond individual businesses to all facets of a destination and needs to be constantly monitored so that the actual customer experience exceeds perception. Planners, marketers, and site managers must work together to ensure that systems are in place to monitor and evaluate visitor readiness and help specific businesses and agencies implement the necessary elements to achieve optimum levels of visitor readiness.

* * * * *

Profile: North Alabama Hallelujah Trail—In Praise of Quality and Diversity

http://www.northalabama.org/explore/hallelujah

For more than a century, churches and other places of worship have marked the countryside in northern Alabama. As Dana Lee Jennings, former president of the Alabama Mountain Lakes

Tourist Association (AMLTA), said, "Nothing is more sacred to a southerner than his cultural and spiritual heritage." This recognition of the importance of ecumenical sites to the region's heritage led to a two-year research process to inventory and document these sacred places. While some are now vacant, others still hold services and are an active part of community life. After cataloging the sacred places, the AMLTA established criteria to recognize the most significant places for visitors:

1. Be at least one hundred years old
2. Be located on its original foundation
3. Still hold services and be accessible to the public

Like a string of pearls, the Hallelujah Trail maps thirty-two sacred sites across sixteen counties in northern Alabama. The trail includes all denominations of Christianity and a Jewish synagogue with varying architectural styles—from recognized architects to construction by members. Some interiors are ornate; others consist only of benches and a wooden pulpit. The settings for these sites also vary—from urban cities to rural countryside.

Grants from the Appalachian Regional Commission ($25,000) and the Alabama Bureau of Tourism and Travel ($25,000) allowed the AMLTA to produce and distribute the regional

Figure 4.3 Hallelujah Trail sign—Northern Alabama. Source: Hallelujah Trail, Alabama Mountain Lakes Tourist Association & Charles Seifried Photography.

Figure 4.4 Corinth Church—Double Springs, Alabama. Source: Hallelujah Trail, Alabama Mountain Lakes Tourist Association & Charles Seifried Photography.

Figure 4.5 Temple B'Nai Shalom—Huntsville, Alabama. Source: Hallelujah Trail, Alabama Mountain Lakes Tourist Association & Charles Seifried Photography.

Figure 4.6 Rock of Ages Trail brochure cover—Northern Alabama. Source: Alabama Mountain Lakes Tourist Association.

Hallelujah Trail brochure in 2007. The organization held a special dedication ceremony—complete with a choir and the lieutenant governor's wife presenting plaques to all participants—to officially launch the Hallelujah Trail. A special section on the website, trail markers, and individual community rack cards expanded the reach of the program. The trail heralded lots of press, with articles in *AAA*, *Alabama Living*, and inclusion on the "Driving Tours of Appalachia" map guide inserted into the April 2008 issue of *National Geographic Traveler*.

Figure 4.7 Amen Trail brochure cover—Northern Alabama. Source: Alabama Mountain Lakes Tourist Association.

"This trail became a great story, resonating particularly with baby boomers," said Tami Reist, president and chief executive officer of the AMLTA. The trail also appeals to photographers, lovers of architecture, and church groups. A lot have been geocached. Reist continued, "The Hallelujah Trail encourages people to spend more time—and money—in the region as they travel through communities and along the backroads to locate and visit these sacred places."

Reist lives by the Helen Keller quote that is included in her e-mail signature: "Alone we can do so little, together we can do so much." This trail, like so many regional programs, requires people working together. The trail starts with an idea and a plan: get a lot of people involved, roll it out, and keep layering to build on the original concept.[3] As popularity of the program grew, the regional association provided $16,000 in grants funds for counties to create its own trail, and the Amen Trail of Morgan County and the Rock of Ages Trail in Colbert County were born. One of the original churches asked to be removed from the brochure due to too many visitors, but another was very excited to be added. In 2015, the AMLTA updated the brochure and driving tour map; 40,000 were distributed in a year, and the association has reordered more.

The AMLTA is gearing up for the Alabama Bicentennial in 2019; Reist serves on the commission. She recognizes that not all history is pretty but that all the stories need to be told. Reist recounts how Sheila Washington helped establish the Scottsboro Boys Museum and Cultural Center in 2010. The museum is located in the former Colored Methodist Episcopal Church of Scottsboro. Former slaves constructed the church, the oldest standing African American church in Jackson County, on the site in 1878, and the structure was rebuilt in 1904. Churches are often a place to help tell these important stories of history and lead us on a path to healing.

* * * * *

Profile: Native Stone Byway—Rebuilding the Legacy
Geary, Riley, Shawnee, and Wabaunsee Counties, Kansas

www.travelks.com/ksbyways/native-stone

This seventy-six-mile state-designated scenic byway showcases the natural limestone formations and stonework used in architecture along Highway K-4 and Highway K-99 in the rolling terrain of the Flint Hills west of Topeka, Kansas. Limestone landmarks dot the route, where expert masonry is evident in houses, barns, commercial buildings, and fences. More than a century ago, farmers and ranchers cleared their pastures and used the abundance of stone to build

Figure 4.8 Interpretive marker for stacked stone—Native Stone Scenic Byway, Kansas. Source: Kansas Native Stone Scenic Byway.

dry-stacked stone fences. Miles of fences found in Wabaunsee County date back to the 1867 proclamation abolishing the open range. Many of these stone fences, though, have deteriorated over the past century; rocks have shifted or fallen over, and property lines have moved. The byway was in jeopardy of losing part of its natural appeal.

In 2007, a local rancher with miles of stone fence on his property saw the need for rebuilding the early fences. He found a dry-stone instructor just one county away and inquired if the byway would offer a masonry class for local property owners. That first class had twenty-two students, and the byway is now enrolling "students" for its nineteenth semiannual workshop. The two-day class costs $100 and includes meals and refreshments. Rocky Slaymaker, a professional dry-stone conservancy mason certified by the Kentucky Stone Fence Conservancy, leads the instruction on the nine elements of successful stone fence building and repair. To date, the Native Stone Byway has renovated or replicated nine fences using the traditional dry-stack method. One location with a 200-foot fence took six workshops to complete. It takes two days for students to complete twenty-eight to thirty-five feet of fence, as each stone has to be chiseled to fit, much like a jigsaw puzzle.

More than 265 attendees have participated in the fence building workshops. "We also host a number of alumni or individuals who have completed more than two workshops. They find the work rewarding and believe in the importance of this project to continue the heritage tourism aspect of the byway," says Sally Stratton, Native Stone Scenic Byway committee chair. About half of the visitors to workshop sites are from surrounding states, and the workshops have also attracted international visitors.

The byway plans to continue hosting the stone fence building workshops due to their uniqueness to the Kansas Byway program and the critical importance to the preservation of the region's heritage. The workshops also contribute an economic impact on the surrounding area. Attendees spend money on food, gas, and lodging, and the tourists visiting the fence sites also stay in the area longer and buy locally.

For additional information on the fence building workshops, contact the Wabaunsee County Economic Development Office (http://www.wabaunsee.com) or committee members Sally Stratton (ssstratton80@gmail.com) or Marsha Ericson (kmarsha@msn.com).

* * * * *

Profile: Lancaster County Planning Commission
Lancaster, Pennsylvania

http://www.lancastercountyplanning.org

What began as an effort to authenticate heritage resources and identify underutilized assets in Lancaster County, the Lancaster County Planning Commission's work evolved into an intensive process to educate, recognize, and promote heritage resources, resulting in a comprehensive designation program. Recognizing that some of the most recognizable images of Lancaster consist of pastoral landscapes and Amish buggies, the county was concerned about overdevelopment of inappropriate and inauthentic attractions. The opportunity to take a proactive approach to tourism development led the planning commission to articulate specific goals and set up a heritage tourism program to oversee progress. One of the goals of the *Lancaster County Strategic Tourism Development Plan* (2005) was to promote tourism development that does the following:

- Complements the county's natural, cultural, and historic resources
- Discourages tourism facilities that inaccurately reflect the county's heritage or that have a negative impact on residents' quality of life

The Lancaster County Planning Commission produced three instructive publications for heritage resource managers: a program manual, an interpretation manual, and a graphic style guide. Recognizing the importance and impact of the Lancaster Heritage program, the neighboring York County Planning Commission established a similar program and mirrored criteria, interpretation, and logos for continuity across county lines.

The *Program Manual for Heritage Partners* offers the background and overview of the heritage tourism program and its purpose and importance to Lancaster County and articulates a process for engagement. Three criteria, established for heritage resource designation, helped focus development activities on this important goal.

1. *Authenticity* is the ability to show a genuine, accurate, and verifiable link to local heritage, defined as the heritage of Lancaster County. Quantifiers for authenticity include the following:
   - Show a direct link to the county's heritage.
   - Offer a genuine Lancaster County experience.
   - Does not have to be old, rare, or unusual to be considered authentic; does have to accurately reflect a tradition that has made a measurable impact on Lancaster County.
   - Must draw on solid research to demonstrate their link to local heritage.
   - Buildings must retain enough features from the significant time period to be recognizable as a product of that time.
2. *Interpretation* is the art of using organized information to explain the natural, cultural, or historic significance of a resource. Qualified interpretation does the following:
   - Relies on sound scholarship
   - Provides an accurate and cultural sensitive portrayal of local heritage
   - Focuses on educating visitors, not simply entertaining them
   - Is easily accessible to visitors through signage, printed materials or other media, exhibits, performances, guided or self-guided tours, or other means
   - Highlights at least one of the five interpretive themes of the Lancaster–York Heritage Region: bounty, ingenuity, freedom, towns and countryside, and natural wonders
3. *Visitor readiness* means being prepared to welcome the public, having the ability to meet their expectations, and exhibiting high standards of appearance and operation. To categorize visitor readiness, the Lancaster County Planning Commission adopted three levels based on services provided:
   - Heritage Partners: Open to the public for a minimum of thirty-two hours per week or more for at least four consecutive months per year. They have public restroom facilities and often have a range of ancillary services, such as full-time staff, exhibits, tours, and programs.
   - Heritage Associates: Generally have regular hours but are open to the public less frequently than Heritage Partners. Heritage Associates may also rely on part-time and volunteer staff to operate. Facilities and services available to visitors may be limited. Visitors should consider calling ahead before visiting a Heritage Associate.
   - Heritage Affiliates: Do not have regular operating hours and may be open to the public only one day or a few days per year or by appointment only. They generally operate with volunteer assistance. Facilities and services available to visitors are either limited or nonexistent. It is strongly recommended that visitors call before they visit a Heritage Affiliate.

The *Program Manual for Heritage Partners* provides more detailed criteria for each type of Heritage Resource. It also includes a designation process for the Lancaster County Heritage Program and Lancaster County Heritage Byways. The five-step process involves (1) an application submitted to Lancaster County Planning Commission staff, (2) review by the Eligibility Committee, (3) recommendation by the Advisory Council to the Lancaster County Planning Commission, (4) approval by the Lancaster County Planning Commission, and (5) official designation, where the resource manager signs a memorandum of understanding.

As raising awareness about the county's authentic resources is also a major goal of the Lancaster County Heritage Program, the *Program Manual for Heritage Partners* outlines specific strategies for marketing and promoting the heritage resources. This includes partnerships with the respective planning commissions, convention and visitors bureaus, and Susquehanna Heritage (www.susquehannaheritage.org) (formerly the Lancaster–York Heritage Region).

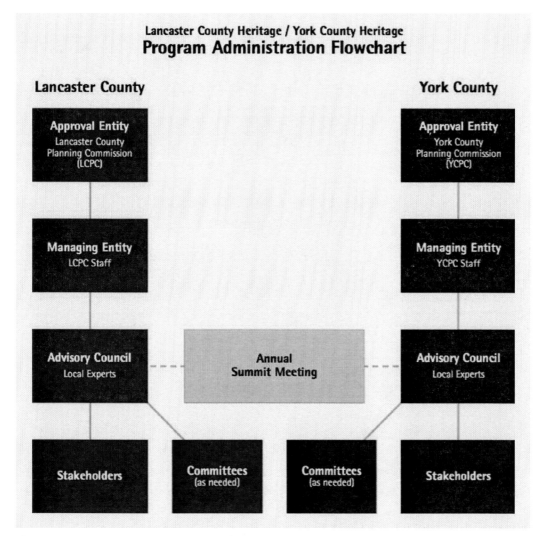

Figure 4.9 Lancaster Heritage Organization Model

Figure 4.10 Lancaster County *Program Manual for Heritage Partners*—Lancaster, Pennsylvania. Source: Lancaster County Planning Commission.

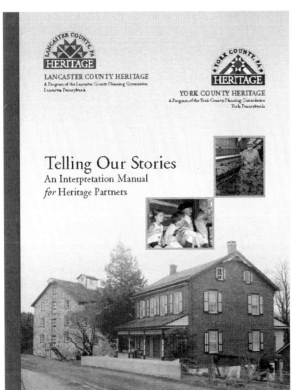

Figure 4.11 Lancaster County *Interpretation Manual for Heritage Partners*—Lancaster, Pennsylvania. Source: Lancaster County Planning Commission.

Figure 4.12 Lancaster County *Graphics Style Guide for Heritage Partners*—Lancaster, Pennsylvania. Source: Lancaster County Planning Commission.

The ninety-page *Telling Our Stories* is a comprehensive manual for heritage partners. In addition to defining interpretation, providing a rationale for a storytelling strategy, and determining the best media for effective results, the manual includes a toolbox that includes the following:

- Research tips on how to find your story
- List of themes and subthemes for Lancaster County and York County
- Advantages and disadvantages of various media (printed, panels and banners, multimedia, displays, Web, and personal interpretation) and tips for each medium
- Good, better, and best practices to review and reference

The *Graphics Style Guide for Heritage Partners* outlines specific use and application for the program symbols—a program logo and a certification seal—to deliver a consistent message. A 1995 version of the logo was updated in 2003 to represent the entire program.

"This is evolutionary not revolutionary. Our CVB [convention and visitors bureau] adopted ideas proposed ten years ago in part because the Planning Commission helped set the stage for this change," said Scott Standish, director of Countrywide Planning, Lancaster County Planning Commission. He continued, "We understood from the very beginning, that if you create a great place to live, you will ultimately create a great place to visit. That is why land use and tourism destination planning must go hand in hand."

Table 4.1 Criteria for Three Levels of "Visitor Readiness"

Local Asset	Visitor Ready	Almost Ready	Not Ready
Attractions: *Cultural* *Historic* *Recreation* *Natural sites* *Man-made sites* *Parks* *Trails*	a) Open a minimum of three days a week including one weekend day	a) Seasonal or more limited but regular hours/days of operation	a) Do not have regular operating hours or only open by appointment.
	b) Staffed	b) Staffed by volunteers	b) Self-guided
	c) Programming, guided tours scheduled at least once a month	c) Limited programming or events	c) No programming or events
	d) Information available on site for visitors (exhibits, brochures, interpretive signs)	d) Limited on-site information	d) No on-site information available for visitors
	e) Visible signage, lighting and well-marked entrance/access	e) Limited signage, lighting and access	e) No signage, lighting. Access at personal risk.
	f) ADA compliant	f) Limited accessibility	f) No accommodation for persons with disabilities
	g) Public parking, restrooms available	g) Facilities and services may be limited	g) Limited or nonexistent facilities
	Bonus: Authentic, Unique to destination		

Accommodations: Hotels Motels Bed-and-breakfasts Inns Campgrounds RV parks	A, E, F, G FT/PT on-site staff includes manager, reception, security, maintenance, housekeeping Central Reservations System (by phone, online); credit cards accepted *Bonus: Significant to/connection with destination*	A, E, F, G Limited or seasonal on-site staff Reservations accepted via e-mail or phone; some/all credit cards may not be accepted	A, E, F, G No on-site staff No advance reservation; no credit cards accepted
Restaurants: Full-service restaurants Fast-food chains Diners Limited service (bakeries, delis)	A, B, E, F, G *Bonus: Specialty connected to the area (heirloom recipe, local sourced food, etc.)*	A, B, E, F, G	A, B, E, F, G
Retail Stores: Locally owned Chains Specialty Art studios/galleries	A, B, E, F, G *Bonus: Inventory includes locally or hand-made objects by local residents*	A, B, E, F, G	A, B, E, F, G
Transportation/Tour Company	Public transportation available (taxis, buses, shuttles)	Limited public transportation available	No public transportation available

(continued)

Table 4.1 (continued)

Local Asset	Visitor Ready	Almost Ready	Not Ready
Visitor Services: Information Guides Transportation Financial services	Previsit Information available (website, brochure, social media) with booking capability	Limited previsit information available (brochure, e-mail)	No previsit information available; no contact for advance information, communication
	Local expert guides available for groups, prebooked tours	Limited availability of local experts	No local experts identified
	Banks and ATMs available	Some Banks and ATMs available	No banks or ATMs available
	Staffed Visitor Center available, signed	Visitor Kiosk or self-service information desk available, signed	No visitor center or information area available or signed
	On-site directional and informational signage	On-site directional signage	No directional or informational signage
Event or Festival: Heritage Music Cultural Sports	Annually scheduled event	Fluctuating date in same month each year	No consistent date
	At least five years old	At least three years old	No records or data available
	Organizational host with staff	Volunteer staff	No consistent management
	Specific theme, focus or goals	Loosely defined goals, theme	No focus or theme
	Operates as a business	Operates with limited funding	Operates without any permanent funding
	Positive ROI, measurable results for community	Some benefit to community	No documented benefit to community (ROI)
	Bonus: Connection to destination (history, tradition, holiday, place-based activities)		

Notes

1. Mark Twain presentation at the Banquet of the St. Nicholas Society, as reported in the *New York Times* (December 1900).
2. TripAdvisor Study (May 2016), https://www.tripadvisor.com/PressCenter-c4-Fact_Sheet.html.
3. Conversation with Tami Reist, June 29, 2016.
4. S. Standish, *Program Manual for Heritage Partners* (n.d.), p. 9, Lancaster Planning Commission, http://www.lancastercountyplanning.org/DocumentCenter/Home/View/136.

Section II

Step Two: Plan and Engage

Chapter 5

Engaging Diverse Stakeholders

Listening offers data. Hearing offers empathy and intelligence. Activity, action, and engagement steer perspective and encourage a sense of community and advocacy.

—Brian Solis, principal, digital analyst, and author, Altimeter Group

Whether you are pondering what to do with a specific building, exploring the potential of a new event or festival, or embarking on a broader community-, city-, or region-wide development project, it is important to have the right people or institutions at the planning table. Consider these steps to achieve optimum engagement: (1) identify the right leaders and partners for your project or planning process, (2) understand their attitudes or knowledge about cultural heritage tourism, (3) define the appropriate level of involvement, (4) create the messages and formats to engage them, and (5) implement a proactive communication and engagement process. Cultural heritage tourism benefits from stakeholder engagement where all partners understand and value their role in planning and implementation and respect other partners' contributions.

Various groups can be tapped in a cultural heritage tourism project. After determining the right stakeholders to include in the planning process, implementing effective communication systems is vital to informing various constituents about the project. These systems also allow for public input and feedback opportunities, if desired. Finally, engagement should lead to action—in forms of public support, ownership, funding, and/or a commitment to implement or adopt the final planning/project outcome. This action often results from persuasive communication where stakeholders buy in to a particular vision or outcome. This chapter explores the kind of stakeholders to tap, how best to involve them for the desired results, and some creative tools to assist in the engagement process. Sometimes, the call to action results in a specific outcome, as in the case of Eatonville, Florida. Community leaders seeking to preserve their heritage and culture from urban sprawl embraced the teachings of a respected hometown author to start a nationally recognized festival. Read the profile of the ZORA! Festival at the end of this chapter to learn more about this community's achievements.

Figure 5.1 ZORA! Outdoor Festival of the Arts—Eatonville, Florida. Source: Ted Hollins Photography.

Identifying Leaders and Partners

As engagement is integral to effective, comprehensive planning, the first task is to identify the primary cultural heritage tourism stakeholders. There are six major groups to involve in planning for cultural heritage tourism: (1) cultural, heritage, and historic preservation organizations and institutions; (2) the travel and tourism industry; (3) cultural leaders, historians, media, and other opinion leaders; (4) government and elected officials; (5) the business community; and (6) civic and educational organizations, and other community and resident groups. These stakeholders are defined in greater depth below.

Cultural, Heritage, and Historic Preservation Organizations and Institutions

This stakeholder group—its related institutions and constituents—is essential to any cultural heritage tourism project or planning process. Without the buy-in, feedback, and support from these entities, the integrity and quality of cultural heritage tourism may suffer. Constituent groups representing the cultural heritage sector include the following:

- Artists, authors, and historians
- Arts and humanities agencies
- Cultural organizations: arts councils, guilds of craftsmen, museum and performing arts associations
- Cultural institutions: museums, performing arts venues
- Historical societies

- Historic sites, house museums, heritage areas
- Historic preservation and conservation agencies
- State historic preservation officers
- Tribal historic preservation officers

The Travel and Tourism Industry

As defined in chapter 1, the travel and tourism industry includes many segments. Identifying the most appropriate components for a specific project or planning outcome is important to ensure the desired result. Just as engagement of the cultural heritage sector is essential, so is involvement of the tourism industry. Cultural heritage tourism does not happen without consideration and engagement by both the cultural heritage sector and the tourism sector. Some of the tourism industry segments include, where appropriate, the following:

- Area attractions
- Destination management companies
- Local convention and visitors bureaus, tourism offices, destination marketing organizations
- State or regional (and multistate) tourism offices
- National tourism offices
- Lodging: hotels, motels, bed-and-breakfasts, campgrounds, RV parks
- Restaurants and restaurant associations
- Tour operators, receptive tour operators, tour guides
- Transportation: airlines, airports, train stations, bus terminals, taxicabs, rental cars

Since development often impacts transportation, parking, signage, and other infrastructure, agencies or entities responsible for these activities (or policies) should also be tapped.

Cultural Leaders, Historians, Media, and Other Opinion Leaders

Often, specific individuals or thought leaders are respected and revered in a community—the people whose opinions matters to large constituent groups or networks. Frequently, these individuals will be asked to lead capital campaigns, lend their influence to secure political or business support, and/or be appointed to chair an advisory committee or a council. Involvement by these leaders may vary, depending on size of the community, type of project, planning outcome, and level of sensitivity or controversy. Key opinion leaders often include the following:

- Local media: journalists, publishers, syndicated columnists, influencer marketers (bloggers)
- Religious leaders
- Tribal chiefs, elders
- Local experts (historians, industry experts, curators)
- Librarians
- Higher education and business executives

Government and Elected Officials

Engagement of government agencies is essential to most cultural heritage tourism projects and certainly should be included in any planning process. Whether as a resource, for referral, or as the coordinator of a project, government agencies serve an important role in cultural heritage tourism. Government agencies can also influence sense of place via design guidelines for compatible in-fill, oversight for historic and cultural districts, and gateways and way-finding signage.

More than one agency may be involved in a given project, especially if permits, policies, zoning, or other planning elements are necessary.

Elected officials often provide the necessary endorsement, recognition, or leadership for successful launch or conclusion of a project or planning process. Understanding the political landscape is important, especially with regard to the sustainability of a project beyond election cycles. Determining the role of elected officials and the various levels of approval required for particular projects or outcomes is necessary to inform the engagement strategy and schedule. Here are some groups to consider for local engagement and support (additional agencies may need to be tapped at the state, regional, and national levels):

- City council
- County commissioners
- Cultural affairs office
- Economic development office
- Historic preservation office
- Planning offices
- Police and fire commissions
- Recreation and parks departments
- Tourism office (tourism ambassadorship, hospitality and events, and other categories)
- Transportation departments
- Other elected officials

Regional entities may also play an important planning, policy, funding, development, or marketing role. Defining the profile and contacts for these agencies or institutions is recommended so that political, human, and financial resources may be leveraged to their fullest potential.

The Business Community

To ensure that cultural heritage tourism products and programs provide the maximum economic impact, the business community must be considered for their support of where visitors will dine, shop, sleep, and visit. The business community often extends the reach of traditional cultural heritage tourism experiences through the lens of their desired "return on investment." Among the business community, these groups may be considered:

- Agriculture (farms, wineries, distilleries)
- Architects
- Chambers of commerce
- Developers
- Downtown business associations
- Financial institutions (banks, investors)
- Health care
- Industry and commerce
- Cultural districts
- Main Street associations
- Marketing firms
- Retail merchants associations
- Parks/recreation/outfitters
- Other business leaders

Civic and Educational Organizations and Other Community and Resident Groups

Local civic and social organizations may provide additional human and financial resources not always considered in cultural heritage tourism projects and planning. These institutions can leverage assets and expand reach through their membership, distribution channels, or in-kind services. Educational institutions, in particular, can be valuable partners for cultural heritage tourism by producing research, studies, and analysis; engaging interns or classes for specific projects; and sharing local expertise. Consider these categories for cultural heritage tourism:

- Academia: universities, community colleges, educational institutions
- Citizen action groups
- Community foundations
- Garden clubs
- Neighborhood associations
- Religious groups
- Civic, social, professional, and fraternal organizations (Rotary Club, Lions Club, Kiwanis)
- Special interest groups

While these are the obvious stakeholders to tap when conducting a broader community-wide planning process, an individual site or project focusing on a narrower geographic scope may not require all of these entities. However, keeping even tangentially related stakeholders informed is important to diffuse any potential roadblocks or issues that might arise later in the process.

Additionally, outliers may exist that do not fall into any of these categories but are critical to the desired outcome—an absentee building owner, an environmental group, a hometown celebrity, or a regulatory agency. Investigating and identifying all the potential influencers and impactors is an important foundation for moving forward with the planning process. Sometimes, collaborations form to create awareness or raise funds. An example is the highly successful farm-to-table dinner in Jonesborough, Tennessee, that has become not only a regional attraction but also a model for other communities. To learn more about the diverse partners banding together for this unique event, read the case study of Jonesborough, Locally Grown, at the end of this chapter.

Developing a Stakeholder Engagement Strategy

> If there is any one secret to success, it lies in the ability to get the other person's point of view and see things from that person's angle as well as from your own.
>
> —Henry Ford

Before appointing or inviting stakeholders to participate in the planning process or development project, determine what role is best suited for their involvement. Who is central to the planning process? These entities (or their representatives) become the core planning team or working group. A project leader is assigned from this small group. Whose support is critical to acceptance or implementation? This group of influencer stakeholders or thought leaders is often convened or appointed as an advisory board or council. Elected officials, funding institutions, and regulatory and policy agencies also need to be involved but may require special strategies for information sharing and comment. Who stands to benefit or will be affected by this process? A broader group of stakeholders—including residents, affinity groups and civic organizations, and visitors—must be included at significant points in the engagement process.

Figure 5.2 Jonesborough farm-to-table dinner—Jonesborough, Tennessee. Source: Photo by Woven Creative Studios.

Don't forget to include future generations as stakeholders: youth and young professionals. Millennials and Gen-Xers are often inadvertently excluded from these planning processes yet will be impacted by and can contribute greatly to planning discussions and decisions. Find ways to engage all generational groups to ensure that the planning process is future seeking and that current needs are addressed. Ethnic and minority groups, indigenous and underrepresented populations should also be consulted and engaged. It may be necessary to go outside traditional meeting locations and seek out audiences where they meet—at churches, civic clubs, neighborhood gathering spots, or local restaurants. Confer with alumni groups, religious organizations, school boards, and young professional organizations to identify potential stakeholders and identify how best to engage their participation. If you are considering family or youth programming, make sure to include representatives from these audience sectors to help advise on or even test ideas and concepts. As indicated in figure 5.3, it may be helpful to list these key constituents according to the desired level of engagement.[3]

People want to share and receive information at various levels of detail and in different formats. Communication is not—and should not be—a one-way street. Thankfully, technology affords an abundance of options and streamlines the process for distribution—via e-mail, online surveys,

1. MOST ENGAGED: Core/ Key Stakeholders

- Project/ Team Leader
- Core Team/ Working Group

2. SOMEWHAT ENGAGED: Advisors/ Regulators

- Advisory Council
- Regulatory Agencies
- Elected Officials
- Funders
- Cultural, Heritage, Tourism Industry

3. LESS ENGAGED: Influencers

- Residents, Visitors
- Media
- General Business, Industry
- Civic Clubs, Organizations

Figure 5.3 Levels of stakeholder engagement. Source: Cheryl Hargrove.

blogs, and document sharing. However, sometimes face-to-face meetings are important (and often required) to gather public feedback or foster robust discussion around a particular subject or issue. Outlining a stakeholder engagement strategy ensures that the right people get the right level of information at the right intervals for decision making with optimum results (endorsement and confirmation). Listening is a vital part of the communication process, and creating specific opportunities for input and feedback is essential to ensure buy-in and avoid potential pitfalls to the project and planning process.

Once a stakeholder engagement strategy is established, in parallel with the planning process or as part of a cultural heritage tourism development project, the next step is creating a communication time line. Sometimes, this schedule will be dictated by predetermined deadlines (grants, council meetings, and fiscal year and budgeting cycles). Other deadlines may also impact the schedule of meetings and/or content reviews: membership meetings, travel schedules, holidays, and public events (school activities, festivals, and elections). Mapping "blackout" dates to avoid and then plugging in benchmarks to conclude specific components of the project and/or planning process will help guide the scheduling of key communiqués and meetings with stakeholders. Defining how content will be shared will also help inform the necessary time to allocate for each activity, especially when requiring comment or approval. Publicizing this schedule can then keep the process on track to realize the desired outcome and ensure that calendars are not compromised by other stakeholder commitments. Table 5.1 at the end of this chapter outlines some specific details and key questions for consideration in establishing an engagement strategy.

Enlisting Key Stakeholder Support

As you identify a vision or determine a desired outcome for a cultural heritage tourism project, crafting a compelling message that engages stakeholders and inspires them to be a part of it becomes an important communication tool—especially for broader constituent groups, such as residents and tourists. Stakeholders will more readily buy into the idea or future vision and choose to participate or help with implementation if they connect with the message or see value in the end result. For cultural heritage tourism projects, compelling messages include the current situation, the desired change, a relatable outcome, and defined benefits for the recipient. An effective message is useful when promoting revitalization projects, preservation and restoration of historic sites, and redevelopment of neighborhoods and/or commercial districts.[4] Key to stakeholder confidence and acceptance is sharing the right message the right way at the right time.[5] The timing, the participation level, and the rationale are all part of "the ask." This instruction should also be considered part of the stakeholder engagement strategy and schedule.

Breaking down the language barriers or diffusing jargon is important to ensure clear understanding and to garner support for cultural heritage tourism. The messages also must have relevant meaning to the audience to help all stakeholders understand how such messages relate to their situation or can provide benefit. The goal is to secure the right stakeholders with the appropriate level of engagement to realize the desired outcome.

Be fully engaged in your community, however you define community.
—Julie Heizer, team lead, industry relations, National Travel and Tourism Office, International Trade Administration, U.S. Department of Commerce

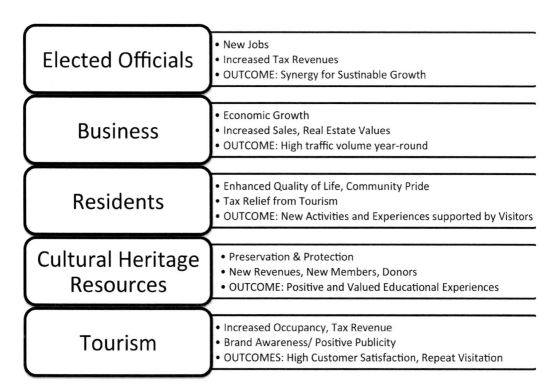

Elected Officials	• New Jobs • Increased Tax Revenues • OUTCOME: Synergy for Sustainable Growth
Business	• Economic Growth • Increased Sales, Real Estate Values • OUTCOME: High traffic volume year-round
Residents	• Enhanced Quality of Life, Community Pride • Tax Relief from Tourism • OUTCOME: New Activities and Experiences supported by Visitors
Cultural Heritage Resources	• Preservation & Protection • New Revenues, New Members, Donors • OUTCOME: Positive and Valued Educational Experiences
Tourism	• Increased Occupancy, Tax Revenue • Brand Awareness/ Positive Publicity • OUTCOMES: High Customer Satisfaction, Repeat Visitation

Figure 5.4 Key messages for key stakeholders. Source: Cheryl Hargrove.

Innovative Strategies to Engage Stakeholders

Traditional planning tools include PowerPoint presentations, facilitated meetings, polls to gauge opinions, surveys to capture ideas, and public forums to capture opinions and prioritize information. However, these are not the only ways to share and receive information—and sometimes not the most effective. The American Planning Association (APA) recommends a number of strategies using arts and culture to enhance community engagement and participation.[6] Why is community engagement important? According to APA,

> Community engagement can bring vibrancy and innovation to the planning practice by strengthening the degree of public commitment to planning processes and making more perspectives available to decision makers.[7]

This is particularly important for destination-wide cultural heritage tourism planning projects but can also be relevant for individual property or site plans. Why is it recommended to utilize a variety of tools when planning cultural heritage tourism projects? Stories and creative projects often appeal to diverse populations that may be more receptive or prone to different forms of engagement.

Various creative tools can help bring the planning process to life and express different stakeholder points of view. A few examples and uses include the following:

- Walking tours to learn more about existing assets, history, culture, place
- Visual art techniques (renderings and illustrations or charrettes) to help portray particular visions.

- Artists to facilitate and interpret the findings and concepts presented during meetings.
- Three-dimensional objects (such as blocks) or imaging to represent the built environment.
- Murals, graffiti, historical photographs, and other images (either existing or created) to help portray opportunities and stories. These visuals can also identify the particular needs and wants of stakeholder groups, concerns, or uses for buildings.
- User-generated content to create digital storytelling for use and consideration in planning.
- Art exhibits, displays of historical artifacts, and educational programs to inform the general public as well as youth (students) in the goals and opportunities envisioned for the project and planning process.
- Quilters to use historic patterns or create contemporary designs to portray the important stories of the community.
- A Flickr site established to catalog resident images of what cultural and historic resources are considered important, sacred, and/or valued.
- A Facebook account to create and engage a community and discuss important issues or content for the planning process.
- Wikiplanning[8] as a creative online resource for the planning process; it facilitates virtual design charrettes.
- Hosting photography, drawing, poster, postcard, or other design competitions (where winning entries are displayed locally at banks, libraries, or other public areas) to involve various ages and demographic profiles in the planning process.
- Microsites (websites) designed to capture information from varied audiences—presenting information in different languages or with various messages.
- Planning sessions scheduled during local festivals, dance performances, music concerts, reenactments, neighborhood gatherings, and other community activities to help access new markets and engage them in the planning process at familiar locations.[9]

These creative tools are just a few ways to use technology, culture, and heritage to involve potential or existing community stakeholders and expand engagement. Make sure that some tools are open or available to visitors; they, too, have a stake in cultural heritage tourism planning or project outcomes.

Chapter Summary

The successful completion and sustainability of cultural heritage tourism projects depend on local leadership and support. Without leaders to champion this effort, the planning process may be stalled or defeated. Without the right stakeholders to foster engagement of others, the process may not realize its full potential. Taking the time to identify and engage the right stakeholders, to understand and deploy a communication strategy to foster their participation, and to use tools to attract creative involvement for cultural heritage tourism projects are important steps in the planning process to ensure optimum outcomes.

* * * * *

Profile: Zora Neale Hurston Festival of the Arts and Humanities (a.k.a. ZORA! Festival) Eatonville, Florida

http://zorafestival.org

Folklorist and anthropologist Zora Neale Hurston (1891–1960), best known for her novel *Their Eyes Were Watching God*, grew up in the small town of Eatonville in central Florida. The oldest

Figure 5.5 ZORA! concert stage—Eatonville, Florida. Source: Ted Hollins Photography.

incorporated African American municipality in the United States, Eatonville constantly faced challenges from urban sprawl along the I-4 corridor near Orlando. When a roadway expansion threatened the heart of the community in 1987, some 200 persons from Eatonville and neighboring communities organized the Association to Preserve the Eatonville Community, Inc. (P.E.C.), to advocate for preservation of the historic town (population 2,243).[1] The nonprofit organization also began organizing a festival to recognize the town and hometown hero, Zora Neale Hurston. The all-volunteer organization was successful in combating the road expansion but, more important, brought attention to Hurston's important work of preserving and perpetuating African American culture. Today, P.E.C. advances cultural tourism as a member of the Historic Black Towns and Settlements Alliance, Inc., and as organizer of a critically acclaimed festival.

What began as a three-day gathering on Main Street in 1990, the Zora Neale Hurston Festival of the Arts and Humanities—the ZORA! Festival—has grown to a nine-day, multicultural, multidisciplinary, award-winning event typically drawing tens of thousands of visitors from all over the world to engage in activities and educational programming in Eatonville, at Rollins College, at the University of Central Florida, and throughout central Florida. At a typical festival, more than 5,000 students from across Florida participate on Friday, "Education Day." More than a quarter of a century later, the ZORA! Festival is one of the most popular cultural events in the region. Held each January, the Outdoor Festival of the Arts features a Children's Corridor, an arts-and-crafts, hands-on activity; the ZORA! Literary Initiative, a book giveaway; a fine arts/master crafters lane; an International Marketplace; a Healthy Lifestyle Pavilion; an International Food Court; an exhibition at the Zora Neale Hurston National Museum of Fine Arts (the Hurston); and much more. The festival continues with its original mission: celebrate the life and work of Zora Neale Hurston, the historic significance of Eatonville, and the cultural contributions that people of African ancestry have made to the United States and to world culture. Famous participants and visitors include Alice Walker, Maya Angelou, Danny Glover, Cicely Tyson, Ruby Dee, and Ossie Davis. Media coverage of the festival is abundant; in 2016, forty-seven journalists attended the event representing twenty local, regional, national, and international media outlets. Two public relations and event executive assistants from Spellman College provided on-ground support.

"Our mission is to educate the public about Eatonville's historic and cultural significance and to use the community's heritage and cultural vibrancy for its economic development," said N. Y. Nathiri, executive director of P.E.C. An eleven-member board of directors brings additional leadership and expertise to the organization. In addition to organizing the annual festival, P.E.C. also provides year-round after-school academic support to elementary and middle school students through its ZORA! STEM Initiative, a decades-long commitment to assist Eatonville students and others become prepared to enroll in science and math classes, which are the prerequisites for the well-paying STEM-related jobs. Since its founding, P.E.C. has recognized how the cultural arts can spur community revitalization and be the catalyst for economic development. P.E.C. developed several revenue-generating programs, including visits from special groups, educational materials, merchandise sales, and rental of a traveling museum exhibit. All these activities contribute to the organization's ultimate goal: developing historic Eatonville into one of America's premier heritage communities.[2]

* * * * *

Profile: A Feast to Remember Jonesborough Locally Grown
Jonesborough, Tennessee

https://jonesborough.locallygrown.net

Farmers markets represent the bounty of summer harvest and an opportunity to buy directly from local vendors. One of the most enticing cultural heritage activities today is the farm-to-table dinner. Chef Alex Bomba of Jonesborough, Tennessee, recognized the power of culinary tourism, especially when prepared with local ingredients from area farms. With help from his wife, Breelyn, owner of Main Street Catering in Jonesborough (along with their families and community volunteers), the farm-to-table dinner concept came to this historic city in 2011. The uniqueness of this particular event, though, was its location at the site of the Jonesborough Farmers Market on Main Street. With cooperation and support of the town, the event received a permit to use Main Street. Volunteers set up and decorated a huge harvest table down a full city block to seat one hundred guests; local flowers adorned the table. Chef Alex and Breelyn donate their time to prepare the five-course meal. Depot Street Brewery donates the beer; Jonesborough Wine and Spirits provides the wine. Tables and chairs are also donated, thanks to Action Rental in Kingsport, while Woven Creative Studios Photography supplies photographic services. These contributions help the bottom line, as all proceeds are donated to the Farmers Market. Tickets sold for $50; $2,500 was raised at the 2011 dinner to help offset operation costs for the market (vendors pay a fee but don't totally cover the costs).

Jonesborough Locally Grown is the community not-for-profit organization that operates the farmers markets (a seasonal Saturday Farmers Market and Boone Street Market, a year-round local food store) and coordinates the farm-to-table dinner. In 2012, additional seats were added, and tickets (increased to $75) sold out in three hours. Net proceeds doubled to $5,000. Now the dinner serves 216; tickets cost $100 and continue to sell out. Direct costs for the dinner pay for food (purchased at full price from farmers market vendors), musicians, rentals (dishware), and incidentals. The event has steadily grown each year to the point that advance tickets are sold to market vendors, volunteers, past dinner servers, and major donors ($3,500 and up). Remaining tickets are sold at the farmers market on a first-come first-served basis, limiting purchase to two tickets per person. Since the first farm-to-table dinner in 2011, a total of $10,000 has been directly returned to local farmers through the purchase of fresh local food used at the dinner, and $40,000 in net proceeds has been contributed to Jonesborough Locally Grown.

In February 2016, Jonesborough Locally Grown produced a fourteen-page event planning guide to detail the process and document the lessons learned from five years of hosting the farm-to-table

Figure 5.6 Breelyn Bomba (Main Street Catering) and Alex Bomba (chef)—Jonesborough, Tennessee. Source: Photo by Woven Creative Studios.

dinner. The guide is now available for a modest $25 donation, with proceeds helping to support the local farmers markets. To date, the popular publication has been shared with thirty-four organizations in twenty states. For more information and to order a copy of the guide, visit http://jonesboroughfarmtotable.blogspot.com/p/info-for-organizers.html.

*****

Table 5.1 Developing a Cultural Heritage Tourism Stakeholder Engagement Strategy

Engagement Steps	Elements/Categories	Action
1. Identify stakeholders	✔ Cultural and heritage groups ✔ Tourism industry ✔ Business community ✔ Community leaders ✔ Media ✔ Government agencies ✔ Elected officials ✔ Residents ✔ Other stakeholders	☐ How and where are key stakeholders found? ☐ Define relationship to project, planning process outcome ☐ Obtain contact information ☐ Secure profile/bio
2. Define desired level of engagement	✔ Core planning team ✔ Advisers ✔ Leadership: elected officials, funders, other influencers ✔ Publics to keep informed	☐ Who is essential to success? ☐ Who has resources (time, money) to contribute? ☐ Who will benefit or be impacted by this project, process?
3. Assess attitude toward cultural heritage tourism	✔ Positive ✔ Negative ✔ Neutral ✔ Uninformed	☐ What is needed to influence, change (or neutralize) their attitude/opinion toward cultural heritage tourism?
4. Determine the best ways to communicate (share and receive information) with each stakeholder group	✔ In-person meetings ✔ Individual interviews ✔ E-mail ✔ E-surveys ✔ Posters, flyers ✔ Direct mail ✔ Other creative techniques	☐ What format is most appropriate for certain types of information? ☐ When is two-way facilitated conversation important, required? ☐ When is feedback essential, and does it need to be written or verbal (or both)? ☐ What content requires group discussion versus individual comment?
5. Establish and implement stakeholder communication system, schedule	✔ Content creator ✔ Content disseminator ✔ Distribution list—coded according to level of engagement ✔ Output schedule: weekly, monthly, quarterly, benchmarks ✔ Feedback and review schedule ✔ Final product/decision/plan announcement	☐ Define distribution frequency ☐ Decide who receives what information ☐ Define key product phases, timeline for response, format for response ☐ Decide who responds to specific content ☐ Decide optimum locations for public and/or stakeholder meetings ☐ List dates/periods to avoid ☐ Decide how much time is required for feedback ☐ Map schedule, working backward from dates of deliverables; adjust as necessary

Notes

1. U.S. Census Bureau.
2. History of the Association to Preserve the Eatonville Community, Inc., from http://www.cs.ucf.edu/~zora/pec_history.html.
3. Modified from Kay Hack, "Three Steps for Perfect Communication Strategy—Developing a Stakeholder Engagement Strategy" (April 2015).
4. K. Hodgson and K. A. Beavers, "Community Engagement: How Arts and Cultural Strategies Enhance Community Engagement and Participation"(2011), Arts and Culture Briefing Papers 04, American Planning Association, in collaboration with RMC Research Corporation.
5. Modified from "Growing Beyond: How High Performers Are Competing for Growth in Difficult Times," EY.com (n.d.), http://www.ey.com/GL/en/Issues/Driving-growth/Growing-Beyond--Stakeholder-confidence.
6. Hodgson and Beavers, "Community Engagement."
7. Ibid.
8. Wikiplanning, http://www.wikiplanning.org.
9. Modified from K. Hodgson and K. A. Beavers, "Community Engagement: How Arts and Cultural Strategies Enhance Community Engagement and Participation," Arts and Culture Briefing Papers 04 (2011), American Planning Association, in collaboration with RMC Research Corporation.

Chapter 6

Establishing a Vision and Plan for Sustainability

Plans are nothing; planning is everything.

—Dwight D. Eisenhower

Planning begins with organizing information around a central purpose. The planning process starts with a specific approach, a leadership structure, methods for engagement and conflict resolution, credible fact-based information for reference in decision making, and a time line for completing significant planning components and phases. To initiate the planning process, communities or institutions must consider what plans have already been created—maybe even dust off a few shelves and review existing documents—to determine *where* and *how* cultural heritage tourism fits into the destination's larger vision and goals. As mentioned in chapter 1, understanding *why* cultural heritage tourism is desired as an economic development strategy is critically important.

Often, the decision to launch into planning comes from a perceived need, required creation or updating of existing plans, or the desire to find solutions for a particular issue or recent crisis. Leadership is always an essential element of a strategic plan, and identifying the right leaders to oversee and engage in the planning process will ensure a greater likelihood for stakeholder buy-in and implementation. Leaders often have great vision, foresight, and perseverance. They often have or may garner political and financial support for their causes. Most important, they never give up despite often insurmountable hurdles or challenges. Leadership and its importance to success and sustainability are explored in greater detail later in this chapter.

Figure 6.1 Carrie Furnace—Rivers of Steel National Heritage Area, Western Pennsylvania.

Planning Models

Several planning models exist for cities and counties, usually in the form of legislated comprehensive plans with both mandatory and optional statutes. In the American Planning Association's *Growing Smart Legislative Guidebook*,[4] economic development (tourism) is traditionally considered a "mandatory with opt-out alternative" component, while historic preservation is viewed as an optional element. Defining the important roles of tourism, cultural resource protection, and historic preservation at the local, county, or state level, vitality and sustainability can be incorporated, at minimum, into the introductory "issues and opportunities" element of the comprehensive plan.

> Key considerations for planning include connections about what makes a place special, the unique characteristic—a lot are historic, cultural or natural. Ignoring them would be detrimental. These are your assets for economic development and quality of life, especially for the younger generation that can live wherever they want.
> —Scott W. Standish, director of Countywide Planning, Lancaster County Planning Commission

Two destination planning models recognized by the UN World Tourism Organization may be utilized for cultural heritage tourism: the sustainable development approach and the strategic planning approach.[5]

1. *The Sustainable Development Approach*

Grounded in the principles of sustainable development, this approach is often recognized as a long-term planning process designed to achieve current tourism goals without compromising the aspirations/needs of future generations. The sustainable development planning process focuses on how the destination navigates its tourism cycles of growth and maturity. An important component of this planning approach is the consideration of tourism's impact on the entire destination and the balance required to ensure the destination's sustainability in terms of positive sociocultural, environmental, and economic impacts. The planning emphasis is on satisfying the triple bottom line (see Figure 6.2). Key "big picture" questions asked and answered during the sustainable development planning process include the following:

- Is a particular development or enhancement project sustainable?
- Do any projects or experiences challenge the destination's ability to preserve and protect its unique resources?
- Do any tourism development programs or activities contribute to the sustainability of one environment yet compromise or negatively impact other environments?
- How does tourism benefit or sustain the respective resources used for or involved in hosting tourists?

This approach ensures an even distribution of benefits, but, most important, it safeguards and sustains (even enhances) the local assets and resources that attract visitors.

Figure 6.2 Sustainable tourism planning model.

In the past decade, this planning approach has gained the most traction globally—initially emphasizing natural resources but expanding to include multiple industry segments. It has now evolved as a process to include global sustainable tourism criteria for destinations with a lens on both tangible and intangible cultural heritage.

2. *The Strategic Planning Approach*

For destinations, this approach is often utilized to solve short-term problems by defining actionable solutions. The planning process outlines specific strategies that accomplish established goals and attain the desired destination benefits for tourism.

An analysis of a proposed tourism development activity or solution begins by identifying its strengths, weaknesses, opportunities, and threats (SWOT) in terms of immediate as well as longer-term impacts for the destination. Strengths and weaknesses are typically internal to the destination and its resources and infrastructure. Opportunities and threats articulate more of the external factors impacting tourists and travel, the destination's competition, or branding. The strategic planning process depends on a current, candid, and realistic assessment of the SWOT and its strategies or actionable solutions to determine their viability and sustainability. Key "big picture" questions to ask and answer during the SWOT analysis of the strategic planning process include the following:

- Can the identified strengths and opportunities help meet the goals articulated in the plan?
- How can the planning strategies be improved, enhanced, or made more effective and inclusive in meeting the destination's tourism goals?

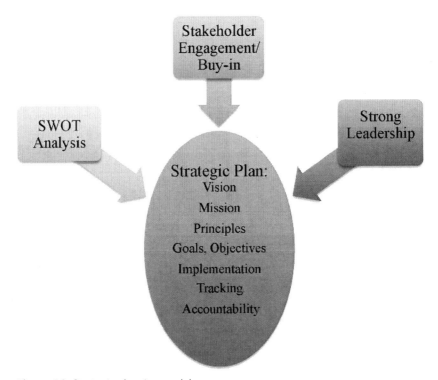

Figure 6.3 Strategic planning model.

- Are specific opportunities leveraged to enhance or sustain tourism growth (and positive impacts on cultural heritage resources)?
- Do external factors or competition from other destinations risk or threaten the successful implementation of any strategy? For example, if a destination seeks to develop its cultural heritage tourism, are neighboring communities or cities already branded as a cultural heritage destination?

Today, most strategic plans don't extend beyond three years—in part due to the rapidly changing tourism environment, technology, and industry's global expansion. However, strategic plans often build a long-range foundation for phased growth and development over a decade or more.

Various destinations have used the UN World Tourism Organization's tourism planning approaches to create their vision, articulate their goals, and define their desired outcomes. When emphasizing cultural and heritage resources for the tourism planning process, destinations often create value statements or principles to guide the planning process to ensure adequate safeguards and management of significant cultural and heritage assets.

For specific sites or projects, destinations may consider planning options that are more aligned with traditional *business models*. Nonprofit organizations, in particular, are seeking new revenue generation models to offset declining availability of government grants and private donations. This business planning approach focuses on market competitiveness, implementation and evaluation of performance measures, and positive return on investment.

This business planning model is becoming more recognized for forecasting sustainability, especially as nonprofit institutions need to diversify revenue sources and operate as more market-facing organizations.

Figure 6.4 Business planning model.

The business model differs from strategic planning models in that it often includes a detailed risk assessment, a more specific phasing and implementation schedule with milestones, success measurement, and much more detailed financial data—a summary of financial needs, a budget, a three-year revenue/expense projection, a break-even analysis, and actual performance statements (balance sheet, profit/loss statement, and financial history). A sample outline of a business plan is available, courtesy of Preserve Rhode Island, at http://culturalheritagetourism.org/wp-content/uploads/formidable/Figure-6.14-PRI-Intern-Business-Plan-Template-July-2009.pdf.

Unique Considerations for Cultural Heritage Tourism Planning

There are some unique factors to address when focusing on cultural heritage resources as part of or as the foundation for a destination's comprehensive tourism plan or even as a stand-alone cultural heritage tourism plan. These considerations can be viewed as challenges or opportunities; however labeled, they must be addressed and resolved during the planning process. Other considerations result from the growth of tourism, the maturation of destinations and aging tourism products, an increase in competition, and external issues, such as terrorism, natural disasters, and global health concerns. Here are some specific factors to consider in the planning process.

Limited Capacity

Unlike manufactured attractions (such as theme or amusement parks), cultural and heritage resources often have a limited capacity. Cultural heritage resources do not always see the measurement of tourism in volume (attendance) as important as the experience or education afforded. Overcrowding may actually have a negative impact on the resource, the destination, and the visitor. Identifying creative strategies to maximize opportunity with minimal invasiveness is central to a positive cultural heritage tourism impact. Capacity management is explored in more detail in chapter 12.

Different Terminology

Cultural heritage resources and institutions use different terms and language than their tourism industry or planning cohorts. Consistent and clear definitions must be established, understood, and utilized. A glossary of terms is included at the end of this book.

Fragmentation

Tourism and cultural heritage sectors are comprised of different constituents. These constituents may be large or small businesses, public or private institutions, for-profit and nonprofit organizations, individuals, or loosely defined groups. Each sector represents a range of entities. For example, the tourism sector includes accommodations, tour operators, attractions, restaurants, retail, and transportation; the culture heritage sector includes museums, historic sites, neighborhoods, performing arts venues, studios and galleries, artists, events, and festivals, just to name a few. These entities come in a range of sizes, budgets, and interests/levels of engagement—ranging from nonprofit, volunteer organizations to small businesses and large institutions and corporations. Elected officials, development authorities, and planning agencies also need to have an understanding of the potential value of tourism and cultural heritage to their local community. Finding common ground among constituents is often a challenge, as indicated in the previous chapter. Collaborating before crisis is important to establish trust and respect for varying opinions or approaches.

Cultural and Historic Integrity Is Paramount to Sustainability

To maintain cultural and historic integrity, resource management policies and procedures have to be included as a priority for the planning process. Costs for preservation and ongoing maintenance to adhere to the Secretary of the Interior's Standards for Historic Preservation (for compliance) must be factored into any type of planning model involving historic structures to determine feasibility for cultural heritage tourism use or reuse. Cultural integrity must respect, represent, and be directed by the peoples whose culture is showcased.

Different Priorities

Cultural heritage resources are often operated by nonprofit organizations or government agencies investing in the mission of education, conservation, and preservation rather than the traditional tourism industry priorities of research, product development, marketing, and profit. Helping each entity mutually agree on the valued outcome(s) is critical to the planning process, implementation, and sustainability.

Fear of Unsatisfactory Outcomes

Tourism, if not properly managed or marketed, can foster homogeneous or inauthentic development, excessive capacity, exploitation, and/or destruction of resources. Conversely, cultural heritage resources may not uniformly provide the consistent access or quality experiences desired by visitors. Clearly defined and mutually approved outcomes help overcome these barriers.

As the tourism industry matures, so have the strategies for cultural heritage tourism planning. Mature destinations may utilize a planning process that reflects the evolution of their tourism product and experiences. As homogenization of products occurs, destinations must redefine their "unique selling proposition" for the desired tourist, often reinvesting or creating cultural and heritage initiatives to reclaim their market share. The destination may conduct a "comparable analysis" to understand how similar destinations are developing and marketing their cultural heritage tourism.

To aid in making informed decisions, destinations may also engage in primary market research to ascertain the value of their cultural heritage resources to key markets or to identify what local residents consider the essential benefits they want to realize from cultural heritage tourism. Cultural heritage resources and institutions may seek strategies to foster sustainability by attracting new audiences or cultivating repeat visitation, especially during off-peak seasons. The emergence of cultural heritage packages, development of cultural entertainment districts, historic neighborhood tours, use of themed itineraries, and focus on anniversaries for commemorations and celebrations expand the engagement of cultural heritage resources in tourism.

Destinations may address and implement specific governance, management, and sustainability policies as part of the planning process. Performance measures may be expanded beyond traditional economic impact and quantity of visitors to ensure that social, cultural, and environmental impacts are evaluated relative to the cultural and heritage institutions and the entire destination's desired outcomes. The pressure to balance visitors' needs with residents' desires and resource impact is paramount. According to the International Conference of Monuments and Sites, "quality" and "creativity" are two distinct new strategies for destinations to embrace. These new strategies focus on how to balance the growth in tourism with the capacity of resources and experience management for positive destination impact.

Typically, a separate cultural heritage tourism planning process is conducted when the destination relies on its cultural heritage resources to be *essential to* or *responsible for* the destination's distinctive brand and experience delivery. At this point, careful coordination of cultural heritage tourism planning and destination planning must occur so that stakeholders (and plans) are not isolated. It is also important not to develop separate cultural heritage tourism strategies that may be at odds with the overall destination vision, mission, and desired outcomes. Leadership becomes the central driving force to enable a cultural tourism strategic plan to evolve, integrate, and ultimately generate a positive impact for the overall destination.

Initiating the Formal Planning Process

Developing a plan requires a local entity or team to inform, instruct, and implement the process. The destination must decide the best structure and participants to oversee the planning process. Scenarios may include an:

- Interagency task force
- Government-appointed leadership council
- Public–private partnership
- Local organization as the lead, with stakeholder participation

A significant early decision is whether to conduct the planning process internally (among stakeholders with input from local partners) or to utilize external assistance (either paid consultants or technical assistance provided by state or educational institutions).

Advantages of a Locally Based Planning Team

- Intimate knowledge of the destination and issues to address
- Ability to navigate across agencies and internal processes
- Access to information and resources
- Easy transfer from planning to implementation

Disadvantages of a Locally Based Planning Team

- Myopia—too "in the weeds" and unable to look at the big picture or potential
- Risk averse
- Bias based on previous activities or agency or team affiliations
- Potential conflict of interest (depending on team composite)

Advantages of Hiring External Consultants

- Recognized expertise
- Objectivity in presenting options and opportunities
- Access to broader networks, relevant examples, and resources
- Neutral facilitator, especially for stakeholder meetings

Disadvantages of Hiring External Consultants

- Learning curve required to understand (or comprehend) particular issues
- Limited availability for planning activities (especially if out of region)
- Perceived as "outsider," restricting acceptance by some stakeholders
- Additional budget required to pay for consulting services
- May not grasp or may miss local issues and nuances

If an external consultant is favored, the typical approach is to create and distribute a "request for proposal" or a "request for qualifications." The first is more detailed with a specific scope of work; the second is a shorter "ask" to narrow the field of potential consultants based on specific expertise. A more detailed scope of work is then shared with the top candidates to prepare a comprehensive proposal and cost estimate.

What to Include in a Request for Proposal (RFP): Twelve Key Ingredients

1. Basics—Share who is issuing, who is eligible to apply, when proposals are due, how to submit, who to contact for assistance, and if there is any window or opportunity to ask questions or request information.
2. Purpose—Explain why the RFP is being issued, what solutions are sought, and the desired outcomes.
3. Background—Provide context for the applicant: offer an overview of the organization or agency issuing the proposal and the destination or location where the work will be conducted.
4. Scope of work—The specific duties to be performed, key points to cover in the proposal, any special instruction for completion, and milestones to accomplish.
5. Deliverables—Explain the final products, format and quantity, and presentation requirements (if any).
6. Methodology—Explain how the work is to be accomplished, with a time line for completion.
7. Cost proposal—Technical, management, and travel budgets for each phase or deliverable, with explanation of any restrictions or exclusions (such as fixed price with a defined payment schedule); licenses and insurance requirements.
8. Credentials—Qualifications of key personnel, relevant prior experience, and references,
9. Copyrights—Define who owns the final products.
10. Evaluation criteria—How each proposal will be evaluated (point score or ranking of specific criteria and what disqualifies a proposal).
11. Opportunity for applicant to raise questions or provide alternative solutions to proposed scope of work.
12. Directions on what to submit, how to submit, and by when.

Both issuers and respondents constantly debate the policy of including a budget in an RFP. The most obvious reason to include a budget is so that respondents can provide a more accurate scope of work for the budget available. The issuer may need to accept lowest bid and therefore not want to propose a fee for services, although this makes the review and evaluation of proposals more difficult, as not all submissions may reflect the same level of services. (Tip: Include a formula similar to what the Appalachian Regional Commission uses. The organization rates the RFP based on the effort required to complete the scope of work. The rating fits into one of four categories—major and large-, medium-, and small-scale projects—and corresponds to a specific budget range assigned accordingly. The commission then shares this rating and budget range to receive more comparable responses.)

Funding is one of the key factors for consideration in the planning process, as the budget may dictate the level of engagement or involvement of external consultants. As a cautionary note, don't expend all your (political and financial) capital on the planning process, as additional human and financial resources will be required to implement the strategies and tasks outlined. Without action, a plan simply sits on a shelf. The goal for a cultural heritage tourism plan is to have a dynamic, living document that becomes a road map for implementation (product development, marketing, and management) and evaluation.

The Importance of Leadership

An inclusive planning process requires someone leading the discussion and deliberation. Ideally, this individual has the political or the community influence to bring other civic groups, governments, attractions, and business leaders to the table for dialogue. Staff of planning agencies or tourism bureaus may be responsible for background research and analysis, but the process requires destination thought leaders to form aspirational ideas. These same leaders have to ultimately reach consensus in order to achieve results. While this may seem an arduous task, especially to get busy high-profile individuals together, the result is invaluable. A vision becomes the foundation that each influencer can champion with his or her colleagues, employees, donors, members, constituents, and publics. This process also requires that leaders make personal commitments or declarations to help move forward. Leaders don't stop once the plan has been created but instead embrace the plan and set out to lend support in necessary ways—financially, with political influence, and/or with staff or other resources.

McKinsey & Company: How to Make a City Great

All city leaders want their local economies to grow. Economic growth, however, does not automatically deliver a better quality of life for citizens and can often harm the environment." Therefore, "smart growth depends upon a strategic approach that identifies the very best growth opportunities and nurtures them, planning so the city and its surroundings can cope with the demands growth will place on them, integrating environmental thinking, and ensuring that all citizens enjoy their city's prosperity.
—McKinsey & Company, "How to Make a City Great" (2013), McKinsey Cities Special Initiative, p. 5, cities@mckinsey.com

Perhaps one of the greatest leaders and visionaries in cultural heritage tourism in the United States is former Mayor Joseph P. Riley Jr. of Charleston, South Carolina. An early advocate for tourism management, Riley recognized the importance of preservation and protection of his city's historic character in building a world-class destination that attracts arts, commerce, and tourism. The delicate balance between delivering residents' high quality of life and meeting changing visitor needs is carefully cultivated through proactive leadership, engagement, performance, and enforcement. Riley has realized a number of achievements and accolades during his ten terms as mayor (since 1975). He forged a remarkable revitalization of the historic downtown business district (a National Historic Landmark), helped create and grow Spoleto Festival U.S.A., and added to the city's park system (including the highly celebrated Waterfront Park), resulting in recognition as one of the most livable and progressive cities in the United States.[7] Charleston received numerous accolades for its tourism product, was named America's #1 City by *Condé Nast Traveller* Reader's Choice Awards for five consecutive years (2011–2015), and was ranked #1 Top City in the U.S. and Canada by *Travel + Leisure* 2015 World's Best Awards.[8] (More information on Charleston is available in chapter 14)

Cultural heritage tourism planning (and the creation of a vision) is conducted for a number of reasons—because of a change in leadership, a shift in the environment, or a change in regulation or to deal with a particular crisis—requiring the need for alternative or innovative solutions to current challenges; bold, new ideas to foster competitiveness; and answers to civic or economic problems. Visionary leaders seek to be part of the solution rather than part of the problem, challenging others to overcome adversity and collaborate toward a common purpose. This leadership requires confidence and integrity but can also be bolstered by information. Great leaders and visionaries will use or obtain data to inform and identify other best practices to forge a course of action. Educating others about opportunities or repercussions (of action or no action) can achieve powerful results and diffuse potentially turbulent discussions, often with greater results than with legislation. Even helping leaders understand others' motivations and realities can ultimately lead to cooperation. Respecting other leaders and their positions as equal partners is also important to building collaborations.[9] Communicating in various ways and with language that resonates to the target audience (as discussed in chapter 5) can also help convey opportunity and forge collaborations.

A business trend that is beginning to influence destination development is collaboration with competitors.[10] Sometimes termed "co-opetition," this concept recognizes the value of working together for a greater (common) good rather than competing with each other and losing valued market share. Heritage areas, thematic trails, and other regional partnerships often bring

Twelve Secrets of Leadership

A leader:

1. Has or earns respect
2. Never loses focus
3. Can clearly articulate the vision
4. Brings passion and enthusiasm
5. Thinks big
6. Empowers others
7. Leads by example
8. Listens
9. Provides thoughtful guidance
10. Cares about people
11. Is committed for the long term
12. Shares the glory

Source: National Trust for Historic Preservation, Share Your Heritage

disparate—even competitive—entities together to create the critical mass or desired activities to achieve greater, more sustainable outcomes. The value is in recognizing that partners can achieve more together than they can separately. Individual needs are weighed against the larger opportunity, and agreed-on compromise ensures that win–win scenarios are developed.

The Value of a Vision

A vision typically establishes a picture of what success will look like in a future period—5, 10, or 20 years from now. Often included in strategic or master plans, a vision is fundamental to establishing goals and strategies to direct and prioritize efforts. A vision may shape how or what kind of development occurs, the level of resource stewardship, and aesthetics to define a "sense of place." Without a vision, planners are rudderless. Or, more critically, to once again quote the infamous Yogi Berra, "If you don't know where you are going, you might wind up someplace else." A vision sets a direction and leads to a purposeful course of action. How to set and act on a vision is explored in this chapter along with the key elements for implementation, including metrics to stay on course.

A vision can bring disparate partners together, helping varied constituents voice a particular desire and work through discourse to a unified end result. Ultimately, the vision articulates a collective image to develop, promote, and sustain the physical and cultural character of a place. Cultural heritage tourism can then be considered a potential strategy to help achieve the vision and define how other forms of economic development may or may not be compatible for sustainable growth. The vision may also underscore key steps to achieve before cultural heritage tourism can be viable. After all, a place must be of value to local residents before visitors can value the city or community.

Some community leaders or elected officials may opt to forge straight ahead to action—to get things done and demonstrate movement. This may provide short-term results but may shortchange or compromise long-term potential. It may also reduce synergy or create silos as disparate groups start initiatives that may not be in harmony—either for the end user or for the destination at large. A vision helps chart a course to better understand compatibility of opportunities, like pieces of a puzzle fitting together. If a building is restored or constructed without context of a larger vision for the destination, the outcome may lack components to optimize results or miss the mark completely. A vision ensures that resources are used effectively according to an agreed-on road map. A vision also sets a course of action for thoughtful cross-platform development and marketing where various agencies and organizations work in tandem to achieve desired goals. The bottom line is that a vision helps leaders, elected officials, and other stakeholders understand and rally around the intentional future outcome—and stay on course to achieve the desired results.

Steps for Articulating a Vision

Different techniques can be used in creating a vision: imagining a future scenario, vision circle, alter ego, and dreaming.[6] The steps are universal, whether establishing a vision for a single business, a district, or a destination. First, you assess the current situation—an exercise accomplished, it is hoped, through the inventory and analysis conducted as described in chapters 2 to 4—as it is important to define the context. For example, you identify similar cities or communities for comparison if visioning for a whole destination, where you may need to look only at uses for other rehabilitated buildings if focusing on a single site. If you have a paper plant or a pristine riverfront, these assets present very different scenarios for a destination vision and for cultural heritage tourism growth. If tourism already exists in the destination, it is hoped that market research (or focus group results) can inform what brings customers now and what specific research can provide further instruction on how to realize future goals. Make sure to include past achievements or successes (especially related to cultural heritage tourism) to demonstrate a can-do attitude and provide a foundation for growth.

The second step focuses on defining desired outcomes—answering the "big picture" questions asked earlier in this chapter. This step articulates exactly why you are embarking on this quest and how success will or should be measured—in terms of economic, social, and environmental

Visions for the Future

Compelling and inspiring visions are often created as part of a planning process to articulate the future opportunity for the institution or destination. A vision embraced by diverse stakeholders helps implement the required activities to achieve the desired results. It can also help articulate the brand promise, especially when included on websites or coupled with value and mission statements.

- Reginald F. Lewis Museum (Maryland): To share globally, and with integrity, the human drama of Maryland's African American experience (http://www.lewismuseum.org/about/mission).
- The Hoboken Historical Museum will continue to benefit the public as a vibrant, dynamic, all-inclusive and exciting organization that is fully involved in the life of the City of Hoboken (New Jersey) (https://www.hobokenmuseum.org/visit/about-us/mission-a-vision). Its vision includes securing additional space for permanent displays, expanding professional staff, creating a $10 million endowment, and effectively utilizing technology.
- Toledo Museum of Art (Ohio): Considering the Museum's aspirations, strengths, weaknesses, opportunities, and current environment, what the Museum can be best at, passionate about, and financially driven by is using our collection to link art and the creative process. If we focus our efforts on becoming the best in the world at linking art and the creative process, we believe that we can successfully achieve the Museum's mission as envisioned in these concepts:
  - Audience Growth: The number of our actual and virtual visitors will increase.
  - Diversity: Our on-site visitors will reflect the economic, social, cultural, and racial diversity of our region.
  - Community Relevance: We will be an integral member of our community and will be responsive to issues of community concern and importance, particularly as they relate to the arts.
  - Art Collection: We will achieve a consistently high level of quality.
  - Professional Leadership: Other organizations will look to us as a model of operational effectiveness, integrity, responsibility to mission, and successful application of innovative solutions to solve real problems.
  - Operational Excellence: Resources will meet organizational needs, be built to realize organizational aspirations, and be allocated to achieve the Museum's mission and vision.

impact (jobs, quality of life, new vitality, enhanced activities, resource conservation and preservation, and thriving businesses) relative to the vision. The third step sets a time line for when to achieve success—typically five but not more than twenty years into the future. The vision is an aspirational compilation of these outcomes, interpreted via imagery or words that describe what, it is hoped, will be realized or achieved by a specific date. Be precise. The details articulated in the vision form the key strategies and priorities to move forward.

Once a vision has been crafted, a plan is outlined to move forward. The planning process can yield important goals and strategies to accomplish for the vision to become reality. Depending on the complexity or comprehensiveness of the vision—requiring many different partners or phases for achievement—principles may be defined to help guide the planning process. It may also be desirable to create criteria for evaluating and prioritizing strategies. The criteria help frame the assessment process. As hundreds of ideas and projects are identified, criteria align concepts according to the vision and ensure consistency in prioritization. As new ideas are presented, criteria also increase efficiency to help stay focused on what is most important. This singular focus is demonstrated best in the origins of the Lower East Side Tenement Museum. Read the accredited museum's profile at the end of this chapter to learn how a vision became a reality and the museum continues to serve its original purpose.

Figure 6.5 Exterior, Lower East Side Tenement Museum—New York City—A Vision to Give Immigrants A Voice.

Figure 6.6 Levine Kitchen, Lower East Side Tenement Museum—New York City.

Developing/Refining A Mission

A *mission* is crafted to move the plan into action and successfully achieve the desired outcomes. Unfortunately, missions are often cumbersome, politically correct verbiage rather than a succinct, powerful statement of purpose. Nonprofit associations and nongovernment agencies designing lengthy and vague or politically correct declarations should instead consider short, memorable mission statements—one that each board member (and staff) can easily remember and recite (the two-minute elevator speech). A destination mission used for marketing identifies the core target audience(s), the experience or product delivered, and what the audience receives (their benefit). For cultural heritage tourism plans, destinations or individual organizations need to articulate their mission as value propositions in terms of authentic experiences, culturally rich resources, and positive impacts on places and people. Thirty-five words is the average length of current mission statements.

Following are some sample mission statements:

- The Delta Blues Museum (in Mississippi) is dedicated to creating a welcoming place where visitors find meaning, value, and perspective by exploring the history and heritage of the unique American musical art form of the blues.[16]
- The Nantucket Historical Association tells the inspiring stories of Nantucket through its collections, programs, and properties. Their strategic plan focuses on four objectives: achieving financial stability; caring for collections, including properties; providing transformative experiences; and providing and promoting a consistent identify and clear brand.

Establishing a Vision and Plan for Sustainability   **121**

- Hill-Stead Museum, a National Historic Landmark, serves diverse audiences in Connecticut and beyond as a welcoming place for learning, reflection, and enjoyment. The museum develops, preserves, documents, displays, and interprets its exceptional impressionist paintings, 1901 historic house, and 152-acre landscape for the benefit of present and future generations.[17]
- The West Virginia State Museum (at the Culture Center) is dedicated to inspiring, educating, and enriching the lives of the public by instilling a deeper understanding and sense of pride through the collection, preservation, and exhibition of diverse cultural and historic traditions, focusing on every aspect of West Virginia history, culture, art, paleontology, archaeology and geology from all geographic regions—representing the people, land, and industries.[18]
- The Broad (in Los Angeles) makes its collection of contemporary art from the 1950s to the present accessible to the widest possible audience by presenting exhibitions and operating a lending program to art museums and galleries worldwide. By actively building a dynamic collection that features in-depth representations of influential contemporary artists and by advancing education and engagement through exhibits and diverse public programming, the museum enriches, provokes, inspires, and fosters appreciation of art of our time.[19]

From an expressive vision and a succinct mission, the planning process sets a course of developing goals and strategies. For destinations and cultural heritage tourism, SMART (Strategic, Measurable, Attainable, Realistic, and Timely) goals are preferred. SMART goals answer the six "W" questions:

- Who is involved?
- What is to be accomplished?
- Where will it occur (location)?
- When will it happen (time frame)?
- Which requirements or conditions are necessary to make the goal happen?
- Why is it a goal (the specific reasons, purpose, or benefits to accomplishing the goal)?

While SMART goals are sometimes harder to articulate, they clearly express the vision and mission of destination planners. For an individual site, the mission may already be established, but context of how this structure contributes to the overall destination experience is important to ensure alignment. A specific site plan should include SMART goals to realize the desired vision and outcomes. Principles or value statements can be introduced to use as an overlay for prioritizing strategies. If, through this process, you create 100 or more good ideas, there needs to be a mechanism to focus on which ideas to pursue first.

Establishing Desired Outcomes

Central to any planning process are well-defined outcomes. The process itself must result in some deliverable—certainly a tangible plan but also to satisfy the original planning purpose. Well-defined outcomes for cultural heritage tourism can keep the planning process on track. Stakeholder consensus on the answers to the following questions can guide the process to successful conclusions:

- How can cultural heritage tourism positively impact the destination? Be specific.
- How will cultural heritage tourism be measured? Be exact.
- When should (new or enhanced) cultural heritage tourism experiences be available? Be precise.

Figure 6.7 The collection, Museum of Northern Arizona—Flagstaff, Arizona.

- Where should cultural heritage tourism be offered or expanded? Provide detailed boundaries.
- What are the cultural heritage tourism priorities? Be explicit.
- Whom should cultural heritage tourism benefit? Provide a detailed list.

Performance measures track activities and ensure that desired outcomes are completed on schedule and to a standard set by the values, principles, or planning guidelines. Performance measures also evaluate the planning process as well as the effectiveness, efficiency, quality, timeliness, and productivity of the planning team. Performance measures may be extended to the implementation phase to require accountability against the planning benchmarks and provide attribution to particular activities. Establishing benchmarks *early* in the cultural heritage tourism planning process is essential to ensure that stakeholders stay focused on priorities, have reference points to help guide the process, and establish systems for evaluation at key periods during implementation. A memorandum of understanding (MOU) may be developed to articulate specific roles and responsibilities among partners. A sample MOU is provided at the end of this chapter. Demonstrating a positive return on investment should be an annual goal for all cultural heritage tourism programs and experiences. As articulated in the profile at the end of this chapter, the Museum of Northern Arizona focuses on mission-centric programs and champions its values in various ways.

Figure 6.8 Young Navajo pollen dancer, Navajo Festival of Arts and Culture—Flagstaff, Arizona.

Acting on the Vision

> Never doubt that a small group of thoughtful, committed citizens can change the world. Indeed, it's the only thing that ever has.
>
> —Margaret Mead, anthropologist

Strong management and oversight must continue beyond the visioning phase. Personal commitments ensure ownership of the vision and the tasks required to achieve the desired outcomes. Voluntary contributions of time and money are always important to demonstrate and recognize support for implementation of the vision. However, assigning roles and responsibilities among individuals, departments, agencies, and organizations—public, private, and nongovernment—is important to ensure continued leadership and coordination. These assignments can instruct how stakeholders are informed and updated on activities related to the vision and also who leads various actions. Memoranda of understanding between key partnership organizations and agencies articulate specific contributions and benefits for each entity based on the vision.

To keep people motivated and energized to move forward, it is important to identify small successes for execution and celebration. Early wins keep enthusiasm high and often attract new partners waiting in the wings. High visibility and strong metrics can generate media coverage and public attention beyond traditional stakeholder networks.

Chapter Summary

While visioning may seem overly important in developing sustainable cultural heritage tourism outcomes, the exercise is perhaps the most important for setting a course of what *is* possible and desired. The vision frames the context of achievement, and then the planning process can address how specific cultural heritage tourism development, marketing, and management can deliver those expectations of success. Establishing systems to monitor and foster growth ensures sustainability, where cultural heritage tourism can achieve its full potential via a specific site, district, community, region, state, or nation. Leadership is key to successfully guide the process to a positive end result/outcome.

★ ★ ★ ★ ★

Saving an Industrial Icon
Profile: Rivers of Steel National Heritage Area—Eight Counties in Western Pennsylvania

http://www.riversofsteel.com

Time can be friend or foe. For the Carrie Blast Furnaces 6 and 7 located just outside of Pittsburgh, Pennsylvania, it has been both. Perhaps the most significant icon for pre–World War II ironmaking technology, the Carrie Furnaces (constructed in 1884 and opened in 1907) produced up to 1,250 tons of steel per day. During its heyday, Homestead Steel was the largest steelmaker in the world. In 1978, parent company U.S. Steel abandoned its operation, and furnaces 6 and 7 closed. Two other sites (furnaces 3 and 4) continued to operate until 1982. Over the next sixteen years, the brownfield site sat empty and neglected. When U.S. Steel sold the site to the Park Corporation in 1998 with permission to scrap it, the two remaining furnaces (6 and 7) experienced a reawakening of sorts—particularly by preservationists recognizing the importance of this structure in telling the story of America's industrial heritage.

Figure 6.9 Graffiti—Rivers of Steel National Heritage Area, Western Pennsylvania.

The uphill battle to reclaim this piece of history took years. A local task force faced continuous liability issues. Local government agencies and the community at large also questioned the viability of saving a behemoth structure with little public access surrounded by a contaminated area. Carrie Furnaces became the relic to save, not only as a significant site and visual reminder of the past but also as a testament to all the men and women who worked for decades in the mill—it was recognition of their contributions and a tribute to their story. Finally, the Redevelopment Authority of Allegheny County purchased the 110-acre site to save Carrie Furnaces from becoming scrap metal. Rivers of Steel entered into a long-term lease to be stewards of the historic site. The next question surfaced: how best to restore and interpret the derelict site? The restoration costs came in at an estimate of $75 million to $100 million for the century-old site that hadn't been maintained for more than four decades.

At the same time that the task force fought to save Carrie Furnaces, momentum was gaining for designation of Rivers of Steel as a National Heritage Area (NHA), which was congressionally approved in 1996. With a mission to "conserve, interpret, and develop historical, cultural, and recreational resources throughout western Pennsylvania, including the eight counties that comprise the Rivers of Steel National Heritage Area," the Rivers of Steel Heritage Corporation set out to help convert Carrie Furnaces from an abandoned, underappreciated site to the main character in its central story:

> According to the National Park Service, a National Heritage Area (NHA) is a designation given by the United States Congress to an area that has places where natural, cultural, and historic resources combine to form a cohesive, nationally important landscape. Through its resources, an NHA tells national important stories that celebrate our nation's diverse heritage area. An NHA is a lived-in landscape.

Consequently, NHA entities collaborate with communities to determine how to make heritage relevant to local interests and needs.[1]

NHAs are a grassroots, community-driven approach to heritage conservation and economic development. Through public-private partnerships, NHA entities support historic preservation, natural resource conservation, recreation, heritage tourism, and educational projects. Leveraging funds and long-term support for projects, NHA partnership foster pride of place and an enduring stewardship ethic.

There are currently forty-nine heritage areas in the NHA program.

The Rivers of Steel Heritage Corporation deliberated on the best short- and long-term uses of the Carrie Furnaces and also began nomination of the site as a National Historic Landmark. It would take another decade to get this designation, in November 2006. During this ten-year period, the heritage area addressed blight, site degradation, vandalism, zoning, and permitting for use. It also dealt with an "energy desert" with no infrastructure in place to power the grid. In 2010, stabilizing the site became paramount. While the intent initially was to restore the facility, the NHA quickly realized that renovating the site as an industrial ruin kept the feel more authentic and real. Several millions have been invested in maintaining its authenticity—rust, rough edges, and all—and will likely require many more millions in future years. Thankfully, federal and state funds, grants from private foundations, state gambling revenue from the casino, and reinvestment of earned income (from tours and rentals) help pay for necessary preservation and environmental issues (asbestos, contaminants, and lead).[2]

Graffiti was rampant at the site, and the heritage area recognized the need to better understand this urban art culture in order to curb destruction and embrace creativity. Two legal wall spaces helped minimize illegal activity and encouraged artistic expression related to the history of the site. As Ron Baraff, director of historic resources and facilities at Rivers of Steel NHA, noted, "Unique partnerships create unique opportunities." No longer do people have to sneak in to get a glimpse of Carrie Furnace; the Rivers of Steel NHA offers tours and special events to encourage visitation and learning.

The NHA also explored the use of solar power to expand the site's footprint and to be more sustainable through a reduction of power consumption. Goats also helped plow through the wasteland in an economic way to manage the landscape. These environmentally sensitive strategies have fostered education tours and attracted new grant opportunities.

Rivers of Steel NHA continues its creative approach to interpretation, partnerships, and sustainability. While it does receive federal funding as a designated NHA, the Rivers of Steel Heritage Corporation is conscious of the requirement to match or exceed the allocated funding, and continues to seek innovative revenue generation strategies.

1. Special events are a major thrust of the NHA to attract new audiences and expand revenue generation opportunities. For example, the NHA hosted Pogopalooza (extreme sports) in 2016; is often booked for weddings (which brought 715 visitors to Carrie in 2015), film crews (an additional 150 people), and photo shoots (attracting 248 people). The NHA also organizes its own events, such as the Festival of Combustion and the Iron Pour (attendance of 594 in 2015), to cast further attention on their central theme. In the more than 1,300 rental fee or hosting agreements negotiated in 2015, all include a general tour for participants or a voucher to return for a tour. Facebook is used to promote events and offers an opportunity to book online. Participation in public events rose from thirty-three in 2002 to 2,489 in 2012 and 3,700 in 2015.

Figure 6.10 Urban art piece—Rivers of Steel National Heritage Area, Western Pennsylvania.

2. Educational programs, such as the Graffiti Workshops, the Abandoned America photographic workshops, and other related instruction, provide more than 500 visitors with unique learning experiences annually and reasons to return.
3. Public–private partnerships offer opportunities for collaboration. Happy hours with local craft brewers and distillers attracted 160 patrons in 2015, while television show productions, when they need a live audience, drew 4,000. The supplemental use of the site generates additional outreach to new businesses and clients as well as customers.
4. Earned income programs include more than 700 private tours and a Receptive Tour program. The NHA Receptive Tour program creates and sells tour packages for eighteen counties in Pennsylvania, Ohio, and West Virginia to North American tour operators. In 2015, receptive tours brought approximately 950 people into the region for tours lasting up to three days. Tour themes include Iron and Steel Heritage, Whiskey Rebellion, The Lincoln Highway, Gardens and Glass, Art and Architecture, and more.

The key to Rivers of Steel's success is in "its innovative partnerships, its market-facing approach to preservation, and never taking 'no' or 'it can't be done' for an answer," according to August R. (Augie) Carlino, president and chief executive officer of the Rivers of Steel Heritage Corporation. Understand what people are looking for rather than telling people what they should experience—and be fluid enough to adapt without compromising the integrity of the story or the site. "Carrie Furnace is core to understanding the industrial and cultural history of Pittsburgh and southwestern Pennsylvania. Without it, Rivers of Steel would be quite sterile," he continued.[3]

Time Line

1884	Carrie Furnaces begins operation.
1907	Furnaces 6 and 7 open (blown in).
1978	Furnaces 6 and 7 are shut down (taken offline).
1982	Last iron made at Carrie Furnaces.
1986	U.S. Steel closes the Homestead Works.

1988	Park Corporation purchases the Homestead Works from U.S. Steel. Heritage Task Force, formed to save Carrie Furnaces and other structures from demolition.
1996	U.S. Congress designates Rivers of Steel as one of nine National Heritage Areas.
2002	Rivers of Steel begins tours of region.
2004	Rivers of Steel works with the Redevelopment Authority of Allegheny County to purchase Carrie Furnaces.
2005	New owners begin assessment of site.
2006	Carrie Furnaces designated a National Historic Landmark.
2010	Rivers of Steel reaches lease agreement with the Redevelopment Authority of Allegheny County.

* * * * *

Profile: the Tenement Museum: A Vision to Give Immigrants a Voice
97 Orchard Street, New York, New York

http://www.tenement.org

> The story of our nation's immigrants is America's defining narrative, and the joys and challenges of establishing new lives and new communities continue for present-day immigrants around the world.
>
> —Morris J. Vogel, PhD, Tenement Museum president

Great accomplishments often begin as a single idea fostered by a visionary leader. Ruth Abram believed in the power of using our nation's history to tell the story of immigration as a conversation starter and opportunity to foster a public dialogue about relevant immigration issues today. She looked for years to find a site to honor America's immigrants. This vision became reality in 1988, when Abram (and cofounder Anita Jacobson) started the Lower East Side Tenement Museum (Tenement Museum) at 97 Orchard Street. The apartments in this historically significant building housed 7,000 working-class immigrants from twenty countries between 1863 and 1935. Shuttered for fifty years, the building, its relatively intact interior, and some 2,000 artifacts left behind provided the perfect foundation for telling the story of a forgotten class.

Recognized as the "first American history museum to give voice to the stories and lives of urban, immigrant working people,"[11] the Tenement Museum uses historically accurate accounts of actual tenants to tell of the strife, sorrows, hardships, and prejudice experienced by nineteenth- and twentieth-century immigrants. Today, the museum brings the building and six restored apartments to life via thematic tours. Focusing on shop life, sweatshops, hard times, and other significant themes, the guided tours explore contemporary issues through the personal stories of tenants (presented by costumed interpreters) residing at 97 Orchard Street. The topics of tours are as diverse and varied as the tenants who lived there and the cultures they brought with them, exploring different religious affiliations and countries of origin.[12] To keep content fresh and relevant, staff (including the museum president) regularly conduct tours. Rated as one of the top non–art museums, the Tenement Museum is listed as number 27 of 997 things to do in New York City, with more than half the reviewers awarding a rating of "Excellent." Visitor comments include "appeals to teenagers—more interesting than the Statue of Liberty," "an important part of our history," and "fabulous stories of New York's beginnings."[13]

As is often the case, the Tenement Museum depends on numerous partners and contributions to fulfill its mission and sustain its operation. Support from city, state, and federal governments and foundations and individuals aided in the development of this nonprofit organization and implementation of its mission:

- The National Endowment for the Humanities funded research on former tenants.
- The National Endowment for the Arts also provided support.
- The New York State Council on the Arts funded the Tenement Museum's Historic Structure Report and development of the sweatshop apartment.
- The New York State Urban Development Corporation gave $500,000 for renovation of 97 Orchard Street.
- The New York City Department of Cultural Affairs contributed more than $800,000 for capital improvements.
- The Tenement Museum received $150,000 from the City of New York, $27,000 from the New York State Council on the Arts, and $20,000 from the New York State budget for educational programs and website development.
- Consultants contributed an additional $78,000 in technical assistance and services.

To broaden the interpretive landscape and extend the organization's vision, the Tenement Museum added neighborhood tours in the early 1990s. The walking tours, when combined with a building tour, provide a comprehensive learning experience. Discounts are offered for visitors to purchase the combo package. The Tenement Museum also recognized a desire for more immersive experiences, extending the popular one-hour-and-ninety-minute tours by adding a posttour discussion to explore relevant topics and issues. Special tours are also available on Thursday evenings. For example, "Tastings at the Tenement" treats visitors to a culinary experience to savor the flavors of the Lower East Side, past and present, interspersed with stories from local purveyors.

Because of the popularity of tours, where some 20,000 visitors annually were turned away due to capacity, the Tenement Museum expanded its operation in 2011 to include a second tenement at 103 Orchard Street. The addition of this property allows the museum to tell post–World War II stories through the lens of approximately 8,000 immigrants who lived here. With space to house permanent exhibits, an official Visitor Center, and a gift shop, the Tenement Museum now attracts more than 220,000 visitors annually.

Beyond its role in cultural heritage tourism, the museum has become a hub for other educational programs on issues related to immigration, including labor, public health, housing, and education:

- Lesson plans are provided for educators from the elementary to the high school level. Tailored lesson plans are provided for teaching with objects, teaching with primary sources, and teaching with oral history.
- An interactive online game helps individuals understand the process, challenges, and logistics for the nearly 23 million people who emigrated to the United States between 1890 and 1924. With narration from an interpretive guide playing Victoria Confino—an immigrant who lived at 97 Orchard Street—and interactive exercises, participants create the necessary steps to emigrate to the United States in 1916 and explore the journey from Ellis Island to Orchard Street. There's even a passport that visitors can complete and have stamped at the museum (http://www.tenement.org/immigrate).

- The "Housing Inspection Program," developed initially by New York City's Department of Housing Preservation and Development, encourages schoolchildren to use building code requirements given to inspectors in 1901 and 1910 to assess conditions in the museum apartments and also their own homes. Reports written by students are submitted to local city housing authorities.

To engage local neighborhood residents (the Lower East Side community is 30 percent Hispanic and 33 percent Asian), the Tenement Museum partners with the University Settlement Society to use its historical research documents in free "English as Second Language" night classes at the museum. The Community Space for Immigrant Arts uses the museum's storefront windows and gallery space to display local works. The New Immigrant Theatre Project performs regularly in the museum's basement, a nineteenth-century beer garden; the Tenement Museum also sells contemporary crafts made by local immigrants along with an extensive collection of books and periodicals on New York housing, immigration, and ethnicity. Through this local outreach, the museum is a vibrant partner in fostering the well-being of the neighborhood and its local residents.

Although Ruth Abram is no longer involved in the day-to-day operations of the Tenement Museum, her vision of a museum as an instrument for social change is now reality.

Mission

For more than two decades, the Tenement Museum has fulfilled its distinctive mission:

- To make tangible the profound role immigration plays in shaping American identity
- To forge powerful emotional connections between visitors and immigrants past and present
- To evoke unforgettably the history of immigration on Manhattan's Lower East Side, America's iconic immigrant neighborhood

Time Line

1863   97 Orchard Street built in New York City. For the next seventy-two years, the apartment building was home to nearly 7,000 working-class immigrants from twenty countries.

1986   Ruth Abram and Anita Jacobson establish the Lower East Side Historical Conservancy.

1988   Cofounders identify 97 Orchard Street as perfect home for the Tenement Museum. They rent the building as office space for the Conservancy, which also becomes formally chartered as the Lower East Side Tenement Museum.

1992   Opened first restored apartment, the 1870s home of the German Jewish Gumpertz Family Building listed on the National Register of Historic Places.

1994   Lower East Side Tenement designated a National Historic Landmark on April 19. Opened Sweatshop Workers tour to tell the story of the Rogarshevsky and Levine families.

1996	97 Orchard Street purchased as permanent home for Lower East Side Tenement Museum.
1997	Launched the Meet Victoria Confino tour (Sephardic Jews from Turkey in 1916).
1998	Museum designated an affiliated area of the National Park Service. Also forged partnership with National Trust for Historic Preservation, the first in New York City.
2001	Awarded Rudy Bruner Award for Urban Excellence (Silver Medal winner) by Bruner Foundation, Inc.
2002	Opened the 1897 home and sweatshop of Harris and Kennie Levine, Jewish immigrants from Poland.
2007	Purchased 103 Orchard Street. Renovations begin on flagship building for Visitors Center, exhibitions, and classrooms.
2008	Awarded the Preserve America Presidential Award and the National Medal for Museum Service.
2008	Restored and opened the home of the Moores, Irish immigrants who lived at 97 Orchard in 1869, for the Irish Outsiders tour.
2011	Museum Shop opens in the Visitor Center at 103 Orchard Street. Recognized by the *New York Times* as the "Best Spot Around for Great New York Gift Shopping," the museum shop stays open late on Thursdays until 8:30 p.m.
2012	Opened the brand-new Shop Life tour within the storefront property of 97 Orchard Street, which tells the stories of the various businesses that occupied the storefront property of 97 Orchard Street from the 1860s until the 1970s.
2014	Museum announces plans for new permanent exhibits exploring the stories of Chinese immigrants, Jewish Holocaust survivors, and Puerto Rican immigrants who began new lives on the Lower East Side after World War II.
2017	New permanent exhibitions on post–World War II immigration open at 103 Orchard Street.

By the Numbers

- 55,000 students visit the Tenement Museum each year.
- 220,000 visitors annually: one-third from the New York tri-tristate area, one-third from the rest of the United States, and one-third international visitors.
- Twelve different tours of 97 Orchard Street and the Lower East Side neighborhood available.
- Fifty-nine full-time staff; 129 total staff.
- $8.7 million annual operating budget, approximately 50 percent of revenue generated from program services.[14]
- More than $1.5 million generated annually from museum store sales (less than $1,000 per square foot).[15]

* * * * *

Figure 6.11 Levine Parlor, Lower East Side Tenement Museum—New York City.

Profile: The Museum of Northern Arizona
Flagstaff, Arizona

https://musnaz.org

A recipient of a Governor's Arts Award and the 2015 National Medal for Museum and Library Science awarded by the Institute of Museum and Library Services, the Museum of Northern Arizona (MNA) considers itself the gateway to the Colorado Plateau. The 200-acre museum campus and its state-of-the-art facilities house more than 5 million Native American artifacts, natural science specimens, and a fine art collection. Founded in 1928, the MNA is a private, nonprofit, member-based institution accredited by the American Alliance of Museums. Its website prominently includes the organization's mission, vision, and values as adopted by the MNA Board of Trustees in June 2004. As the only accredited museum within 150 miles of Flagstaff, the MNA has become a regional learning center interpreting the natural and cultural heritage of the Colorado Plateau.

The mission, vision, and values of the organization are readily available on the MNA's website:

Mission

The mission of the Museum of Northern Arizona is to inspire a sense of love and responsibility for the beauty and diversity of the Colorado Plateau through collecting, studying, interpreting, and preserving the region's natural and cultural heritage.

The Museum reaffirms the core tenets of the mission established by the founders in 1928:

- Research—"to increase knowledge of science and art"
- Collections—"to collect and preserve objects of art and scientific interest"
- Education—"to diffuse knowledge and appreciation of science and art"
- Conservation—"to preserve and protect the region's historic and prehistoric sites, works of art, scenic places, [plants], and wildlife from needless destruction"
- Place—"to maintain a museum in the city of Flagstaff that provides facilities for research and aesthetic enjoyment"

Vision

The Museum of Northern Arizona is a warm and vibrant place of ideas, with a strong local identity, a regional focus, and an international perspective. The vision for the museum is that:

- It is a welcoming place where people are drawn together to share their knowledge, love of learning, and sense of innovation.
- It is a place that supports and gives voice to the region's diverse cultural perspectives.
- It has sustainable, state-of-the-art facilities while retaining its traditional character.
- Its educational programs and exhibits are beautifully presented, inspiring, and intellectually challenging.
- Its collections are conserved with great care and respect, and will provide a continuing source of inspiration and learning.
- It sets the standard for ongoing regional research that is solid and significant.
- Its staff and volunteers are creative, enthusiastic, and supportive of each other, the museum's mission, and the wider museum community.

Values

The Museum of Northern Arizona is committed to:

- Openness—of purpose, governance, and communication
- Integrity—in fair and ethical practices, and the respectful treatment of all
- Excellence—in leadership, cooperation, and in use of highest museum standards
- Relevance—in identifying and responding to new challenges
- Stability—of its mission, vision, and resources, particularly its collections
- Respect—for different viewpoints, diverse cultural values, and the traditions of the museum

The MNA carries out and achieves its mission in a number of strategic ways. The museum's values are integrated into delivery of various programs and services. The museum offers regularly scheduled tours of its campus as well as special group tours and educational programs. Many of the MNA's collections are housed in the award-winning LEED Platinum–certified Easton Collection Center; preregistration is required for walking tours of Collections held at 4:00 p.m. on select Fridays between March and November. The museum is open 362 days per year; more than 100,000 visitors partake in tours and programs annually. The Discovery Program offers enriching programs for children of all ages. The MNA also launched a Navajo-language summer camp for Diné youth and hosted forums to foster dialogue about critical community issues and the future of the region. The museum recently introduced a new summer after-hours series in partnership with community organizations to program different events. "Thirsty Thursdays" offer unique cultural offerings—music, dance, storytelling, and hands-on activities—from 5:00 p.m. to

Figure 6.12 Navajo Festival of Arts and Culture—Flagstaff, Arizona.

8:00 p.m. weekly from Memorial Day to Labor Day. Attendance hovers at around one hundred at each weekly gathering.

The Heritage Program Festivals celebrate the arts and culture of the people of the Colorado Plateau. The Annual Hopi Festival of Arts and Culture represents a unique collaboration between the museum and Hopi artisans, native scholars, and performers. The Fourth of July tradition held on the museum grounds since the 1930s includes Hopi dance performances, lectures, art pieces for sale, and other activities to help educate the public. Heritage Insight programs by Hopi educators, scholars, and artists offer insights into the tribe's ancestry and efforts to preserve the language, arts, and agricultural traditions. The festival receives financial support from the State of Arizona and the National Endowment for the Arts through the Arizona Commission on the Arts, City of Flagstaff Better Business Bureau revenues, and the Flagstaff Arts Council. A Zuni Festival is also scheduled each May, and a Navajo Festival is held in August.

Sample MOU
[Applicant Letterhead]

WHEREAS, **[Applicant X]**, **[Partner 1]** and **[Partner 2]** have come together to collaborate and to make an application for **[name of Grant Program]** grant; and

WHEREAS, the partners listed below have agreed to enter into a collaborative agreement in which **[Applicant X]** will be the lead agency and named applicant and the other agencies will be partners in this application; and

WHEREAS, the partners herein desire to enter into a Memorandum of Understanding setting forth the services to be provided by the collaborative; and

WHEREAS, the application prepared and approved by the collaborative through its partners is to be submitted to the Office on Violence Against Women on or before **[application due date]**;

I) Description of Partner Agencies

For each member of the collaborative, provide some background on the agency or organization and its work regarding domestic violence, dating violence, sexual assault, and/or stalking.

II) History of Relationship

- *Provide a brief history of the collaborative relationship between the partners, including when and under what circumstances the relationship began and when each partner joined the collaboration. Specify how often the collaborators meet.*
- *Describe any changes in the collaboration, including an explanation or description of any new or additional partners that have been added, or any partners that would no longer participate.*
- *Describe the critical and long-range goals of the collaboration.*

III) Development of Application

- *Discuss the circumstances under which this application began and how recent collaboration aided in the development of the application.*
- *Specify the extent of each party's participation in developing the application.*

IV) Roles and Responsibilities

NOW, THEREFORE, it is hereby agreed by and between the partners as follows:

- *Clearly state the roles and responsibilities each organization or agency will assume to ensure the success of the proposed project.*
- *Describe the resources each partner will contribute to the project either through time, in-kind contribution or with the use of grant fund, e.g. office space, project staff, training.*

Figure 6.13 Sample memorandum of understanding (credit: U.S. Department of Justice).

- *Identify the representatives of the planning and development team who will be responsible for planning, developing, and implementing project activities and describe how they will work together and work with project staff.*
- *Demonstrate a commitment on the part of all partners to work together to achieve stated project goals and to sustain the project once grant funds are no longer available.*

1. **[Applicant X]** will provide **[specify type of program/assistance/service]** to:
2. **[Partner 1]** will provide **[specify type of program/assistance/service]** to:
3. **[Partner 2]** will provide **[specify type of program/assistance/service]** :
1. **[Applicant X]** and **[Partner 1]** will collaborate in the following manner:
2. **[Applicant X]** and **[Partner 2]** will collaborate in the following manner:
3. **[Partner 1]** and **[Partner 2]** will collaborate in the following manner:

V) *Time Line*

The roles and responsibilities described above are contingent on **[Applicant X]** receiving funds requested for the project described in the grant application. Responsibilities under this Memorandum of Understanding would coincide with the grant period, anticipated to be **MM/DD/YYYY** through **MM/DD/YYYY**.

VI) *Commitment to Partnership*

1. The collaboration service area includes **[specify region in your state, tribe, territory, county, or multijurisdictional area]**.
2. The partners agree to collaborate and provide **[specify type of service/assistance]** to victims of **[specify crimes]** pursuant to the program narrative of the grant application attached to this agreement.
3. Compensation for [non-lead] partners' contribution to this project will be provided as outlined in the attached budget detail worksheet.
4. We, the undersigned have read and agree with this MOU. Further, we have reviewed the proposed project and approve it.

By_____   By_____
                Director, **Applicant X**   Director, **Partner 1**
Date _____   Date _____

By_____
                Director, **Partner 2**
Date _____

cc: Agencies and Interested Parties

Figure 6.13 *(continued)*

Outline of a Cultural Heritage Tourism Plan

(Based on Strategic Planning Model)
Executive Summary
Situation Analysis
SWOT—including

- Visitor research—Obtain in six weeks or as can and analyze for gaps, findings
- Old and relevant new plans
- Asset Inventory + Additional assets—important or contributing
- Environmental Scan—external issues impacting success (political, social, demographic, etc.)
- Competitive analysis—other cities, sites doing a good job—Benchmarks for success
- Current heritage tourism—collaborative analysis; secret shoppers
- Additional assets: Corning Preserve, Pine Bush, others? Asset inventory—need complete list
- Restaurants, retail, regional restaurants, transportation—opinions on HT impacts
- Strengths, Weaknesses, Opportunities, Threats Analysis

Vision/Mission
Goals/Objectives
Develop, enhance, expand Cultural Heritage Tourism experiences—

- Interpretive plan
- Infrastructure (wayfinding, signage, interpretative panels, safety/security, gateways, beautification, aesthetics)
- Enhanced, New Products
- Visitor Services

Market for Success—

- Target Audiences
- External marketing, distribution
- Internal market distribution—before and on-site

Capacity Management

- Budget
- Oversight—Roles and responsibilities
- Schedule for implementation
- Short-term, long-term sustainability

Measurement

- Systems and schedule to evaluate success
- Controls for realignment to meet key performance indicators

Appendices

Figure 6.13 *(continued)*

Outline for a Sustainable Tourism Plan

1. **Executive Summary**
2. **Overview**
   - Background, purpose of plan
   - Geographic boundaries for plan
   - Description of lead agency, organization, key stakeholders
3. **Situation Analysis**
   - Economic
   - Sociocultural (historic, cultural)
   - Environmental
   - State of current tourism
4. **Conduct a Conservation Threat Assessment**
   - Direct
   - Indirect
   - Tourism impact analysis
5. **Define Target Conditions for Cultural, Historic, and Natural Resources**
   - Preservation
   - Conservation
   - Integrity
   - Perpetuation
6. **Establish Goals, Objectives, and Target Conditions**
   - Set benchmarks
   - Define success measures
7. **Describe Sustainable Actions to Achieve Target Conditions**
   - Education, awareness programs
   - Policy adaptation and mitigation
   - Adoption of sustainable management practices—government, private sector
   - Incentives to reward sustainable actions
   - Marketing, promotion
8. **Define Resources Required**
   - Human: management, leadership, stakeholders
   - Financial: public, private
9. **Develop a Sustainability Plan Budget**
10. **Generate a Detailed Action Plan (One to Two Years)**

Figure 6.14 Outline for Sustainable Tourism Plan.

Notes

1. "What Are National Heritage Areas?," National Park Service, U.S. Department of the Interior (n.d.), https://www.nps.gov/heritageareas/FAQ.
2. According to a report, the National Heritage Area secured $19,908,281 in local funding to match $13,687,188 in National Park Service funding (145 percent matching funds). Myers, M.A. + Ogubiyi, Fortuna, Dubsky and Solarz (September 2012), "Rivers of Steel National Heritage Area Evaluation Findings," Westat for the U.S. National Park Service, p. 15, http://www.nationalheritageareas.us/documents/Rivers-of-Steel-Final-Findings-Report-Final.pdf.
3. Correspondence with Augie Carlino, July 13, 2016.
4. American Planning Association, *Growing Smart Legislative Guidebook*, 2002 Edition, p. 7-61, table 7-3: Local Comprehensive Plan Elements in Model Statutes.
5. UN World Tourism Organization, "Sustainable Tourism for Development," http://cf.cdn.unwto.org/sites/all/files/docpdf/devcoengfinal.pdf.
6. "Visioning Techniques," Innovation Styles (2014), Values Center Innovation, http://innovationstyles.com/isinc/content/toolstechniques0.aspx.
7. Biography of Mayor Joseph P. Riley Jr., City of Charleston, http://www.charleston-sc.gov/DocumentCenter/View/4.
8. Charleston Convention and Visitors Bureau, http://www.charlestoncvb.com/media/press_releases.
9. UNWTO/UNESCO World Conference on Tourism and Culture: Building a New Partnership (Siem Reap, Cambodia, 4–6 February 2015), p. 56 http://www.e-unwto.org/doi/book/10.18111/9789284417360.
10. G. Hamel, Y. Doz, and C. K. Prahald, "Collaborate with Your Competitors—and Win," *Harvard Business Review*, January–February 1989, Joint Ventures.
11. Richard Wener with Emily Axelrod, Jay Farbstein, Robert Shibley, and Polly Welch, *Placemaking for Change: 2001 Rudy Bruner Award for Urban Excellence* (2001), p. 43, http://www.brunerfoundation.org/rba/pdfs/2001/02_LowerEastSide.pdf.
12. Sophia Dembling interview with Ruth Abram as reported in "Ruth Abram: Explaining Today through Stories of Yesterday" in National Trust for Historic Preservation blog (November 19, 2014), https://savingplaces.org/stories/ruth-abram-explaining-today-stories-yesterday#.V5Pbf46exgo.
13. TripAdvisor, rating comments downloaded July 22, 2016, from https://www.tripadvisor.com/Attraction_Review-g60763-d104369-Reviews-Tenement_Museum-New_York_City_New_York.html.
14. Form 990 via Guidestar, 2014. www.guidestar.org
15. http://www.thenonprofittimes.com/news-articles/smooth-selling-nonprofits-reap-big-dividends-in-smart-retail.
16. http://www.deltabluesmuseum.org/about.asp.
17. http://www.hillstead.org/about-us.
18. http://www.wvculture.org/museum/State-Museum-Index.html.
19. http://www.thebroad.org/about/mission-statement.

Chapter 7

Setting Policies and Procedures to Preserve and Protect Integrity

> Preservation/conservation is not a series of rules but a process whereby a community examines its history and determines what it must bring into the future.
>
> —Vince Michael, heritage executive and thought leader

Policies set the definitive course or method of action; they also steer procedures for ensuring that cultural and heritage assets are preserved and conserved for future generations. Designed as clear, simple, high-level statements, policies are formulated when it is necessary to articulate specific instruction or benefit. Good policy can also provide strategic leadership as well as a legislative framework for developing or restructuring an industry or community.[1] This policymaking is particularly true in places where tourism is perceived as an alternative to more traditional industries.

For cultural heritage tourism, guiding principles are often the precursor to policies that dictate oversight for nonlegislative or legally binding activities. Principles remind organizers, developers, planners, and implementers of the quality, values, and intent of cultural heritage tourism—often related to a destination's or organization's vision. National and international organizations frequently convene and prepare principles to inform intentions for growth and to address trends. In this chapter, the types and effective development of policies are discussed along with the value of established principles to protect the assets at the heart of cultural heritage tourism. Codes, standards, and guidelines are also defined and described in the context of cultural heritage tourism and management.

Types of Policies

Various public policy instruments exist and are often dictated by the governing body. Typically, policy instruments are classified three ways: economic (market based), regulatory (command and control), and institutional. Economic policies include special-use taxes, user fees, financial incentives, and market permits. Many of these financial-related policies are described in detail in chapter 10. Regulatory policies issued by an executive authority or governing agency focus on laws enforcing usage quotas and zoning, adopted through legislation, regulation, treaties, agreements, or court decisions. Institutional policies are established to label or grade to a specific standard. For cultural heritage tourism, a combination of policy instruments may be appropriate, depending on the needs or maturity of the destination.[2] Businesses and nonprofit organizations may adopt policies to instruct employee behavior or relationships with external customers and vendors, as noted later in this chapter.

Government policies may also restrict the operations and actions of international or transnational organizations by controlling certain operational procedures, prohibiting or limiting ownership and management, and mandating a local financial impact. Tourism policies require more broad-based support and external focus. Clare Gunn, noted authority on tourism planning, provides the following insights on tourism policy:[3]

1. The formulation and administration of tourism policy must take place by all sectors.
2. Tourism policy development is the prerogative of all levels, national to local.
3. Tourism policy is hollow without support by action.
4. Better integration of tourism policies is needed—directed toward all goals.
5. Tourism policies must be flexible because tourism development is dynamic, not static.
6. Tourism policies of the components of the tourism supply side are interrelated and interdependent.

While national policies may influence the facilitation of cultural heritage tourism across political or geographic borders, state and local policies may more significantly impact the planning, development, and management of cultural heritage tourism. Here, policy decisions enhance or impede the growth and sustainability of cultural heritage tourism. Management policies may ensure the stewardship of natural and cultural heritage resources, while policies for infrastructure regulate usage of roads and other infrastructure. Building codes can dictate setbacks, accessibility, egress, height restrictions, and in-fill. Fire and police protection, as well as health and safety policies, are fundamental to preserving residents' quality of life and meeting tourist expectations.

Section 106 Regulations Summary

Section 106 of the National Historic Preservation Act of 1966 (NHPA) requires federal agencies to take into account the effects of their undertakings on historic properties and afford the Advisory Council on Historic Preservation (ACHP) a reasonable opportunity to comment. The historic preservation review process mandated by Section 106 is outlined in regulations issued by ACHP. Revised regulations "Protection of Historic Properties" (36 CFR Part 800) became effective August 5, 2004.

Source: ACHP, http://www.achp.gov/106summary.html.

Creation of policies is not limited to government. In fact, policymaking by the private sector and nonprofit organizations is very important to sustainability. Lobbying for cultural, heritage, or environmental stewardship, design and development guidelines, historic preservation, and other issues impacting the advancement of cultural heritage tourism is an important priority for many organizations and businesses. A memorandum of understanding between entities can also out-line specific policies or procedures to enact for achieving a specific purpose or goal (see example provided at the end of chapter 6). Successful cultural heritage tourism policies crafted at the local level require the following:

- A clear and mutually agreed-on definition of issues and intent
- A consensus on principles for cultural heritage tourism
- Information-based analysis and decision making
- Protocols for engaging and representing all sectors affected by policy preparation
- A system for implementing and measuring outcomes

As policies set the stage for all other implementation strategies, they should be carefully and thoughtfully created with clear intent and language.

Policies, Standards, Codes, Guidelines, Procedures

Definitions can help clarify intention and appropriateness. Understanding options to create the desired results is important, especially depending on the level of enforcement required.

If policies are high-level statements, standards are the second level of mandatory controls to enforce and support the consistency of action. Often, standards support or conform to a policy. For example, the *Secretary of the Interior's Standards for Rehabilitation* determines qualification for a certified rehabilitation eligible for federal tax programs.[4]

Codes relate to regulations and technical requirements proposed by third-party entities for en-forcement. The International Code Council (ICC) has a family of codes related to construction and renovation of buildings, including historic sites.[5] The ICC also includes codes for energy con-servation, green construction, exemptions for historic buildings, and fire safety.

Guidelines are general statements or recommendations that provide a framework to achieve policy objectives; as they are not mandatory, they can be changed frequently to reflect specific concerns or issues. The European Association of Historic Towns and Regions created Guidelines for Sustainable Cultural Tourism in Historic Towns and Cities (2009) to describe a recommended course of action to interpret and flow from a set of cultural heritage tourism principles. These guidelines address policy objectives, processes, delivery, and appraisal of cultural heritage tourism, considering the relationship between visitors and destination stakeholders.[6]

Procedures are the practical steps and instruction required to enact the guidelines, codes, stand-ards, and policies—transforming instruction into action. Procedures describe the process and mechanisms to implement and enforce the policy—who does what, when they do it, and under what circumstances or criteria.

Through my two terms on the U.S. Travel & Tourism Advisory Board (TTAB), a group of us were formed into a Cultural Subcommittee which was my honor to co-chair to help advance cultural tourism at the federal level. The TTAB board consists mainly of traditional tourism companies and leaders from the travel industry, but as the arts representative I found in-terest and support among these corporate leaders for expanding the traveler experience beyond the traditional offerings. More importantly, I found that federal tourism-related officials were keen to expand government support for authentic tourism experiences, especially cultural tourism, because of its reach into all corners of the country.

Through formal recommendations to the Secretary of Commerce, the TTAB highlighted how cultural tourism could be supported through the federal government, and leveraged by other government and nonprofit sector partners. Key to these recommendations was to engage in data collection, tourism research, and marketing efforts that are specific to diverse populations in the U.S. in order to bring to light the importance of minority and cultural sectors in domestic tourism.
—Robert L. Lynch, president and chief executive officer, Americans for the Arts

Types of Policies, Standards, Guidelines, and Procedures

Good stewardship doesn't just happen. Historic and cultural preservation is achieved through specific statements and official instruction on how buildings, sites, and traditions are protected, maintained, revived, and/or restored. For cultural heritage tourism, planners and developers must consider broader issues that impact visitor experiences—beautification of streetscapes, curation of artifacts, and architectural design guidelines. What do specific policies related to cultural heritage tourism address? Here are some of the categories of policies impacting cultural heritage tourism growth and sustainability at the local, state, and national levels.

Accessibility/Safety

Policies related to the Americans with Disabilities Act include code relief for historic buildings related to access to multistory facilities and grand staircases. Understanding how to afford access to persons with disabilities at historic structures is important to ensuring that all visitors are able to experience, in even limited ways, cultural heritage sites and programs.

Beautification/Aesthetics

Aesthetics of place is important to visitors' first impressions. Tree ordinances, litter control, signage, and transportation policies can impact the visual appearance of cities and communities, gateways, and corridors. The International Society of Arboriculture offers guidelines to consider for developing and evaluating tree ordinances with regard to protection, planting, and barriers.[7] The Federal Highway Beautification Act also addresses billboard and signage regulations.[8]

Building Codes

Understanding how building codes impact the renovation and restoration of historic buildings, as well as the density and construction of new facilities, is important in planning for and sustaining cultural heritage tourism. Compliance is essential and provides opportunities for sustainable practices—even with historic buildings.

In-Fill Development

When vacant lots sit between historic buildings, the space is usually desirable for "in-fill." How the new building or land is developed (sometimes as a park, garage, or other uses) can enhance or detract from the historic character of the commercial district or neighborhood. Compatible in-fill and other policies to ensure compliance require zoning and design standards that define setbacks for yards, architectural design, and building guidelines (height, width, orientation, materials, entrances, windows, rooflines, and other construction components). In-fill development should be sensitive to existing architecture and appropriate for the lot, especially if located in a historic district.

Collections Management

This set of policies addresses various components of collections management and how specific historic and cultural institutions or museums address how they preserve and protect precious artifacts. A collections management policy ensures that the artifacts held in trust for the public are made accessible at the highest legal, ethical, and professional standards (as recommended by the American Alliance of Museums and other organizations). Good stewardship with integrity does not happen without rigorous policies and procedures.[9]

Conservation Easements

According to the American Planning Association, a conservation easement "is a non-possessory right of a person or entity over the real property of another." Basically, an easement defines what a person(s) can or cannot do on a piece of a property that they don't own. For example, an easement may allow rights-of-way or permission to cross another's premises (to access a public park). It can also prohibit development or specific uses. Typically, most easements are created by agreement between private individuals, businesses, and nonprofit organizations. Different from a regular contract, an easement binds future owners even if they were not part of the original agreement.

A conservation easement is considered a "negative easement," where the owner of the property cannot engage in development activities that may typically be performed. "A conservation easement can prohibit all future development, or it can specify particular development activities that are prohibited."[10] For example, a scenic easement may prevent obstruction of the view by prohibiting construction above a particular height.

Development Agreements

A development agreement is a "statutorily authorized, negotiated agreement between a local government and a private developer that establishes the respective rights and obligations of each party with respect to certain planning issues or problems related to a specific proposed development or redevelopment project."[11] Some states, such as Arizona, California, Florida, Hawaii, Idaho, Maryland, and Nevada, have specific statutes on governing development agreements, impacting their structure and level of detail. It is recommended to review state laws regarding development agreements before embarking on authorization.

Columbus, Indiana, is a master at considering the impact of quality architecture on aesthetics. Read the profile at the end of this chapter to learn the history of the community's architecture program and its long-term impact on the community.

Historic Preservation Ordinances

Historic preservation ordinances are established to preserve and protect the historic character of structures or buildings in a community. Typically, the ordinances follow the eligibility guidelines for designating a historic site or building on the National Register of Historic Places: association with a significant person or a significant event, significant architecture, archaeological significance, or being at least fifty years old. Historic preservation ordinances often focus on retaining the historic integrity of the site and ensuring that proposed renovations, repairs, reconstruction, or additions do not negatively impact extant sites. Historic preservation ordinances exist in almost every state, "either as a permissible objective in zoning and other land-use regulations or as a separate statute."[14]

Historic and Architectural Design Review

Considered a standard for communities with historic resources, historic preservation ordinances and architectural design review work in tandem to retain a city's, community's, or neighborhood's sense of place. Design review regulations define criteria and standards for what the architecture should look like (either a specific style or a diverse interpretation of styles). Examples are usually provided to help interpret the criteria. For cultural heritage tourism, typically the architectural review informs how new construction (contemporary architecture) fits within the character and integrity of existing historic sites and buildings.

Both historic preservation and architectural design review ordinances typically have independent boards appointed to guide the process for application, review, approval/compliance, or dismissal (for amendment or reapplication of proposal). An example of the review process for exterior alterations of historic structures is provided in figure 7.1, courtesy of the City of Santa Fe, New Mexico.

Parking Ordinances

A parking ordinance regulates usage and establishes a schedule of fines for violations. Parking ordinances are prevalent in high-density areas and historic districts, where on-street parking may be limited. Depending on the zoning, a minimum number of off-street parking spaces may be required for new development. Parking is often an issue for municipalities, especially seasonal destinations. Parking ordinances should be considered in the context of a larger transportation plan (think multimodal, focusing on pedestrian and bicycle use plus public transport) and density of commercial downtowns or historic neighborhoods.

Resource Conservation

Like historic preservation ordinances, resource conservation focuses on protecting the existence and integrity of natural resources—greenspace, wetlands, landscapes, barrier islands, mountaintops, and so on. The Resource Conservation and Recovery Act (42 U.S.C. § 6901 et seq. [1976]) protects against the negative impacts of hazardous waste. The act gives the Environmental Protection Agency the "authority to control the generation, transportation, treatment, storage and disposal of hazardous waste"; manage nonhazardous solid wastes; and address environmental impacts associated with storage of hazardous substances.[15]

What is the process for working with the Historic Preservation Division regarding exterior alterations?

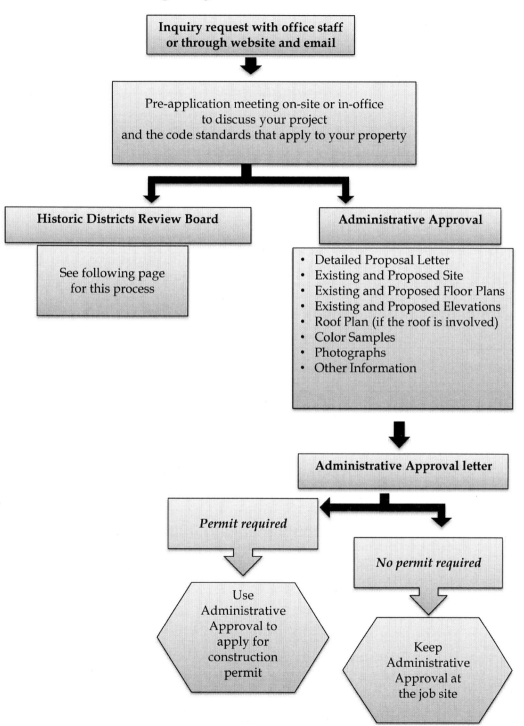

Figure 7.1 City of Santa Fe historic preservation flowchart—Santa Fe, New Mexico.

Safety

The International Existing Building Code, developed by the ICC, has been adopted throughout the United States. Updated annually, the code includes a chapter on safety at historic buildings and at related renovation or restoration activities.

Tourism Ordinances

Charleston, South Carolina, has always been a leader in proactive planning for tourism and historic preservation. In 1931, Charleston was the first city to adopt a zoning ordinance for its historic district. The city council adopted a tourism ordinance in 1983 to address the impact of increased number of tourists to the city. The purpose of the regulation is

> to maintain, protect and promote the tourism industry and economy of the city and, at the same time, to maintain and protect the tax base and land values of the city, to reduce unnecessary traffic and pollution and to maintain and promote aesthetic charm and the quality of life for the residents of the city.[16]

Significant issues that surfaced during the city's tourism growth in the late twentieth century justified a separate ordinance and organization beyond the administration of the arts-and-history interests of the city. The ordinance responded to and addressed the following impacts:

> the numbers of unregulated tour vehicles and other commercial vehicles entering the city for the purpose of touring the historic districts are having adverse effects upon the health, safety, and welfare of the citizens of the city and that traffic accidents, damage to property, traffic congestion and other problems require the enactment by the city of a comprehensive tourism management ordinance.[17]

Charleston's tourism ordinance includes specific rules for the following:

- Operation of motorized vehicles by peddlers in the old and historic district (Section 29-3).
- Limitation on operation of vehicles on Battery and White Point Gardens (Section 29-4).
- Limitation on operation of vendors near churches or places of worship (Section 29-5).
- Tour guide: application, examination, and grant or denial of license (Section 29-59).
- Limitation on number of small buses in operation (Section 29-114).
- Special permit required: no large buses may conduct a tour in the districts without a touring permit duly authorized by the manager of arts and history/tourism commissions (Section 29-142).
- Touring limitations: recreational vehicles, school buses, and church buses twenty-five feet or less in length may travel freely in the districts but must park in compliance with applicable ordinances of the city (Section 29-173).

This ordinance also established a fourteen-member Tourism Commission comprised of elected officials, private residents, business leaders, tourism industry representatives, and experts in architecture/history. The Tourism Commission oversees

> the broad range of tourism-related matters that affect the economic and general welfare of the citizens of the city in order that visitors can enjoy the historic and cultural aspects of the city's heritage consistent with the maintenance of the environmental quality of its citizens.[18]

The Tourism Commission has the opportunity to recommend policies to the mayor and the city council that further the goals of tourism management, particularly in the areas of parking and

Figure 7.2 Rainbow Row—Charleston, South Carolina.

routing of tourism-related traffic activities, the qualification and licensing of tour guides, the determination of vehicle appropriateness, and the enforcement of tourism management regulations."[19] The city's Office of Tourism administers all aspects of the tourism ordinance and management plan.

Zoning Ordinances

In its *Growing Smart Legislative Guidebook*, the American Planning Association states that the contents of the zoning ordinance focuses on many topics—floodplains, storm water, landscaping, and signage—as well as both maximum and minimum densities.[20] Zoning also typically indicates the type of use for existing structures or parcels of land—commercial, residential, and industrial. Ensuring that zoning adequately protects the cultural and historic character of place is important to the development, marketing, and management of cultural heritage tourism.

The Policymakers

Policies and procedures are often formed at the highest levels of the federal government and then trickle down to states and local municipalities. "Open skies" agreements between countries, security protocols, and visa requirements are also regulated at the federal or the executive level. At the state level, policies over land use may be instituted or to address privacy related to accessing, browsing, or viewing a state website. Policies regarding copyrights, trademarks, intellectual property, and limited permissions—especially for digital content and images—are commonly found in destination marketing. Government agencies may also establish policies regulating travel and reimbursement of expenses. These are standard policies related to the tourism industry.

In addition to government officials and regulatory bodies, other national and international organizations oversee codes and standards to guide preservation, protection, renovation, or new development. These institutions set the bar for destinations small and large to meet when instituting policies for cultural heritage tourism. Perhaps one of the most widely used standards is the Global Sustainable Tourism Council (GSTC) Criteria, organized into four pillars:

1. Sustainable management
2. Socioeconomic impacts
3. Cultural impacts
4. Environmental impacts

The GSTC Criteria are considered the global standard for sustainability in travel and tourism, with specific baseline criteria for hotels and tour operators (second version adopted March 2012) and destinations. The GSTC Criteria for Destinations (November 2013) build on other certification standards, such as the UNWTO destination-level indicators. Of the forty-one performance indicators outlined in the GSTC Criteria for Destinations, almost half pertain directly to cultural heritage tourism development, marketing, and management. In particular, Sections B ("Maximize economic benefits to the host community and minimize negative impacts") and C ("Maximize benefits to communities, visitors, and culture; minimize negative impacts") deal with specific aspects of cultural heritage tourism—visitor management, visitor behavior, attraction protection, cultural heritage protection, site interpretation, community support, tourism awareness, and education. The full list of GSTC Criteria and corresponding indicators is provided at the end of this chapter in table 7.1. To learn how one city offered incentives to attract artists, read the profile of Paducah's Artist Relocation Program at the end of this chapter.

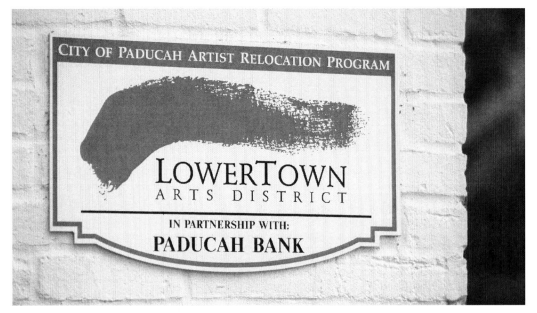

Figure 7.3 Artist relocation sign—Paducah, Kentucky.

Chapter Summary

Policies and related regulatory instruments can help safeguard the availability, integrity, and sustainability of cultural and heritage resources. While voluntary stewardship and preservation and conservation ethics are revered, they don't always surface to the extent necessary to protect historic sites and cultural assets for future generations. Futuristic planning requires strong policies to protect what's important to a community, city, state, nation, and people and to maintain a level of quality and authenticity respectful of the resources. Policies can be both pro-development and pro-preservation if comprehensive planning is at the heart of their creation and enforcement. Understanding and demanding a balanced approach to growth is vital to cultural heritage tourism; enacting policies of protection and preservation help strengthen sense of place and the potential for a positive tourism impact.

* * * * *

Profile: Columbus, Indiana—Designing Sense of Place

http://www.columbus.in.us

Architecture by Eero Saarinen, I. M. Pei, Kevin Roche, and Cesar Pelli. Art installations by Henry Moore, Jean Tinguely, and Dale Chihuly. Seven National Historic Landmarks. Seven buildings designed by Pritzker Architecture Prize winners. Understandable for large metropolitan cities but for a Midwestern town of 45,000? Indeed, thanks to a visionary corporate leader in Columbus, Indiana. More than fifty years ago, J. Irwin Miller (former chairman and chief executive officer of Cummins, a Fortune 200 company with headquarters in Columbus) recognized the need to attract the best talent to Columbus. Rather than let boring (or uninspired) public buildings be built and subsequently set the aesthetic tone of place, Miller set out to recommend leading architects and provide funds for the design portion of architectural fees for selected public projects. With an initial focus on school buildings (remember, this was the start of the baby boom, and communities were focused on expanding facilities to accommodate the escalating number of students), the Cummins Foundation made its first grant in 1957 to support architecture fees for the Lillian C. Schmitt Elementary School designed by Harry Weese.

The Architecture Program, designed to encourage architectural excellence in Bartholomew County, continues today as part of the Cummins Foundation. To date, the Cummins Foundation has sponsored more than fifty projects—expanding from schools to include the Roche-designed post office, a Robert Trent Jones–designed golf course, the Edward Charles Bassett–designed city hall, the Venturi-designed Fire Station No. 4, and other public buildings, including the county jail and parking garage. Other significant works have been privately commissioned, including Eero Saarinen's North Christian Church, the Irwin Conference Center, and the Miller House and Garden.

Public art installations complement the city's building design, with works by Bernar Venet, Jean Tinguely, and Henry Moore. Dale Chihuly's *Persians* are installed at the Columbus Area Visitor Center, along with the magnificent *Yellow Neon Chandelier*. His work can also be seen at the Columbus Learning Center (as part of the Indiana Glass Trail). The Columbus Visitors Center Gift Shop sells Dale Chihuly studio editions and limited-edition prints.

Today, Columbus is routinely listed as one of the top American cities for architecture, taking a place alongside urban centers such as Chicago and New York. "We take seriously the responsibility of sharing the Columbus architecture story with locals and visitors alike, because it is so inspiring—the idea that an entire community can be elevated by the presence of good design," said Karen Niverson, executive director of the Columbus Area Visitors Center, which conducts more than 1,000 public tours each year and executes a broad range of programs designed to grow the local tourism industry. Their efforts are working, with national and regional media recognition from the *New York Times*, the *Wall Street Journal*, the *Chicago Tribune*, *Midwest Living*, and *Dwell*. In 2005, *Smithsonian* magazine called Columbus a "veritable museum of modern architecture." The same year, *USA Today* said, "Columbus is one grand, landscaped park." In 2008, *National Geographic Traveler* ranked Columbus first of all U.S. destinations and number 11 of 109 destinations worldwide.

Given that the architecture program started more than half a century ago, many of the buildings are now individually recognized as National Historic Landmarks. The important architectural fabric of this community has attracted visitors from around the world. Perhaps one reason is the intimacy of the experience, being able to see a density of great architecture in a relatively small area. Thanks to the Cummins Foundation, "architectural excellence in Bartholomew County continues as an important part of the development, prosperity and vitality of the community."[12] Visitors help contribute to this economic growth. "While the presence of extraordinary buildings and public art create an enviable quality of life in our small city, these assets also provide the community with a lucrative tourism industry. Visitors spend nearly $260 million annually in our local economy and support approximately 4,400 jobs," said Niverson.

The Architecture Program Process

1. The qualified community entity (projects owned and operated by public tax dollars) completes a project qualification form (scope of the project, building, purpose, budget, and other key details).
2. The completed form is submitted to the Cummins Columbus Committee representative and reviewed by the Cummins Architecture Program core team.
3. If the project is appropriate and meets the qualifications under the Architecture Program, the core team makes a recommendation on funding to the Cummins Foundation Board of Directors. At the next meeting, the foundation board votes on the request.
4. If approved, the core team generates a list of architects and provides this to the requesting community entity.
5. The core team representative meets with the community entity to help facilitate architect selection using Six Sigma tools.[13]
6. On completion of the selection process, the Cummins Foundation provides funds for the design portion of the architect's fees. (The fees of the project architect are the responsibility of the community entity.) The Architecture Program may choose to pay for a project consultant to ensure that the design vision is executed to the desired quality standard, on time and on budget.

The ultimate selection of the architecture team is up to the community entity. All final decisions are made by the community entity, and they become the client of the chosen architectural team. Also, a new list of architects is generated for each client. No permanent list is maintained.

★ ★ ★ ★ ★

Profile: Paducah, Kentucky—The Artist Relocation Program (ARP) and Cultural District Designation

http://www.Paducahky.gov
http://www.paducahmainstreet.org/lowertown-arts-district.htm

The Lower Town Arts District, listed on the National Register of Historic Places in 1982, is one of Paducah's oldest neighborhoods. Despite its varied architectural styles (Queen Anne, Romanesque, Italianate, gothic, and folk Victorian) and historic significance, the Lower Town neighborhood fell into decline and neglect. Recognizing the potential for redevelopment, the district became the pilot for Paducah's Artist Relocation Program (ARP) established in March 2000. Community leaders actively sought out artists to infuse creativity and restore the city's oldest residential neighborhood.

Through ARP, the City of Paducah offered incentives to attract artists: reduced-price property sales (some at $1) and reimbursements of up to $2,500 for architectural and other professional services with approved proposals. Paducah Bank, a community partner, also provided below-market financing for qualified proposals. Artists helped build a thriving artistic community over the next ten years. Since ARP began, artists and residents have invested more than $30 million in the arts district. ARP's success has become a national model for arts-based economic development. The district also began attracting visitors as the Convention and Visitors Bureau promoted the colorful revitalization of the historic neighborhood. In 2008, the Paducah Arts Alliance founded the Artist-in-Residence Program, which continues to successfully bring artists from diverse backgrounds to Paducah for two to four weeks to share their work and skill. It has become an ideal way to create cultural diversity and interaction between the artists and residents.

Figure 7.4 Lower Town Arts District—Paducah, Kentucky.

However, redevelopment has had some bumps in the road in the past decade. Following the Great Recession, several art galleries closed, and buildings stood empty. Fortunately, the revitalization of the Lower Town Arts District has continued, as noted by certification as a Kentucky Cultural District in 2012. The Kentucky Arts Council designates cultural districts to "encourage city and county governments to partner with a local community nonprofit or for-profit organization, businesses, and individuals to enhance the quality of life for its citizens." Zoning of this cultural district afforded new uses for the neighborhood, including living and work spaces. According to the National Trust, "This zoning effectively enables residents, artists, and non-artists alike to create mixed-use space consisting of galleries, studios, restaurants, cafes, and living space under one roof."[21]

In 2013, Paducah leveraged its recognition as the home of the National Quilt Museum and American Quilter's Society, its success of the ARP, and its wide-ranging cultural attributes to receive designation as a UNESCO City of Crafts and Folk Art.[22] Approximately twenty artists now live and work in the Lower Town Arts District. The campus of the Paducah School of Art and Design, a division of West Kentucky Community and Technical College, is the latest addition to the Lower Town Arts District featuring visual arts education in photography, drawing, painting, 2D graphic design, ceramics, sculpture, jewelry, metals, and 3D design. The anchor 2D and Graphic Design Building represents a $10 million expansion and a 22,000-square-foot studio facility, which opened in 2016. *Creative Collaborations*, a special event series launched in 2016, provides opportunities for the public, art lovers, and art collectors to experience the creativity and diversity of Paducah's arts community—often free of charge—through Meet the Artists programs and the Lower Town Arts and Music Festival.

Figure 7.5 Paducah School of Art and Design—Paducah, Kentucky.

The Paducah Artist Relocation Program, Lower Town Arts District, and UNESCO designation have generated new platforms to put the city on the map through destination branding:

- Major media outlets around the world have spotlighted Paducah's creative economy. The city's cultural pedigree and smart strategies to leverage culture have drawn attention with national and international coverage, including *National Geographic*'s listing of Paducah fifth on its list of the Traveler 50: World's Smartest Cities.
- The Paducah Convention and Visitors Bureau worked with Opportunities Unlimited to guide local nonprofit attractions in leveraging authentic destination stories and experiences to develop five new unforgettable and immersive experiences exclusively for groups.
- Tourism continues to grow in Paducah, with direct expenditures rising from $203.9 million in 2013 to $211.6 million in 2014 and 223.6 million in 2015, increases of 3.8 percent and 5.4 percent, respectively.
- Paducah Economic Development's launch of Forward Paducah, a citywide strategic vision and plan that incorporates arts and tourism as economic drivers and provides a road map for the city's smart growth, cultural integrity, and sustainable development.

 Laura Oswald, marketing director for the Paducah Convention and Visitors Bureau, said, "Cultural heritage has been a platform and creativity a driver to realize the economic benefits of the arts in Paducah. From the 'Wall to Wall' Floodwall Murals project as a catalyst for Historic Downtown development to the famed Artist Relocation Program's revitalization of Lower Town and the destination's continued evolution with global UNESCO Creative City designation, these initiatives have generated new platforms to translate creative tourism value." She continued, "That value transcends the economic impact of tourism by also contributing greatly to quality of life and the sustainability of our community.

* * * * *

Table 7.1 Global Sustainable Tourism Criteria for Destinations

SECTION A: Demonstrate sustainable destination management

A1 Sustainable destination strategy
The destination has established and is implementing a multi-year destination strategy that is publicly available, is suited to its scale, that considers environmental, economic, social, cultural, quality, health, and safety, and aesthetic issues, and was developed with public participation.

A2 Destination management organization
The destination has an effective organization, department, group, or committee responsible for a coordinated approach to sustainable tourism, with involvement by the private sector and public sector. This group is suited to the size and scale of the destination, and has defined responsibilities, oversight, and implementation capability for the management of environmental, economic, social, and cultural issues. This group's activities are appropriately funded.

A3 Monitoring
The destination has a system to monitor, publicly report, and respond to environmental, economic, social, cultural, tourism, and human rights issues. The monitoring system is reviewed and evaluated periodically.

(continued)

Table 7.1 *(Continued)*

A4 Tourism seasonality management

The destination dedicates resources to mitigate seasonal variability of tourism where appropriate, working to balance the needs of the local economy, community, cultures and environment, to identify year-round tourism opportunities.

A5 Climate change adaptation

The destination has a system to identify risks and opportunities associated with climate change. This system encourages climate change adaptation strategies for development, siting, design, and management of facilities. The system contributes to the sustainability and resilience of the destination and to public education on climate for both residents and tourists.

A6 Inventory of tourism assets and attractions

The destination has an up-to-date, publicly available inventory and assessment of its tourism assets and attractions, including natural and cultural sites.

A7 Planning Regulations

The destination has planning guidelines, regulations and/or policies that require environmental, economic, and social impact assessment and integrate sustainable land use, design, construction, and demolition. The guidelines, regulations and/or policies are designed to protect natural and cultural resources, were created with local inputs from the public and a thorough review process, are publicly communicated, and are enforced.

A8 Access for all

Where appropriate, sites and facilities, including those of natural and cultural importance, are accessible to all, including persons with disabilities and others who have specific access requirements. Where such sites and facilities are not immediately accessible, access is afforded through the design and implementation of solutions that take into account both the integrity of the site and such reasonable accommodations for persons with access requirements as can be achieved.

A9 Property acquisitions

Laws and regulations regarding property acquisitions exist, are enforced, comply with communal and indigenous rights, ensure public consultation, and do not authorize resettlement without prior informed consent and/or reasonable compensation.

A10 Visitor satisfaction

The destination has a system to monitor and publicly report visitor satisfaction, and, if necessary, to take action to improve visitor satisfaction.

A11 Sustainability standards

The destination has a system to promote sustainability standards for enterprises consistent with the GSTC Criteria. The destination makes publicly available a list of sustainability certified or verified enterprises.

A12 Safety and security

The destination has a system to monitor, prevent, publicly report, and respond to crime, safety, and health hazards.

A13 Crisis and emergency management

The destination has a crisis and emergency response plan that is appropriate to the destination. Key elements are communicated to residents, visitors, and enterprises. The plan establishes procedures and provides resources and training for staff, visitors, and residents, and is updated on a regular basis.

A14 Promotion

Promotion is accurate with regard to the destination and its products, services, and sustainability claims. The promotional messages treat local communities and tourists authentically and respectfully.

SECTION B: Maximize economic benefits to the host community and minimize negative impacts

B1 Economic monitoring

The direct and indirect economic contribution of tourism to the destination's economy is monitored and publicly reported at least annually. To the extent feasible, this should include visitor expenditure, revenue per available room, employment and investment data.

B2 Local career opportunities

The destination's enterprises provide equal employment, training opportunities, occupational safety, and fair wages for all.

B3 Public participation

The destination has a system that encourages public participation in destination planning and decision making on an ongoing basis.

B4 Local community opinion

Local communities' aspirations, concerns, and satisfaction with destination management are regularly monitored, recorded and publicly reported in a timely manner.

B5 Local access

The destination monitors, protects, and when necessary rehabilitates or restores local community access to natural and cultural sites.

B6 Tourism awareness and education

The destination provides regular programs to affected communities to enhance their understanding of the opportunities and challenges of tourism, and the importance of sustainability.

B7 Preventing exploitation

The destination has laws and established practices to prevent commercial, sexual, or any other form of exploitation and harassment of anyone, particularly of children, adolescents, women, and minorities. The laws and established practices are publicly communicated.

B8 Support for community

The destination has a system to enable and encourage enterprises, visitors, and the public to contribute to community and sustainability initiatives.

B9 Supporting local entrepreneurs and fair trade

The destination has a system that supports local and small and medium-sized enterprises, and promotes and develops local sustainable products and fair trade principles that are based on the area's nature and culture. These may include food and beverages, crafts, performance arts, agricultural products, etc.

SECTION C: Maximize benefits to communities, visitors, and culture; minimize negative impacts

C1 Attraction protection

The destination has a policy and system to evaluate, rehabilitate, and conserve natural and cultural sites, including built heritage (historic and archaeological) and rural and urban scenic views.

C2 Visitor management

The destination has a visitor management system for attraction sites that includes measures to preserve, protect, and enhance natural and cultural assets.

(continued)

Table 7.1 *(Continued)*

C3 Visitor behavior
The destination has published and provided guidelines for proper visitor behavior at sensitive
   sites. Such guidelines are designed to minimize adverse impacts on sensitive sites and
   strengthen positive visitor behaviors.
C4 Cultural heritage protection
The destination has laws governing the proper sale, trade, display, or gifting of historical and
   archaeological artifacts.
C5 Site interpretation
Accurate interpretive information is provided at natural and cultural sites. The information
   is culturally appropriate, developed with community collaboration, and communicated in
   languages pertinent to visitors.
C6 Intellectual property
The destination has a system to contribute to the protection and preservation of intellectual
   property rights of communities and individuals.

SECTION D: Maximize benefits to the environment and minimize negative impacts

D1 Environmental risks
The destination has identified environmental risks and has a system in place to address them.
D2 Protection of sensitive environments
The destination has a system to monitor the environmental impact of tourism, conserve
   habitats, species, and ecosystems, and prevent the introduction of invasive species.
D3 Wildlife protection
The destination has a system to ensure compliance with local, national, and international laws
   and standards for the harvest or capture, display, and sale of wildlife (including plants and
   animals).
D4 Greenhouse gas emissions
The destination has a system to encourage enterprises to measure, monitor, minimize, publicly
   report, and mitigate their greenhouse gas emissions from all aspects of their operation
   (including emissions from service providers).
D5 Energy conservation
The destination has a system to encourage enterprises to measure, monitor, reduce, and
   publicly report energy consumption, and reduce reliance on fossil fuels.
D6 Water management
The destination has a system to encourage enterprises to measure, monitor, reduce, and
   publicly report water usage.
D7 Water security
The destination has a system to monitor its water resources to ensure that use by enterprises
   is compatible with the water requirements of the destination community.
D8 Water quality
The destination has a system to monitor drinking and recreational water quality using quality
   standards. The monitoring results are publicly available, and the destination has a system to
   respond in a timely manner to water quality issues.
D9 Wastewater
The destination has clear and enforced guidelines in place for the siting, maintenance and
   testing of discharge from septic tanks and wastewater treatment systems, and ensures
   wastes are properly treated and reused or released safely with minimal adverse effects to
   the local population and the environment.

D10 Solid waste reduction

The destination has a system to encourage enterprises to reduce, reuse, and recycle solid waste. Any residual solid waste that is not reused or recycled is disposed of safely and sustainably.

D11 Light and noise pollution

The destination has guidelines and regulations to minimize light and noise pollution. The destination encourages enterprises to follow these guidelines and regulations.

D12 Low-impact transportation

The destination has a system to increase the use of low-impact transportation, including public transportation and active transportation (e.g., walking and cycling).

Source: Global Sustainable Tourism Council, https://www.gstcouncil.org/en/gstc-criteria/criteria-for-destinations.html.

Notes

1. Conversation with Scott Wayne, SW Associates for Cultural Tourism Course, University of British Columbia (2009).
2. Modified from "Policy Instruments for Sustainable Tourism, Environmental Justice Organizations, Liabilities and Trade," http://www.ejolt.org, 2012.
3. Clare A. Gunn, with Turgut Var, *Tourism Planning* (2002). New York: Taylor & Francis, p. 117–118.
4. U.S. Department of the Interior, *Secretary of the Interior's Standards for Rehabilitation*, http://www.nps.gov/tps/standards/rehabilitation/rehab/stand.htm, 1995.
5. International Code Council, http://www.iccsafe.org, 2009.
6. European Association of Historic Towns and Regions, "Guidelines for Sustainable Cultural Tourism in Historic Towns and Cities" (September 2009), http://www.historic-towns.org/documents/downloads/SustainableTourismGuidelines.pdf.
7. International Society of Arboriculture, http://www.isa-arbor.com/education/onlineResources/treeOrdinanceGuidelines.aspx, 2001.
8. American Planning Association, *Growing Smart SM Legislative Guidebook*, 2002 Edition, p. 8-45.
9. Modified from American Alliance of Museums, "Collections Management Policy," http://www.aam-us.org/docs/default-source/continuum/developing-a-cmp-final.pdf?sfvrsn=4.
10. American Planning Association, *Growing Smart SM Legislative Guidebook*, 2002 Edition, p. 9-66.
11. Erin J. Johnson, "Development Agreements: Planning Perspectives," in *Development Agreements: Analysis, Colorado Case Studies, Commentary*, 3, as reported in American Planning Association, *Growing Smart SM Legislative Guidebook*, 2002 Edition, p. 8-191.
12. Cummins Foundation, *How the (Architectural) Program Works* (n.d.), p. 2.
13. Six Sigma is a quality program with a disciplined, data-driven approach and methodology for eliminating defects (driving toward six standard deviations between the mean and the nearest specification limit); https://www.isixsigma.com/new-to-six-sigma/getting-started/what-six-sigma.
14. American Planning Association, *Growing Smart SM Legislative Guidebook*, 2002 Edition, p. 9-25.
15. U.S. Environmental Protection Agency, "Summary of the Resource Conservation and Recovery Act," http://www.epa.gov/laws-regulations/summary-resource-conservation-and-recovery-act.
16. Tourism Ordinance No. 1983-22 § 1, 5-10-83, as provided by Vanessa Maybin, Appendix to the City of Charleston Tourism Management Plan (2015 update), p. 108.
17. Ibid.
18. Ibid., p. 110.
19. Ibid.
20. American Planning Association, *Growing Smart SM Legislative Guidebook*, 2002 Edition, p. 7-170.
21. Rebecca Chan, *Main Street Story of the Week* (March 21, 2012), National Trust for Historic Preservation, http://www.preservationnation.org/main-street/main-street-news/story-of-the-week/2012/120321artsand-entertainment/arts-entertainment.html.
22. wUNESCO, http://www.paducahky.gov/news/paducah-unesco-creative-city-crafts-folk-art.

Section III

Step Three: Develop Authentically

Chapter 8

Developing and Enhancing Authentic Experiences

Sustainable development is the pathway to the future we want for all. It offers a framework to generate economic growth, achieve social justice, exercise environmental stewardship and strengthen governance.

—Ban Ki-moon, secretary-general of the United Nations

At the heart of cultural heritage tourism is experience engagement. Developing authentic and appropriate experiences to enhance the overall destination appeal for visitors is perhaps the most important foundation for cultural heritage tourism. Development relies on a number of factors, however. Strong preservation policies, cultural integrity, defined "sense of place," and desired vision should drive all development decisions related to cultural heritage tourism.

Tourism "product development" is the foundation for destinations seeking to attract visitors and their spending. It is the process where the assets are molded to meet the needs of national and international customers.[1] Yet product development takes many forms. For cultural heritage tourism, the focus on asset-based or place-based development must ensure authenticity, compatibility, and, it is hoped, sustainability. Placemaking centers on what already exists, and expansion complements the essence—the character—of a community or a city. As discussed in chapter 2, placekeeping ensures that the specific characteristics of place remain. Important to remember in developing any kind of tourism are the key components of a visitor experience: a place to eat, a place to shop, a place to tour, and a place to sleep. These activities, when combined, provide the economic drivers for tourism—out-of-town (domestic and international) visitors spending money locally, generating sales tax and other revenues for businesses and cultural heritage institutions. How these experiences are created depend on the products available. A tourism development plan allows the local destination marketing organization (DMO) or city or county manager to effectively schedule and fund development activities in a holistic way, making sure that the right priorities are aligned with the overall vision of cultural heritage tourism. And development may happen many times during the life cycle of a site. For example, the Hotel de Paris Museum has changed ownership and evolved over time, as reported in the profile at the end of this chapter.

Figure 8.1 The restored Hotel de Paris Museum—Georgetown, Colorado. A profile of this museum and its life chapters is included at the end of this chapter.

Sustainable cultural heritage tourism development occurs three ways: (1) renovation, expansion, or enhancement of existing physical products (sites and buildings); (2) construction of new facilities for cultural and heritage activities (performance venues, museums, and art centers); and (3) added products and services to complement the physical space (festivals, programs, and tours). Capitalizing on interest in niche markets—such as food or culinary tourism, music tourism, literary tourism, and adventure tourism—affords opportunities to develop products and services catering to visitors' specific tastes and interests. Of course, infrastructure impacts all tourism development growth, and understanding the importance of signage, roads, parking, and the availability of public restrooms is paramount to sustainable growth. As mentioned, traffic congestion, litter, or lack of convenient parking can negate the best experiences in the world. Planning for infrastructure development is essential when considering sustainable tourism of any kind.

Understanding the purpose for tourism product development is important. For communities seeking to grow tourism, the focus may begin on using existing resources as the basis for products, attractions, or activities for visitors. The outcome may be a greater critical mass of attractions and/or additional activities appealing to different audiences. For cities where tourism is already a main form of economic development, the desire may be to create new facilities to enhance the capacity or availability of cultural heritage activities—especially to attract visitors during slower or off-peak seasons. For seasonal destinations, a goal is to become "evergreen" or have year-round appeal and sustainable business. This chapter defines tourism product development with an emphasis on cultural heritage, explores the ways to develop new or expand existing tourism products for cultural heritage experiences, and addresses potential challenges to sustainability. Developing a tourism product development plan is recommended, and a sample process is included in figure 8.7 at the end of this chapter for reference.

Defining Product Development for Cultural Heritage Tourism

As cultural heritage tourism relies on authenticity and sense of place to attract and sustain visitation, the lens for product development is slightly different than for mass-market, manufactured tourist attractions and destinations. Repurposing existing building stock, adding new products (parks, museums, performing arts centers, and memorials), and clustered activities (trails and districts) all focus on expanding and recognizing the physical character of a place. By utilizing intangible cultural heritage assets and resources, destinations can develop or enhance festivals and other local traditions and expressions. Wayfinding and information centers ensure that visitors can navigate the destination with ease and assurance. Infrastructure improvements also contribute to the safety, security, and needs of visitors.

Existing Buildings

The historic building stock of a city or community is often the foundation for cultural heritage tourism. Indeed, historic downtowns became the nexus for a commercial revitalization movement known as "Main Street," which focuses on neighborhood commercial districts. Museums, hotels, restaurants, galleries, retail shops, visitor information centers, and theaters can all call historic buildings home. When historic buildings are restored for a new contributing use to tourism, the history of the site can enhance its unique selling proposition. Famous people who passed through its doors or slept overnight become accolades to attract new visitors ("George Washington slept here!"). Read about the colorful past of the Occidental Hotel and its appeal to visitors today in the profile at the end of this chapter.

Iconic architecture, old or new, is consistently used as a signature for a destination to differentiate it from all others. Consider your favorite destinations. Often, a landmark church, county courthouse, or fountain is the signature structure associated with the place. Compatible design is important to ensure that old and new fit together like vintage garments adorned with sparkling new gems.[6]

Intangible Assets

Beyond buildings, the cultural intangibles—such as food, music, language, or dance—also shape the character of a destination. As discussed in chapter 2, these cultural assets are equally important to providing desired authentic experiences for visitors. UNESCO defines *intangible* as "cultural expressions that have passed from one generation to another, have evolved in response to their environments and contribute to giving us a sense of identity and continuity."[7] UNESCO's definition of intangible cultural heritage includes oral traditions, performing arts, social practices, rituals, festive events, knowledge and practices concerning nature and the universe, or the knowledge and skills to produce traditional crafts.[8] According to UNESCO, intangible cultural heritage is characterized as follows:

- Traditional, contemporary, and living at the same time
- Inclusive
- Representative
- Community based

Therefore, when developing products and services based on or including intangible cultural heritage, local tradition bearers must be included in the process to ensure sensitivity and appropriateness. At risk is commodification of culture, exploitation of indigenous peoples, or staged authenticity. These concerns are addressed later in this chapter.

Developing cultural heritage tourism products and experiences goes beyond the physical and intangible resources. How existing or new attractions are packaged or bundled can also shape the appeal to and receptivity from visitors. Packaging often affords the visitor a better value and greater convenience, as multiple activities are combined into easy-to-purchase or easy-to-experience products. Bundling activities and attractions around a particular theme or along a linear corridor can often create the critical mass necessary for a more immersive experience and promote collective learning.

Enhancing Existing Assets and Products

The most viable development strategy for cultural heritage tourism is to start with what you have. Existing buildings (vacant or occupied), festivals, museums, monuments, parks, and other assets (as identified in chapter 2) often provide the foundation for cultural heritage tourism. Some structures or activities may require substantial investment to make them visitor ready; others require nominal tweaking to enhance existing cultural heritage tourism experiences.

Restoration, Renovation, and Reuse

The ultimate form of recycling occurs when a historic structure is restored or renovated for a new purpose. Infusing new life into abandoned building stock serves two purposes. The blighted structure becomes a contributing part of the community's or city's economic infrastructure and also adds to the critical mass of cultural heritage attractions available to the visitor. However, as with any development project, the return on investment must be calculated along with the cost of maintaining and operating the structure. Sustainability is the key to long-term success.

Dynamic, Immersive Programming

Engaging programming is necessary to attract today's traveler and sustain interest by key audiences. Museums that don't refresh content, that present static "one size fits all" programs, or that lack compelling content are at risk of losing customers—and viability. As mentioned in chapter 3, today's visitors want engagement and immersive experiences. Providing these types of interactive, varied programs requires creativity, commitment, and out-of-the-box applications.

What constitutes dynamic, immersive programming? Certainly, it includes an engagement opportunity, whether the experience incorporates meeting local residents or involves participating in some sort of educational activity. Dynamic, immersive programming must be relevant for the audience and, it is hoped, stimulates the senses via a photography class, an artist demonstration, pottery lessons, a controlled archaeology dig, a "tasting tour" that combines culinary stops and history, or a local brewpub tour. The concepts are based on authenticity and local assets; the programming is limited only by creative application. Experiences that engage not only are desired by visitors but also can be more lucrative (a valued purchase); most important, these immersive experiences are more memorable and are often shared with others, thereby creating a buzz or interest by future patrons.

Dealing honestly with history, warts and all, is vitally important to the integrity of place and visitor education. While engaging is sometimes interpreted as fun and entertaining, some periods of history require more sensitive presentation. Enslavement, the civil rights movement, women suffragettes, immigration, terrorism, military, and other social, political, and environmental issues should be respectfully presented without compromise of integrity. Powerful messages can help heal wounds, evoke greater understanding and empathy, reveal atrocities (with hopes that dark periods of history will not be repeated), and give voice to underrepresented or silenced populations. The responsibility to present difficult stories is great; making sure that the information and delivery is accurate, sensitive, and appropriate is of utmost importance. Ownership and attribution of history are particularly important to maintaining integrity of messages. Interpretation is explored more fully in the next chapter.

> Keep digging, turning things over, looking at them from different angles. Don't be afraid to experience. If you are in a rut, try something new. Reinterpreting the Davenport House to include the experience of urban slavery has an element of risk—but it's worth taking.
> —Daniel Carey, president and chief executive officer, Historic Savannah Foundation

The move away from strict hours of operation to preset programs—especially for small museums or sites run by volunteers—allows a more flexible offering of experiences for visitors and diminishes staffing hardships. Rather than waiting all day for a visitor to show up, a site can schedule a program or special tour and market it for advance registration. While this is not always an optimal or preferred operating practice, it serves both the site and the visitor better than being open "by appointment" (which is never a good option). Museums with limited resources may find that consistent programming (every Thursday evening or Saturday afternoon) affords a better way to reach visitors and to be a contributing asset until more frequent access is available. This permanent schedule may also be more attractive to marketers who need confidence in a site's ability to host visitors on a regular basis.

Offering programming on days and times when visitors are in town may require a change of staffing schedules. Weekends are still prime time for leisure travelers; a museum or site open weekdays only may find empty halls and miss out on hosting visitors. Many smaller or rural towns and destinations need evening activities, a ripe opportunity for museums to offer special programming. Local DMOs or convention and visitors bureaus can identify the travel patterns of leisure visitors and cite the days or times most needed for experiential engagement.

Expansion to Existing Businesses

Private businesses or nonprofit organizations may also enhance their tourism potential through expansion of existing facilities or additional products and services. This strategy is particularly prevalent in agricultural and traditional manufacturing businesses seeking to generate additional (year-round) revenues from visitors. The addition of a gift shop selling local "farm-to-table" products or scheduled demonstrations to "watch it being made" can enhance visitation, increase revenues from product sales, and expand awareness through education.

The addition of a gift shop, café, or meeting space (rental for specific events, weddings, or special programs) can also generate revenue beyond admissions. While the sales and profitability of museum stores can vary widely depending on the size and location of the facility, the Museum Store Association reports that they can contribute as much as one-third of the institution's operating budget.[9] The institution may operate the on-site facility, contract with a concessionaire, or sell licensed products to other retail merchants to increase sales and extend its brand. As shopping continues to top the list of activities of leisure travelers and taking home a locally made memento appeals particularly to the cultural heritage traveler, sites and destinations see shopping as a strong economic driver. What do travelers want? A study produced by the Office of Travel and Tourism Industries, U.S. Department of Commerce, found the following:[10]

- Seventy-three percent visit stores that they don't have at home.
- Sixty-seven percent seek out items that travelers can't get at home.
- Fifty-three percent purchase items that represent the destination that travelers are visiting.
- Fifty-two percent favor a unique shopping atmosphere.

Local merchants can enhance their appeal to visitors by clustering locally made items in a special area of the shop. Working with local artists to display work and share their information (through photos, scripted hangtags, or biographies) may further connect the visitor to the destination. And these displays can reach beyond the traditional retail store to sell at restaurants, hotels, or spas. (A personal example—I saw a carousel with locally made earrings at a diner's cashier stand in Montana, and, just like at grocery stores, product placement worked. My dinner concluded with a purchase of jewelry made by one of the waitresses.) Adorning walls of restaurants with local art or photographs adds authentic personality to a place but also provides another distribution channel for the artists. Hotels, airports, train stations, shopping malls, and other places where people gather can be transformed into new spaces for showcasing and/or selling cultural heritage tourism products and services.

Creating Compelling New Products and Experiences

A destination seeking to expand its cultural heritage tourism or product has, it is hoped, conducted market research to understand the feasibility of these new attractions and activities. In the planning process, the viability and availability of new attractions—museums, performing arts venues, public art, and other physical products along with festivals and events—are considered in the greater context of destination development. Before initiating any development project, consider how this new product will do the following:

- Contribute to the realization of the destination's cultural heritage tourism vision (outlined in chapter 6)
- Add to the economic vitality of the community, city, or region
- Enhance resident quality of life or provide other benefits
- Offer an additional marketing opportunity for the destination
- Expand the length of time visitors spend in the destination
- Fill a gap in the current experience offering (as an evening, weekend, weekday, or indoors, "rainy day" activity or for a particular audience, such as kids, seniors, or groups)

Additionally, the new product or facility should complement or enhance the destination's brand. As mentioned previously, iconic new architecture often makes a statement about the personality of place and can become an attraction in its own right—beyond the functionality of the space.

Critical considerations for any type of physical development include the location, the scale, the purpose, and the impact on surrounding infrastructure and the community at large. Zoning, parking, egress, and signage must be considered for new development, as must the environmental and social impacts related to future use. Managers of public facilities need to consider costs beyond the development phase, including operations and maintenance, public safety, and transportation impacted by the new facility. How long will it take to recoup initial investment or begin generating revenue? The time line at which it makes a profit (or at least breaks even) should be determined before proceeding so that investors and stakeholders can make informed decisions. If some other metric is used to evaluate success, such as public need, quality of life, or greater revitalization impact, the benchmark should still be established before development.

Saturation may also occur if development is not well managed. Too many hotels or an abundance of visitor services in relation to local businesses and residential housing, especially in historic districts, can tip the livability of a destination. Often, this imbalance occurs in popular, more mature destinations (such as the New Orleans French Quarter) when tourism planning and management is not enforced in a holistic way.[11]

Public Facilities

The U.S. government operates a number of public facilities related to cultural heritage tourism. The national park system (through the U.S. Department of the Interior), national wildlife refuges (through U.S. Fish and Wildlife and the Department of the Interior), and marine sanctuaries (through the National Oceanic and Atmospheric Administration and the U.S. Department of Commerce) offer visitors an opportunity to experience our nation's culture and heritage via specific sites, interpretive programs, and experiences. The Department of the Interior also administers the National Register of Historic Places, the National Historic Landmark program, and World Heritage Site designation. This ownership offers businesses and destinations opportunities for gateway development and public-private partnerships.

The U.S. Congress designates national museums (such as the National World War I Museum in Kansas City, Missouri) and National Heritage Areas (NHAs), recognizing significant regions of the country. The forty-nine NHAs "further the mission of the National Park Service by fostering community stewardship of our nation's heritage." The National Park Service oversees the NHA program and provides technical assistance to NHA staffs, boards, and partners; the National Park Service does not own any land or impose land use controls within NHA boundaries.[12] Nonprofit organizations or other private corporations usually administer national museums and heritage areas.[13]

States also use public lands and develop public facilities for cultural heritage tourism. Parks, museums, and monuments commemorating wars and legendary explorers or patriots attract visitors seeking to learn about the respective state's history. States traditionally manage a "state museum" with art collections, artifacts, and exhibits related to the state's origin, geography, settlement, industry, and/or growth often located in the capital city. States may choose to develop or designate specific sites to showcase a specific set of artifacts or recognize a certain genre related to the state's history, such as the Music Hall of Fame or Sports Hall of Fame.

States may provide incentives or support local jurisdictions in the development of other public facilities for use by cultural and heritage tourists:

- Museums
- Performing arts venues
- Public art in parks
- Festivals
- Parks and recreation kiosks
- Trails
- Visitor information centers

Funding from the state arts council (as appropriated by the National Endowment for the Arts), tourism development grants, or tax credits can help offset some of the costs for developing these new products. The Commonwealth of Virginia has one of the most robust tourism development financing programs in the nation, with specific requirements in place to receive funding. The submission criteria, including the recommended components of a tourism development plan, are provided at the end of this chapter in figure 8.7.

Local governments may spur creation of these new products through donations or a $1-per-year lease on currently vacant structures, especially if developed by a nonprofit or a public–private organization. Visitor information centers frequently marry local government (transportation agency, city, or county) and private investment (from a chamber of commerce, DMO, or convention and visitors bureau) to acquire the site, build the structure, and operate the facility.

As with any new product, due diligence must be conducted to determine feasibility and sustainability. The process for developing new cultural heritage tourism sites and attractions is similar to planning processes for other public buildings.

Private Development

Private developers provide the vision and expertise to convert derelict structures or blighted neighborhoods into contributing assets for local and visitor use. Renovating historic buildings

Figure 8.2 Exterior, Ka'ili's Restaurant—Santa Clara, Utah.

into boutique hotels, using commercial warehouses for retail galleries, transforming old gas stations into hip diners, and restoring former pump houses into art museums are only a few examples of successful private development projects. Often, private investors seek additional incentives—in the form of tax credits, workforce development, infrastructure, land purchase or lease—to realize the project. The investor's request for incentives may occur at the local municipality level or directly to development authorities, county commissioners, regional commissions, or the state's department of economic development. The same analysis process applied to public projects should be used for private development to determine appropriateness, feasibility, and sustainability.

Some developers have a personal interest or passion for a particular project. Often, this labor of love yields a new attraction or activity that enhances a destination and is profitable for the developer or business owner. In the profile of Ka'ili's Restaurant in Santa Clara, Utah, at the end of this chapter, read about one man's personal journey to show honor and respect.

Infrastructure Inspired by a Destination's Cultural Heritage

One area often overlooked for development is inspired infrastructure. It is true that safety standards must be met when constructing roads, bridges, and intersections, yet some of the most significant public projects transport people every day—the Golden Gate Bridge, the Blue Ridge

Figure 8.3 Gateway welcome sign—Lucas, Kansas.

Parkway (designated by the U.S. Department of Transportation as an All American Road), and the Pacific Coast Highway. The careful planning and execution of these infrastructure projects provide an enduring legacy, demonstrating how the journey can also be part of the attraction.

Gateways present the most obvious opportunity to define the personality of place. The welcome sign and landscaping establish a first impression of the destination. The condition and architecture of these elements present a visual message about the place. If it is attractive, well maintained, and interesting (in display and design), the destination may lure more visitors to spend time and money (see the accompanying feature for a unique example). If it is not maintained or, worse, it includes no distinguishing element other than a standard highway sign, the visitor may drive by due to a lack of interest and appeal.

Transportation hubs—airports, train stations, subways, bus stations, and rental car facilities—also serve as gateways. Considering ways to visually brand these facilities via banners, public art, distinctive architecture and use of local building materials, or other cultural treatments helps visitors become familiar with the essence of place. Hartsfield–Jackson International Airport in Atlanta uses its moving walkways between concourses as a time line for the city's history, as shown in figures 8.4 and 8.5.

Figure 8.4 A walk through Atlanta history, Hartsfield–Jackson Atlanta International Airport—Atlanta, Georgia.

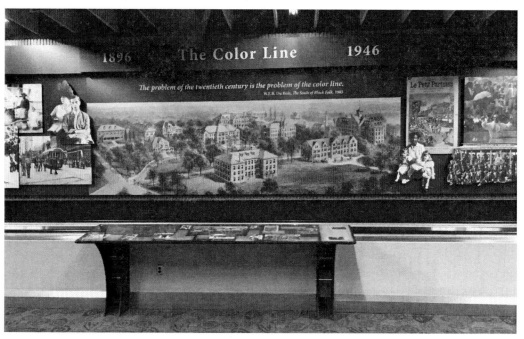

Figure 8.5 Interpretive exhibit on tram concourse, Hartsfield–Jackson Atlanta International Airport—Atlanta, Georgia.

A destination's entrance is traditionally part of a larger way-finding system to help direct and inform visitors on how to navigate around the municipality. A way-finding plan, developed locally and approved by the state department of transportation (if highway or interstate signage is required), is the first step in a cohesive signage system. Signage does not have to be boring, though. It can be designed to reflect the destination and its cultural heritage. What do you want your signage to say about your site or destination? Are there local elements you want to include to recognize a particular expertise or architectural feature of your destination or site (such as iron-work, granite, or other materials)? Sign ordinances, as covered in chapter 7, should be reviewed as to their impact on gateways and way finding.

Beyond signage, interesting infrastructure design applies to bridges, overpasses, and transportation hubs. Just as "big box" retailers do not have to follow a single design, bridges and overpasses also benefit from interesting architecture or features. Murals, environmental art, and other design features enhance the visual appeal of the infrastructure. Road access is also a telling statement about destinations. Are you bicycle friendly, with paths clearly marked and accessible? Do you have setbacks or buffer zones to create green space between roads and development? Are bill-boards prevalent? Do tree-covered medians invite travelers to slow down in downtown districts or neighborhoods? Are traffic-calming circles integrated into the road design to encourage safety and also to "linger longer?" While transportation plans may be part of a municipality's comprehensive plan, the opportunity to include signature elements that speak to the cultural heritage of the destination should not be lost. Investing in proactive design may not require extra resources to make signature statements that flow through a site, city, town, county, region, or corridor. The winding road to Monticello, Thomas Jefferson's home in Virginia, set up the experience and education about this expansive site.

Parking structures also require consideration as to their visual impact on the visitor. While parking is necessary for all commercial and residential plots, the size, scale, location, and architecture vary greatly from place to place. How a parking structure looks (design or materials used) impacts the overall feel or impression of a commercial district. The creative approach to masking a massive city parking garage (described in the profile at the end of this chapter) demonstrates how a sterile structure can be transformed into an iconic attraction. Whether a historic site's or a museum's parking lot is shaded and situated off to the side or located in front of the building changes the first impression and probably the site's photo opportunity. Parking meters versus free parking are also a consideration for every downtown or busy commercial district. Understanding the cost-benefit analysis and purpose of parking meters (perhaps as a tourism management strategy) is important and unique to each destination. Parking issues should be addressed as part of an overall comprehensive tourism management and transportation plan.

Clustering Activities and Attractions

An industry standard for aggregating activities and attractions is packaging. For cultural heritage tourism, most packages center around blockbuster exhibits, music events, performances, or special festivals. The advent of these occasions leads to the creation of time-sensitive promotions, value-added programs, and packages that make purchasing easy. Packages usually include the cultural or heritage activity, lodging, and other admissions or complementary programs. A significant aspect of packaging is prepurchase, usually via the website of a hotel, destination, or attraction. The one-price package allows visitors the convenience to choose various activity options and prepay for the bundled experience (with lodging).

Figure 8.6 The Community Bookshelf masks the Kansas City Public Library's parking garage—Kansas City, Missouri.

Great packages may be developed to attract off-season visitors or midweek or weekend travelers to fill attendance lulls. These packages, often cleverly titled and targeted to a specific market, again provide convenience through preplanned itineraries or special discounts at various attractions, retail shops, and/or restaurants. The travel packaging process includes eight elements:

1. Package design (components—typically hotel, attraction, and experience)
2. Package pricing (what makes it valued—discounts and added value)
3. Distribution (where and how it will be sold and for how long?)
4. Marketing (who is it for, and how will it be promoted?)
5. Selection (buyer purchase)
6. Delivery (notification and presentation of vouchers or instruction for redemption)
7. Administration (systems for paying partners)
8. Evaluation (measurement of return on investment)[17]

If they charge admission, many historic sites do not have a commissionable rate (wholesale or discount) for use in packaging. Therefore, it may be more appropriate to use the same process to create compelling itineraries. Three elements are important in developing itineraries:

- Provide a route that is easy to follow—include addresses or major GPS coordinates for customers to input for directions.
- Include how much time it takes to get from point to point, and also how much time should be allowed at each historic or cultural attraction.
- Remember to connect the dots: recommend places to eat, shop, and sleep to enhance the visit.

Often, these itineraries can be mapped according to a half day, a full day, forty-eight hours, or a long weekend in a destination, using the themes and/or subthemes identified in the interpretive plan (see chapter 9).

Trail Development

Linking assets like a string of pearls provides destinations—especially smaller towns and rural areas—the potential to enhance a critical mass of activities for visitors. While many trails are repurposed old railroad routes now used for recreational purposes, cultural heritage trails connect historic sites or cultural landscapes into interpreted corridors. Using criteria to qualify or cull contributing attractions or activities, cultural heritage trails stimulate visitation into artist studios, galleries, museums, historic sites, local diners, and bed-and-breakfasts. The final product—a qualified cluster or themed corridor—can be promoted as a single entity. Local or regional "passports" are frequently developed to entice travelers to visit all contributing sites and locations, with incentives or prizes awarded on completion. The trail structure allows for research to be conducted with participating sites and activities to collectively determine visitor profiles, spending, and satisfaction. Federally designated National Historic Trails and National Recreation Trails afford an opportunity for local collaboration.

Steps and Considerations for Creating a Cultural or Heritage Trail

1. Define the theme.
2. Define the geographic area or boundaries of the trail. Will it be a linear trail or clusters? Will it follow a specific route, either historic or contemporary (existing road)?
3. Define the criteria for inclusion. Is the determining factor related to the theme, the level of visitor readiness (see chapter 4), or a combination of the two?
4. Determine additional assets for inclusion, such as tours, lodging, dining, and retail, that complement the theme or enhance the trail experience (and impact).
5. Define the desired outcomes. Increase visitation, increase awareness, expand critical mass to attract customers, and provide an opportunity for partner collaboration and marketing.
6. What are the participants' responsibilities (on-site surveys, maintaining a certain level of experience based on criteria, cross marketing, and fees for participation)?
7. How will the trail be signed (window clings, private signs, or highway signage)?
8. How will the trail be marketed and to whom?
9. How will measurement be conducted and attributable to the trail project?
10. How will the trail (creation, marketing, management, and expansion) be funded?
11. Who is responsible for organizing and managing the trail (verifying compliance, maintaining signage, marketing and measuring the trail's impact on the community at large, and attribution from tourism)?
12. What policies are in place for noncompliance?

Challenges to Sustainable Cultural Heritage Tourism Product Development

Several key issues challenge cultural heritage tourism as a viable and sustainable strategy for economic and community growth. Development dictates the appearance, capacity, density, aesthetics, and character of place. Inappropriate development can negatively impact the economics as well as the cultural integrity of a destination. Standardization, commodification, and staged authenticity can occur when planning or policies are not in place to safeguard cultural resources and/or dictate terms for development.

Standardization

In cultural heritage tourism, standardization or homogenization occurs when "distinctively authentic resources and experiences become subject to global criteria or are modified to meet international expectations."[18] This approach most frequently begins with marketing and adapting the products and services to appeal to the perceptions or desires of international tourists rather than customizing market strategies and retaining the cultural integrity of resource experiences.

Coupled with a tendency to "museumize" cultural resources, where historians and curators create exhibits to interpret cultures or display artifacts outside their original environment, cultural standardization dilutes or often removes the inherent uniqueness and even quirkiness of authentic cultural expression and activities.[19]

In heritage terms, the standardization often results in a sameness of architecture, where everyplace looks like anyplace. Even some "Main Streets" begin to look alike when similar styles of benches, lampposts, and banners are used. Understanding how to protect the aesthetics of place becomes as important as how to present and offer unique experiences and market the authentic messages to distinguish one destination from another.

Commodification

As cultural heritage tourism becomes more recognized as a viable and sustainable growth strategy, the value of cultural and historic resources to commercial enterprises and the tourism industry increases. Cultural heritage becomes a commodity measured in market terms and valued in the context of trade. The packaging of cultural "goods and services" for commercial consumption and gain is defined as commodification.

Cultural commodification can compromise authenticity of story and tradition, especially when focused on indigenous peoples. To safeguard against this threat, tribes sometimes establish protocols or policies to protect the cultural integrity of information, interpretation, and presentation. Tribal protocols may also suggest modifications or cancellations of scheduled activities in certain situations; for example, the Tlingit do not consider dancing appropriate when a family (clan) member passes on. While cultural heritage tourism can serve as a vehicle for education and understanding and also generate local revenues, destination planners, marketers, and visitors must be respectful of local cultural traditions and values. Providing alternative cultural activities is important to honor tribal traditions and also meet the tour obligations for the visitor while maintaining the authenticity and integrity of the cultural tour program.[20]

The island state of Hawaii has suffered from commodification for more than half a century. In the 1950s, the modern tourism industry transformed true Hawaiian traditions into "Kodak moments" of hula dancers in grass skirts and coconut bras. Sacred traditions and Native Hawaiian values were hijacked to establish a mass-marketed brand of hospitality and entertainment. In recent years, Native Hawaiians have encouraged cultural sensitivity and visitor and industry education to enhance respectful engagement.

Examples of historic commodification can best be visualized at the themed casinos in Las Vegas. The Venetian, Luxor, New York/New York, and other casino hotels use architectural replicas to theme their exteriors. Another example of historic commodification is "Disney's America." In the early 1990s, the Walt Disney Company attempted to sell the concept of a "historically themed" park in northern Virginia, the home of significant Civil War battlefields (including Manassas). The attempt to use this historic area to contrive a historic experience was thwarted.[21]

Perhaps the most egregious use of commodification is where no historic asset or culture exists and yet it is created to satisfy tourist interests. Such is the case of the fictional Main Street at Walt Disney World, which has no historical content or context. Commodification can be realized in more personal ways where an artist's work is recognized and celebrated but then subjected to requests for mass production or price reduction to meet demand.

Staged Authenticity

Former *New York Times* architecture critic Ada Huxtable was an outspoken opponent of the sanitation of history and architecture for tourism or economic development. In her book *The Unreal America: Architecture and Illusion*, Huxtable states,

> The replacement of reality with selective fantasy is a phenomenon of that most successful and staggeringly profitable American phenomenon, the reinvention of the environment as themed entertainment.[22]

She further challenges the historic preservation community's and the tourism industry's development of "authentic reproduction" as a "total upending of values and a great moneymaker for historic restorations, museums, and assorted coattail enterprises."[23]

In *Authenticity: What Consumers Really Want*, authors Gilmore and Pine explore the evolution of how goods and services are now packaged and sold as transformational experiences. "With the rise of authenticity as the new consumer sensibility, what customers really want is the real from the genuine, not the fake from the phony, and therefore increasingly make the distinction between the two."[24] Destinations are instructed to seek out specific strategies where tourists are encouraged to engage in the creation of authentic experiences. The authors suggest that destinations employ a chief experience officer to help define, develop, market, and host these authentic experiences for visitors.

Chapter Summary

Developing cultural heritage tourism experiences requires ongoing research and analysis to best understand what visitors want, what residents care about, and how these jive with the vision for the site, organization, community. How to develop experiences focusing on culture and heritage depends on numerous factors, including available assets, desired outcomes, funding, infrastructure, and creativity. Sustainability for this industry segment means ensuring that development does not compromise the integrity and authenticity of existing cultural heritage. Focusing on existing resources first helps retain sense of place, scale, and history. Complementing extant resources, new development allows the destination to expand capacity and diversity. Understanding the development process and prioritizing efforts are key to maximizing return on investment and making smart decisions for adding new trails, services, programs, or products alongside strong and sustainable existing cultural heritage tourism resources. Packaging these individual activities allows partners to offer and sell value-added experiences, especially during desired seasons.

While several government entities fund tourism product development, the Commonwealth of Virginia has one of the more comprehensive and proactive programs. To foster sustainable

The Commonwealth of Virginia's Tourism Development Financing Plan

https://www.vatc.org/TDFinancingProgram

One of the requirements to receive financing from the State of Virginia is submission of a Tourism Development Plan. The purpose of the plan is to:

1. Outline the specific deficiency (void) the proposed project will fill.
2. Provide accurate representations of a locality's current tourism product and assets, infrastructure, marketing efforts and visitor profiles.
3. Show the return on investment the proposed project will have to the local tourism economy.

Existing tourism plans may be submitted, however applicants will need to complete and submit the official Tourism Development Plan online form to continue with the TDFP application. The form is available at (http://lis.virginia.gov/cgi-bin/legp604.exe?081+ful+CHAP0462).

SECTION 1: PROPOSED PROJECT

- Briefly describe the overall scope and concept of your proposed project
- What perceived deficiency (void) in your local tourism economy will this proposed project fill?
- Will this proposed project fit into an existing Tourism Zone? Virginia Code § 58.1-3851. Creation of local tourism zones
- What is the projected number of jobs and local tax revenue created from this specific project?

SECTION 2: PRODUCT ANALYSIS

- Attributes—which best describe your area, such as nature & outdoor recreation, history & heritage, epicurean & experiential, arts & culture, entertainment & amusement
- Drivers—such as major lures that attract tourists to your area including attractions, activities and experiences
- Uniqueness—which makes your destination truly different; a particular attraction, history or cultural experience, or a combination of several
- Competition—such as a community, attraction or travel experience with similar product within 150+ miles

SECTION 3: S.W.O.T. ANALYSIS

A tourism development plan will need to include a gauging of your tourism infrastructure, economy and business community, as well as a community's social and cultural assets.

S.W.O.T. Specifics

- TOP 3 STRENGTHS—characteristics of community or area that give it an advantage over others

Figure 8.7 The Commonwealth of Virginia's Tourism Development Financing Plan.

- TOP 3 WEAKNESSES—characteristics that place your community or area at a disadvantage relative to others
- TOP 3 OPPORTUNITIES—external chances to achieve greater success and profits in your industry
- TOP 3 THREATS—external elements in the environment that could cause trouble for business or community

SECTION 4: MARKETING PLAN

- You will be asked to submit a current or existing marketing plan adopted by your community.
- A marketing plan is an official, adopted plan by which an organization or community can maximize its tourism potential. It answers key questions which provide direction for a community's tourism marketing activities. A marketing plan brings together an organization's research, particular goals, measureable objectives, brand ideals and other important considerations in one concise, executable directive.

Figure 8.7 *(continued)*

business practices, the Commonwealth of Virginia's Tourism Development Financing Program requires plans that articulate not only the product purpose and viability phase but also the implementation phase (including marketing, management, and measurement).

* * * * *

Profile: The Hotel de Paris Museum: A Touch of France in the Rockies
Georgetown, Colorado

http://www.hoteldeparismuseum.org

The Hotel de Paris has changed hands six times in its life since Frenchman Louis Dupuy opened his hotel and restaurant in 1875. The lavish European-inspired hotel expanded to half a city block to accommodate business from the silver boom before the housekeeper inherited it on Dupuy's death in October 1900. The hotel was leased by Sarah Harrison and James Burkholder in 1901 and purchased by them in 1903. It maintained its reputation as a fine hotel and first-class French restaurant into the 1920s.

When private automobiles arrived in the mountains, Louis Dupuy's French menu was retired, and managers who leased the hotel from the Burkholder's daughter (Hazel Burkholder McAdams) began serving a more modern and American offering of trout, steak, and chicken dinners in a more casual diner-style format (much like the 1945 American film noir *Mildred Pierce*). Hazel retired from the Clear Creek County School District in the 1940s and ran the hotel as a boarding house until 1949. The National Society of the Colonial Dames of America in the state of Colorado purchased the hotel in 1954 for $15,100 and restored the site to its 1890s appearance. The Colonial Dames still own and operate the site, now as a museum. The building was listed on the National Register of Historic Places in 1970. Famed western author Louis L'Amour fictionalized the setting in his 1978 novel *The Proving Trail*.

Figure 8.8 Antique travelers' trunks are placed around the Hotel de Paris Museum to give visitors a sense of movement and activity within the historic site—Georgetown, Colorado.

Figure 8.9 1878 commercial kitchen open storage, Hotel de Paris Museum—Georgetown, Colorado.

In 2007, the museum became an affiliate site of the National Trust for Historic Preservation (NTHP) through a ten-year Historic Site Operating Agreement. "We have imposed a museum model on a hotel and restaurant, and have done very well with this approach; however, we want to be more competitive in order to continue to thrive," says Kevin Kuharic, executive director of the Hotel de Paris Museum.[2] A benefit of the NTHP partnership is technical assistance to help professionalize the site and raise funds for an endowment (a requirement of the agreement). The operating agreement also addresses governance; personnel and volunteers; finance and fundraising; collections management; facilities, safety, and emergency preparedness; an interpretive plan; education; and marketing and membership. Interest on the endowment pays for most of the staff salaries and other benefits (such as professional development) for the executive director. "Our relationship with the NTHP is viewed as a 'Good Housekeeping Seal of Approval' and this credential can influence the casual visitor to take a tour, or donor to contribute funds," says Kuharic.[3]

The current NTHP agreement requires the museum to be open a minimum of 140 days per year. While the current visitation is around 7,000 per year, the potential is about double with current staff and infrastructure. Admission, which increased from $5 to $7 in 2015 (with no apparent negative impact), accounts for about 11 percent of the museum's annual budget. For every dollar spent in admission, another $0.50 is collected in gift shop sales. With an annual budget of less than $150,000, visitors not only help satisfy the museum's mission but also generate revenue for the organization.

The museum's mission is to collect, preserve, and share history associated with Louis Dupuy's Hotel De Paris and serve as a catalyst for heritage tourism in Georgetown, Colorado. Like many museums, the Hotel de Paris moved away from decorative arts and room-specific descriptions to a more theme- and story-based interpretation. Docent-led tours of about forty-five minutes are currently the big attraction, where visitors learn about Louis Dupuy as well as workers and guests as they explore the three levels of the former hotel and restaurant. Stories of the workers and guests contribute to the Content which has also expanded to focus more on the Chinese and Jewish contributions at Hotel de Paris. Printed translations of tours are available in French, German, Japanese, and Spanish. The museum still depends on grants and contributions to help fund interpretation and preservation. An exhibit in the 1878 commercial kitchen was not funded, so the staff elected to use "visible storage"[4] to make the artifacts more accessible to visitors. This cost-effective strategy has generated positive comments from first-time and repeat visitors as well as board members and volunteers. Use of iPads to provide a 365-degree view of the hotel's multiple floors is currently under consideration to provide greater access for the mobility challenged.

With a full-time year-round staff of one, plus two seasonal full-time and one seasonal part-time employees for the 140-day tour season, volunteers are important to managing and expanding operations. Volunteers often staff the admissions area and gift shop, allowing staff to offer more tours. However, the number of permanent residents and new citizens in Georgetown is declining as the number of vacation rentals and second homes escalates. This impact has not been fully realized, but it is something that staff are paying attention to—especially in the quest to expand the time and money a visitor spends on-site.

"We hope to find a business to occupy a building behind the museum, yet within our historic site. By offering a café that acknowledges our culinary history, we will not only create rental income that we don't presently have, we will also brand build the museum by reawakening the original use of the property," said Kuharic. He continued, "Perhaps going back (in part) to the former function of site may be what we do."[5]

* * * * *

Profile: The Occidental Hotel—If Walls Could Talk
Buffalo, Wyoming

http://www.occidentalwyoming.com

Not many hotels boast outlaws, presidents, authors, and generals on their guest list, but such was the prestige of the historic Occidental Hotel located near the Bozeman Trail at the foot of the Bighorn Mountains. Butch Cassidy and the Sundance Kid, cattle detective and killer Tom Horn, Buffalo Bill Cody, Martha "Calamity Jane" Cannary Burke, Presidents Theodore Roosevelt and Herbert Hoover, Ernest Hemingway, and General Phil Sheridan are just a few of the famous—and infamous—who stayed at the Occidental, built in 1880. Owen Wister, author of *The Virginian*, spent time in the hotel, basing many characters in his book on the cowboys and gunslingers he came across from his vantage point in the lobby.

Like many historic hotels over the past century, hard times fell on the Occidental. Business declined during the Great Depression, and motels began taking business away after World War II. The doors closed in 1986, and demolition by neglect seemed imminent. However, when Dawn and John Wexo bought the property in 1997 and began an exhaustive restoration process, the glamour of the Occidental shined through. False ceilings installed in the 1940s were removed to reveal original wainscoting and intricately embossed wall coverings. Decorated tin ceilings on the first floor proved to be in excellent condition. When the carpets were pulled up, wooden floors needed little repair. While years of neglect required new electrical wiring; new plumbing, heating, and cooling systems; and roof and ceiling repairs from water damage, overall the building was in better shape than many abandoned century-old structures. The reason for this and for the discovery of original furnishings and artifacts lies with former caretaker Margaret Smith. Margaret was the wife and mother of John and Al Smith, who won ownership of the Occidental Hotel in a poker game in 1918. Margaret was asked to take over running the hotel until John and Al could sell it. Instead, Margaret ran the hotel for fifty-eight years until she died in 1976 at the age of ninety-two. A frugal but loving caretaker, Margaret rarely threw anything away. Many of the photographs and artifacts stashed away by Margaret are on display today at the Occidental Hotel Museum.

The hotel itself has been lovingly restored thanks to Wexo and current owners David and Jackie Stewart. The Stewarts originally moved to Wyoming in 1977 and vacationed at the Occidental as a restful getaway. The couple began volunteering at the hotel when they moved to Clear Creek in 2002. The Stewarts invested in the Occidental in 2005 to continue renovation of the North Wing and increase the number of rentable rooms to eighteen. To meet the debt service on the building, special events—such as the "Thursday Night Jam"—were scheduled to bring in people and revenue. Today, the Occidental is a meeting place for the community. PBS has visited numerous times, using the Occidental to film various shows. *National Geographic Traveler* considers it one of the Top 129 Hotels in North America (2009 Stay List), and *TrueWest Magazine* awarded it the title of "Best Hotel in the West" twice.

Today, guests experience both authenticity and comfort during their stay at the Occidental Hotel. The Old West still lingers here and invites patrons to step back in time. Even the bullet holes in the saloon are original.

* * * * *

Profile: Kai'li's Restaurant: Tribute to a Hero
Santa Clara, Utah

http://www.kailisrestaurant.com

Tributes come in various forms. Herb and Wendy Basso, owners of Kai'li's Restaurant, honor the past and present in three unique ways. The Santa Clara couple purchased the Greek Revival building on Main Street in 2002 and lovingly preserved the 1870s adobe structure as a commercial home for several businesses and apartments upstairs. In 2012, the Bassos recognized the need for further rehabilitation and invested in refinishing the original floors, making additional repairs, stripping off layers of wallpaper, and adding central air conditioning. The Utah Heritage Foundation recognized their preservation effort with a Heritage Award in 2015. However, the respect for the past doesn't end with the restoration of the building.

Herb Basso, a Native Hawaiian, always loved to cook and decided that the renovated ground floor was perfect for his own restaurant. In respect to his culture, he named the restaurant after Herbert "Kailieha" Pililaau—Basso's uncle. In 1951, Pililaau was drafted—along with 4,000 other Hawaiians—to serve in the Korean War. A Christian of deep faith, Pililaau decided to put aside his reservations and fight in the war. He joined the 23rd Infantry Regiment as private first class, even volunteering as the company's automatic rifleman. Pililaau and company fought valiantly in the Battle of Bloody Ridge that August, yet his heroism would be recognized the following month.

Figure 8.10 Private First Class Herbert Ka'ili Pililaau display, Ka'ili's Restaurant—Santa Clara, Utah.

In the Battle of Heartbreak Ridge, as platoons of North Korean soldiers attacked and threatened to overrun the U.S. soldiers, Pililaau elected to stand ground and cover the withdrawal of his comrades. While his company safely retreated to lower ground, Pililaau pelted North Koreans first with ammunition, then with grenades, and finally with rocks until the enemy was on him. Even then, he did not give up, stabbing and punching North Korean soldiers before he was shot dead on September 17, 1951, shortly before his twenty-third birthday. The next day, U.S. soldiers found Pililaau's body and about forty North Korean soldiers he had killed in the area that he defended. President Harry Truman awarded the Congressional Medal of Honor to Pililaau's parents, recognizing him as the first Hawaiian to receive this prestigious award. A photo of Basso's uncle and a story of his heroics are on display at the restaurant.

Ka'ili's Restaurant pays tribute to the local community by serving fresh, locally grown food whenever possible. The Bassos operate two gardens in Santa Clara year-round—growing fresh herbs to flavor and garnish dishes, fruits and vegetables for salads, and sauces. Fresh flowers at the tables also come from the gardens, except in winter months. The historic granary on the property serves as overflow for dining and also as restaurant storage. Ka'ili's also supports local businesses by accessing produce from Frei's Fruit Market.

A historic building, a restaurant named after a national hero, and a business supporting other local businesses, Ka'ili's Restaurant has consciously made a commitment to respecting heritage and fostering sustainability. As Basso says, this is "a very special place with great food enjoyed with great company." Pililaau would be proud of his nephew.

* * * * *

Profile: Lucas, Kansas— A Welcoming Statement

http://www.lucaskansas.com

Founded in 1887, this quirky town of 407 (2010 census) is known as the "Grassroots Art Capital of Kansas." This distinctive welcome sign at the north end of Wilson Lake on the Post Rock Scenic Byway in north-central Kansas directs visitors to a thriving downtown.

"Distinctive signage makes people stop!" according to Connie Dougherty, director of the Lucas Chamber of Commerce. She continued, "They stop to photograph the sign and they stop in town to see what other unique things you have to see."[14]

Boasting the volunteer-built and -run Lucas Area Community Theatre, the Garden of Eden (an attraction since 1907, listed on the National Register of Historic Places), the Grassroots Art Center, and the Deeble Sculpture Garden, other notable attractions in Lucas include the World's Largest Collection of the World's Smallest Versions of the World's Largest Things Museum, the fourth-generation–operated Brant's Meat Market, and Miller's Park. To make sure bathrooms are available to visitors, local residents built Bowl Plaza as a public restroom with "Bling!" in 2012. Covered with locally created mosaics inside and out, Bowl Plaza was named the "Second Best Restroom in the United States" in 2014.[15]

Figure 8.11 Lucas Bowl—Lucas, Kansas.

The welcome sign cost $500 and took more than forty locals to construct; Bowl Plaza cost $117,000 and took locals four years to build. The Grassroots Arts Center served as administrative coordinators. Financial support for the Bowl Plaza Project came from the following:

Contributor	Cash	In-Kind
City of Lucas	$10,000	$15,000
Kansas Attraction Development Grant	$43,000	
Dane G. Hansen Foundation Grant	$5,000	
National Endowment for the Arts Grant	$10,000	
Merrill Foundation Grant	$2,000	
Toilet Seat Auction	$3,000	
Grassroots Arts Center	$3,500	
Land donation		$9,000
Landscaping (local volunteers)		$2,000
Artists (artistic design)		$2,500
Volunteers (labor, design, workshops)		$3,000
Bottles/mosaic materials (donated)		$2,000
Kansas Arts Commission (pending)[16]	$7,500	
Total = $117,000	$84,000	$33,500

"Lucas has always been fortunate to have people that could see the value a project would bring to Lucas and work together to accomplish it," says Dougherty. Lucas receives approximately 15,000 visitors annually. People from every state and seventy countries have signed the "Bowl Plaza" guest book. A group of volunteers maintain both the welcome sign and the Bowl Plaza.

★ ★ ★ ★ ★

Profile: Kansas City Library—The Community Bookshelf
Kansas City, Missouri

http://www.kclibrary.org/community-bookshelf

You can tell a lot about a book from its cover. The same can be said about a community: its appearance is what often defines our first impression. The Central Branch of the Kansas City Public

Library took this concept to heart and considered a way to mask its parking garage exterior with a more representative view than the standard concrete and pilings. In 2004, the library completed a "Community Bookshelf" to cover the south wall of its parking garage, located on 10th Street between Wyandotte Street and Baltimore Avenue.

The library invited Kansas City readers to suggest a list of representative books to reflect the entire city's story on a Mylar signboard. Suggestions for titles were solicited from the community through the library's website, the *Kansas City Star* newspaper, local bookstores, and schools. In March 2014, the Kansas City Public Library Board of Trustees selected forty-three titles for inclusion on twenty-two book spines measuring twenty-five by nine feet. Among them were two volumes of Kansas City–connected stories and a collection of children's stories as well as *Catch 22, Silent Spring, O Pioneers!, Cien Años de Soledad, Their Eyes Were Watching God, Fahrenheit 451, Adventures of Huckleberry Finn, The Collected Poems of Langston Hughes, To Kill a Mockingbird,* and *Charlotte's Webb.*

The Community Bookshelf is featured in a self-guided downtown walking tour of twenty-two commercial buildings dating from 1881 to 1950. With a mission of serving as "a doorway to knowledge for all people in our community," the Kansas City Public Library, established 1873, has extended this hospitality and education to visitors and residents alike.

* * * * *

Notes

1. Peter MacNulty and Cleverdon, *Handbook on Tourism Product Development* (2011). UN World Tourism Organization.
2. Correspondence with Kevin Kuharic, July 27, 2016.
3. Ibid.
4. A concept used by museums to display artifacts and objects on shelves sometimes called open study centers, similar to how a library has open stacks.
5. Correspondence with Kevin Kuharic, July 27, 2016.
6. Mark Twain comments at the Banquet of the St. Nicholas Society, as reported in the *New York Times* (December 7, 1990), http://www.twainquotes.com/19001207.html.
7. "What Is Cultural Intangible?" Intangible Cultural Heritage, UNESCO, http://www.unesco.org/culture/ich/doc/src/01851-EN.pdf.
8. UNESCO (n.d.), http://www.unesco.org/culture/ich/en/what-is-intangible-heritage-00003.
9. Museum Store Association, "Frequently Asked Questions" (n.d.), https://museumstoreassociation.org/about-msa/faqs/#toggle-id-3.
10. Shopping and the Cultural/Heritage Tourism Report (1999) Office of Travel and Tourism Industries, U.S. Department of Commerce http://tinet.ita.doc.gov. Archive #990316162013
11. Elizabeth Becker, author of *Overbooked: The Exploding Business of Travel and Tourism*, lecture in Savannah, Georgia, February 16, 2016.
12. National Heritage Area program (n.d.), http://www.nps.gov/heritageareas/FAQ.
13. Ibid.
14. Correspondence with Connie Dougherty, July 11, 2016.
15. In the fall of 2014, the Cintas Company sponsored a "Best Public Restroom" contest for the United States.
16. Grant pending for community arts project support.
17. Modified from Opportunities Unlimited (2014), http://www.opportunityguy.com.
18. L. Nguyen "Marketing Mix across Cultures: Standardization or Adaptation" (2011), Lahti University of Applied Sciences.

19. Modified from C. Hargrove Module 2, "Cultural Tourism: Impacting Communities Worldwide" (January 2013), University of British Columbia.
20. Input from Camille Ferguson, AIANTA, August 10, 2016.
21. P. Brink, "Experiencing America through Heritage Tourism," *Forum Journal* (Summer 1999), National Trust for Historic Preservation.
22. Ada L. Huxtable, *The Unreal America: Architecture and Illusion* (New York: New Press, 1997).
23. Ibid.
24. James H. Gilmore and B. Joseph Pine II, *Authenticity: What Consumers Really Want* (Cambridge, MA: Harvard Business School Press, 2007), pp. 250-51.

Chapter 9

Interpreting for Engagement

Look at things from the other person's point of view. Step outside yourself to discover what's important to someone else.

—Dale Carnegie, *The Leader in You*

The contemporary play *Hamilton: An American Musical* powerfully demonstrates the impact of relevant storytelling. With its hip-hop music and diverse cast, the 2016 Tony Award–winning play is attracting not only accolades but also new audiences eager to experience the musical— and learn more about one of our founding fathers and first secretary of the treasury. Based on Pulitzer Prize–winning author Ron Chernow's book, the play brings to life the issues and drama of the early immigrants, resonating with audiences today through their messages and content. The popularity and press coverage of the blockbuster Broadway musical have fostered several spin-off tours and programs at historic sites and destinations across the country. The Alexander Hamilton Awareness Society even developed an online database to locate "All Places Hamilton" by region (New York State, New Jersey, Pennsylvania, Philadelphia, and others).[1]

Every day, museums, historical societies, and cultural organizations seek to make their cause or purpose relevant and important to their respective audiences with the same level of engagement as patrons to *Hamilton: An American Musical*. The communication process that is designed to connect visitors to a site or place is called interpretation. Common techniques include tours, exhibits, lectures, interactive displays, podcasts, and other methods to engage audiences. Previous chapters focused on various audiences and their motivations or interests in traveling to historic and cultural activities. This chapter, on interpretation, identifies the content and delivery techniques most appropriate for each target market. The chapter explores the art and process of interpretation and the different strategies that organizations and sites can use to educate and engage audiences through high-quality, high-valued cultural heritage experiences. How to identify and create informative content, select the most appropriate techniques for conveying the information, and then develop the interpretive program is discussed thoroughly, with additional instruction and tools provided at the end of the chapter.

Tilden on Interpretation

Definition: An educational activity that aims to reveal meanings and relationships through the use of original objects, by firsthand experience, and by illustrative media, rather than simply to communicate factual information.

Corollaries used to strengthen the destination:

- Interpretation is the revelation of a larger truth
- Interpretation should capitalize mere curiosity for the enrichment of the human mind and spirit

Principles of Interpretation

1. Any interpretation that does not somehow relate what is being displayed or described to something within the personality or experience of the visitor will be sterile.
2. Information, as such, is not interpretation. Interpretation is revelation based on information. But they are entirely different things. However, all interpretation includes information.
3. Interpretation is an art, which combines many arts, whether the materials presented are scientific, historical, or architectural. Any art is in some degree teachable.
4. The chief aim of interpretation is not instruction but provocation.
5. Interpretation should aim to present a whole rather than a part and must address itself to the whole person rather than any phase.
6. Interpretation addressed to children (up to age of twelve) should not be a dilution of the presentation to adults but should follow a fundamentally different approach. To be at its best it will require a separate program.

Source: Freeman Tilden, National Park Service, *Interpreting Our Heritage*, 4th ed. (1957). Chapel Hill: The University of North Carolina Press.

What is interpretation? Several official definitions and organizations focus on this act. One of the founding fathers of interpretation was Freeman Tilden. In 1957, he published *Interpreting Our Heritage* as an instructive guide for National Park Service rangers and other resource managers on how to uncover relevant content and deliver valued visitor experiences; Tilden's book continues as one of the most informative guides on interpretation. His definition, corollaries, and principles are still applicable (and used) today.

In many ways, Tilden is responsible for casting aside the litany of boring names and dates as traditional guide presentations utilize new strategies for connected engagement. While Tilden's focus was initially on individual sites, interpretation has evolved to encompass entire destinations, select neighborhoods, and trails and routes (see table 9.1).

The National Association for Interpretation has modified Tilden's original definition to describe interpretation as a "mission-based communication process that forges emotional and intellectual connections between the interests of the audience and the meanings inherent in the resource."[2]

Table 9.1 The Evolution of Interpretation

Old	New
Names and dates	The story of "why"
Focus on "things"—artifacts, decor	The people and their lives
Passive	Interactive
Only the good	The good, the bad, the ugly
Static exhibits	Immersion of the scenes

The national organization has established *Standards and Practices for Interpretive Planning*[3] to help guide destinations and sites in developing their interpretive strategies (see table 9.2).

Destinations or host organizations often conduct a comprehensive interpretive planning process to establish the principles, themes, and strategies for developing and delivering quality experiences. A government agency, planning office, cultural or heritage organization, destination marketing organization, or community foundation may spearhead the interpretive planning process. Good interpretation should result in three outcomes: (1) provide a message that the visitor understands, (2) give a valued and relevant learning experience, and (3) achieve mission (and/or business or stewardship) objectives.[4] As with other planning processes, a key to success is ensuring that all appropriate stakeholders are engaged.

The interpretive process includes four key steps: (1) content investigation and prioritization, (2) audience analysis, (3) message development and delivery, and (4) evaluation. (This process condenses the National Association for Interpretation's recommended interpretive planning framework comprising management, message, market, mechanics, and media.) Conducted internally by a cultural or heritage institution or with the aid of consultants, the interpretive plan provides a long-term guide to effectively communicating key messages via appropriate formats to obtain maximum engagement with the visitor. Most important for any cultural heritage institution or destination is the completeness of the process, especially the investigation of content so that no relevant or important information is inadvertently missed.

> For every place man has walked—and places he hasn't walked—there is a story. That story can be made attractive for others if you can figure out what the story is and how to tell it.
> —Robert Billington, PhD, president, Blackstone Valley Tourism Council

Interpretive Process Step 1: Content Investigation and Prioritization

Identifying significant information to convey begins the process for creating an interpretation plan for a particular site or destination. Often, this information is readily available in archives, historical records, local newspapers (for periodically published articles), artifacts and collections, annual reports, interviews, and other documents maintained or cataloged by the organization. More broadly, buildings, landscapes, and streetscapes provide the foundation for understanding important social, industrial, environmental, political, diplomatic, intellectual, and economic history of a place. To begin the investigative process, create a list of all available resources. Culling

Table 9.2 National Association for Interpretation Standards and Practices for Interpretive Planning

Advocacy	Interpretive organizations must have advocates and be advocates for their resources.
Audience Analysis	Understanding the audience is critical to the success of the plan.
Civic Engagement	Successful interpretive plans usually include stakeholder involvement and/or public input.
Evaluation	Evaluation should be built into the planning process at multiple stages.
Management Objectives	Interpretation methods and content should align with management objectives.
Marketing Factors	Understanding the market climate and niche can help in achieving success.
Media Descriptions	The interpretive plan clearly indicates the mix of media required to convey the message(s) to specific audiences.
Message Elements	Message elements include central theme, subthemes, and storylines. Themes and message elements clearly align with specific interpretive plan objectives.
Operational Commitment	The best plan cannot be implemented without (financial and operational) support.
Partnerships	Most interpretive programs/organizations require partners for cost-effective operations.
Staff/Volunteer Training	Staff and volunteers are usually responsible for implementation of the plan. The interpretive plan should identify specific outcomes and/or impacts for training.
Stakeholder Involvement	Stakeholders may include partners, volunteers, staff, governance, user groups and others. An engagement strategy (for updates, review progress) can help ensure success.
Terminology	Consistent vocabulary helps avoid costly misunderstandings.
Visitor Experience	Ultimately, the interpretive plan defines and clearly describes the visitor experience. Optimally, it should provide opportunities for peak experiences and self actualization, encourage a commitment from visitor beyond immediate experience (further thought or action), and be planned holistically to include the decision to visit, the entry, connections, the exit, and resulting commitment to action/change in attitude or behavior.

Source: National Association for Interpretation, https://www.interpnet.com/docs/BP-Planning-Jan09.pdf.

through currently available material can reveal perhaps overlooked information, data of interest to particular audiences, or even insights about particular people, places, or products that may resonate with (or parallel) a particular issue today.

Peter Shaffer's Broadway play *Lettice and Lovage* brought comedic focus to the challenge of staying true to content and on message. The 1990 play starred Dame Maggie Smith as the flamboyant docent who often exaggerated her narrative at the house museum where she gave tours, much to the chagrin of the heritage interpretation specialist. The declaration that "nothing happened here" thrust the play into a detective-style exploration to uncover little-known—sometimes tawdry and macabre—facts about the people who lived, worked, and died at the English country estate. This play resonated with its emphasis on authentic research for historic sites and making the past more engaging for the visitor.

Certainly, information needs to be local or relevant to your cause or intent to create the greatest impact and connect with the audience. Traditionally, the more impactful messages have a personal connection to your community, your organization, or your project. A recent trend is to use heritage as a vehicle to make the past relevant to the present.[5] When conducting research, here are some questions to answer:

- Why is the site or destination significant?
- What makes this place or site different from all others?
- What are potential sources of information to tap (not currently used)?
- Was the site or destination featured in local society columns or photographs?
- Is there a business, political, or environmental connection to explore?
- Are descendants of the original families, owners, or workers currently living? Do they have diaries, records, or other written documents to review? Have oral histories been recorded of these individuals?

Think broadly and delve into all aspects of a site or destination. Some of the most interesting stories are about little-known (or unknown) facts resulting from a particular voice or angle. For example, the perspective of a gardener or a local artist is an unusual lens not always shared in traditional interpretation of a historic site or structure. Is there an individual or group (labor, social, sporting, religious, or fraternal) that has a unique or different perspective of historical events and activities? These connections are important when developing the content for presentation and sharing; their voices also may attract a new potential audience.

The investigation process should not be hurried, as it is the foundation for your interpretive program. Develop a list of questions to ask and answer around a particular topic or broadly for a site and then seek out information from a wide spectrum of sources. Conduct focus groups, record conversations with community thought leaders or individuals, search through archives and records, and delve into collections of artifacts to uncover potential information for sharing. This investigation phase may require traveling to state or national archives, other museums or societies connected by a person or industry, and/or destinations with similar topography or architecture. Grants from the National Endowment for the Humanities can often provide the academic expertise to conduct extensive research if content is not currently available. Local universities and colleges may also be good sources to tap, as may content is independent historians and field experts.

As content is uncovered, review the research and information to see if themes or topics begin to arise. Interpretive planning sorts out the most significant stories or themes for further

Figure 9.1 UNESCO City of Literature logo—Iowa City, Iowa.

investigation and development. Can content be bundled as a more robust and rich collection of information and stories when coupled with artifacts or tangible assets? Has new information been identified to add to or debunk previous content? (This is often the case at archaeological sites or as ancestral documents are discovered.) Curious researchers may unveil a new thread of information that links to other material or that completes a missing piece of a historical puzzle. As identified in the profile of Iowa City, Iowa, recognized that its literary foundation provided a unique selling proposition. Read Iowa City's profile at the end of this chapter to learn more about how they present and interpret their literary heritage for residents, authors, and visitors.

The end result for this step is a primary interpretive theme to focus on when developing programs and tools to educate and engage the visitor. A main theme may also yield related subthemes or supporting themes to broaden the content messaging and relevance to audiences. Interpretation is a key component of any national park unit or National Heritage Area. Typically, interpretive themes are based on an organization's mission statement and derived from the foundation statement in a required management or comprehensive plan.

The Mississippi Hills National Heritage Area (MHNHA) has an overarching theme, "The Mississippi Hills—Where Appalachia Meets the Delta," and four primary themes for interpretation: Native American heritage, African American heritage, the Civil War, and the arts. Subthemes are developed into interpretive statements to describe their contribution and focus. Below are two examples of how these themes and subthemes are crafted for an interpretive plan. Mississippi Hills National Heritage Area Management Plan: Interpretive Plan (July 2014), p. 58.

Theme: Native American Heritage

Interpretive Statement: Complex Native American societies that inhabited the region for thousands of years before European exploration and settlement have left physical vestiges on the landscape in the form of mounds, archaeological sites, and traces, which help tell their stories of cultural development and conflict, among each other and with the United States.

Subtheme: Prehistoric Era

Interpretive Statement: The region's rich ecosystem with numerous streams provided sufficient sustenance to nurture Native American cultures during the Paleoindian, Archaic, Woodland, and Mississippean periods that culminated in relatively complex mound-building societies prior to European occupation.

Subtheme: Historic Era

Interpretive Statement: The MHNHA is perhaps the most significant region in the country to the Chickasaw Nation, which included the 1832 Pontotoc Creek Treaty whereby the Chickasaws gave up all lands east of the Mississippi River in exchange for lands west of the Mississippi.

Theme: African American Heritage

Interpretive Statement: The complete story of African American history in the United States can be told through the MHNHA, as much of the most significant facets of it occurred within the region. That story progresses from slavery, to freedom and contraband camps, to the formation of United States Colored Troop (USCT) regiments, to admirable performance of USCT soldiers at battles such as Brice's Crossroads, to the Reconstruction era political achievements of Hiram Revels and the establishment of Shaw University (now Rust College), to the twentieth century Civil rights gains through nationally prominent heroes such as Ida B. Wells and James Meredith.

Subtheme: Freedom Arrives

Interpretive Statement: The Union Army's occupation of North Mississippi beginning in the spring of 1862 resulted in freedom for most of the area's slaves. The Contraband camp in Corinth was the first model for such camps that was replicated by countless Contraband camps across the South by the end of the war.

Subtheme: Reconstruction and Post-Reconstruction

Interpretive Statement: Following the Civil War, the Hills region saw some of the most significant—yet short term—educational and political gains for African Americans in the country, including the establishment of Shaw University in Holly Springs in 1866 (later Rust College) and Hiram Revels filling the U.S. Senate seat once held by former Confederate President Jefferson Davis. Rust College graduate Ida B. Wells became one of the country's most important civil rights activists and writers in the early twentieth century.

Subtheme: Civil Rights—An Arduous Journey

Interpretive Statement: The Hills region is one of the most significant places in the country relative to the civil rights movement, including the early activism of Ida B. Wells, James Meredith's tumultuous enrollment into the University of Mississippi in 1962, and Grenada's

1966 Southern Christian Leadership Conference, which featured icons such as Dr. Martin Luther King Jr., Andrew Young, and singer Joan Baez.

Additional interpretive statements for themes and subthemes for the Civil War and the Arts are also provided in the MHNHA interpretive plan. The plan also outlines current approaches to interpretation by theme and location, and also recommended approaches to interpretation to link themes, sites, and events. Specific strategies describe how the MHNHA will research, create, and educate target audiences utilizing a variety of tools and media. Mississippi Hills National Heritage Area Interpretive Plan: http://www.mississippihills.org/wp-content/uploads/2015/06/MHNHA%20Management%20PlanSMALL%202_1_15.pdf

Interpretive Process Step 2: Audience Analysis

This step was discussed in chapter 3 but should be considered again in light of the information gathered in step 1 of the interpretive planning process. Which audiences are most inclined to be receptive to or interested in the main themes or topics? Are there themes or topics that require

With assistance from Randi Korn & Associates and funding from the Allen and Kelli Questrom Foundation, the Dallas Museum of Art conducted seminal research in 2008 to determine "levels of engagement with art" for current visitors and teachers. The study built on previous research to better understand the behavior of various audiences and their preferred interpretive tools for education and enlightenment. Analysis revealed four clusters of visitors and their preferences for meaningful experiences:

- Tentative observers—New to art and most interested if they can connect it to a personal interest
- Curious participants—Active art consumers who like to take guided tours and use reading areas in the galleries and want to connect with works of art in various ways, including performances and readings
- Discerning independents—Knowledgeable about art but like to view art on their own terms without explanations and interpretations
- Committed enthusiasts—Confident, enthusiastic, and emotionally and intellectually connected to works of art and desire interpretive materials; some want to see a diverse audience (including children)

The research findings provided new insights into the preferences of the museum's customers and fostered creation of new interpretive programming and tools to achieve the learning objectives of both visitor and institution. A "Late Night Series" (third Fridays, 6:00 p.m. to midnight) caters to Millennials, working professionals, and insomniacs. Lectures, performances, and related films expand the theme of art exhibitions. An expanded array of social activities (demonstrations, performances, and readings) cultivate the curious participants. The DMA app also provides access to more than 23,000 works of art and updates users on what's happening at the museum. For mor information, visit https://www.dma.org/sites/default/files/file_attachments/dma_310864.pdf

additional investigation if focused on a particular market? The selection of audience will also dictate how best to deliver the message and what tools and techniques will resonate with the particular group. For example, Millennials are much more inclined to use technology as part of their learning process.

Selecting key audiences—the individuals or groups of people or organizations—to cultivate or keep as customers is vital to making sure that the programming can be designed appropriately. Armed with visitor profiles, motivations, experience needs, and expectations, the site or destination can proceed with creating compelling programs, exhibits, trails, or other interpretive strategies.

Interpretive Process Step 3: Message, Media Development, and Delivery

As themes are set and audiences identified, step 3 focuses on finding the right messages to marry with the right delivery tools (media) to achieve the desired learning, behavioral, and emotional objectives. Interpretation has proven impacts on visitation. According to certified interpretation specialist and veteran destination interpretation planner John Veverka, every dollar spent on interpretive programs and services yields about $5 in benefits to the organization or business.[8] Quality interpretation is founded in fact but delivered through varied means and methods. According to Veverka, the interpretive planning process traditionally has three objectives for tourists. These objectives focus on what is hoped will happen to the tourist through the interpretive experience.

1. *Learning Objectives*

Learning objectives are achieved through successful and powerful education. Successful education happens when information *of interest to the tourist* is used to provoke tourists, relate information (about the site or destination that is relevant) to their lives, and reveal lessons they will remember. Learning objectives change what a visitor *knows*.

2. *Emotional Objectives*

Emotional objectives are realized when information is presented in inspiring and motivational ways. Market research helps destinations understand what visitors care about and how information is presented to them (as a personal story, through hands-on exhibits, through performance, or simply as quiet reflection) so that they can put the event into the perspective of their own daily lives. Emotional objectives change the way a visitor *feels*.

3. *Behavioral Objectives*

Behavioral objectives are accomplished when visitors are compelled to action. The behavioral changes usually occur after a strong learning and emotional experience, and a connection is formed with the site, destination, or organization. Behavioral objectives compel visitors to *act*.[9]

Content development offers an intentional way to convey important messages or calls to action to visitors and stakeholders (elected officials, donors, and community leaders). Personal stories, in particular, captivate, compel us to relate, become introspective, and then share.[10] Good storytelling and presentation skills are paramount for the guided tour. Data can inform the head, but storytelling tugs at the heart or a person's emotional core.[11]

Various mediums are available for interpretation, especially to share content in ways beyond the personal guided tour. Technological advancements bring information to the fingertips of all mobile device users (via apps, podcasts, and responsive websites). Augmented reality, blogs, social media, video, and other digital media are increasingly popular tools for interpreting sites and locations. More advanced technology can also transform flat visual exhibits into three-dimensional imagery or holograms to convey what a site may have looked like (particularly useful for helping visitors better understand archaeological sites or ruins). Traditional interpretation techniques are still utilized, particularly the historic marker, outdoor wayside exhibits interpreting the site via text and graphics, printed brochures, special events, thematic programming, reenactments, lectures, concerts, films, and books.

The development phase for each of these techniques is unique and requires consideration of space, visitor access, budget, and staffing. Some tools are more labor intensive (tour guides, requiring both training and staffing for delivery); others require extensive creative expertise. The complexity of the message may also dictate the choice of medium. The budget also can impact the decision for more affordable low-tech options of information delivery. Audience preferences or uses may dictate fabrication, as program tools for children—especially when interactive exhibits or replicas of artifacts are considered—need to be durable and safe. An interpretive plan will highlight the best strategy to reach the audience and achieve the desired outcomes. Stratford Hall, profiled in a case study at the end of this chapter, took a hard look at its own interpretation during a two-day symposium in 2009. The findings helped the house museum become more customer-centric.

Figure 9.2 Great House, Stratford Hall—Stratford, Virginia.

Delving into interpretive subthemes can increase the opportunity to offer programs that entice visitors to return for more substantive learning. The sweet spot where message and media intersect for a powerful connective experience may compel the visitor to action or seek additional instruction. Evaluating the impact of interpretive programs is important to ensure that the techniques resonate with audiences and achieve the desired outcomes. Monitoring their use and effect on audiences can help planners determine the most valued interpretive strategies and techniques. This data may also help inform additional needs or instruction to achieve interpretive goals. As new audiences are cultivated, markets evolve, technology advances, and sites mature, the interpretation program may need refreshing or further evaluation. Recognizing the important role of Hispanic Texans to the Lone Star State, the Texas Historical Commission (THC) set out to compile a comprehensive guide about places and people of significance. The profile of the agency's new guide "Hispanic Texans: Journey from Empire to Democracy" at the end of this chapter shines a light on this important segment of the population and their stories past to present.

Figure 9.3 *Hispanic Texans Travel Guide*—Texas Historical Commission.

One of THC's signature heritage tourism efforts is the award-winning Texas Heritage Trails Program. Since 1998, the THC has helped establish the ten independent heritage trail organizations that work at the local and regional levels to develop and promote heritage tourism. A large component of the program funding came from federal transportation enhancement dollars accessed through the Texas Department of Transportation. Those funds, which are no longer available, allowed THC to produce the trail region travel guides as well as various thematic guides. In 2010, THC significantly expanded and redesigned an older African American heritage guide to produce *African Americans in Texas: A Lasting Legacy*. Following that model, THC developed *Hispanic Texans* and the *German Texans* mobile tour in 2017.

Chapter Summary

As organizations, sites, and destinations seek to attract new audiences—Millennials and underrepresented audiences (particularly ethnic groups not currently frequenting mainstream museums and historic sites), interpretation that relates to the customer and creates both intellectual and emotional connections will become even more important. Understanding how best to build and establish this connectivity requires research. Recognizing that all customers are not the same or don't learn the same way will require cultural heritage institutions to identify and utilize various techniques to interpret their content and deliver relevant messages. This interpretive planning becomes an integral part of the cultural heritage tourism planning process and the foundation for experience development and engagement.

* * * * *

Profile: Iowa City, Iowa—Power of the Word

http://www.iowacityofliterature.org

Seeking out the homes of favorite authors or visiting places mentioned in books bring the pages to life. Well-known sites, such as William Faulkner's Rowan Oak in Oxford, Mississippi, or Ernest Hemingway's home in Key West, Florida, receive thousands of visitors each year. These literary landmarks and others connect readers to the author through artifacts and place-based stories. Other cities capitalize on their role in novels to attract literary tourists. Savannah, Georgia, built a whole tour program based on the popularity of the 1994 John Berendt book (and 1997 film of the same title) *Midnight in the Garden of Good and Evil*. Some destinations—such as Iowa City, Iowa—recognize the importance of literary history to its identity and secure that designation to recognize this legacy.

Since 1936, this Midwestern town has hosted the Iowa Writers' Workshop on the University of Iowa campus. Recognized as the world's first master of fine arts degree program in creative writing, the Iowa Writers' Workshop played a substantial role in how literature, first in America and then around the world, evolved to its present-day form.[6] The pedigree of the University of Iowa is impressive; graduates and faculty have won more than twenty-five Pulitzer Prizes in literature since 1955. Authors Kurt Vonnegut, Philip Roth, John Irving, and Flannery O'Connor either lived, taught, or studied in Iowa City. An international writing program, a series of literary festivals, libraries, eleven literary presses, bookshops, and reading programs build on that strong heritage. According to noted poet and playwright Paul Engle, "All writers in the world ought to come to Iowa City."

Figure 9.4 Writers' Workshop, Dey House, University of Iowa—Iowa City, Iowa.

To showcase this literary heritage and excellence, community leaders applied for—and received—the UNESCO City of Literature designation in 2008. With this recognition, Iowa City became the only city in the United States and the third worldwide (Edinburgh, Scotland, and Melbourne, Australia, were named before Iowa City) to be an official City of Literature and included among the 116 members of the global Creative Cities Network as of 2016. Criteria for the Creative Cities and City of Literature designation include the following:

- "Existence, at the time of application, of a development strategy or actions and initiatives aimed at strengthening the role of creativity in the socio-economic development of the city and in urban renewal
- Historical importance and place of the creative field concerned for the candidate city as well as within its contemporary economic and social context
- Potential contribution of the cultural and creative assets of the candidate city, particularly in the creative field concerned, towards achieving the Network's objectives
- Expertise of the city in organizing local, national and/or international fairs, conferences, exhibitions and other activities aimed at professionals as well as the general public."[7]

The designation allows Iowa City to celebrate and promote its rich literary history and current programming. A staff of two oversee the nonprofit organization, funded by the City of Iowa City, the University of Iowa, other civic entities, and donors and sponsors, and directs its programs,

Figure 9.5 One Book Two Book Children's Literature Festival—Iowa City, Iowa.

outreach, and networking. Since its designation, the city has added extensive literary programming and both events run by the UNESCO organization, such as the One Book Two Book Children's Literature Festival, and those run by others, such as the Mission Creek Festival and the Witching Hour.

"Iowa City didn't need UNESCO to tell us we were a City of Literature. Anyone who has spent any time here already is aware of that fact. But the designation does help us to tell that story to those outside the area or who are less familiar with our country's literary culture," said John Kenyon, executive director of the Iowa City UNESCO City of Literature organization. "Recognition from a respected international organization like UNESCO validates what we say about our community and can raise awareness globally. It also has empowered residents to pursue audacious ideas. New festivals, new nonprofit organizations, writing groups, and other programs have popped up since we earned the designation, enhancing what already was one of the best literary communities in the world. It also has helped us to build more and stronger bridges with other literary cities around the world as we collaborate with other members of our network," he continued. Time to book a trip to Iowa City!

★ ★ ★ ★ ★

Profile: Stratford Hall
Stratford, Virginia

http://www.stratfordhall.org

Since first introduced by Mount Vernon in 1852, the docent-led house tour has been the mainstay of historic house programming. A stagnant model for more than a century, the rise in competition—both from new museums and other attractions—led, in part, to declining attendance and lackluster reviews. Changing audience expectations, expensive preservation standards, and over-head costs also contributed to lower visitation and financial instability.

Stratford Hall, the eighteenth-century home of the Lees of Virginia and birthplace of Robert E. Lee, was not immune to these trends. The site encompasses around 1,900 acres along the Potomac River, including the Great House, a public dining room, a gift shop, a research library, and a visitor center. Guests can also stay overnight in modern guest houses and more rustic cabins. To identify solutions, the Robert E. Lee Memorial Association (owners and operators of Stratford Hall) hosted a two-day "Rediscovering the Historic House" symposium in October 2009 using its own site as a case study. The findings became a road map for implementing new techniques and strategies to make the site more customer-centric, more engaged with the community, more in-viting to nontraditional audiences, and more interactive. The art of storytelling, gaming strategies, smartphone technologies, sensory elements, and new media content are all part of enhancing the visitor experience.

Stratford Hall receives approximately 28,000 visitors each year. School groups are prevalent from March to May, families visit mostly in summer months, and seniors and empty nesters frequent the site in fall. The house is open year round. Located two hours from Washington, D.C., and forty-five minutes southeast of Fredericksburg, Virginia, visitors purposely decide to visit Stratford Hall. Knowing their visitors are already motivated by history, decorative arts, or the Civil War (to name a few), the staff is keenly focused on better understanding peoples' interests for greater engagement.

A "Geek Tour" is now available to visitors as a result of the curator's and education staff's interest in quirky facts—from how people went to the bathroom to what you can learn in a single carpet fiber or how historic paint is made—and the interest by visitors to learn more of these historic fun facts. The staff film pieces of stories of interest to them ("staff picks") that don't fit anywhere else in the tour, make a video of the content, upload them to the app, and then change the tour. The program is constantly evolving, keeping it fresh for visitors and staff. The digital "Geek Tour" has influenced the museum's use of social media and provided the staff an opportunity to share why they love the museum and what often can't be seen on a tour—what's under the bed, behind the door, viewed from the chimney stack, and so on.

"Using different storytelling methods and using technology are two ways we hope to engage new audience segments," says Abigail Newkirk, director of interpretation and education. "We are not trained digital content producers so we focus on the stories rather than a polished video clip," she continued.[12] A new landscape app allows visitors to record audio stops and add them to the tour. Two apps are available—one for people with their own smartphones and another for access on devices provided by Stratford.

Events are a mainstay for attracting new audiences and repeat visitors, with visitations per event ranging from thirty to 5,000. The Fourth of July event draws a lot of families, especially because the site is free to the public on that holiday. Robert E. Lee's birthday is also a free day, with high attendance from first-time visitors. The staff overlay other activities, especially on free days, to help visitors understand the bounty of experiences available—enticing them with a reason to re-turn. More than a third of the visitors to the Fourth of July event engaged in other activities while they visited the beach or the gristmill or toured the Great House.

Figure 9.6 School group looking for fossils on the beach, Stratford Hall—Stratford, Virginia.

Some programs have been around for years. A Grandparent/Grandchild Summer Camp offers multigenerational activities packed into a three-day all-inclusive on-site package. The interactive program often attracts repeat visits (sometimes four years in a row) and includes flashlight tours, a bonfire, and intimate engagement with the site. The popular Wine and Oyster Festival offers a distinctive way to enjoy the grounds each September; *Virginia Wine Lovers Magazine* named it "Best of" in 2016.

Figure 9.7 Gristmill, Stratford Hall—Stratford, Virginia.

Stratford Hall is exploring more programming and interpretation about its natural history. A new paleontology program started as a result of finding a six-foot whale's skull on the grounds. Utilizing various historic resources reports, heritage landscape plans, and archaeological studies, staff engage visitors in on-site learning about the site's geology as part of the broader site experience.

Since the organization attracts a wide range of visitors, marketing communications must utilize multiple platforms. The traditional e-newsletter still appeals to older audiences, while videos are becoming increasingly important. "We have a digital footprint across a lot of different platforms," says Jim Schepmoes, director of marketing and public relations.[13] Facebook, Twitter, and Instagram are all important media for Stratford Hall.

"Our job is to generate authentic content and make it both available and engaging. Social media allows us to push information to existing and new audiences," says Newkirk. "We can also use the forum for explaining why changes are made, especially as we learn more about the site. It becomes an opportunity to engage with our online community and generate a conversation; hopefully, they are inspired to care about the story and care about the museum—not just a one-time visit."[14]

* * * * *

Profile: Hispanic Texans: Journey from Empire to Democracy

Texas Historical Commission
http://www.thc.texas.gov/public/upload/publications/hispanic-heritage-travel-guide.pdf

The Texas Historical Commission (THC) recognizes that in the past fifty years, cultural identity has become even more complicated. With this publication, the THC set out to introduce the first 500 years of the rich and colorful Hispanic experience in Texas.[15] The guide also celebrates the important Hispanic contributions to the Lone Star State's birth and growth while recognizing their hardships and challenges. This one-hundred-page guide for heritage travelers showcases sixty-one sites of Hispanic significance across the state. Specific sites include designated National Historic Landmarks, listings on the National Register of Historic Places, recorded Texas historic landmarks, state antiquities landmarks, Texas historical subject markers, designated historic cemeteries, and the THC's own historic sites. Historical context in this colorful and comprehensive guide is organized according to seven themes: Spanish settlement of Texas; independence; civil rights; architecture and urban design; immigration, industry, and commerce; and military service.

The complementary mobile tour that was developed concurrently with the print guide includes additional sites but also, more significantly, the ability to enrich the visitor experience with video, audio, and historic images. Ten scripted videos relate the historical context using a storytelling approach illustrated through artwork and historic images. The field video on such topics as the 1966 Starr County Farm Workers' Strike, Club Victoria, the Sheep Shearers, and Del Rio's School District Battles feature compelling stories told through individuals' personal experiences and heritage. The THC promotes the mobile tour through social media channels by featuring appropriate videos to commemorate an anniversary or celebrate an event. This strategy has increased the agency's Facebook following, as these videos are shared beyond the existing preservation audience, often garnering thousands of views and significant shares. Texas Time Travel Tours can be accessed on the Web or downloaded to iOS or Android devices (http://www.thc.texas.gov/explore-texas).

The THC, working with scholars and site professionals, researched more than 1,000 architectural and visitor sites beginning in 2013. Contractors and a Texas scholar assisted with writing and photography. THC conducted extensive editing in-house and with several subject matter experts. Design, Spanish translation, and printing took more than a year with the guide launching in April 2015. THC produced the guide to help Texans and non-Texans understand the impact and influence of Hispanic culture on the state. The Texas Department of Transportation's Statewide Transportation Enhancement Program provided funding together with THC matching funds for printing of the 2015 guide, totaling $267,767 for the English version and $110,574 for the Spanish version.

"Texas would not be Texas without the influence of Hispanic leaders and citizens, whose legacies form an essential pillar of Texas history," said Mark Wolfe, THC's executive director. "The THC's new travel guide—our biggest and most comprehensive cultural heritage guide yet—allows travelers to explore places statewide and discover their own connections to the diverse and deeply rooted Hispanic history of Texas," Wolfe continued. The educational component derived from the guide is critical, but ultimately, all of the THC guides are produced to maximize the economic impact of heritage tourism as the means for protecting the state's historic sites and communities.

General Interpretive Plan Outline

I.   Introduction and Scope of the Plan.
A. What was the scope of work the plan was to cover?

II.   Main Interpretive Theme and Subthemes.
(These themes are derived from focus workshops and site resource analysis.) Main interpretive theme and rationale.
A. Main subthemes and rationale.
B. Interpretive story-line flow bubble diagram.

III. Total Interpretive Program/Services Objectives (Learn, Feel, Do).
(This is for the total interpretive program/services effort—site and/or visitor center combined. This usually comes from a focus workshop, and edited based on the interpretive site resources review.)
A. Learning objectives
B. Behavioral objectives
C. Emotional objectives

IV.   Visitor Analysis.
(This is usually based on existing visitor data, as doing new visitor surveys is both time consuming and expensive.) Sections of this part of the plan can include:
A. *Visitation numbers and trends over the past three to five years.* Graph these data.
B. *Basic market profile.* Who are the visitors, where are they traveling from, how long are they staying, gender and age variables, etc.
C. *Visitor experience desires or focus.* Specify why they are visiting this site.
D. *Seasonal visitation trends or issues.*
E. *School group and curriculum based interpretive planning needs and issues.*
F. *Visitor management issues.* Relate to behavioral objectives.

V.   Individual Site Interpretive Inventory and Story Development Forms.
A. *Site resource location/inventory map.* This map would show the locations of each interpretive site, feature, facility, etc. that an interpretive planning form set would be completed for (existing or proposed).
B. *Interpretive site index list.* This is a list of all of the interpretive sites inventoried and included in the interpretive planning form sets that follow.
C. *Interpretive planning form sets.* This information is for each interpretive site inventoried including orientation sites, facilities, trails, demonstration areas, historic sites, natural resource areas, etc. (existing or proposed).
For each planning form set include:
    a. Site Inventory Form:
       1. Site index number (keyed to map)
       2. Site name
       3. Site location (reference site index map, etc.)
       4. Site description (refer to photos if available)Interpretive significance (why are we interpreting this site?)Story Development Form Set:
       5. Main interpretive theme/topic for each individual site.
       6. Site objectives. *These are physical development objectives such as building a stair way, add a viewing deck, etc.*

Figure 9.8 General interpretive plan outline.

7. Interpretive program/services objectives. *These are the specific objectives (learn, feel, or do) that interpretive programs, services, or media are to accomplish at this specific site.*

8. Recommended interpretive media for this location. *This is a list of the interpretive media that could best be used to accomplish the stated objectives (i.e., self-guiding trail, interpretive panel, outdoor demonstration, guided walk, exhibit in a visitor center, etc.).*

9. Any budget issues or estimates. *This helps make each individual interpretive planning form set a "mini" work plan for each individual site or feature that is part of the interpretive plan.*

VI. Five-Year Implementation and Operations Strategy/Matrix.
This includes: site index number; each interpretive media or site development needs; fiscal year for implementation; estimated cost for each site/item listed. This allows us to plan priorities and costs for actually implementing the total interpretive plan five years down the road.

VII. Evaluation Recommendations.
How will you know if the interpretive media you are going to purchase actually works (accomplishes its objectives), such as pretesting interpretive panels in draft form etc.

VIII. Appendices as Needed.

Note: This includes the minimum content that nay interpretive planning document should contain. A different set of planning forms are used for visitor center/museum exhibit planning.

Source: John Veverka & Associates, http://www.heritageinterp.com/interpretive_plan_outline.html.

Figure 9.8 *(continued)*

Notes

1. AllThingsHamilton.com, an information portal to Alexander Hamilton, http://allthingshamilton.com/index.php/alexander-hamilton/all-places-hamilton/77-aph-additional-locations/175-aph-other-locations.
2. National Association of Interpretation, *Standards and Practices of Interpretive Planning* (2009). http://www.interpret.com/nai/docs/BP-Planning-Jan09.pdf.
3. Ibid.
4. J. Veverka, as referenced in Cultural Tourism Workshop for University of British Columbia (2012).
5. P. Newton, "7 Top Storytelling Trends" (December 2014), http://www.intelligenthq.com/marketing/7-top-storytelling-trends,
6. City of Literature, http://www.cityofliterature.com/cities-of-literature/cities-of-literature/iowa.
7. http://en.unesco.org/creative-cities/sites/creative-cities/files/Designation_Procedure_2015Call_UNESCO_Creative_Cities_Network.pdf.
8. J. Veverka, interpretation services proposal to State of Kansas Scenic Byways Program (2013).
9. Ibid.
10. M. Smith, "The Storytelling Trend" (May 2012), http://proofbranding.com/the-storytelling-trend.
11. H. Monarth, "The Irresistible Power of Storytelling as a Strategic Business Tool," *Harvard Business Review* (March 2014), https://hbr.org/2014/03/the-irresistible-power-of-storytelling-as-a-strategic-business-tool.

12. Conversation with Abigail Newkirk and Jim Schepmoes, July 8, 2016.
13. Ibid.
14. Ibid.
15. Texas Historical Commission, "Hispanic Texans: Journey from Empire to Democracy," p. 6, http://www. thc.texas.gov/public/upload/publications/hispanic-heritage-travel-guide.pdf.

Chapter 10

Funding Your Focus

Making money is art and working is art and good business is the best art.

—Andy Warhol

The important decision about funding your focus (vision, mission, and goals) is defining the need for funding. Do you want to convert an existing building into an attraction? Do you want to generate revenue to fund operations? Is identifying funding sources for new exhibits a priority? All of these projects and activities may be funded by different sources on varied giving cycles.

Several funding sources exist for place-based projects and cultural heritage tourism if you know where (and when) to look for sources at the national, state, and local levels. Private sector funding can also yield high results if the "ask" is a good fit. In fact, crowdfunding sites, such as Kickstarter and Kiva, have proven the power of individual giving to fund specific projects. Capital campaigns for large acquisitions typically capture both individual investments and contributions with well-planned case statements. In-kind donations—in the form of services or products—may also assist with the bottom line.

Today, most organizations and planners recognize the value of a diversified funding approach to sustain cultural heritage tourism, especially given the volatility of "soft money"—grants, endowments, and donations—and the time line required for longer-term financing options (bonds, specially designated taxes, and capital campaigns). In this chapter, the various funding options for cultural heritage tourism, as well as revenue generation from earned income, are explored.

Understanding when and whom to ask is important to funding your focus as well as building a continuous revenue stream to support—and sustain—existing projects.

Partnership is the most important thing you can do, especially if you have limited resources.
—Rosemary McCormick, publisher, *Cultural Traveler Guide*

Establishing a Funding Plan

A failure by many institutions and agencies is to "chase the money," letting sources of money dictate the project scope or activity. This approach may help satisfy short-term needs but often diverts funding away from priority projects (to achieve the long-term vision). These funds, often a one-time grant or donation, may be used to save a structure or help a start-up but then do not cover ongoing operations or maintenance. Without defining all funding needs and sources to satisfy important project phases (development, launch and ongoing operation and possible future growth or enhancement), the maximum outcomes may not be realized. The first step in funding your focus is to understand the full cost required to accomplish the desired result.

It is also important to review funding for cultural heritage tourism—either as a specific project or at the destination level—in the context of its overall economic infrastructure. As stated in a recent UNESCO fund-raising proposal, "The historic environment is a key driver of footfall to many tourism destinations, but on its own delivers few economic benefits."[1] Therefore, most cultural and historic sites cannot sustain operations and consistently deliver quality visitor experiences on tourism admissions or program fees alone. However, they can be the catalyst for increasing spending on other business products and services—hotels, restaurants, retail shops, tour companies, transportation, and so on. Understanding the potential contribution that the renovated historic site or new cultural attraction can provide to the overall destination experience and revenue base (through tax generation and consumptive spending) is important to factor into the return on investment. A dynamic cultural heritage infrastructure, combined with strong tourism infrastructure, is the sustainable model most destinations seek when focusing on cultural heritage tourism.[2] Working together, they create the revenue and foot traffic required to grow at a sustainable level.

A funding plan is initiated once a project has been identified. For example, a historic school is now vacant and needs renovation, but a feasibility study deemed it perfect for a performing arts and community center. The questions to ask in creating a funding plan include the following:

- Who owns the site currently? (include purchase price or transfer of title costs [if it is to be deeded to a new owner])
- What is the cost to restore the building into its new use? (include costs of architectural plans, contractor fees, permits, construction costs, landscaping, streetscape, and signage)
- What is the cost to operate the facility? (include staff, maintenance, programming, marketing, and general operations)
- What revenue can be generated from the site? (facility rental, retail sales, ticket sales, membership fees, and other sales)
- Will the site or facility generate revenue for other businesses, services, and the community at large? (sales tax revenue, jobs, and vendor agreements)

Some of this information may have been determined in the feasibility study or during case statement development (for a capital campaign or annual fund), but detailed itemization is important to understand the specific amounts and schedule of capital required to complete the project. This exercise can also help identify where in-kind contributions or donated products and services may offset overall costs. Armed with this information and the determination to proceed with the project, the planner can begin a focused fund-raising effort.

Determining the Right Types of Funding

Several categories of funding are available for cultural heritage tourism. Admissions, gift shop sales, rental income, licenses and permits (for photography, filming, and merchandise), grants, donations, loans, and tax-based revenue generation are the most frequently used strategies today. A majority of programs fund project development (physical or programmatic). Other programs may allow funds to be used for the marketing of existing or proposed projects. Many grants do not fund operations or administration exclusively.

Grants

Grants are the most widely used form of funding for cultural heritage tourism, especially by cultural and historic institutions. Unfortunately, funds have decreased over the years—as federal and state program budgets get cut—and the grants become more competitive. Often, the application requests exceed the amount of funding available by ten to one.[3]

Federal

Currently, more than 900 grant programs are offered by twenty-six federal agencies. While not all of these grants are appropriate and available for cultural heritage tourism programs, they offer an opportunity to understand the types of projects and programs of interest and funding requirements. The availability of funds and technical assistance is based annually on the federal appropriation to various agencies. In some years, Congress may also allocate funds to special projects or themes such as Civil Rights. The best place to start an investigation is at http://www.grants.gov.

National Nongovernmental Organizations

Most nongovernmental organizations involved in cultural heritage tourism have grant programs as well as professional development, research, and/or technical assistance opportunities to consider as in-kind contributions. A resource directory outlining the current programs and funding opportunities available from organizations such as Americans for the Arts, the American Alliance of Museums, the National Association of State Arts Agencies, and the National Trust for Historic Preservation, is now available at http://www.culturalheritagetourism.org.

State

Agencies involved in tourism, economic development, the arts, historic preservation, conservation, education, and other related cultural heritage activities may have specific funding programs available for communities, nonprofit organizations, and sometimes private businesses. These are typically smaller-scale grants ($2,000 to $20,000) that require a local match (often one to one) and documentation of results. Monies are dispersed based on performance and satisfying the terms of the grant. Seek out your individual state tourism, state historic preservation, state arts, and humanities councils. The Grantsmanship Center also offers online access to lists of funding by state at https://www.tgci.com/funding-sources.

Third Party

National and state heritage areas, regional economic development authorities, cultural districts, business improvement districts, utilities, and other entities may have monies to re-grant, provide technical assistance, or serve as a fiscal agent for cultural heritage tourism activities. Contact the National League of Cities for a list of members and also state municipal leagues for technical assistance and funding information at http://www.nlc.org/about-nlc/state-league-programs/state-municipal-leagues/state-municipal-league-director.

Donations

Philanthropy in the United States is "big business." *Giving USA*, the most recent report by the Lilly Family School of Philanthropy at Indiana University (Indianapolis), noted that charitable contributions totaled $373.3 billion in 2015, an increase of 4.1 percent from the previous year. This represents 2.1 percent of gross domestic product, a rate that—except for the recent recession—has remained fairly constant for the past ten years.[4]

Individual

Most of the contributed support (71 percent) is from individuals, with foundations representing 16 percent, corporations 5 percent, and bequests 8 percent. Most of what is given benefits faith-based organizations (32 percent), followed by support for education (16 percent), human services

Figure 10.1 Cemetery Gate—Virginia City, Nevada.

(12 percent), and gifts to foundations (11 percent), health-related causes (8 percent), and international affairs (4 percent), with 2 percent going directly to individuals. Contributed support for those sectors most likely to be engaged in cultural heritage tourism (public-sector benefit; arts, culture, and humanities; and—to a lesser extent—environment and animals) represent collectively 15 percent of the total given. Rising 7 percent from the previous year, giving to arts, cultural, and humanities organizations saw the third-highest increase in giving among all subsectors.[5]

Visitors are often tapped for individual donations, either in voluntary contribution jars at historic sites and museum or via purchase of a product where proceeds directly (or partially) benefit a particular cultural heritage institution. One such model is Cemetery Gin, a fundraiser for the Virginia City Cemetery Foundation. To learn about this project, read the profile at the end of this chapter.

Foundations

There are 86,726 foundations in the United States with an estimated $865 billion in assets. According to the Foundation Center, the estimated giving in 2015 was $60.2 billion—a 9 percent increase over 2014.[6] Individual and family foundations are anticipated to continue growing at a higher rate than corporate and other types of foundations.[7] Two sources of foundation information are the Foundation Center (http://www.foundationcenter.org) and the Grantsmanship Center (http://www.tgci.com).

Crowdfunding

According to the Small Business Administration of the U.S. Department of Commerce, "Crowdfunding is a collective cooperative of people who network and pool their money and resources together, usually online, to support efforts initiated by other organizations. Crowdfunding gathers multiple, smaller investments as opposed to a single source of funding."[8] There are four models of crowdfunding platforms:

1. **Donation-based model:** Funders donate to causes they want to support, with no expected compensation i.e. charities and non-profit organizations (e.g., Crowdrise).
2. **Reward-based model:** This is the most popular and largest platform to date, where the funder's primary objective is to receive nonfinancial rewards (e.g., Kickstarter and Indiegogo).
3. **Lending-based model:** Funders receive fixed periodic income and expect repayment of the original principal investment; often provides peer-to-peer lending (e.g., KIVA).
4. *Equity-based model:* Funders receive compensation in the form of the fund-raiser's equity-based revenue or profit-sharing arrangements.[9]

Most online campaigns are successful when a well-formulated concept is marketed socially, creating interest and familiarity and thereby driving potential investors to the site during a specific time period. Texts sent to provide updates, prompt action, and acknowledge gifts can spur further support and engagement. One crowd funding example (profiled at the end of this chapter) helped save a sweet tradition in Cleveland, Ohio.

Loans/Incentives

Loans are often an attractive option for private investors or municipalities seeking to finance development costs at below-average rates, with incentives or more favorable lending terms.

Figure 10.2 Mitchell's Fine Chocolates—Cleveland, Ohio.

Another use of loans is to parcel lending out for various aspects of the project development based on the financial terms of the loan agreement. The U.S. Economic Development Administration (http://www.eda.gov) offers a resource directory and other services through its planning and local technical assistance program. The U.S. Small Business Administration also provides financial assistance with loans, grants, and tax-exempt bonds (https://www.sba.gov/content/economic-development-agencies). Rural areas and businesses should consider the U.S. Department of Agriculture's Rural Economic Development Loan and Grant program for favorable rates and repayment terms (http://www.rd.usda.gov/programs-services). Nongovernmental entities sometimes offer loan programs for specific purposes. Private businesses may also want to explore the various funding mechanisms available (including traditional and alternative lending and start-up funding) and other funding strategies via Dun & Bradstreet's Access to Capital (http://accessto-capital.com/sources-small-business-funding).

Tax-based funding is available at the national, state, and local levels. Public funding sources usually require legislation to approve, amend, or reward monies. New initiatives require both political and community support to introduce an option and therefore need to be carefully researched and drafted for approval.

Tax Credits/Incentives

The Federal Historic Preservation Tax Incentives program has been one of the most popular incentives for restoration, renovation, and protection of historic sites and areas. According to the

National Park Service, the program has leveraged more than $73 billion in private investment to preserve 40,380 historic properties since 1976. Three program types are available:

- A 20 percent tax credit for rehabilitation of certified historic structures that are income-producing buildings is available.
- Nonhistoric, nonresidential buildings constructed before 1936 are eligible for a 10 percent federal tax credit for rehabilitation.
- Tax benefits are also available for historic preservation easements, a voluntary legal agreement permanently protecting a historic property.[10]

Thirty-four states offfer some sort of historic tax credit program. For more information on the positive impact of historic tax credits, read the profile of Georgia's enhanced tax credit (HB 308) at the end of this chapter.

Some states also offer tax rebates as part of an economic development incentive. For example, the State of Georgia offers a ten-year sales tax rebate on approved new tourism products (such as cultural centers or museums) with an investment of more than $1 million and the intent of attracting at least 25 percent of out-of-state visitors after three years.

Local Option Sales Tax

The local option sales tax (LOST) has different iterations, depending on the state and the purpose. Variations relevant to cultural heritage tourism include T-SPLOST to finance transportation-related projects and SPLOST to direct funds to a "special purpose" (such as a new cultural center or performing arts venue). Typically, this additional sales tax (1 percent on top of local county or city sales tax) funds building of public projects in the municipality. Revenue cannot be used for operating or maintenance expenses.[13] The Tax Foundation records and compares state and local option sales tax for reference and transparency.[14]

Percent-for-Art Projects

Ordinances for municipal capital improvement projects often fund public art projects. According to Americans for the Arts, local percent-for-art ordinances have existed since 1959. Traditionally applied to publicly funded capital improvement projects, some cities today are expanding their programs to include private development.[15]

The City of Chicago Percent-for-Art Ordinance

Chicago's Percent-for-Art Ordinance, adopted in July 2007, creates a fund for commissioning or purchasing artwork, administration of the Public Art Program (through the Department of Cultural Affairs), and maintenance of the artwork in the program. Funds are generated from a 1.33 percent appropriation on the original budgeted cost of construction or renovation "affecting 50 percent or more of the square footage of a public building to which there is or will be public access built for or by the City of Chicago." To review the actual ordinance, visit http://www.cityofchicago.org/city/en/depts/dca/auto_generated/public_art_program_publandreports/new_art_on_pink_line.html.

Tourism Development Fund

A tourism development fund (TDF) is often a special fund for capital improvements or building projects to grow tourism in a destination. In some cases, the TDF is funded by a dedicated tax or fee added to the local occupancy or accommodation tax used for marketing a municipality. One of the first municipalities to establish a TDF fund was Asheville in Buncombe County, North Carolina. Read their profile at the end of this chapter to understand the process employed to develop the area's tourism product.

Tax Increment Financing

Municipalities use tax increment financing (TIF) as a local redevelopment tool to fund specified public and private improvements, typically in a designated area (district). TIF earmarks property tax revenue generated from redevelopment of a blighted area.[20] The increment of ad valorem taxes generated from net increase in assessed values (year to year) is used to finance project costs. District creation includes four steps: (1) preplanning (defining the reinvestment area, historic preservation, enterprise area, whether it's project specific or area specific, and urban renewal area), (2) appointment and establishment of a TIF review committee for the proposed district, (3) development of a project plan (identify the district area, define basis for eligibility, budget for TIF expenditures, and indicate an implementation designee), and (4) approval of project plan (TIF review committee and city and county planning commissions).[21]

Tourism, Business, and Parking Improvement Districts or Areas

These improvement districts or areas are a specially designated geographic boundary whereby property owners can finance services and improvements through self-assessment. Businesses and property owners within the borders are assessed a fee on specific revenue (such as short-term room rental) for a defined period of time (such as five years). Annual funds are collected for an explicit purpose—marketing, infrastructure improvements, or operations—as decided by the property and business owners. Annual costs are apportioned to eligible property owners in

Figure 10.3 The Orange Peel received a tourism product development fund grant and loan to expand and update its facility—Asheville, North Carolina.

the district.[22] There are numerous iterations of these districts, most recently the formation of cultural districts to cross municipal boundaries or parcel a section of a neighborhood. Some historic districts also assess fees for beautification, lighting, and other improvements. Business improvement districts are also popular for clustering and managing new growth areas, such as Main Streets or urban hubs, for commercial revitalization. A business improvement district cannot replace existing city services but instead are in addition to existing city services.

Napa Valley Tourism Improvement District

With tourism as the second-largest industry in Napa County, California, generating more than $1.4 billion in annual spending, the Napa Valley Tourism Improvement District "ensures that funding for Visit Napa Valley's targeted marketing, selling, and promote of the Napa Valley as North America's premier wine, food, arts and wellness visitor destination is maintained at competitive levels." For specific information on how the Tourism Improvement District works and its impact, visit https://www.visitnapavalley.com/about-us/napa-valley-tid.

Bond Financing

Bonds are legally binding loans where municipalities serve as the bank. A city may sell bonds to raise money for a public building or structure. States have various legal restraints on issuing bonds (such as the amount of new debt incurred or the length of the term.) There are different kinds of bonds, depending on the issuer. Treasury bonds are issued by the U.S. government for maturity in thirty years, and municipal bonds are issued by states, cities, and local governments (municipality) and, if you live where the bonds are issued, may also be exempt from state taxes. Development authorities and housing authorities may also issue bonds, aptly called authority bonds. Often, bonds are proposed to fund large-scale transportation projects (airport expansions and public transit) that add to overall destination growth and access.

Several references are available to help sort out existing funding sources and technical assistance to aid in the development of cultural heritage tourism products. The *Catalog of Federal Domestic Assistance* is an online listing of all federal programs available to state and local governments; it contains detailed program descriptions for 2,315 federal assistance programs—grants, loans, and other types of assistance.[23]

Other Revenue Generation Strategies

This section would be incomplete if it did not include other ways for historic sites, cultural institutions, nonprofit organizations, and businesses to earn income. Certainly, retail shops can generate revenue from visitor spending. Throughout this book, the importance of local merchandise to a valued shopping experience has been recognized. The opportunity for museums, in particular, to attract visitor spending is important, as it extends the experience with the purchase of a special place-based memento and allows the visitor to support the organization's mission. Other ways to cultivate revenue generation—beyond admissions, programs, and gift shops—include product licensing (of artifact reproductions, books, and other tangible assets), food service (where available or as a percentage of vendor sales), permit fees (for photography shoots or filming [see chapter 12]), and space rental (for events, residencies, overnight guests, or contractors). Building in earned-income strategies is important in seeking diversification of revenues for long-term sustainability.

Understanding Funding Protocols

Each funding mechanism has its own terms and conditions as well as a schedule for application review and approval. Some are more complex than others; several require public input or legislative action. The simpler tools, even for small amounts of money, often involve community support or securing matching funds. Understanding the process and protocols for each funding strategy is important to determine the best tool(s) to pursue.

Funding sources, especially grants, often require matching funds. Community support or private or institutional funds—cash or in-kind donations—are often mandated for approval and must be defined in the application. Determining eligibility of in-kind donations (how volunteer labor or contributed materials are calculated as a fee) is important for compliance. Letters of support for the proposed project are also important documents to secure in advance of the grant deadline. Many grant applications require official signatories or designation of a fiscal agent as well. Obtaining these local commitments is vital and must be secured before submission.

Soliciting contributions from individuals and foundations, whether online or in person, requires well-crafted, compelling fund-raising materials. Identifying and obtaining prospect lists of potential donors is the lifeblood of most nonprofit development offices to understand giving levels and goals. Boards of nonprofit organizations must demonstrate support for projects through their own donations. Capital campaigns often require securing a majority of pledges before introducing the giving opportunity to the general public. Read the profile at the end of this chapter to learn how one heritage area is inviting individuals, companies, and groups to commemorate the nation's history in a unique lasting way.

Funding tools requiring legislative and community action deserve careful consideration and planning. Understanding the time and resources necessary to successfully adopt these funding mechanisms is important in a holistic planning effort. Weighing the outcomes against other funding strategies should be factored into the decision-making process.

Most destinations require multiple funding models to develop and sustain viable projects or districts. Planners should work with public and private entities to complete funding plans to identify and outline appropriate mechanisms to raise the necessary capital from a variety of sources. Utilize federal, state, and regional resources to map funding schedules (time lines for grant applications and legislative agendas) and tap national organizations to help identify the best strategies for cultural heritage tourism priorities. To get started or for reference, a fund-raising primer is provided in figure 10.7.

* * * * *

Profile: Cemetery Gin—A Thirst for Preservation
Virginia City, Nevada

http://www.visitvirginiacitynv.com/attractions/virginia-city-cemeteries/cemetery-gin.html

Safe drinking water was not readily available in the 1850s, so it's said that residents of Virginia City, Virginia, often mixed tap water with two parts gin. Hazardous working conditions to mine

Figure 10.4 Cemetery Statue—Virginia City, Nevada.

gold and silver deposits of the Comstock Lode contributed to the harsh lifestyle. While some became multimillionaires, death was a more frequent end result—an average of one miner a day. Combine these two threats, and you understand the context for Cemetery Gin, carrying the tagline "guaranteed to embalm you while you're still breathing."

To help preserve the history of the Comstock Lode, Virginia City Tourism brought to life Cemetery Gin on Nevada Day (October 28, 2015) with a donation of $1 from the sale of each bottle benefiting the Comstock Cemetery Foundation. The foundation preserves and protects the historic cemeteries in the National Historic Landmark district. An initial donation helped restore a public visitor center at the entrance of the Silver Terrace cemeteries. Quarterly contributions generated from the sale of Cemetery Gin will further support the mission of the local foundation.

Figure 10.5 Cemetery Gin—Virginia City, Nevada.

Named the official spirit of Virginia City, Cemetery Gin is 100 percent produced and bottled in Nevada by Frey Ranch Estate Distillery. The gin's signature ingredient is Nevada pine nuts found exclusively in the region and, laced with lavender, is guaranteed to be much tastier than the historic swill. Today, visitors and residents alike can purchase Cemetery Gin at the Virginia City Visitors Center, all of the town's saloons, and more than a dozen locations throughout northern Nevada.

"We wouldn't have developed this product if we couldn't donate a portion of the funds to the Cemetery Foundation," says Deny Dotson, director of tourism for the Virginia City Tourism Commission. "It's important to us to help preserve the history of our town, and this is a fun way to do it where everybody wins."

★ ★ ★ ★ ★

Profile: Mitchell's Fine Chocolates—Saving a Sweet Tradition
Cleveland Heights, Ohio

https://www.mitchellschocolates.com

Family owned and operated since 1939, Mitchell's Fine Chocolates is an institution in Cleveland Heights, Ohio. Greek immigrant Chris Mitchell opened the neighborhood soda fountain and candy store that soon became Mitchell's Fine Chocolates. Located next to a neighborhood movie theater, Mitchell's Chocolates became a favorite of movie patrons. The sweets are still hand-crafted in small batches, just like they were four generations ago.

The current owner, Chris's son Bill, decided to retire in 2016 and planned to close the store after Memorial Day unless he could find a buyer ready to carry on the chocolate-making tradition. Enter Jason Hallaman and Emily Bean, a local Millennial couple prepared to launch a $60,000 Kickstarter campaign to raise operational and marketing funds. Specifically, the couple needed to buy boxes and raw materials (Bill had been winding down business in anticipation of closing) and also set aside funds for possible equipment repairs.

"To me, this was a no-brainer. I was ready to quit my job the next day to save Mitchell's Chocolates. Who would let a seventy-seven-year-old business go the wayside, one that isn't even floundering?" said Jason Hallaman. "Ever since I was a kid, I've had a fondness for Mitchell's Chocolates. Our families attended the same Greek Orthodox Church. I used to stop in after elementary school for a treat, and Mrs. Mitchell [Bill's mom, Penelope] was always so nice. It wasn't until I was in my teens that I discovered our families have a closer link—Penelope was from the same Greek Island, Limnos, as my grandparents," said Jason. "Now, my wife and I are embarking on a journey with Bill to acquire his artisan business. There is no greater honor that could be bestowed upon us than to have him consider us worthy of continuing his family's legacy."

The crowdfunded campaign ran for twenty-six days (May 4 to 30, 2016) and sought pledges in increments from $5 to $1,000. The couple did not explore other financing options; they needed cash fast and determined that this was the best way to engage other people who wanted to save Mitchell's too. In appreciation of the contributions, donors received, of course, chocolates. Custom-created chocolates named for the donor are the ultimate thank-you. At the end of the campaign, the couple had raised $62,893 and became the new partners to keep Mitchell's Fine Chocolates operating, it is hoped, for several generations to come. Bill will continue to mentor the couple for several years, but Jason and Emily are already at work adding wine parings with local businesses, expanding social media presence, and staying open late. Probable reasons for their crowdfunding success include a great story, giving thresholds attractive to varying levels of investment, great incentives (the product worth saving), and a sound rationale for the "ask."

"We value the tradition and heritage of this business, one based on quality and integrity. The high standard of product and the nostalgic atmosphere in the showroom will always be maintained," said Hallaman.

* * * * *

Profile: Georgia HB 308—Peach of a Deal

http://georgiashpo.org/incentives/tax

Historic tax credits represent one of the best incentives for developers of historic properties to renovate buildings for new or existing uses. While some states have eliminated or reduced historic tax credits, the State of Georgia elected to increase its existing state income tax credit program for a rehabilitated historic property. HB 308, signed into law on May 12, 2015, creates two new project categories and allows earned credits to be sold. The law, which went into effect on January 1, 2016, increases the allowance of tax credits from $300,000 to $5 million for any taxable year. If a project creates 200 or more full-time, permanent jobs or $5 million in annual payroll within two years of opening, the project is eligible for credits up to $10 million for any certified structure. This bill, authorized for 2017–2021, particularly helps redevelopment of large historic projects, such as power stations and other megacommercial structures.

Carole Moore, tax incentives coordinator for the Historic Preservation Division (HPD) of the Georgia Department of Natural Resources, which administers the state and federal tax incentives program, said, "HB 308 is having exactly the economic effect on Georgia that its proponents hoped for. The new tax credit categories have already sparked and increased significant developer interest in undertaking large rehabilitation projects in Georgia. To date, HPD has precertified fifteen higher-credit projects planned for completion in 2017 and 2018, with total estimated rehabilitation expenses of almost $300 million. These projects, located in Athens, Atlanta, Augusta, Savannah, Macon, and Lookout Mountain, will potentially create almost 5,000 jobs and generate approximately $200 million in salary and wages for Georgia workers in the roughly two-year period it will take to complete the projects." Moore continued, "Our hope is that the legislation will be renewed again in 2021 once the legislature sees the economic development that comes from the credit."

In Georgia, "every $1 million in historic preservation creates 16.3 jobs during construction with a payroll of $811,000. It also provides 7.5 permanent jobs and ultimately adds $558,000 to Georgia state tax revenues."[11] According to the Historic Savannah Foundation, 140 historic tax credit projects were completed between 2001 and 2013 in Savannah, resulting in $85,857,556 in development expenditures, 1,318 jobs created, and $47,456,100 generated in household income.[12] To review the entire bill with amendments, visit http://georgiashpo.org/s.

★ ★ ★ ★ ★

**Profile: Tourism Product Development Fund—Investing in the Past, Focusing on the Future
Buncombe County, North Carolina**

http://www.ashevillecvb.com/product-development

Nestled in the Blue Ridge Mountains of western North Carolina, Buncombe County is home to Asheville, the Biltmore Estate, the Thomas Wolfe Memorial, and the Blue Ridge Parkway. In 1983, local tourism industry leaders established one of the first occupancy taxes in North Carolina. This allowed for dedicated funding to market Asheville and Buncombe County to potential visitors. Since the inception of the tax, visitor spending has grown from $183 million to $1.7 billion. However, the city and county began to lose market share and experienced declining occupancy rates in the late 1900s and needed to identify ways to jump-start visitation and its economic impact.

Four of Asheville's key business organizations—the Buncombe County Tourism Development Authority (BCTDA), the Asheville Area Chamber of Commerce, Carolina Power and Light (the regional power utility), and Advantage West (the regional economic development authority)—joined together to hire consulting firm Arthur Andersen to conduct a tourism product assessment and development program. The consulting report recommended "a combination of enhancements and scaled projects as the optimum strategy" for tourism product development.[16] A task force charged with implementation faced a serious concern—how to fund the product development plan. Asheville is not home to a major employer or corporate headquarters. To turn the recommendations into reality, industry leaders once again determined that the best strategy was to have hotels tax themselves. They lobbied for the North Carolina State Legislature to amend the existing law to increase the Buncombe County occupancy (room) tax from three cents to four cents and establish a fund for tourism product development.[17] Revenue collected from the one-cent additional tax were placed in the appropriately named tourism product development fund (TPDF) to seed capital projects and enhancements outlined in the report. The first three-fourths of the tax continues to be used solely for out-of-market advertising of the Asheville area.

The new legislation (drafted by the local task force and the staff of the Asheville Convention and Visitors Bureau) included language to garner support from local stakeholders and elected officials. To affirm the fund's objective of increasing overnight visitation at lodging facilities in Buncombe County, particularly in slower or quiet months of travel, the following stipulations were included:

- TPDF had to be used for capital project expenses to build evergreen (year-round) products rather than events (expressly prohibited for any occupancy tax supports).
- The BCTDA maintained complete control over the funds and how they were distributed.
- Projects for consideration had to demonstrate that they would generate new and incremental room nights in Buncombe County.
- Restrictions were placed on the distribution of funds so that no one project could receive full allocation of the fund for either one or subsequent years.
- TPDF allocations were to supplement other funding, not be a sole source for projects.
- The BCTDA could either grant or loan funds to a project.

In August 2001, the bill passed (on an off-election year), and the TPDF became reality.[18]

The detailed management and implementation phase began with the goal of establishing a fair process. The enabling legislation mandates that a TPDF committee review all funding applications and make recommendations for approval of the BCTDA. It took more than a year to establish the nine-member review committee (five of which are occupancy tax–collecting lodging properties), the application process, and suggested criteria to measure all applications.

In 2013–2014, the BCTDA set out to refine the application process and address other key issues for the decade-old program. The TPDF Application Improvement Study focused on clarifying guidelines, criteria, and implementing more accountability in the process. The application process now includes two phases, well-defined requirements, and board-adopted criteria. Other changes to the TPDF include adoption of a Strategic Priority List and the Major Tourism Works Pathway to proactively fill strategic gaps in the market.

In June 2015, an additional 2 percent was added to the occupancy tax (raising it to 6 percent) with 1.5 percent dedicated to funding the TPDF. HB 347 modified the existing legislation so that for-profit entities are no longer eligible for funding. During a standard funding cycle, the nonprofit or government applicants may request a grant, loan guarantee, or funds for debt service.

Since the fund's inception in 2001, $23 million have been awarded to twenty-seven community projects. Annual grants and loans range from $16,500 to $2 million. Several of the funded projects are historic or cultural: the Grove Arcade, the Western North Carolina Veteran's Memorial at Pack Square Park, the Buncombe County Civil War Trails, the Asheville Art Museum, and the Riverglass Public Glass Studio and School. Requests annually far exceed funds available; sixteen projects applied for the 2015 grant cycle with a total amount requested of more than $9 million. Two TPDF beneficiaries demonstrate the benefit of this fund:

- From 2004 to 2009, three grants totaling $2.5 million were awarded for the construction of a signature park and performance venue: Pack Square Park and Pavilion. The project created a cultural icon in the heart of Asheville's central business district. The park features a covered stage used for dozens of cultural events annually, including its longest running and most beloved, Shindig on the Green.
- A $250,000 loan guarantee was awarded, along with a $50,000 grant, in 2009 to the Orange Peel to enable the venue to expand its capacity to meet the requirements of touring acts. Since its expansion, the Orange Peel has become one of the most well-known concert venues in the southeast, attracting top-tier acts and national audiences.

"Buncombe County's tourism development model has enhanced Asheville's appeal to visitors without disrupting its cultural identity," said Stephanie Pace Brown, executive director of the Asheville Convention and Visitors Bureau. She continued, "This balance is achieved by investing in home-grown projects enjoyed by both citizens and visitors."

The TPDF Process

A program guide is available online to describe the process and provide application materials.[19] (Note: The content below has been extracted from the current program guide for easy reference.) Phase I application is a short form outlining key project information to help the review committee assess the viability of the application, compliance with eligibility requirements, and conformity to the goals of the fund. Successful Phase I applicants are invited to move forward in the process and prepare a more comprehensive application in Phase II. In addition to submitting financial documents, business plans, and feasibility studies, the applicants also have the opportunity to present projects in person to the TPDF Committee. Site visits may also be planned at the TPDF Committee's discretion:

March	TPDF Program Guide and Application available for download
April	TPDF hosts information session for interested applicants
June 1	Phase I applications due
June 29	Phase I applicants notified
August 31	Phase II applications due
September	Project presentations
September to October	Site visits

Late October	Grantees announced
January 15	Grantee annual report due to TPDF

Eligibility

Applicants must meet the following grant requirements:

1. Funding must be for capital investments ("bricks and mortar") only. Design fees and operational expenses may not be funded.
2. A project must demonstrate that it will create substantial new and incremental hotel room nights in Buncombe County.
3. Must secure a minimum one-to-one funding match prior to the funding request (excluding in-kind goods and services). Design fees already expended may count toward the one-to-one match.
4. Projects that either directly increase hotel room nights by themselves or support a larger initiative that will increase room nights will be evaluated equally.
5. Projects may not solely benefit a single hotel owner or hotel property or be situated on a hotel property.
6. Other funds must be secured before submitting an application. TPDF funds cannot be the first funds committed to a project.
7. For-profit entities are not eligible for TPDF funding.

Evaluation Criteria

- *Financial stability of the requesting organization*, including perceived ability to raise additional funds to complete the project
- *Ratio of room nights generated to funding requested*, as an indicator of return on investment
- *Ability to serve as a contributing asset*, demonstrating how the project may be a catalyst for other tourism product development
- *Strength of business planning*, based on an accurate and complete business plan
- *Strength of sales and marketing plan*, evaluating the budget and likelihood for drawing visitation to the destination
- *Generator of new and incremental room nights*, especially from out-of-town markets rather than displacing existing visitors to Buncombe County
- *Association with an identified need period*, whereby greater consideration is given for those projects for quieter travel seasons rather than peak and established travel periods
- *Size of market to be served*, based on the project's capacity to fill many hotel rooms or draw new and untapped niche markets to the county
- *Scope of impact on the lodging market*, based not only on number of hotel room nights generated but also the geographic impact and types of hotels filled by visitors
- *Timeliness of the project*—"shovel-ready" projects preferred
- *One-to-one funding match exceeded*, whereas special consideration is afforded to projects that go beyond the mandatory one-to-one match
- *Uniqueness and innovation of project*, particularly those attractions and activities new to the region or currently not available to visitors living in key feeder markets
- *Strength of brand alignment*, to show consistency with the Asheville destination brand and to support the brand promise

Figure 10.6 Shindig on the Green, one of the many festivals enjoyed at Pack Square Park in downtown Asheville—Asheville, North Carolina.

- *Projects already funded*, as long as the application is for a new project with additional incremental room nights

Once a contract is signed for construction of the project, three equal disbursements of the awarded fund are made on scalable progress—after one-third completed, after two-thirds completed, and on date of completion. A third-party engineering firm is retained to validate contract compliance prior to authorization of each payment. Grantees must submit annual reports each January to the Asheville Convention and Visitors Bureau (grant administrator) during the term of the agreement and continuing four years after the completion date. The annual report must include marketing plans and methodologies for capturing annual and out-of-market visitation, up-to-date room night projections, and copies of survey instruments used for data. Other materials may also be required.

The legislation is available via the following links:

HB 105: http://www.ncga.state.nc.us/Sessions/2001/Bills/House/HTML/H105v3.html

HB 347: http://www.ncleg.net/Sessions/2015/Bills/House/HTML/H347v4.html

★ ★ ★ ★ ★

Profile: The Journey through Hallowed Ground National Heritage Area—Living Legacy Project

https://www.hallowedground.org/Get-Involved/Plant-a-Tree/About-Living-Legacy

In her poem *Trees*, twentieth-century poet Joyce Kilmer wrote about how a tree looks at God all day. The Journey through Hallowed Ground National Heritage Area pays a fitting tribute to a tree's majesty and purpose through its Living Legacy Project. The organization aims to plant one tree for each of the 620,000 soldiers who died during the American Civil War. In November 2012, the inaugural tree planting for the Living Legacy Project occurred at Oatlands Historic House and Gardens to provide an opportunity for remembrance of the fallen, for patriotic celebration and commemoration, and for appreciation of partners for this endeavor. Since the initial tree planting ceremony, the partnership has hosted eighteen different tree-planting ceremonies along the 180-mile corridor spanning from Charlottesville, Virginia, through western Maryland to Gettysburg, Pennsylvania. Approximately 4,000 trees have been planted or tagged to date.

In some instances, the Journey through Hallowed Ground tags existing trees as part of the project. "A witness tree on Seminary Ridge in Gettysburg was tagged and included as part of the Living Legacy Project. This tree was there during the first day of the Battle of Gettysburg and had special meaning to the site as well as to the importance and goals of this project," said William W. Sellers, president and chief executive officer of the Journey through Hallowed Ground Partnership.

Not surprisingly, the Living Legacy Project garners a lot of media attention. National and regional media—including the Associated Press, *USA Today*, the *Washington Post*, and Voice of America—and major network affiliates have covered the project, bringing attention to new audiences across the country.

Members of the tourism industry, through a voluntary tourism program organized by Tourism Cares, contributed to the Living Legacy Project in May 2015. More than 300 professionals worked at the largest single planting to date—more than 1,000 trees in one day. In 2005, Tourism Cares[24] gave a grant to the Journey through Hallowed Ground, so a partnership to plant trees seemed a natural fit. In addition to the Tourism Cares delegation, the partnership also hosted the Vans Warped Tour for a Living Legacy program. "Individuals from across the country traveled to our region to help plant trees. In both cases, the participants needed hotel accommodations, meals, and other goods and services. Their visits generated a direct economic impact on our local communities," said Sellers. "In addition, these individuals are now more familiar with the tourism assets in our National Heritage Area and very well may come back to visit—or even check out 'their' trees," he continued.

The Journey through Hallowed Ground's educational programs also benefit from the Living Legacy Project. Through a partnership with Ancestry.com, the partnership has trained teachers across the country to conduct soldier research. The partnership used this research content to populate the online memorial page created for each soldier honored with a tree through Fold3.com. To date, students from Vermont, Massachusetts, and Connecticut have traveled to the corridor to help plan or dedicate trees.

A project of this scale needed thoughtful planning. Through a grant from the Federal Highway Administration, the Journey through Hallowed Ground hired the nationally renowned firm of Rhodeside & Harwell to create the master plan for the Living Legacy Project and also established three criteria for tree species selection. First, only native species are used. Second: A plant palette gives weight to key symbolic tree offer a range of trees to allow for clustering and also for seasonal blooming. The primary palette includes four trees: red oak, red maple, redbud, and red cedar. Finally, the primary palette will comprise at least 75% of the species within the right of way. The choice of red in the primary palette was also intentional, as the color symbolizes the sacrifice, courage, and bravery of the soldiers honored through this tree-planting project.

Key partners in the Living Legacy Project include the Virginia Department of Transportation, the Virginia Department of Forestry, and the Pennsylvania Department of Conservation and Natural Resources. Individuals may also donate $100 to plant a tree. Private foundations and business-sector support has been significant. Employees at Bartlett Tree Experts participated in three large-scale tree-planting events, mobilizing other community volunteers—from the National Guard to high school students—to participate in similar activities along the corridor. Bartlett Tree Experts manager Greg Bradshaw led environmental science students at Tuscarora High School through a soil sample testing during a recent planting program, tying the tree planting to the local science curriculum, while history students conducted research on fallen soldiers to whom the trees were dedicated. The overall maintenance and management of trees is the responsibility of the site where the tree is planted. Currently, only one employee is dedicated to this project. Recognizing the long-term effort required to accomplish the project goal, the Journey through Hallowed Ground staff are examining ways to scale up its efforts.

Stewardship of our landscape is important. When this preservation can be combined with a memorial of recognition for fallen heroes, the landscape becomes even more sacred. The opportunity to participate in a project that acknowledges the ultimate sacrifice paid on American soil makes the Living Legacy Project a valued cultural heritage tourism experience for both current and future generations.

* * * * *

FUNDRASISING PRIMER

The opportunity to generate philanthropic support varies greatly from organization to organization depending on their level of fund-raising sophistication, board and other volunteer involvement, public profile, staffing, the solicitation mechanisms used, and other factors. Below are some generally accepted guidelines regarding terminology, staffing, consultants, volunteer involvement, fund-raising expenses/return on investment, and special campaigns.

Terminology

- "Development" is often used interchangeably with the term "fund-raising;" many large nonprofit organizations (notably colleges and universities) use the term "advance-

Figure 10.7 Fund-raising primer

ment" when combining their fund-raising operations with other functions, such as alumni services and/or public relations.

- "Annual" or "unrestricted" fund-raising refers to those gifts and grants that may be used for any purpose by a nonprofit organization.
- "Restricted" contributions are designated by the donor or the recipient organization for a specific function and must be used solely for that purpose.
- "Endowment" gifts are generally deposited in a nonprofit's endowment fund, with the earnings from those funds used for either unrestricted or restricted purposes, as determined by the stipulations of the gift and the organization's investment policies.
- "Planned gifts" are those funds that are given to an organization by way of any combination of bequest, insurance plan, annuity, or any of several types of trusts.
- "Major gifts," "leadership gifts," or "pacesetter gifts" all refer to a fairly arbitrary set of criteria designed to identify those donors—usually high-net-worth individuals—who, by way of their past or potential giving, represent an organization's top prospects; depending on the scale of a nonprofit's fund-raising, the threshold for a major gift might be as little as $1,000 or as much as $100,000 or even more.

Staffing

- Professional staff (salary and benefits) will usually be the largest component of the fund-raising budget.
- Organizations can expect to spend $100,000 to $150,000 (in salary and benefits) for an experienced director of development or chief development officer. An effective professional fund-raiser can be expected to generate as much as $500,000 or more in annual cash and pledges after the first twelve to eighteen months of employment, assuming the organization's case for support is strong and there is supporting fund-raising infrastructure in place.
- An experienced development officer can be expected to actively manage about 100 prospects at any given time.
- Support staff is crucial to success, enabling the more senior development staff to focus on personal cultivation, solicitation, and stewardship of major gifts.
- Organizations generating $500,000 to $1 million in annual contributions should have at least 1.5 to 2.0 full-time equivalent (FTE) in dedicated development staff; you should plan on increasing that staffing level by 1.0 to 2.0 FTE for each additional $1 million raised.
- Organizations interested in "ramping up" their fund-raising need to front-load that effort with additional development staff; expanded development staff is a means to an end.
- Even the most experienced director of development will have only limited success without the active support of the organization's chief executive officer and other staff.

Consultants

- Many nonprofit organizations utilize consultants for a variety of purposes, including the following:
    - Development audits—evaluating a nonprofit's current fund-raising operations
    - Feasibility studies—determining an organization's ability to raise significant support for a major campaign
    - Governance—assessing a board's current capabilities

Figure 10.7 (continued)

- Strategic planning—helping organization's chart their future
- A few consulting firms have specialized in outsourced development, providing some or all of an organization's fund-raising operations on a fee-for-service basis.
- When hiring a consultant, it is important that each party's expectations be clearly stated in a written agreement.
- Qualified fund-raising consultants can be found through online searches or via the Chronicle of Philanthropy (https://www.philanthropy.com) or the Association of Fund-raising Professionals (AFP) (http://www.afpnet.org).
- Check references and be sure that your fund-raising consultant is a member of the AFP and adheres to its guidelines, code, and standards of ethics.

Volunteer Involvement

- Fund-raising is generally accepted as one of a governing board's key areas of responsibility.
- While each member of the board should play an active role in fund-raising, by both cultivating support and making personal gifts, the primary responsibility lies with the organization's Development (or Fundraising) Committee.
- While not every board member will be comfortable soliciting gifts for the organization, each member should be expected to help identify prospects, introduce potential supporters to key staff and board leadership, assist with ongoing cultivation, and play an active role in stewardship—making sure all donors are appropriately thanked and acknowledged.
- The Governance Committee should factor the board's fund-raising responsibility into its work, seeking out and recruiting prospective members with the necessary skills and experience.
- With recent trends toward smaller governing boards, many organizations have formed ancillary boards, such as honorary or advisory boards, to help broaden their base of support and strengthen their fund-raising capability.
- While it is very difficult to cite an accurate average for board giving, due to the wide range in the size of governing boards and other factors, some sources suggest that an organization should be able to count on its board contributing about 20 percent of total charitable giving. At minimum, every board member should gift some sort of annual amount so that when submitting grant applications and seeking funding from outside sources, the organization can report 100 percent board participation.

Fund-Raising Expense—Return on Investment

- The national average cost for fund-raising is $.20 for each dollar raised.
- Fund-raising costs for major gift fund-raising from individuals and capital campaigns tend to be significantly less, averaging about $.05 to $.15 per dollar raised.
- Benefits and special event fund-raising costs, on average, $.40 per dollar raised (when mature).

Figure 10.7 *(continued)*

- Direct mail renewal is generally $.20 per dollar raised, although smaller and less mature programs can spend as much as $.30 or $.40 per dollar raised.
- New donor acquisition costs by direct mail are often between $1.00 and $1.25 per dollar raised.
- Corporate and foundation efforts often cost between $.15 and $.25 per dollar raised; those efforts can take twelve to twenty-four months to mature and often require that the recipient organization match the donor's grant.
- Planned giving costs run about $.25 per dollar raised—with significant delays in any return on that investment.
- While organizations vary widely depending on the nature of their fund-raising, below is an example of how those costs might be allocated across six generally accepted expense areas.

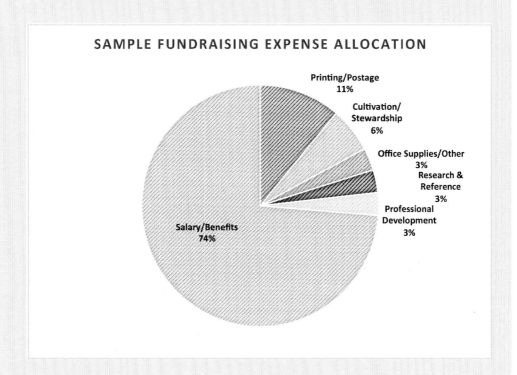

SAMPLE FUNDRAISING EXPENSE ALLOCATION

Printing/Postage
11%

Cultivation/
Stewardship
6%

Office Supplies/Other
3%

Research &
Reference
3%

Professional
Development
3%

Salary/Benefits
74%

The table below summarizes the cost and both annual and return on investment for each type of fund-raising, detailing the level of board and staff involvement required and other key requirements.

Figure 10.7 *(continued)*

	Direct Mail	Events	Corps & Fdns	Major Gifts	Planned Giving*
Cost/Dollar Raised (At Maturity—5 yrs)	$.35	$.40	$.20	$.15	$.25
1st Year of Annual Net Gain	2	1	2	2	4
1st Year of Cumulative Net Gain	2	1	3	2	4
Five Year ROI ((Gain—Cost)/ Cost))	.98	.41	1.47	2.68	0.03
Relative Level of Board Involvement		ttt	t	tt	t
Relative Level of Staff Involvement	tt	ttt	tt	tt	t
Other Requirements	Broad-based appeal; Recognizable signatory / spokesperson	Large volunteer base; Highly-regarded honoree(s)	Well connected Board; Research capabilities	Well connected and affluent board	Established endowment and planned giving vehicles; large donor base

Will require 6—8 years to reach maturity ("Cost" based on total known bequests and irrevocable planned gifts)

The two charts below illustrate the potential annual and cumulative impact of each type of fund-raising over a five-year period as each effort matures, based on the assumptions detailed in the table on the preceding page.

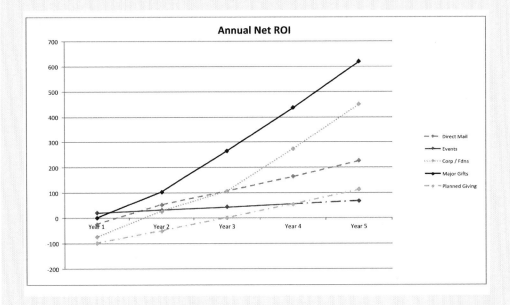

Figure 10.7 *(continued)*

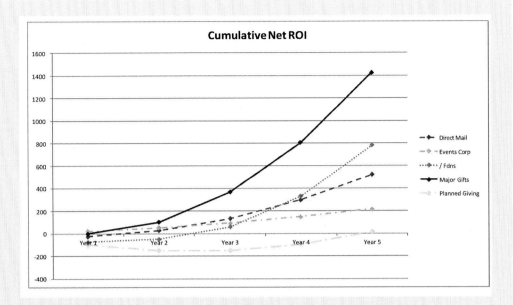

Cumulative Net ROI

Legend: Direct Mail · Events Corp · / Fdns · Major Gifts · Planned Giving

Special Campaigns

- Special campaigns are those unique fund-raising initiatives with a specific dollar goal conducted over a discrete period of time for a designated purpose.
- There are typically four types of special campaigns:
  1. Capital campaigns are for "bricks and mortar" initiatives.
  2. Endowment campaigns are designed to establish or grow an organization's the corpus of an organization's restricted investments.
  3. Project campaigns help launch special new programs or initiatives.
  4. Comprehensive campaigns incorporate two or more of those components.
- In order for any type of special campaign to be successful, five dynamics must be addressed. The nonprofit must have the following:
  - Compelling case for support (a document that details what the organization hopes to accomplish by way of the campaign and articulates the benefits that will accrue to the nonprofit and the community it serves)
  - Dedicated campaign leadership
  - A sufficient number of qualified prospects
  - Enough staff and volunteers to solicit those prospects
  - Effective staff support
  - Organizations will often commission a feasibility study to test the case for support and ascertain whether the proposed goal is achievable. These studies often include the following:
  - Confidential interviews with staff, board, current donors, opinion leaders, and/or key stakeholders
  - An assessment of the organization's current fund-raising capabilities
  - An analysis of the nonprofit's donor base
  - A study to identify other major campaigns that might represent competition

Figure 10.7 (*continued*)

- An environmental scan to ascertain overall charitable giving in the community-While estimates vary, it is generally accepted that a campaign's lead gift (i.e., largest contribution) should represent 10 to 20 percent of the goal; if an organization cannot generate a lead gift of that magnitude, it might suggest that the goal is unrealistic.
- The long-held adage that 80 percent of what will be given will be given by the top 20 percent of donors has shifted toward a 90 percent/10percent ratio.
- Depending on an organization's fund-raising prowess, it is prudent to identify two to four times as many individuals or institutions for identified *potential* support as the nonprofit hopes to raise since not every prospect will make a gift or contribute at the level hoped for.
- Campaigns often have a "quiet phase" when soliciting support from the organization's board and key prospects and a "public phase" when contributions are solicited from the community at large.
- The most successful campaigns generate at least 60 percent of their goal during the quiet phase before they launch the public phase.
- While the length of time required to conceive, organize, implement, and conclude a major campaign varies greatly depending on the nature and scope of the project and magnitude of the fund-raising goal, such efforts can easily take up to several years:
  - Feasibility study: Three to four months
  - Campaign plan development: One to two months
  - Volunteer leadership recruitment*: Two to three months
  - Prospect identification and research*: Two to four months
  - Volunteer training and prospect assignment: One to two months
  - Collateral materials design and production*: Two to three months
  - Quiet phase fund-raising: Four to twelve months
  - Public phase fund-raising: Six to eighteen months

*Can occur concurrent with other initiatives

- In general, it is difficult to sustain an intensive campaign for more than two years, unless professional staff primarily drive that effort, as is often the case with higher education, major health care organizations, and the largest nonprofit organizations.

Figure 10.7 *(continued)*

Notes

1. J. Redbanks, "World Heritage Tourism: The Potential for a New Fundraising Model for World Heritage Destinations" (2012). whc.unesco.org/document/121350
2. Ibid.
3. Based on analysis of two state granting programs over the past five years.
4. http://givingusa.org/giving-usa-2016.
5. https://www.philanthropy.com/article/Donations-Grow-4-to-373/236790.
6. Foundation Center, "Foundation Stats" (July 2016), http://data.foundationcenter.org/#/foundations/all/nationwide/total/list/2014.
7. Foundation Center, "Key Facts on U.S. Foundations" (November 2014), http://foundationcenter.org/media/news/20141105.html.
8. Small Business Administration, U.S. Department of Commerce, http://www.sba.gov. Introduction to crowdfunding for Entrepreneurs, SBA Learning Center https:///www.sba.gov/tools/sba-learningcenter/training/introduction-crowdfunding-entrepreneurs

9. Crowdfunding, LLC, "Glossary of Terms" (2012) Crowdfunding Industry Report, p. 25. www.crowd-funding.nl/wp-content/uploads/2012/05/92834651-massolution-abridged-crowd-funding-industry-report1.pdf

10. Tax Incentives for Preserving Historic Properties, Technical Preservation Services, National Park Service, U.S. Department of the Interior, http://www.nps.gov/tps/tax-incentives.htm

11. Sourced from Georgia's Savannah historic tax credit map and economic impacts and list provided by the National Trust for Historic Preservation and reported in Historic Savannah Foundation's June 30, 2014, newsletter article, "Federal Historic Tax Credit Threatened." http://www.myhsf.org/newsletter/historic-tax-credit-threatened.

12. Ibid.

13. G. Burge and B. Piper, "Strategic Fiscal Interdependence: County and Municipal Adoptions of Local Option Sales Taxes," National Tax Journal 65, no. 2 (June 2012): 387–416.

14. Tax Foundation, "Updated State and Local Option Sales Tax," http://taxfoundation.org/article/updated-state-and-local-option-sales-tax.

15. Public Art Network, Americans for the Arts, "Percent-for-Art Programs," http://www.americansfort-hearts.org/sites/default/files/pdf/2013/by_program/networks_and_councils/public_art_network/PublicArtAdvocacy_talkpnts.pdf.

16. Arthur Andersen study, December 1997.

17. As stated in the case study of Asheville in DMAI Essentials: Destination Product Development (n.d.), "North Carolina does not allow county taxing jurisdictions to create or change occupancy tax amounts. All room tax creations or changes for any County need to be voted by the Legislature."

18. Ibid.

19. The 2016 program guide is available at http://www.ashevillecvb.com/wp-content/uploads/TPDF-2016ProgramGuide.pdf. For more general information, see http://www.ashevillecvb.com/product-de-velopment.

20. Modified from a presentation by Cathy O'Connor, president of the Alliance for Economic Development of Oklahoma City, http://www.theallianceokc.org/sites/default/files/files/images/Blog/Streetcar%20Subcommittee_BID-TIF_072413.pdf, and Richard Dye and D. Merriman, "Tax Increment Financing," Land Lines 18, no. 1 (January 2006), http://www.lincolninst.edu/pubs/1078_Tax-Increment-Financing.

21. Ibid.

22. Ibid.

23. General Services Administration, Catalog of Federal Domestic Assistance, http://www.cfda.gov.

24. Tourism Cares is the charitable community of the travel and tourism industry with a mission to preserve and enhance the travel experience for future generations; see http://www.tourismcares.org/mission.

Step Four: Market for Positive Impact

Chapter 11

Marketing to Visitors

Traveling is not just an activity, it's the art of broadening your vision through the priceless experience.

—Wayne Chirisa, author

Marketing generates interest, conveys uniqueness, and compels action. Great marketing helps destinations and sites distinguish themselves from the competition through dynamic images, targeted messages, and engaging content. Effective marketing begins with solid research to instruct design and distribution. Optimally, the integrated marketing activities cross platforms to present a consistent brand.

While traditional marketing focuses on four Ps—product, price, place, and promotion—the advent of social and digital media brought a new component to the marketing mix with the consumer's desire to engage with a community of peers. The emphasis on tourism requires marketing to focus outwardly, where cultural and heritage institutions or destination marketing organizations (DMOs) seek to attract visitors from beyond their geographic borders. Organizations may create promotions and other strategies to connect with residents and local leaders, but primary emphasis should support the overall destination's goal to increase the economic, social, or environmental impact from targeted domestic and international visitors (to generate new money from outside the community). For cultural heritage tourism, marketing must be sensitive, appropriate, and representative of the site or destination. Without this lens on authenticity, the destination or site may misrepresent the significant experience(s) available. This chapter reviews the process and unique considerations for marketing cultural heritage products and experiences to visitors.

Sustainable Marketing Begins with a Plan

A consistent thread throughout this book is the need to plan, to be informed in decision making and proactive in implementation, and to understand what desired outcomes are to be achieved. A marketing plan is often created after a destination or organization has determined its vision and overall goals for cultural heritage tourism. The sophistication required to reach audiences above the din of the competition (from destinations as well as other entertainment options) requires marketing skill and customization. No longer is a "one-size-fits-all" marketing strategy able to penetrate the various psychological and behavioral differences or motivations of today's traveler. Generating a positive call to action involves knowing the following:

- Where travelers get their information
- How travelers want to receive information
- When travelers want to access and receive information
- What information will motivate them to travel to the destination
- Why they would be interested in the destination site's culture or heritage

A comprehensive cultural heritage tourism marketing plan for a destination or organization will answer all these questions for *each target market*. Along with the consumer strategy, the planner must also recognize the travel trade distribution system and design specific marketing approaches to engage tour operators, online travel agencies, traditional travel agencies, global distribution systems (GDS), receptive tour operators, destination management companies, influencer marketers, media, and meeting planners to help realize the cultural heritage tourism goals.

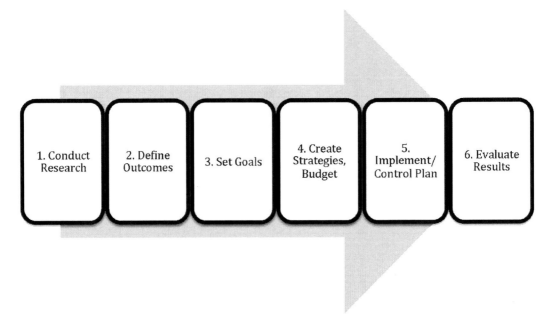

Figure 11.1 Process for creating a cultural heritage tourism marketing plan.

The good news is that marketing budgets do not need to be large to be effective, only focused and measurable. To get started, consider what you want to achieve and review the vision to identify what activities will help advance the objectives—greater attendance at special events, attracting new audiences, increasing gift shop sales, and/or generating off-season travelers. Examine the destination's or organization's situation analysis, if available, to understand the current marketing landscape and performance before creating overall marketing objectives and tactics.

Targeted research, "controls" to stay on course, and detailed expenses to execute marketing activities must be outlined and followed. Make sure the budget includes both human and financial resources, as dedicated staff or consulting time to implement and manage marketing activities—especially social media—are critical to success.

Research Helps Make Informed Decisions

Research is a conversation. If a destination asks the right questions and listens to the customer (the visitor), the responses may prove insightful, instructional, and informative. The more you know about your customer, the better equipped you are to create appealing messages, design attractive materials, and produce compelling promotions. Market research begins with identifying the right questions that an organization or destination wants answered and then selecting the correct methodology and survey instrument to obtain those answers from the desired audience. Research is (or should be) the foundation for all organizations and destinations embarking on a marketing initiative.

Types of Tourism Research

A challenge for cultural heritage tourism planning is the lack of consistent data available, not only from destination to destination but also in the definition of "culture" or "heritage" categories and when research is planned. Destinations (national, state, and local) often do not use the same methodology, making it difficult to compare data. The lack of nationally credible and current data is also problematic to defining benchmarks given the quickly changing profile of customers. Due to the size and diversity of the United States, national data may not be relevant or applicable to local areas. Despite these challenges, planners must proceed by cobbling together existing (secondary) data and conducting original (primary) research when possible. Various research tools are defined in chapter 15. For a cultural heritage tourism destination, a marketer may want to know the following:

- When attendance rates are lowest (days of the week or months of the year) to plan special promotions or packages or to develop new attractions, products, and activities
- The motivation for travel—how culture and heritage rate among other motivations for travel (such as visiting friends and relatives or attending sporting events)
- Whether and how the availability of culture and/or heritage impacted the visitor's decision to stay longer in the destination
- Whether the visitor plans to return and what would enhance future visits

For a cultural heritage event or attraction, a marketer may want to know the following:

- Overall attendance
- Ratio of local residents to out-of-town visitors
- Distance traveled and origin cities (where visitors live and reside)
- Behavior patterns (activities and spending) of attendees
- Visitor satisfaction and areas for improvement
- Plans to attend future events
- Economic impact and return on investment (cost of creating and hosting the event vs. revenue generated)

For a cultural heritage promotion or advertisement, a marketer may use research to determine the following:

- How different messaging tests with visitors
- Preferred incentives for promotions
- Best months to hold special events or promotions

- Favored graphics or images in various advertisements
- Where to advertise
- The appeal and value of timed admissions or other online booking tools for special exhibitions, concerts, and programs

Often, private market research firms or universities are hired to develop, deploy, and analyze primary market research. Some destination marketing organizations (DMOs) and convention and visitors bureaus (CVBs) have research staff who may oversee these functions or contract with outside experts for objective data collection. Cultural heritage institutions may find it advantageous to partner with CVBs when assembling specific information (dedicated research) or to participate in destination-wide research (ongoing market studies). Ask local destination marketing experts about their research program to learn more about methodology, their schedule for collecting and analyzing visitor data, and special studies that may be planned to capture specific information. Cultural and heritage institutions may prefer to join (perhaps at a nominal cost) with the CVB or its market research firm to capture primary data. This may be in lieu of or to complement conducting their own independent market research.

Market Segmentation

As mentioned previously, most destinations cannot afford to market to everyone—nor is this an effective approach. Therefore, cultural heritage tourism planning begins by identifying a target market via *market segmentation*:

> The process of defining and subdividing a large homogenous market into clearly identifiable segments that have similar needs, wants, or demand characteristics. Its objective is to design a marketing mix that precisely matches the expectations of customers in the targeted segment.[1]

Since the market for tourism is global, a planner must begin to segment audiences based on one or more characteristics. The five main characteristics of markets are the following:

1. Geographic (where the visitors live)
2. Demographic (visitor profile—age, race, sex, education, and income)
3. Motivational (purpose for visiting the destination)
4. Psychographic (interests, activities, and opinions)
5. Behavioral (actions, manners, and loyalty to brands and destinations)

The cultural heritage tourism marketing planning process begins with identifying the audience characteristics that are most appropriate or the best fit for the existing and proposed experiences. This market segmentation does not preclude understanding the current visitor; the process focuses on what *new market* could be attracted to visit. Perhaps the geographic area is limited to a drive market (typically within a 250-mile radius of the destination) or airport origin cities, the preferred demographics may be families or seniors, or the motivation may be leisure rather than business and/or include visiting friends and relatives. It is hoped that the target market has an interest in culture, history, and heritage.

Existing marketing profiles and trends help narrow the field, as evidenced in chapter 2. Using consumer data and behavioral traits, planners sift through the myriad profiles to identify the most likely visitors for the destination and cultural or heritage site. This market intelligence guides creation of specific goals to advance cultural heritage tourism through collateral materials, advertising, sales and promotions, public and media relations, and digital and social media marketing strategies.

> Millennials and cultural sites can be a natural and compelling fit, especially if the site remembers two important components of the Millennial experience. First, the site must create a way for these visitors to share experiences through the technology channels necessary for peer-to-peer communication. Second, cultural locations can connect and create long-lasting loyalty through opportunities to share the site's future with restoration projects in which Millennials can participate. This sense of pride in knowing they made a difference is a powerful driver for this audience. Marketing will be compelling if it's disruptive and conveys the site through an authentic, nontraditional lens.
> —Claudia Vecchio, director, Nevada Department of Tourism and Cultural Affairs

About Branding

Collectively, the cultural heritage experiences should enhance the destination's brand and contribute to its unique market appeal. In recent years, destinations have spent tremendous amounts of resources on developing their brand. "Branding," however, is more than a slogan or a tagline. In fact, a destination brand is really how the customer perceives, imagines, or considers the place or product. No amount of marketing can replace the impact of the actual experience. Without the delivery of exceptional (and, it is hoped, authentic) experiences and service, the brand promise focusing on cultural heritage cannot be fulfilled.

Cultural heritage branding differs from traditional consumer product and destination branding in five ways: (1) culture is not always "tangible" and therefore may be more difficult to express or interpret visually; (2) authenticity is important in establishing a value proposition with meaning for both destination and customer without compromising cultural and historic integrity; (3) it is fluid and may change with the local culture; (4) it may require different icons, images, and messages to associate with different audiences; and (5) it is only as strong as how residents feel about the destination and its culture, heritage, and tourism. Resident and stakeholder buy-in is essential to "selling" the brand.

The Impact of Technology

Technology has transformed the way people plan and travel. The swift rise of Internet use for travel planning quickly changed marketing strategies as destinations consider the value and impact of traditional print materials and shift emphasis to mobile technology. Understanding the impact and staying ahead of the technology curve requires persistence and skill. Engaging professionals to help navigate changes in customer trip-planning behavior and on-site usage of technology when traveling may be a wise investment. Monitoring research on technology preferences and trends may also provide insights into how best to market your site or destination. Knowing your customer profile is vital; helping customers flow through travel cycles is critical to ensure that actions culminate in the sharing of positive experiences. According to Google,

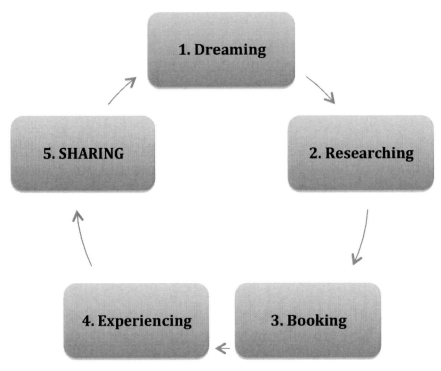

Figure 11.2 The five stages of travel.

there are five stages of travel: dreaming, researching, booking, experiencing, and sharing (see figure 11.2).[2]

Marketing strategies must address each of these stages, ideally using integrated promotions and platforms most appropriate for each target audience. Incorporating benchmarks to measure transition from one stage to another determines the effectiveness of marketing tools and strategies. Tailoring messages and visual cues can also spur consumers from one stage to another. Providing forums and formats—especially via social media—allows visitors to participate in the marketing process by sharing images or commenting on experiences.

As mobile devices grow in popularity and use, responsive design—where content adapts to any format—is essential. According to the *State of the American Traveler* report, 44.6 percent of millennials prefer to use their mobile phone to access travel information. Travel-related apps are also often used on tablets or mobile devices (15.4 percent).[3]

Digital Marketing: Social Media and Beyond

In the twenty-first century, the website is the front window for a site, event, or destination. The architecture, design, and user-friendliness of the website influence whether a consumer stays on the site and plans a trip to a cultural heritage destination, attraction, or event or searches for other places to visit. While the DMO website is the single most popular trip-planning tool, user-generated content and social media are increasingly revered for travel planning.[4] Facebook, Twitter, Pinterest, Instagram, YouTube, Tumblr, Periscope, and Snapchat are popular portals used for trip planning and are growing rapidly as trusted sources of information from peers and valued experts.

Emphasis may currently focus on social media, yet digital marketing goes beyond this medium to build awareness and promote a brand by using all available digital channels. Specifically, digital marketing includes the following:

* Internet marketing (Web, search engine marketing [including search engine optimization and pay-per-click advertising], smartphones, mobile markets, e-mail marketing, online banner advertising, and social media)
* Non-Internet digital channels (television, radio, Short Message Service [text messaging], and digital billboards)[5]

Expanding distribution of content across multiple digital channels ensures that cultural heritage is recognized on the Internet but also seen (or heard) on other media. In 2015, half of Americans used a mapping site to plan leisure travel.[6] Non-Internet digital channels may be more appropriate if you want to drive customers to a special event or off the highway. To establish goals for digital marketing, here are two questions to consider:

1. What are the specific outcomes desired for the destination, event, or site?
2. How can digital marketing help you realize these cultural heritage tourism goals?

Once goals are established, create a digital marketing campaign that includes these four components:

1. Search engine marketing—through content strategy and search engine optimization or through paid search advertising (such as AdWords)
2. Social media promotions—paid advertising on Facebook or promotion on Twitter, Pinterest, and Google+
3. Mobile market promotions—creation of native apps and submission to Google Play and the Apple Store
4. E-mail marketing—promotion of products or services through e-mail marketing campaigns[7]

Building in the correct metrics for other digital marketing strategies is also important. For example, how will your presence on mapping sites influence travel decisions or generate positive response from a travel-related e-mail newsletter? These digital marketing platforms can often enhance brand awareness and create buzz by new or potential visitors. One small destination decided to engage its youth in the creation of an app to showcase its cultural heritage and nature-based attractions and also establish a tracking mechanism to reward visitation. Read the ProjectWA case study at the end of this chapter to learn how technology is influencing behavior.

Figure 11.3 Teacher Anthony Rovente, left, and Tim Fry, far right, with students from Lopez Island—Washington State.

Focusing on Social Media

The World Bank considers a good website as your home country and social media as your embassy.[8] When preparing a marketing plan with social media and digital marketing strategies, understanding social media is critical. How destinations and their cultural heritage tourism experiences can be promoted to foster visitation, followers, and fans begins with understanding the size and scope of the segment. According to Statista, 1.79 billion people use social networks worldwide, and 73 percent of the U.S. population has a social network profile.[9] The statistics company expects the number of social media users worldwide to reach 2.5 billion by 2018.[10]

Social media may prove useful if you want to find new customers or educate existing customers. Understanding which market profiles match to social media platforms is important for designing content (for social media) and determining distribution channels. For example, Pinterest has more female users and is most appropriate for showcasing images. Twitter requires brevity (140 characters) but also frequency and "news to use" for cultural heritage marketers to garner the size of followers necessary to produce a loyal fan base.

During the 2011 Iowa City Book Festival, attendees helped write a "Twitter Novel" during the three-day event. Individuals from around the world were also encouraged to contribute content via tweets to build the story; seventy-two authors wrote 878 tweets during the creation of Novel IC. The Iowa City of Literature organization helped promote the project, which drew extensive media coverage that shined a light on the festival and the organization.

Seven Things to Remember when Building Your Social Media Strategy

By Lauren Cleland, digital media strategist and one of the "Top 20 Most Influential Tourism Professionals on Twitter," July 2016

1. Do one and do it well.

   With new social networks popping up each month, it's tempting to join each one. However, this is not a best practice. It's better to identify the best social network for you (based on your goals, audience, and content) and build a strategic plan for success. Only once you feel as though you have a strong hold on the first social network is it appropriate to begin looking for another network to add to your marketing repertoire.

2. You have to fail to succeed.

   Not every Facebook post, tweet, or Instagram photo is going to result in thousands of likes. With each new post you publish, you get a better understanding of your audience, which will, in turn, lead to more engaging social media content. Always take note of the engagement and reach of each social media post. If it's successful, identify what made the post successful and implement those tactics in future posts. If the post fails, analyze why it didn't resonate with your audience and avoid those pitfalls when crafting future posts.

3. Social media is not the story.

   Social media is integral to the storytelling process; however, social media itself is *not* the story. Your content, whether it is a photo, video, or article, is the story. Social media is simply a vehicle for these stories. Your social media strategy is only as strong as your content.

4. Become an "info-tainer."

   There is more competing for consumer attention than ever before. The only way to rise above it all is to create content that adds value to the lives of your customers. Your content must inform as well as entertain. Those who share "info-taining" content on social media are more likely to see an increase in organic engagement.

5. Follow the "Five Rule."

   On average, only 2.6 percent of your social media audience sees your content.* To maximize the reach of your story, share it at least five times. Share it on Facebook one day. Then, several days later, share the same piece of content on Twitter. A month later, share it on Facebook again—but use a different featured image and headline.

6. The only thing constant in social media is change.

   The digital media landscape is constantly changing. What works one month may fall flat the following month. To stay afloat on the ever-changing digital tides, educate yourself. Sign up for relevant newsletters, identify influencers in your field to follow, and have open communication with your counterparts at other organizations. The only way to stay afloat is to prepare yourself with proper knowledge.

7. Followers and fan numbers do not matter.

   Understanding your analytics is the most important part of your social media success. With that said, do not fixate on the wrong analytics. Instead of concentrating on your follower count, pay close attention the reach, impressions, and engagements that your content receives. These numbers are a much stronger reflection of your success.

---

* Marshall Manson, "Facebook Zero: Considering Life after the Demise of Organic Reach" (March 2014), Social@Ogilvy.

Figure 11.4 Seven things to remember when building your social media strategy.

As social media sites mature, the rules for engagement may change. Destinations and institutions are developing protocols and guidelines for social media postings and usage. Monitoring (and responding to) content on TripAdvisor, Facebook, Twitter, and other user-generated content sites becomes increasingly important to brand management. The World Bank says,

> Social media guidelines are meant to empower staff to engage through social media about their own work, not to make statements on behalf of the Bank that are outside their scope of work or expertise, or where they may purport to speak for other departments or for management.[11]

Therefore, the planning process and cultural heritage tourism social media marketing goals include *what social media should be used* as well as *who shall use it* (on behalf of the company) and *how it shall be used* (for official statements vs. personal time). Having protocols in place for engagement ensures brand consistency and avoids potential problems with inappropriate content generation or postings.

You may want to evaluate the number of Facebook fans or likes; the total size of your fan base on social networking websites; positive reviews on Trip Advisor, Yelp, and so on; or the number of conversions resulting from social media. Yet cultural heritage marketers must think more strategically. The results should be measured by the action generated, not only on volume of use. After you posted, tweeted, or engaged, did you accomplish the following:

- Grab attention
- Cause people to want to share
- Initiate a discussion
- Cause people to take an action
- Deliver economic value[12]

According to Avinash Kaushik, author of two books on Web analytics, Google's Digital Marketing Evangelist, and cofounder of Market Motive (online marketing training), there are four social media metrics to use:

1. Conversation rate—the number of conversations per post
2. Amplification rate—the number of reshares or retweets per post
3. Applause rate—retweets, likes, +1s, and so on
4. Economic value—the sum of short-term revenue, long-term revenue, and cost savings[13]

A comprehensive social media marketing strategy begins with great content, a schedule of placement to appropriate platforms, constant engagement with customers, and evaluation tools to measure impact against original goals.

Two areas often overlooked in the social media marketing plan are training and evaluation. Several websites can help track statistics, but time for training as well as uploading and managing content and analyzing statistics is necessary to ensure that social media networks work to their full potential. The *Chronicle of Philanthropy*[14] recently published several strategies to help nonprofits advance skills in social networking. These strategies, when adapted and enhanced, apply to cultural heritage resource managers and destination tourism staff as well. Suggested strategies include the following:

- Training employees how and when to interact on social networks
- Empowering them to engage during prime peak interaction periods (such as Sunday evenings for Facebook) as well as business hours

- Establishing different strategies for campaigns to ensure that everyday interactions are kept separate and maintained for loyal followers
- Learning how to use mobile devices to take and post images of important happenings
- Creating a social calendar to inform staff on when, what, how, and where to post
- Following thought leaders of cultural heritage tourism (on Twitter, Facebook, and LinkedIn) to add value to your own network (through retweets and "likes" or "shares")

As plentiful and diverse as social media sites are, so are the tools used to evaluate them. A comprehensive marketing plan must include social media strategies as well as evaluation methodology to monitor impact and make adjustments to plans as necessary. Successful media strategies are: useful, timely, informative, relevant, practical, actionable, generous, credible, brief, entertaining, and fun.

Some of the most prevalent and relevant social media engagement tools also build in sustainability mechanisms. Here are a few management and evaluation tools:

- Google Analytics is the most popular choice for analyzing Web traffic and evaluating social media. Some measurement tools are free, and others are for a fee.
- HootSuite.com is a (mostly) free social media management dashboard; it helps manage various accounts and posts in advance.
- Keyhole.co measures a brand's impact on Twitter, Facebook, and Instagram.
- Klout quantifies your influence on each major social platform (your "Klout" score).[15]

In the fast-paced world of social media, it is also important to track trends on technology and their applications—social, mobile, video, and local. Follow blogs and technology sites to learn the most current news and impacts of digital media. Planning for social media is as important and requires as much consistency as actually engaging in social media. A comprehensive marketing plan for cultural heritage tourism will consider both these factors and allocate the necessary financial and human resources to accomplish the desired digital marketing goals. Refer to figure 11.4 for more instruction on building a social media strategy.

Compelling Collateral Materials

The advent of the Internet posed a potential challenge for producers of collateral materials—visitor guides, brochures, maps, rack cards, and so on. With the Internet maintaining its lead as the primary source of information for tourists planning a trip, where do collateral materials fit in the marketing mix? Research indicates that brochures and maps, in particular, are still viable travel marketing tools, especially during trips. Brochures positively impact visitor behavior, often influencing where to travel and in what activities to engage.[16] Brochures and other collateral materials are often shared with others; a 2014 report indicates that 62 percent of all visitors share brochures with at least one to four people in their group.[17] Brochures or guides also provide an opportunity to introduce new information or through a new lens. The profile at the end of this chapter shows a strategy for visitors interested in learning about Route 66 from the American Indian perspective.

Ten Tips for Creating a Perfect Tourism Brochure

Travel marketing guru Judy Randall has reviewed thousands of travel brochures during her career of more than thirty years in the industry. Here are ten recommendations she makes for creating a compelling brochure to promote your cultural heritage tourism attraction or business:

1. First, You Must Determine How Your Visitors Describe You. If your brochure does not match what your tourists say about you, you are on the wrong track.
2. The Top Front 1/3 Must "Hook the Reader. The sole purpose of the front top 1/3 of the brochure is to catch the reader's attention.
3. Make an Emotional Connection. After you have gotten the reader's attention, the next step is to make a strong emotional connection.
4. Now Tell Them the "Must-Sees," Highlights and Specifics. You've won a brief few seconds to tell them about your product. Capture the overview quickly.
5. Use Design to Strengthen Your Message. Use fresh, updated photography that tells a story.
6. Maps Are a Must. Accurate maps show the site or destination in relation to the rest of the region or the country.
7. Tell Them How to Get Additional Information. Make your brochure do as much work as possible but always give them a way to access more information—website address, phone number, e-mail address.
8. Create a Complete Package and Make It Easy to Say "Yes." Packaging your destination or attraction with a complete one-price itinerary works.
9. Inquiry and Fulfillment Pieces Must Match. Have your fulfillment pieces match your inquiry-generation pieces (ads, brochures, etc.) for maximum effect—with the same color, design, message on the outside of the envelope, etc.
10. Sell the Experience, Not the Room or Ticket. People will come to buy a unique experience. Your job is to package "the experience" to compel them to visit.

Source: Randall Travel Marketing, Inc., http://www.rtmnet.com.

The brochure or rack card[24] is the quintessential marketing tool for most cultural and heritage institutions. Given the plethora of brochures distributed today, marketers must answer three important questions:

1. Who is the brochure's or rack card's audience?
2. What message or call to action do you want to convey?
3. Where will the brochure or rack card be distributed?
4. How will you measure the impact (or obtain a conversion rate—cost of production vs. visitors generated)?

Once these questions are answered with enough specificity to instruct content and design, the process can proceed. A design philosophy and graphic guidelines are paramount for visually presenting an organization or destination persona. For cultural heritage tourism, the brochure planning process begins with the desire to present information in a compelling, attractive way representative of the quality experiences available. Engaging experts to facilitate the process of interpreting the vision into visual elements and colors may be appropriate so that politics and/or favoritism do not dilute effective brochure development.

Advertising

There are multiple advertising media available for destinations and cultural heritage tourism sites: television/cable, radio, print media, and digital media (including social media). Super Bowl television advertisements may take center stage at award shows and generate lots of buzz, but effective advertising can be produced at all price points. A destination or cultural heritage resource may purchase advertising or media buys for a few reasons:

1. To present or tell your story in your own words—for example, to share your brand promise, inform readers and listeners about your unique cultural heritage experiences, thank the audience for support in times of crisis, or request or appeal in times of need
2. To inform the audience about new attractions or developments, deals, and opportunities—for example, if there is a new heritage trail, a new museum, a culinary tour package, a newly renovated hotel, or a trolley tour
3. To promote a time-sensitive activity or event—for example, a festival or special concert, a theater performance, or a special exhibition

The selection of media is dependent on the audience. There are two markets for advertising to consider: travel trade and consumer. Travel trade magazines and business-to-business media are used when targeting tour operators, industry partners, and consolidators. Consumer media reach the target audience directly via newspaper, magazines, television, radio, Internet, social media, outdoor billboards, and specialty sources (such as advertising on taxicabs, buses, stadiums, and convention centers). Knowing where the target audience (current or potential visitor) prefers to receive their travel information is vital research to secure before preparing and purchasing advertising. Defining the frequency required for a call to action is also important intelligence to secure in advance. Identify and plan for the method of evaluation to determine the effectiveness of the advertising media buy(s).

Radio is a great choice to promote area events. Television/cable is a better medium when compelling visuals and video convey the call to action. Billboard advertising and signs in transport stations (in bus terminals, airports, and train stations and in train cars, buses, and taxis) and via auto routes are effective as local reminders for travelers going to or already at the destination.

Digital advertising is gaining ground, with social media advertising in particular becoming more targeted and providing cost-effective ways to build awareness. As new channels are added and formats change, the most important consideration is defining the desired advertising outcome—more leads (potential visitors) or more conversions (actual visitors). Facebook allows granular focus on demographics, interests, and behavior to marry your message with the right audience. Instagram, surpassing Twitter and Snapchat with more than 600 million users (as of December 2016), links ad campaigns to Facebook accounts. Twitter and LinkedIn are perfect for building a community with business-to-business content. As discussed briefly in the section "Digital

Figure 11.5 Museum and tourist leaders launch Seattle Museum Month 2016—Seattle, Washington.

Marketing: Social Media and Beyond" earlier in this chapter, website advertising can be measured three ways:

- Search engine optimization—improve the ranking of Web pages through content, linking, and search engine–friendly design. This results in search engines ranking pages in the website higher for various search terms.
- Pay-per-click—use key word bidding through Google to display sponsored text ads and image ads for targeted key words and phrases.
- Cost-per-click—Facebook ad rates, driven by click-through rates.

The advertising component of a marketing plan will outline specific media buys and the frequency and cost for these purchases as well as the creativity required to produce a compelling ad. The outcome is measured not only in audience exposure but also in the conversion rate to actual visitors.

Sales and Promotions

Promotions provide a unique opportunity for cultural heritage tourism marketers to collaborate and extend their traditional reach to customers through time-sensitive packages—thematic offerings crossing geographic borders and enticing repeat visitation with incentives and value-added benefits. Marketed directly to consumers or through the travel trade (tour operators, travel agents, and convention and meeting planners), promotions are most effective when offered for a limited time with special offers and value-added benefits that destinations or organizations can track and measure for impact. The example profiled at the end of this chapter demonstrates the opportunity for cultural and heritage institutions to collaborate with area hotels to help increase business during a traditionally slow season.

Events are popular and potentially profitable activities for cultural heritage destinations or organizations. Many cities or communities host annual events and festivals as a way to celebrate their culture and heritage, offer a unique gathering of activities for residents and visitors, and provide a consistent marketing opportunity for the destination. As these cultural heritage events mature, they often attract large audiences from around the world; consider the visitation to the Annual Gettysburg Civil War Battle Reenactment, Pasadena's Tournament of Roses Parade, the Kentucky Derby, or the National Cherry Blossom Festival in Washington, D.C. Some events appeal specifically to group tours. For this audience, the American Bus Association annually publishes its "Top 100 Events in North America" for tour operators to consider including in their annual itineraries (http://www.buses.org/news-publications/top-100).

To sell cultural heritage tourism products and experiences, destinations or cultural and heritage institutions may do the following:

- Attend international travel trade shows, such as World Travel Market in London (November), ITB in Berlin (March), the U.S. Travel Association's IPW (June), and domestic marketplaces organized by the American Bus Association, the National Tour Association, or Travel Learning's Educational Travel Conference.
- Participate in consumer promotions hosted by automobile clubs, bank clubs, and local or regional sponsors.
- Host on-site familiarization tours for tour operators or research visits for journalists and influencer marketers to learn more about a destination or cultural heritage site.

- Establish e-commerce and Internet links with other travel industry partners (hotels, restaurants, and airlines) to encourage advance online booking for packages and promotions.
- Host sales missions or media blitzes (where destination representatives go to these origin cities and meet with local tour operators, travel planners, and journalists).

The variety of promotions is limited only by the creativity of the partners, the budget for implementation, and the fit between the customer and the experience. Each promotion should contribute to a specific marketing goal and help achieve the greater cultural heritage tourism vision. Metrics to measure success should be built into each promotion and analyzed for their return on investment. A successful promotion based on a destination's heritage can help increase both visitation and education. Read the profile of Lincoln City, Oregon, at the end of this chapter to learn more about how one community used its past industry to promote present-day experiences.

Public and Media Relations

Public and media relations foster third-party reporting or commentary about a destination's cultural heritage tourism. Identifying and building relationships with journalists is fundamental to a successful media relations campaign. Various organizations—such as the Society of American Travel Writers (http://www.satw.org, which includes both U.S. and Canadian members)—can help streamline the process of identifying editors, photographers, freelance journalists, broadcasters, and videographers interested in cultural heritage tourism.

A comprehensive public and media relations campaign will include a special "media" section on the destination's or cultural heritage resource's website with the following information:

- List of story ideas for the journalists' consideration and exploration
- Press releases featuring news prepared by the destination or resource
- Image gallery
- Selection of published media articles featuring the destination or cultural heritage resource
- Accolades for the destination or cultural heritage organization or resource (as recognized by other media and respected sources)
- Fact sheet about the destination or cultural heritage resource
- Media assistance guidelines—how the destination or cultural heritage resources can help the journalist with story research, fact checking, quotes, interviews, on-site research, hosting, and so on
- Contact information for specific questions, quotes, etc.

Some destinations or cultural heritage managers ask journalists to register to obtain some or all of this information as a way of controlling usage (especially photographs), to provide more customized service, and to track inquiries. As journalists are frequently on deadline when researching information, this extra step may be a deterrent to their schedule.

Public relations plans expand the reach of media relations by focusing on additional ways to reach target markets and communicate effectively with both internal and external audiences. The major elements of a public relations plan include the following:

- Media list
- Press kit (detailed above)

- General presentation on cultural heritage tourism (economic impact, unique stories, overview of historic and cultural importance or value to community, and visitor experience)
- Speaker's bureau (list of experts to tap for interviews and presentations)
- Crisis communications plan

A public and media relations strategy is usually planned in context with other marketing components.

Distribution Channels for Cultural Heritage Tourism

The tourism industry has six traditional external marketing distribution channels. These are important networks to understand, utilize, and compare with the impact of the destination's website. When creating a marketing plan, the choice(s) of distribution channels can affect the market reach and also the outcomes based on who is traveling and how the cultural heritage experience is purchased. The six external marketing distribution channels are:

1. Travel agencies: Specialists who plan itineraries or assist with booking specific destination or travel packages for consumers.
2. Online travel agencies (OTAs): Self-service online booking portal for consumers to directly reserve and purchase airline tickets, hotel rooms, car rentals, and other travel items (Travelocity, Expedia, Orbitz, and Kayak are examples).
3. Global distribution systems: A worldwide computerized reservation system for use by travel agencies and/or corporate travel departments to reserve airline seats, hotel rooms, rental cars, and other travel components (Sabre, Amadeus, Galileo, and Worldspan are the leaders).
4. Airline consolidators: Brokers who buy airline seats in bulk and then resell them to travel agents.
5. Tour wholesalers and operators: Specialists in group travel, tour wholesalers will create and market all-inclusive or independent tours for sale through travel agents, tour operators will create and market group tours for sale directly to customers, and receptive operators provide the ground operations and coordination for groups in a destination.
6. Specialty channels: Meeting and incentive tour planners, educational travel planners, and volunteer tourism planners, to name a few.

A marketing plan focusing on a destination's cultural heritage tourism vision may include all six distribution channels but will normally balance these distribution systems with selling directly to their target audience via the destination or cultural heritage manager's other marketing strategies. The three most relevant to cultural heritage tourism are described in more detail below.

Online Travel Agents (OTAs)

Online travel agents are popular browsing sites, such as Expedia, Travelocity, and Trivago, with airline tickets and lodging being the most frequently sourced information, followed by rental cars, events tickets, theme park passes, travel packages, and cruises. Typically, online travel agents charge a fee for inclusion. Cultural heritage tourism destinations and institutions must weigh the booking fees against the promotional value of the global distributor. Understanding the sites preferred by market segments and how a destination (and its cultural heritage offerings) is currently represented on these sites provides good intelligence when creating a marketing plan.

Tour Wholesalers and Operators

Tour wholesalers and tour operators are important distribution channels, especially for destinations and cultural heritage resources interested in group tours or packages for their cultural experiences. A tour wholesaler assembles the tour components at a discounted rate (usually 10 to 20 percent off transportation, lodging, attraction tickets, entertainment, and meals) and then markets it for sale through their own company or resells it to travel agents and other distribution channels for a fee. A tour wholesaler may also be a tour operator, marketing and selling the package tour directly to consumers or as a group. A receptive operator handles all of the logistics and hosting of the group locally for a tour operator at a destination.

A number of travel trade shows focus directly on the wholesale and group tour operator market. These business-to-business conventions or shows often have set appointment schedules between buyers (operators and tour planners) and suppliers (destinations and attraction representatives). A marketing plan using tour wholesalers and operators requires further understanding about the specific needs of these specialists. Tour wholesaler operator trade organizations include the following:

- National Tour Association: http://www.ntaonline.com
- American Bus Association: http://www.buses.org
- United States Tour Operators Association: http://www.ustoa.com
- Canadian Association of Tour Operators: http://www.cato.ca
- European Tour Operators Association: http://www.etoa.org

Receptive tour operators are represented by the International Inbound Travel Association (http://www.inbound.com).

Specialty Channels

A cultural heritage tourism destination that utilizes specialty channels must have the critical mass and level of quality experiences to attract and host these discriminating tour specialists (and their customers). The marketing plan can outline specific strategies to attract this influential travel buyer if the incentive, luxury, meeting, corporate, or educational market is favored by and suited to the destination or cultural heritage resource.

Creating a marketing plan for these specialty channels requires an extensive knowledge of the requirements to host these groups and the tools to reach them. Each specialty segment is different and has its own organization, trade show, contracting, and hosting requirements. To be effective in securing this business, the destination's cultural heritage tourism marketing strategies must be tailored for each channel. Specialty channel and travel associations include

- Incentive Marketing Association/Incentive Travel Council: http://www.incentivemarketing.org
- Meeting Professionals International: http://www.mpiweb.org
- Educational Travel Conference: http://www.travelearning.com
- Student Youth Travel Association: http://www.syta.org

Chapter Summary

Sustainability of cultural heritage tourism is threatened if visitors don't know that you exist. As important as overall planning is to sustainability, strategic marketing is also critical. Whether working with a limited or robust budget, destinations and cultural heritage institutions must define the most desired audiences and determine how best to reach them—through compelling messages and/or visuals or via specific media or marketing activities (promotions, public relations, advertising, or digital and social media).

Once research has been completed and analyzed, target markets have been identified, goals have been defined, and budget has been established, the specific components of the cultural heritage tourism marketing plan can be created. Sifting through the various tools and distribution channels, cultural heritage tourism marketers must prioritize strategies to achieve optimum results both for return on investment and for contribution to overall organizational and destination goals and vision. Rather than siloed activities, integrated marketing strategies move the customer through the five stages of travel, resulting in a positive sharing of cultural heritage tourism experiences.

Not only does a strong marketing plan lay out what tools and distribution channels will be used, but adhering to the plan also helps the organization or destination stay the course by avoiding pitfalls and distractions. Implementing controls in the form of evaluation and backup strategies also ensures that high performance is maintained and a positive return on investment is realized. A cultural heritage tourism marketing plan, based on sound research, is fundamental for all destinations and institutions seeking to advance their goals, brand, and vision.

* * * * *

ProjectWA

http://www.ProjectWA.org

The power of the road trip is alive and well thanks to a group of students and new technology from a mobile marketing entrepreneur in Washington State. While many students learn about history via a field trip to a historic site or museum, five Lopez Island Middle School students made history. Calling it ProjectWA, the eighth graders embraced technology and designed a way to reward people for seeking out unique, historic places around Washington State. Led by history teacher Anthony Rovente with technical assistance from Tim Fry of 468 Communications, the students created an app in their "Northwest History" class. They selected heritage-based locations to be included in the app, conducted historical research about each site, and wrote content for "Washington State Insider," a free download on Google Play and the iOS App Store.

Once the app was launched, Fry and his family promoted the app via a 2,000-mile history tour of Washington State in a ProjectWA-branded RV. Along the way, they invited state residents to suggest other historic places to be added to the Washington State Insider app.

A unique feature of the app platform, called 468 Insider, is its reward program for users. In May 2016, Fry launched a visitor's app for the San Juan Islands based on this platform. The San Juan Islands Insider app highlights 130 locations—including historic sites, recreation spots, and businesses—where users can collect points. Visitors physically go a site listed in the app, and GPS verifies one's presence at that location so that points can be accrued for redemption at reward locations. Not only does this app incentivize exploration, but it also encourages visitors to frequent local businesses to redeem their points. For example, fifty points could translate to a 50 percent discount at a local restaurant or retail store.

Instead of discounts at businesses, the Washington State Insider app, created by the Lopez Island students, offers discounted admission to the Washington State History Museum as its user reward. The history-for-students-by-students Washington State Insider app went live in June 2016 with nearly one hundred sites. Within a month of launch, it had been downloaded 1,500 times, generating significant media attention across the state—for both ProjectWA and the off-the-beaten-path historic sites that it was designed to promote.

The long-term goal for the project is threefold: (1) listings for this app will continue to expand to include all the unique and lesser-traveled historic sites and communities in Washington State; (2) other educators will adopt the ProjectWA platform and encourage a class project that uses technology to make history more relevant to today's mobile generation; and (3) consumer downloads will raise awareness about history and increase preservation of the state's distinctive heritage sites.

While Fry and his family were promoting ProjectWA across the state in the summer of 2016, the world was introduced to Pokémon Go, an app based on similar location-aware technology as 468 Insider. For Fry, this instant craze validated his approach to applying gamification to communities that he took with the Insider platform. It also helped illustrate the varying degrees of engagement that result from different applications of mobile technology.

"The emergence of these types of apps shows that games appeal to people of all ages," said Fry. "It's important to keep in mind, though, that the best use of mobile technology is one that contributes to *actual*, not *virtual*, presence—leading to more meaningful engagement in the real world."

* * * * *

Figure 11.6 Tim Fry and family depart on Team ProjectWA road trip—Washington State.

Profile: American Indians and Route 66
Guidebook produced by the American Indian Alaska Native Tourism Association

http://www.americanindiansandroute66.com

Route 66 has many names: the Will Rogers Highway, Main Street of America, and the Mother Road. Designated in 1926, Route 66 stretches more than 2,400 miles from Chicago to Santa Monica, California, and became known as a major east–west artery. As the economy improved in the late 1930s, Route 66 fueled travelers' interest in scenic natural wonders and American Indian culture as portrayed (incorrectly) in "cowboy and Indian" movies. Business owners along the route perpetuated the stereotype of Indian tribes in the form of teepees and war bonnets.[18] After World War II, Route 66 regained public notoriety and almost iconic fame via a television show of the same name in the early 1960s. By this time, commercial development along the route was rampant to accommodate one of the most heavily traveled roads in the country as the main vacation route to Los Angeles. The advent of the modern interstate system—particularly construction of I-40—initiated the decline of Route 66. However, the allure of the Mother Road continues, especially with international visitors to the United States.

A new guidebook, *American Indians & Route 66*,[19] seeks to share the distinct cultures and histories of the more than twenty-five tribes living along the route. With more than half of Route 66 crossing Indian country, the guidebook debunks myths and stereotypes about American Indians living along the infamous route. Produced by the American Indian Native Alaska Tourism Association (AIANTA),[20] the guidebook provides a historical account on the impact of an interstate highway system on the tribal lands and people and context for the creation of Route 66 in relation to other events negatively affecting American Indians—the passage of the Indian Citizenship Act, early tourism and its misrepresentation of cultural identity, the Urban Indian Relocation Program of the 1950s, and use of eminent domain.[21]

"At AIANTA, we feel there is no better way for tribes to share their stories than to tell them themselves. It's important that our peoples' cultures and traditions are kept alive through our own voices and perspectives, and tourism can truly perpetuate the traditions that are still thriving today," said Camille Ferguson, executive director of AIANTA. "By welcoming and educating visitors, through projects like the American Indians and Route 66 Guidebook and Native America. travel website, tribes are able to share stories that they want others to know while still maintaining the privacy and sanctity of certain aspects of their traditions," she continued.

The sixty-eight-page guidebook shares a compelling, easy-to-follow narrative about the distinctive American Indian nations located along the route, describing by state the significant tribal events and notable attractions available to travelers today. Little-known facts, historical and contemporary photographs, and cogent quotes complement personal profiles and stories of American Indians past and present. The "Did You Know?" sidebars on each page provide historical accuracy and context on a range of subjects—from soapstone and birdsongs to the Grand Canyon Skywalk, Tribal Sovereignty, the Sandia Bison Herd, and Laguna Pottery. Contact information and other pertinent trip-planning information are included for reference. A map of the Native American nations with tribal names and locations occupies the guidebook's center spread.

An instructive "Before You Go" section provides general etiquette and information to help visitors respectfully experience Route 66 and the American Indian lands. For example, when attending

Figure 11.7 *American Indians & Route 66* guidebook cover.

a powwow, the guidebook suggests being observant and recognizing that protocols may vary. Some standard guidelines include the following:

- Recordings are not allowed without the permission of the master of ceremonies and the lead singer.
- Ask a dancer's permission before taking a photograph.
- Be respectful of regalia.
- Do not touch or handle an eagle feather; if one has fallen, let the dancer or powwow staff member know.
- The dance circle is sacred; do not walk across the circle and do not permit children to run in or around the circle.[22]

Rules of etiquette are also provided for visiting pueblos, tribes, and American Indian ruins. Tips are also offered for buying American Indian arts and crafts. The free digital guide is available online, offering the most updated tribal tourism information available and an interactive map of tribes along the route.[23]

While we can't go back and undo history, we can certainly learn from the past and correct errors or misconceptions to deal honestly with the events that shaped the country's relationship with American Indians. This guidebook provides an opportunity to experience Route 66 from a different perspective for a whole new more enlightened, informed, and respectful experience.

* * * * *

Profile: Museum Month
Seattle, Washington

http://www.visitseattle.org

What began as a weeklong promotion in conjunction with the conference of the American Alliance of Museums in Seattle, Washington, in 2014, Museum Month has now grown into a full-blown annual event, launched in 2015. The February 2016 campaign focused on increasing overnight visitors, especially among arts, culture, and heritage travelers. Families were also targeted to visit the city during this traditionally quiet travel month. Visitors staying at one of the fifty-nine participating hotels located in the Seattle Tourism Improvement Area (STIA) were eligible for half-price admission at forty-one participating museums (twenty-five in Seattle and sixteen regional museums).

The second annual STIA-funded Museum Month has garnered impressive results:

- 16,862 paid discounted admission redemptions during the twenty-nine days of Museum Month, a 50 percent increase over 2015

Figure 11.8 Chihuly advertisement, Seattle Museum Month—Seattle, Washington.

- Almost 200,000 unique visitors to the dedicated Seattlemuseummonth.com website, a 327 percent increase
- More than 328 million earned media impressions, nearly a tenfold increase over the year
- The 2016 public relations campaign, which resulted in 538 stories featuring Museum Month, including the *Los Angeles Times*, the *Oregonian*, *The Province* newspaper (Vancouver, BC), About.com, and the *Alaska Dispatch* newspaper—almost double the number of stories from 2015

Visit Seattle, the city's official DMO, directs and manages the program. They promote Museum Month with a significant paid media campaign (radio, outdoor, social, digital, and movie theater trailers) and integrated the campaign into all Visit Seattle channels. The program was featured on the Visitseattle.org home page (exposure to more than 100,000 unique visitors monthly) and in Visit Seattle's *No Umbrella* travel blog. It was also included as an event in the *Seattle Localist*, Visit Seattle's monthly consumer e-newsletter sent to more than 93,000 recipients, and as a video wall takeover at Visit Seattle's Visitor Information Center and was promoted on all Visit Seattle social media channels (456,000 fans on Facebook, more than 24,000 followers on Twitter, and more than 48,000 followers on Instagram); it was also part of a targeted media relations campaign. Digital ads performed more than four times the industry standard at 0.34 Click Through Rate (CTR—0.08 is standard), and paid social advertising not only drove site visits but also sparked conversation around Museum Month.[25]

How Museum Month Works

Spring/Summer: Visit Seattle's director of cultural tourism completes prior-year analysis of Museum Month campaign and distributes it to participants.

Summer: Visit Seattle—led by the director of cultural tourism, along with the organization's ad agency, marketing, and public relations teams—defines the campaign, funding, and promotion strategy for next year's Museum Month. Creative work begins on campaign advertisements and Museum Month collateral.

Figure 11.9 Counter card, Seattle Museum Month—Seattle, Washington.

Figure 11.10 Guest pass, Seattle Museum Month—Seattle, Washington.

September: Visit Seattle invites hotels and museums to sign up to participate in the February promotion. Museum participants do not have to be members of Visit Seattle, and there is no fee for participation. The only requirement is that museums extend an admission discount of 50 percent per person to Museum Month pass holders every day they are open in February. Free museums are also invited to be included in the campaign and are noted as such for consumers. Museums submit an invoice and documentation of the number of passport users for the month of February to Visit Seattle. On receipt, Visit Seattle reimburses half of the discounted amount from funds provided by the STIA member hotels. (Museum participants absorbed 25 percent of the discount.) All museums are encouraged to offer special programs and to promote Museum Month via their own communication channels—such as newsletters, websites, media outreach, and social media.

During Museum Month: Participating hotels distribute Museum Month packets to all guests at check-in. Hotels are also encouraged to promote the program on their websites, newsletters, e-mail, and social media. Visit Seattle provides each participating hotel with tabletop desk signs and Museum Month packets that include a map of participating museums and the passport for discounted admission. Pull-up banners are available on request.

While the intent of this campaign is to encourage out-of-town visitation and overnight stay at downtown hotels, a "For Locals" page on the Museum Month website offered the option of promoting a Museum Month membership discount. While many museums expressed enthusiasm for this, participation levels of both museums and consumers have so far remained low.

"We are thrilled with the expansive growth of Seattle Museum Month in only its second year," said Tracey Wickersham, director of cultural tourism for Visit Seattle. She continued, "Redemption rates, particularly for our largest and most well-known museums, have exceeded our expectations."

Wickersham continued, "We anticipate that, as the program becomes an established annual event, we will attract more visitors who will plan their trips in advance specifically to partake in Museum Month and we will see an increase of guests who visit more diverse museums across the region. And of course, we hope that the kind of increased awareness fostered by the reach of the campaign will benefit all our museum partners throughout the year. Over and over we hear variations of 'I had no idea the Seattle region had *so many* interesting and unique museums!' This program aims to change that."[26]

* * * * *

Finders Keepers
Lincoln City, Oregon

http://www.oregoncoast.org/finders-keepers

Along Oregon's 360 miles of coast, many communities are using the arts to take the beach experience beyond sand, surf, and scenery. Lincoln City draws from its past to create new ways to showcase its contemporary culture. As early as 1910, Japanese deep-sea fishing crews used blown-glass globes to float their nets. By the 1940s, European fisherman replaced the more traditional wood and cork with glass floats. Beachcombers scoured the sand to find this deep green or blue sea glass. Now that plastic bottles have replaced the glass floats, the sea glass is a rare find except along Lincoln City's more than seven miles of public beaches. Since 1999, each year from mid-October to Memorial Day, volunteers hide more than 2,000 new floats for visitors to find and keep as a reminder of the destination's heritage and also increase off-season business. The quantity of gloats hidden is equal to the year (2,016 floats in 2016).

The "Finders Keepers" project began in 1999 when a local artist wanted a project to launch the new millennium. The city saw it as a mechanism to expand glass arts in the area as an economic development strategy. Lincoln City Visitor and Convention Bureau funds and promotes the program; the city hires eight to twelve artists to handcraft signed and numbered glass floats. "Float Fairies" hide more than 2,000 floats above the high-tide line and below the beach embankment. "Official" floats carry numbers reflecting the current year and can be registered to receive a certificate of authenticity and information about the artist. A drawing is held monthly for those who are physically unable to comb the beach for their own chance at finding a float. Other glass art (sand dollars, starfish, and crabs) are also occasionally hidden in special drops on holidays or other signature occasions. Glass floats also reward volunteerism; visitors may bring a bag a beach trash to the visitor center to enter a monthly "Trash for Treasures" drawing. Glass floats are also available for purchase in most galleries and gift shops, and a blow-your-own glass float experience is available throughout the year at the Jennifer L. Sears Glass Art Studio.

"Finders Keepers is a phenomenon, generating national awareness of Lincoln City as a Pacific Northwest beach destination. In the past year, the program has produced articles in *Smithsonian*, *USA Today*, and TripAdvisor," said Edward Dreistadt, director of the Lincoln City Visitor and Convention Bureau. He continued, "Finders Keepers also boosts awareness and drives significant visitation in our off-peak seasons."

* * * * *

Notes

1. *Business Dictionary*, http://www.businessdictionary.com/definition/market-segmentation.
2. Modified from Sarah McDonald's presentation on the customer journey from the World Travel Market "Travel Perspective" session 2013 (slide 5), "Inspire and Inform Consumers to Ensure Your Brand Makes It into the Initial Consideration Set," http://www.slideshare.net/socialtrav/google-the-customer-journey-wtm-travel-perspective-2013
3. Destination Analysts, *State of the American Traveler* (Fall 2016), Destinations Edition, vol. 22.
4. Destination Analysts, "Travel Media and Technology" section of the *State of the American Traveler* (January 2016), Destinations Edition, vol. 19, reports that DMO websites were used by 36.4 percent, while 59.4 percent used user-generated content and 49.8 percent used social media for travel planning.
5. A. Chris, "Difference between Digital Marketing and Social Media" (n.d.), https://www.reliablesoft.net/difference-between-digital-marketing-and-social-media.
6. Destination Analysts, "Travel Media and Technology."
7. Chris, "Difference between Digital Marketing and Social Media."
8. J. Rosenberg, Slide 13—Digital Strategy in 71 Words, "Social Media at the World Bank—Content, Analytics, Strategy, Engagement," Accion (May 2013), http://www.slideshare.net/jerotus/world-bank-social-media-summary-jim-rosenberg-may-2013.
9. Statista, "Social Media and User-Generated Content Statistics and Facts," http://www.statista.com/topics/1164/social-networks.
10. Ibid.
11. J. Rosenberg, Slide 15—Staff: What Should I Talk about Online?, "Social Media at the World Bank" (2011), http://siteresources.worldbank.org.
12. K. Lee, "5 Unique Ways to Measure and Evaluate a Social Media Campaign" (September 2015), https://blog.bufferapp.com/how-to-evaluate-and-optimize-social-media-content.

13. A. Kaushik, "Occam's Razor" (2011), http://www.kaushik.net/avinash/best-social-media-metrics-conversation-amplification-applause-economic-value.
14. @raymund23@Philanthropy (n.d.).
15. Modified from information compiled from a presentation by Sree Sreenivasan, "The Top 25 Social Media Analytics Tools," http://keyhole.co/blog/list-of-the-top-25-social-media-analytics-tools.
16. I. Cross, "Brochure Distribution Research" (July 2014), p. 3, https://www.certifiedfolder.com/assets/cfdsusa/wms/2014-Brochure-Distribution-Research-i1135.pdf.
17. Ibid., p. 5.
18. National Park Service Road Segments: Arizona, Discover Our Shared Heritage Travel Itinerary: Route 66. Online history brief part of the DOSHTI series. https://www.nps.gov/nr/travel/route66/arizona_road_segments.html
19. Written, photographed, and designed by Lisa Hicks Snell, Cherokee. Snell is the publisher and editor of the *Native American Times* (http://www.nativetimes.com).
20. AIANTA is a 501(c)3 national nonprofit association of Native American tribes and tribal businesses, incorporated in 2002 to advance Indian country tourism. The association is made up of member tribes from six regions: Alaska, Eastern, Midwest, Pacific, Plains, and Southwest. AIANTA's mission is to define, introduce, grow, and sustain American Indian and Alaska Native tourism that honors traditions and values.
21. "History of the Tribes," *American Indians & Route 66*, http://www.americanindiansandroute66.com/history.
22. Adapted from Lisa Hicks Snell, "Powwow Etiquette," *American Indians & Route 66*, p. 10. http://www.americanindiansandroute66.com
23. *American Indians & Route 66* was produced by AIANTA, with partial funding from the Route 66 Corridor Preservation Program, National Trails Intermountain Region, National Park Service.
24. A brochure typically includes one or more folded pages; a rack card is a single four-and-a-half-by-eleven-inch vertical card printed on both sides.
25. In-person interview with Tracey Wickersham, April 27, 2016.
26. E-mail correspondence with Tracey Wickersham, July 29, 2016.

Step Five: Manage for Growth and Sustainability

Chapter 12

Managing for Consistency, Quality, and Sustainability

Effective leadership is putting first things first. Effective management is discipline, carrying it out.

—Stephen Covey

Quality experience delivery ensures customer satisfaction; quality tourism management, especially when focusing on local culture and heritage, safeguards the character of place. Sound management practices focus efforts and policies to guarantee benefits for residents, stewardship of resources, and a balance between culture and commerce. An integrated approach is required when managing tourism. Whether for an individual site, a neighborhood, a city, a county, a state, or a region, tourism management requires planning and oversight.

Tourism management can be directed by the individual site or destination at large. For individual cultural heritage sites (or events), tourism management explores the capacity for visitation and the host's ability to provide consistent and quality visitor experiences without damage or negative impact on the site or community at large. Yes, this is tied to the service delivery of the brand promise, but tourism management anticipates the necessary controls or policies to cultivate and direct appropriate growth and sustainability. At the destination level, tourism management takes a more inclusive approach to ensure that livability and character of place are not compromised or negatively impacted by growth. As demonstrated in the Corning, New York, example at the end of this chapter, tourism management requires strong leadership and ongoing oversight.

What does tourism management include? How is a plan or ordinance created and used to anticipate and monitor tourism impacts? Why is tourism management particularly important to cultural heritage tourism? These questions are answered in this chapter. And while not all destinations may consider tourism management important, especially for emerging destinations or sites seeking to grow visitation, planning for success has proven to help anticipate challenges and define proactive solutions to potential problems. Tourism management seeks to maintain the host–guest balance, implement controls for service delivery, preserve sense of place, and align marketing with community or organizational vision.

Figure 12.1 21 East Market Street, Corning's Gaffer District—Corning, New York.

Figure 12.2 Aerial view of Corning's Market Street—Corning, New York.

The first step toward sustainability is development and implementation of a tourism management philosophy. The *Tourism at World Heritage Sites: Site Manager's Handbook*[2] defines the essential elements to consider: (1) type of site and its use, (2) conservation policy, (3) relationship with living communities, (4) types of visitors, (5) carrying capacity and access, (6) security and insurance (liability) considerations, and (7) visitor services. The handbook recognizes special considerations for historic towns and urban areas. Tourism management must defend against "demeaning commercialization, damage to the historic fabric and other inappropriate developments."[3]

Capacity Management

Tourism management begins with understanding capacity. Negative impacts typically occur when a site (or place) exceeds tourism carrying capacity (TCC). Defined by the UN World Tourism Organization, TCC is "the maximum number of people that may visit a tourist destination at the same time, without causing destruction of the physical, economic, socio-cultural environment and an unacceptable decrease in the quality of visitors' satisfaction."[4] Some critics see this as an antiquated way to manage visitation. However, most planners and managers easily grasp the concept of TCC. Too many people engaging in an activity, especially at a historic or cultural site (not traditionally designed for mass tourism), can produce adverse effects. Consider elevators for public venues; for safety reasons, fire departments limit the number of people permitted. Cultural heritage sites require no less consideration as to the negative impact(s) from exceeding capacity and must address ways to minimize or mitigate these impacts to the physical condition of the site, the visitor experience, the desecration of facilities, and/or cultural assets. Another realization is that not all tourists want or need the same level of experience; some are satisfied with a cursory visit, while others may desire a more immersive experience (Garfield, 1993).

An alternative to using TCC as a tourism management strategy is setting "limits of acceptable change (LAC)."[5] These are not interchangeable approaches, as TCC establishes capacity and then devises policies to counter excess visitation. LAC is often used for nature-based tourism. However, it can also be used as a planning and management framework for cultural heritage tourism as it changes the question from "how many is too many?" to "what are the appropriate/acceptable conditions for hosting visitors?"[6] LAC proactively deliberates the questions about visitor access and use and goals for tourism, the site, and the community at large. As McCool states, "Limits of Acceptable Change is focused first on identifying and securing agreement on the outcomes of management."[7] The procedure includes defining and describing opportunity, which address the following:

1. Type of impact
2. Severity of impact
3. Prevalence and extent of impact
4. Apparentness of impact (extent to which impact is noticeable to visitors)[8]

Ultimately, site managers need to proactively consider and plan for impacts related to tourism. Setting policies to restrict access, schedule closures for renovations and maintenance, and intentional instruction to foster positive behavior are all accepted strategies to enhance tourism management and minimize negative impact. Read the profile at the end of this chapter to learn how Shangri La has incorporated special strategies to manage visitation.

Figure 12.3 Mughal Suite exterior, Shangri La—Honolulu, Hawaii.

Tourism Management for Cultural Heritage Destinations

Charleston, South Carolina, is the national standard-bearer for how to manage tourism in a destination. In 1979, Charleston became the first city in the United States to adopt a tourism management plan. The first plan was revised sixteen years later (in 1994) and then updated again in 1998.[12] Now in its seventh edition, Charleston's tourism management plan is a model for other destinations and contributing cultural and heritage institutions. Developed by major public–private stakeholders, based on credible data and market research, and infused with resident input and forward-thinking standards, this plan demonstrates a destination-wide, public–private approach to tourism management as part of the city's overall vision. The plan is fluid so that it can consider unanticipated threats—such as hurricanes, overcrowding, or loss of major employers—and leverage opportunities, including new niche market growth, such as culinary tourism and music tourism. Has long-term tourism management planning paid off? Absolutely, if accolades are any indication. National consumer magazines and traveler choice award lists regularly recognize Charleston as a "Top Destination" or "Best American City."[13]

Longtime Charleston mayor Joseph P. Riley Jr. called this "an important blueprint identifying the impact of tourism on downtown Charleston and solutions for its management."[14] Management planning is not for the fainthearted, however. The process can easily take a year to allow ample time for transparent broad-based community input and consensus and to digest research and inspire thoughtful resolutions. A good plan is only as good as the dynamic process required to generate desired outcomes; dedicating sufficient resources—both time and money—is important to a workable tourism management plan for oversight and implementation.

Figure 12.4 City Market—Charleston, South Carolina.

Figure 12.5 Carriage Tour—Charleston, South Carolina.

Charleston's plan update involved a twenty-six-person Tourism Advisory Committee, representatives from the various departments at the City of Charleston—Planning, Preservation and Sustainability, Office of Cultural Affairs, Department of Parks, Clerk of Council/Tourism, Department of Recreation, Police Department, Legal Department, and Traffic and Transportation—and the College of Charleston's Office of Tourism Analysis in the Department of Hospitality and Tourism Management as well as an independent consulting team to keep the project focused toward productive outcomes. The result: a thirty-four-page plan outlining public–private partnerships and support, with appendices to guide Charleston into its next decade of tourism.

Components of a Destination Tourism Management Plan

Using Charleston as a model, a tourism management plan should be research based and involve inclusive engagement for overarching outcomes and long-term implementation. As the process moves forward to synthesize and prioritize issues and craft specific solutions, the final recommendations resonate with the public at large while protecting the authentic (historic, cultural, and natural) resources that provide the optimum benefits for both guests and residents. Beginning with a vision statement (see chapter 6), the tourism management plan describes the planning process and identifies current issues to address. Charleston articulated five key areas of focus: (1) tourism management and enforcement, (2) visitor orientation, (3) quality of life, (4) special events, and (5) mobility and transportation. The Tourism Management Plan Advisory Committee proclaimed a *Charleston Charter* to serve as guiding principles for a structured approach to sustainable cultural heritage tourism, as defined by considering:

- Community—respecting the values and quality of life of the residents
- Environment—conserving the cultural and physical environment
- Visitors—their needs, aspirations, and well-being
- Industry—the need for tourism businesses to be profitable[15]

Santa Fe, New Mexico, designated in 2005 as the first city in the United States to be recognized as a UNESCO Creative City of Folk Art, Crafts, and Design, also has a long history of tourism management and focus on sustainability. From the preservation and protection of adobe structures to careful stewardship of the city's unique cultural identity, Santa Fe leaders collectively cultivate strategies to retain authentic character while stimulating a creative economy. For this thoughtful approach to tourism management, Santa Fe also receives its share of accolades.[16] The Santa Fe County Sustainable Growth Management Plan[17] includes a vision and purpose for creating the plan as well as principles for sustainable growth, concentrating on environmental responsibility, economic strength and diversity, and community livability and quality of life:

> Sustainable for Santa Fe County means meeting the needs of the present while preserving our land, our history, our culture, our resources, and our communities for future generations. Sustainable development maintains or enhances economic opportunity and community well-being while protecting and restoring the natural environment upon which people, natural systems and economies depend.[18]

Santa Fe's focus on sustainability goes beyond the traditional tourism management strategy, where respect for nature and culture is integrated into policies and practices. The plan centers on thirteen elements: (1) land use; (2) economic development; (3) agriculture and ranching; (4) resource conservation; (5) open space—trails, parks, and recreation areas; (6) renewable energy and energy efficiency; (7) sustainable green design and development; (8) public safety; (9) transportation; (10) water, wastewater, and storm-water management; (11) adequate public facilities and financing; (12) housing; and (13) governance. Like Charleston, Santa Fe uses principles to guide the planning process and growth management. Placemaking is the recognized strategy to create sustainable communities where identity is recognized and celebrated, not duplicated. Partnerships and public input were also significant components of the plan preparation; the result is a comprehensive work program with goals, policies, and strategies for implementation.

> A trap to avoid is to measure success only by attendance. If you do this, you risk not being good stewards of what you are charged to preserve, or to provide the right educational opportunity. Look at a variety of criteria for which to measure success in accordance with your mission.
> —George W. McDaniel, executive director emeritus, Drayton Hall Preservation Trust

Global Sustainable Tourism Criteria

As mentioned in chapter 7, the Global Sustainable Tourism Council (GSTC) defines the minimum requirement for sustainability as "any tourism business or public destination management authority should aspire to reach in order to protect and sustain the world's natural and cultural resources."[19] GSTC criteria are available for hotels, tour operators, and destinations. The destination criterion "demonstrate sustainable destination management" includes fourteen specific criteria, many of which are the tenets discussed above in existing destination management plans. Two destinations in the United States are early adopters of the GSTC's destination criteria: Jackson Hole, Grand Teton, and Yellowstone, Wyoming, along with St. Croix, Virgin Islands.

Brand Management

Destination marketing organizations and cultural heritage institutions focus on brand management to build equity with customers and ensure that the experiences afforded to visitors deliver on their brand promise. Ultimately, consumers define a destination's or organization's brand. Therefore, there is a need to make sure that the visitor experience is exceptional. Brand management is the process of maintaining, improving, and upholding a brand so that the name is associated with positive impressions. Establishing a good relationship with the target markets—the guests, whether domestic or international—is essential for brand management. Staying current is also important, as brands must remain recognizable to preserve brand equity.[20] Destinations, like people, have life cycles; planning for the various stages of tourism impact is important. As discussed in chapter 11, listening to the customer (visitor) and analyzing opinions about (it is hoped favorable) experiences is part of the brand management and marketing process.

A positive, sustainable brand should not be cultivated at the expense of residents or cultural heritage resources. Destination marketing organizations must convey the importance of tourism to local communities, hosts, government agencies, elected officials, and civic organizations while also addressing any negative impacts—through enforcement, engagement, and education.

Additional Cultural Heritage Tourism Management Considerations

Two other areas to address in managing cultural heritage tourism include special event and film permitting and crisis communications. While these elements are often included in other comprehensive plans—tourism management plans, marketing plans, or municipal plans—they are gaining ground in importance and are worthy of further exploration, especially for cultural heritage institutions.

Special Event and Film Permitting

Major events, such as parades or festivals, often require road closures, increased safety and security (police, fire, and emergency medical services), special permits (for vendors and entertainment), and additional public services. Public policies and procedures for organizations and government agencies hosting or contributing to these events are vital to appropriate scheduling, engagement, and compliance. These events also require impact data to ensure that increased visitation, congestion, noise, and other impacts do not negatively affect residents or resources.

Photographers and film producers find cultural heritage sites and destinations particularly attractive due to their uniqueness and character. Establishing permit and filming policies and fees is instructive and informs the photographers or producers of guidelines (regulations or restrictions) surrounding the use of the site or location. These guidelines, when communicated and published broadly, help managers plan for on-site shoots and minimize the impact on visitors and residents. Institutions (and destinations) must weigh the benefits and challenges to determine the viability of these earned revenue and marketing activities.

Crisis Communications

Unfortunately, the potential for a crisis—either natural or man-made disaster—is likely in the life of a cultural heritage site or destination. Even if a crisis never occurs, having a plan is a good risk management strategy. The need to respond promptly, confidently, accurately, and consistently on message is vital—not only for public safety but also for broader audience perception. A crisis communications plan, which may be part of a broader tourism management or communications plan prepared by a public agency or destination marketing organization, informs, at minimum, the persons or agencies involved and the following protocols:

- What constitutes a crisis and when the plan is activated
- Appointment of a crisis communications team
- Internal communications procedures
- Identification of official spokesperson(s)
- Compilation of emergency contacts and media list
- External communications procedures: systems to reach or communicate with affected audiences (visitors, businesses, and residents)
- Instructions for informing and managing communications outflow to traditional, digital, and social media and other key distribution channels

A crisis communications plan, like many long-term projects, often gets tabled or pushed to a future date. However, a fire at a historic site or an accident or severe weather–related event at a cultural festival occurs at random. Every cultural heritage institution and destination needs to have a crisis communications plan in place, and invest in the appropriate training and trial implementation for

Figure 12.6 Historic Mission San Juan Capistrano—San Juan Capistrano, California.

preparedness. Some crises happen over time, as in the case study of Mission San Juan Capistrano in the profile at the end of this chapter. Identifying solutions becomes paramount to sustainability.

Tourism management is a complex, comprehensive process requiring both time and money to compile, communicate, and implement. Without management plans, protocols, and procedures in place, cultural heritage sites and destinations risk adverse impacts. These concerns were discussed more than twenty years ago at a gathering convened by the Historic Annapolis Foundation. A more recent Heritage Tourism Summit (convened in Savannah, Georgia, during the annual meeting of the National Trust for Historic Preservation in November 2014) revisited a number of the initial issues discussed regarding tourism impacts on historic districts. As reported in *Living with Success Revisited: Summit on Heritage Tourism in Our Nation's Most Beloved Historic Cities* (compiled by the National Trust in May 2015), historic and cultural destinations raised these top concerns:

1. Inadequate parking
2. Congestion in high-tourism areas
3. Loss of neighborhood character and quality of life
4. Loss of resident amenities and services
5. Inappropriate behavior and noise
6. Consequences of short-term rentals
7. Impact of cruise ships
8. Lack of adequate transportation
9. Decrease in market-rate and workforce housing[22]

Managing for Consistency, Quality, and Sustainability

This list demonstrates how the more successful a destination or site is (either in the volume of visitation or in the influx of external or national chain businesses and second-home rentals), the more important tourism management is for sustainability. Plans need updating to reflect changing development and resident concerns, changes in heightened visitation, and other external impacts.

Chapter Summary

Taking the time and dedicating resources to create a comprehensive management plan for cultural heritage tourism is a worthwhile exercise. Community and visitor input allows managers—of an individual site or a large city—to better inform, enact, and enforce appropriate strategies for maximum economic, sociocultural, and environmental benefit and to articulate ways to minimize negative impact. Tourism management plans, especially for destinations showcasing place-based cultural heritage resources, must address key issues, including:

- Visitor access and orientation
- Training and workforce development
- Partner engagement
- Mobility and transportation
- Resource management
- Enforcement

The management plan also includes ordinances, policies, procedures, and guidelines for monitoring, measuring, and controlling impacts. Pro-active planning and tools to manage grows helps ensure long-term sustainability and positive outcomes from cultural heritage tourism.

* * * * *

Corning's Gaffer District
Corning, New York

http://www.gafferdistrict.com

Corning's Gaffer District gets its name honestly. A gaffer, also known as top glassblower, epitomizes the foundation for the cultural district. This south-central New York town is headquarters for Corning (since 1868) and home to the world-famous Corning Museum of Glass. Aptly named "America's Crystal City," Corning leverages its historic and contemporary connection to glass to enhance its distinctive brand. The city, population 10,993,[1] hosts more than half a million visitors annually.

A commercial revitalization strategy launched more than forty years ago has paid off handsomely in the form of accolades and sustainable growth. *Travel + Leisure* named Corning "One of America's Most Beautiful Town Squares" in 2013, and in the same year, the American Planning Association designated Market Street as "One of 10 Great Streets." In 2013, the reopening of the Centerway Bridge led to national recognition as the American Public Works Historic Restoration and Preservation Project of the Year. Annual events offer high-quality, often heritage-based activities for residents and visitors alike. The American Business Association selected the four-day GlassFest (presented by the Chemung Canal Trust Company) three years in a row—2014, 2015, and 2016—as one of the "Top 100 Events in North America."

"We are uniquely positioned as the southern gateway to the Finger Lakes Region of New York State and the home of the Corning Museum of Glass to welcome visitors from all over the world. It is an opportunity that we are deeply invested in and committed to as a part of our strategy for a sustainable downtown economy," said Coleen Fabrizi, executive director for Corning's Gaffer District. She continued, "Although our footprint and population is that of a small city, our vitality and extraordinary variety of dining, shopping, and cultural experiences makes us a place where people are drawn to again and again."

The Gaffer District is home to 253 businesses, operating at 90 percent storefront occupancy on Market Street and 94 percent occupancy on Bridge Street. The Corning Intown District Management Association protects the historic and cultural integrity of the commercial district while strengthening existing business and fostering private investment. A staff of eleven oversee preservation and design compliance, organize and promote more than a dozen annual events, and serve as the public face for the district. The management association administers a facade grant program, a sign design incentive of $500 for new businesses, and a free visual merchandising program to help install storefront displays to reflect the local business image and attract pedestrian and street traffic. The beautiful custom window installations often become a favorite "selfie" backdrop for residents and visitors year-round. A new *Buildings Alive! Historic and Architectural Walking Tour* pays homage to more than fifteen distinctive sites along Main Street. The narrated tour (available online and for download) tells of Corning's illuminating past through its historic buildings.

"The key to our success has been based on communication, collaboration, and cooperation. Although there have been varying opinions along the way, the commitment to success has

Figure 12.7 Summer in Centerway Square, Corning's Gaffer District—Corning, New York.

remained steadfast," said Fabrizi. She added, "My best advice to other downtown organizations is to determine the right leaders to look toward overall downtown success and build a team of committed collaborators to make things happen."

The success of Corning's Gaffer District is galvanizing revitalization across the river. Corning's Northside brings the neighborhood back into urban development, transforming the live–work–play concept in harmony with Gaffer's vibrant business district.

* * * * *

Profile: Shangri La
Honolulu, Hawaii

http://www.shangrilahawaii.org

Doris Duke, heiress to the American Tobacco Company and Duke Energy Company, fell in love with historic monuments during her travels across North Africa, the Middle East, and South Asia. Sites like the Taj Mahal, built during the Mughal dynasty, inspired Duke. She began to collect Islamic art in India, including jade objects with inlaid stones, Central Asian *suzanis* (embroideries), carpets, and metalwork. The final stop on her around-the-world honeymoon in August 1935 was the then-American territory of Hawaii. Duke and her husband, James Cromwell, became close friends with a prominent Native Hawaiian family—the Kahanamokus—and by the time they left four months later, Duke decided to build a house in Hawaii. In April 1936, with the help of the Kahanamokus, Duke purchased 4.9 acres on the south shore of Oahu with stunning views of the Pacific Ocean and Diamond Head Beach. She hired architect Marion Sims Wyeth to design a home that would marry her love of Islamic art with Hawaii's tropical landscape. The couple moved into Shangri La in December 1938. Construction was completed in early 1939, and the couple separated in the spring of 1940. The cost of the project was $1.4 million.[9]

For the next fifty years, renovations would be done to the house to accommodate the expanding collection. Duke not only purchased pieces but also commissioned work from living artisans in Morocco, Iran, and Syria. She continued to expand the collection until her death in 1993. In her will, she established the Doris Duke Foundation for Islamic Art (DDFIA) to own, manage, and share Shangri La with the public and "promote the study and understanding of Middle Eastern Art and Culture."

Even though Shangri La is broadening access to the collection through digital and off-site exhibits, visitation remains one of the central ways to learn about the site and the collection. "There is much about Shangri La that is best appreciated by being on-site, namely, the intentionality with which Doris Duke chose to situate the house and the care that she took in displaying the collection," said Dawn Sueoka, Shangri La's archivist. "The physical spaces at Shangri La—the harmonies and vistas, as well as the contradictions and juxtapositions—activate the imagination and create opportunities for visitors to engage with the global culture of Islamic art. Our visitation program, which encompasses guided tours and on-site public programs, seeks to encourage these kinds of encounters.

"Since Doris Duke left little correspondence and no journals or diaries, the house and the collection are two of the primary ways that we've come to understand and interpret her vision. In transforming Shangri La from a private residence into a museum, we kept this in mind," said Sueoka. "Guided by national standards and best practices for rehabilitation and conservation, as well as

Figure 12.8 Syrian Room, Shangri La—Honolulu, Hawaii.

by our 2008 Historic Structures Report, we made every effort to retain and, in some cases, restore the site's character-defining features while also making the property safe and accessible for visitors. The stewardship of the collection has taken on greater urgency especially in recent years, when comparable works are being destroyed by conflict and war. As the house ages and as our institution adapts to meet the needs of increasingly diverse communities in a rapidly changing world, we are guided by the idea that stewardship of the house and collection are closely aligned with the stewardship of Doris Duke's legacy and connecting our work with contemporary issues that broaden the civic imagination," Sueoka continued. The former bedrooms in the Playhouse are now used as short-term living quarters for scholars and artists in residence. Starting in 2004, DDFIA has partnered with the Winterthur University of Delaware Program in Art Conservation to conserve several rooms at Shangri La. In 2014, DDFIA expanded its Summer Internship Program to provide practical experience for graduate students training to become conservators.

The museum is open four days a week (Wednesday through Saturday), with a maximum of ninety-six visitors per day.[10] "Welcoming visitors to Shangri La is central to our mission. Yet we are a small staff, in a largely open-air historic house that is located in a residential area. Further, we invite guests to experience historic interiors by walking through them rather than observing them through a doorway or from behind a stanchion," said Sueoka. Managing visitation through the conditional use permit issued by the City and County of Honolulu and a partnership with the Honolulu Museum of Art enables Shangri La to make the house accessible while at the same time sustaining the integrity of the site over the long term. "Our Wednesday-through-Saturday tour schedule, for example, allows us to limit the exposure of certain vulnerable collections to sunlight and the ocean breeze. It also affords conservation staff the time to complete cyclical maintenance routines that keep collections looking their best. Modulating the flow of foot traffic

Figure 12.9 Jali Pavilion, Shangri La—Honolulu, Hawaii.

through the house ensures that collections that are not behind glass—most of our collections—can be safely enjoyed," she continued.

The guided tours last approximately two and a half hours (including transport) and depart at 9:00 a.m., 10:30 a.m., and 1:30 p.m. from the Honolulu Museum of Art in groups of twenty-four by shuttle bus. Tickets must be purchased in advance and may be bought online at http://honolulumuseum.org. Tickets include admission to the Honolulu Museum of Art and its permanent exhibitions. Shangri La also holds a variety of creative public programs that feature international scholars and visual and performing artists that are usually free of charge with advance reservations.[11]

★ ★ ★ ★ ★

Profile: Flight of the Swallows San Juan Capistrano, California

http://www.missionsjc.com

The miracle of migration adds to the majesty of California's Mission San Juan Capistrano. Each spring, cliff swallows arrive and rebuild their mud nests in the ruins of the mission's Great Stone Church. At dawn on St. Joseph's Day, March 19, the tiny birds begin their summer nesting period after wintering in Argentina. The arches of the ornate vaulted Great Stone Church, exposed and bare following the earthquake of 1812, provide an ideal shelter for the swallows. The mission and historic town celebrate the arrival of the swallows with a two-month-long "Fiesta de las Golodrinas" to welcome both the birds and the visitors seeking to experience the migration. Another celebration is held on the Day of San Juan, October 23, to bid farewell to the "Jewel of the Missions."

Figure 12.10 Cliff swallows return annually to Mission San Juan Capistrano—San Juan Capistrano, California.

Figure 12.11 Signature bell tower, Mission San Juan Capistrano—San Juan Capistrano, California.

Figure 12.12 Renovated wall, Mission San Juan Capistrano—San Juan Capistrano, California.

The Mission Preservation Foundation, the nonprofit organization responsible for the long-term preservation and stewardship of this historic landmark, charges admission to help generate funds for care of Orange County's only mission. (The Spanish mission, listed on the National Register of Historic Places, receives no funds from the Catholic Church or the State of California.) The foundation recently completed the final phase of the $650,000 Sala Preservation Project with conservation of the original eighteenth-century building, the Sacred Garden, and the historic bell wall. The mission hosts more than 73,000 California fourth-grade students, teachers, and chaperones for hands-on learning. While the mission offers a plethora of historical tours, educational programs, and events for adults and children, the legend of the swallows resonates globally.

In the past two decades, though, after preservation of the ruins removed the old nests, hundreds of swallows have taken up residency elsewhere. Swallows tend to reuse nests and now nest along bridges and overpasses in other parts of Orange County. Mission officials recognize the impact of the swallow migration to attracting visitors, as tourism is one of the key revenue generators for preserving this California historic landmark mission, museum, and chapel. In fiscal year 2015, tourism-related spending accounted for more than 68 percent of the mission's annual revenue.[21] Without visitors and their spending, the Mission Preservation Foundation would be more dependent on grants and individual contributions to provide funding for essential preservation activities.

The Mission Preservation Foundation is now exploring ways to attract and keep the world-renowned swallows coming back to the mission, founded by Saint Serra in 1776. Working with ornithologist Dr. Charles Brown, foundation staff erected a fifteen-by-fifteen-foot temporary wall adjacent to the ruins of the Great Stone Church to lure the birds back. The wall, containing a dozen nests made from dental plaster, is designed to tempt the swallows to nest again at the mission. If successful, the wall can be removed as swallows again use the ruins as their summer home. And visitors can continue to enjoy this wonderful spectacle, with their attendance supporting the preservation and stewardship of this important landmark.

Notes

1. U.S. Census, 2014 population estimate.
2. D. Garfield, *Tourism at World Heritage Sites: The Site Manager's Handbook* (2nd ed.) (Madrid: World Tourism Organization), pp. 9–12.
3. Ibid., p. 13.
4. United Nations World Tourism Organization, UNEP/MAP/PAP (1997). Jovicle, D. and Dragin, A. (2008) The Assessment of Carrying Capacity-A Crucial Tool for Managing Tourism Effects in Tourist Destinations, TURIZAM Volume 12, p. 4-11, www.dgt.uns.ac.rs/turizam/arhiva/vol1-1.pdf
5. G. Stankey, D. Cole, R. Lucas, M. Peterson, and S. Frissel, "The Limits of Acceptable Change (LAC) System for Wilderness Planning," General Technical Report INT-176, U.S. Forest Service, U.S. Department of Agriculture, Washington, D.C.
6. S. F. McCool, "Limits of Acceptable Change and Tourism," in A. Holden and D. A. Fennel, eds., *Routledge Handbook of Tourism and the Environment* (Oxon: Routledge, 2013), pp. 285–98.
7. Ibid.
8. Ibid.
9. S. Littlefield, *Shangri La—Islamic Art in a Honolulu Home* (n.d.), http://www.shangrilahawaii.org/globalassets/research/publications/pp01-13---5.pdf.
10. https://www.honolulumuseum.org/4883-tours_shangri_la.
11. http://www.sfgate.com/living/article/Doris-Duke-s-Shangri-La-museum-4339907.php.
12. Tourism Management Plan (2015 Plan Update), Charleston, South Carolina, Executive Summary.

13. *Travel + Leisure* ranked Charleston the "#1 City in the United States and Canada" in 2015 for the third consecutive year; Charleston also ranked number 2 on the list of "Top 10 Cities in the World" in the annual readers' poll (Charleston Convention and Visitors Bureau, July 2015). In 2014, Charleston was listed among the top twenty travel destinations in the world by *Telegraph Travel*, voted number 2 on the list of "Best Girls' Trips" by readers of *USA Today* and 10Best.com, ranked the fourth "Most Romantic City" in the world by *Fodor's*, and named number 4 among the "Best American Cities for Foodies" by *Condé Nast Traveller* (Charleston Preferred Properties.com, January 2015).
14. Tourism Management Plan (2015 Plan Update), Charleston, South Carolina, Letter from the Mayor.
15. "Charleston Charter for Sustainable Tourism," Appendix to the City of Charleston Tourism Management Plan (2015 Update), p. 35.
16. The city of Santa Fe was named number 2 "Best Small City in the United States" and number 6 "Best City Overall Among World Cities," one of the "22 Best Small Town Family Weekend Destinations," and number 10 "Architecturally Impressive Small Towns in America" by *Condé Nast Traveller* Reader's Choice (2015). Booking.com named Santa Fe one of the "Top 7 Emerging Food Capitals in the U.S." (Santa Fe Convention and Visitors Bureau, https://santafe.org).
17. Santa Fe County General Plan adopted by the Board of County Commissioners by Resolutions 2010-210 and 2010-225 (November 2010).
18. Section 1.2.1.1, "What Is Sustainability and Sustainable Development in Santa Fe County?," Santa Fe County Sustainable Growth Management Plan (2010), p. 15.
19. Global Sustainable Tourism Council, "Our History," https://www.gstcouncil.org/en/about/gstc-overview/our-history.html.
20. M. Di Somma, "5 Ways to Keep Your Brand Current" (February 2016), http://www.brandingstrategyinsider.com/brand-management.
21. Financials, Mission San Juan Capistrano 2014–2015, Annual Report, p. 5; total tourism spending calculated as 25 percent from admissions, 17 percent from merchandise sales, 13 percent from tours and photos, and 13 percent from signature events and educational program fees (http://www.missionsjc.com/wp-content/documents/about/MSJC_AnnualReport2015.pdf).
22. National Trust for Historic Preservation, "Living with Success Revisited"(May 2015).

Chapter 13

Delivering Valued Cultural Heritage Tourism Experiences

Travelers always buy experiences which no books can give.

—Anonymous

Once visitors select a destination, based on marketing or recommendations from friends and family, the responsibility falls to the local community at large to deliver exceptional experiences. Unfortunately, travel—particularly transportation—to a destination has become fraught with its own challenges of potential delays, security concerns, and congestion. The destination, therefore, has the onerous task of overcoming these heightened frustrations—by providing a culture of exceptional hospitality—to give visitors a worthwhile experience.

The person arriving for the last lighthouse tour or late check-in at a local bed-and-breakfast deserves the same hospitality and service level as the first customer of the day. Delivering high-quality, consistent cultural heritage tourism experiences is not only expected but also required to meet (or, it is hoped, exceed) expectations. For cultural heritage tourism to thrive and be sustained, a holistic approach to experience delivery must be embraced. Indeed, all stakeholders—from residents to resource managers and elected officials to tourism industry leaders—must define and understand their important role in delivering desired cultural heritage tourism experiences. Remember, cultural heritage tourism is part of a service industry at every level; it's a commitment. A commitment to quality delivery of cultural heritage experiences depends on the day-to-day actions of residents, docents and guides, transportation escorts (Uber, taxi, trolley, and bus drivers), front-desk staff and concierges, restaurant servers, cashiers, and every person involved in the service distribution chain. Defining the role of cultural and heritage resources in this engagement is a vital part of quality experience delivery. This chapter explores key areas where experience delivery should be orchestrated and evaluated in concert with the community-at-large needs and expectations from visitors.

Experience delivery includes RESPECT:

- **R**espectful hosts, tourists
- **E**vergreen (year-round) experiences
- **S**tewardship
- **P**ride of Place
- **E**xceptional Quality
- **C**onsistency
- **T**rust

The Initial Welcome

Gateway signage and access form a visitor's first impression. As discussed in chapter 8, welcome signs and the surrounding landscape properly present the visual image reflective of the culture and heritage of the destination or site. "Hospitality," a term first used in the fourteenth century, focuses on the "generous and friendly treatment of visitors and guests."[1]

The Initial Contact: The Visitor Information Center (or Information Desk)

Visitor information centers (VICs)—also known as visitors' centers, welcome centers, tourist information centers, and, more recently, tourism experience centers or tourism sales centers—are intended to serve as the first point of contact for visitors to a destination. Designed to promote the destination, provide orientation and instruction about attractions and activities, and control and filter visitor flows, the location of VICs affects their functionality.[2] As such, VICs have typically been located at destination gateways, such as entrances to states or cities, major interstate highways, or main traffic thoroughfares. More recently, VICs are also located at key intersections where tourists gather—parks, convention centers, shopping malls, and major tourist attractions.

According to the 2013 "Visitor Information Centers Study" by Destination Marketing Association International, eight out of ten destination marketing organizations (DMOs) offer some type of official VIC to visitors. With an average net cost per walk-in visitor at $2.72, DMOs seek ways to make the VIC more relevant in high-traffic areas and also demonstrate a greater return on investment. Diversified revenue streams have become increasingly important to contribute to the DMO's bottom line. Merchandise sales represents 48 percent of all direct revenues generated by VICs.[3] Most prevalent merchandise includes souvenirs (53 percent), clothing (42 percent), books (42 percent), local arts and crafts (31 percent), prints and posters (31 percent), jewelry (20 percent), and food and drink (20 percent).[4]

As DMOs seek to convert traditional information centers into sales centers, the opportunity to showcase a destination's distinctive culture and heritage is significant. This emphasis on authentic local assets and historical milestones may also increase browsing time—and foster greater connectivity to the customer. Consider how interpretive exhibits, locally made items, and unique artifacts can complement and reinforce the sales opportunity for the visitor information staff seeking to help a visitor stay longer (and spend more).

The VIC also provides a great partnership opportunity for local arts and history organizations to provide distinctive items for sale, set up exhibits, or schedule demonstrations. If a purpose of the

VIC is to sell to and service visitors, these unique cultural and historical components may offer additional reasons for visitors to stop in the center. Outsourcing retail or renting portions of the VIC space to businesses that can sell attraction tickets and tours or book hotel rooms can help offset operating costs while offering direct sales access to industry partners or cultural heritage institutions. The visitor is able to purchase direct or complete a transaction on-site with assistance from travel experts; the DMO can track sales and benefit from the partner collaboration with additional staff on premises and revenue generation. Increasingly, providing iconic "selfie" spots for visitors to snap and post pictures to social media is important.

A welcoming staff is central to any VIC. Appealing, interesting displays can quickly be overshadowed if the staff are not hospitable and instructive. Friendly, knowledgeable staff are foundational for an effective VIC. According to a recent article in the *tourGUNE Journal of Tourism and Human Mobility*, VIC staff particularly play a key role in urban tourism destinations, serving as local experts who can tailor personal information to visitor wants and needs.[5] VICs act as a motivation element, affecting the destination's competitiveness by offering added value: expert information with human interaction. While technology—in the forms of apps and mobile guides—may aid in information delivery, nothing can replace personal interaction with the visitor. VIC staff provide the local knowledge—about the destination as well as everyday news—valued by the traveler. Often, this personal interaction will result in a transactional return on investment. Cultural and heritage institutions can help provide information and reference materials for VIC staff to use in conversation with visitors. This instruction can also enhance the knowledge and affirm the integrity of information shared by local VIC counselors. Specific ways in which cultural and heritage institutions can support VIC staff include:

- Creating a chronology of destination or site history, with supporting stories about major events, people, architecture, commerce, sports, culture, and society
- Conducting training for specific historic or cultural themes to provide additional knowledge and insights about the site or destination
- Hosting local familiarization tours to historic and cultural sites
- Sharing information about upcoming events, activities, and programs (at least thirty days ahead for optimal sharing with visitors)
- Setting up local displays and offering to schedule demonstrations to provide additional and refreshed activity
- Presenting special awards to recognize individuals and VIC staff for their cultural heritage knowledge
- Offering locally made items for sale in the gift shop (Visitors, especially those interested in cultural heritage, often purchase items and crafts by a local population or unique to the destination [37 percent] and artwork [15 percent] in addition to traditional souvenirs [49 percent].)[6]

These partnership strategies can extend beyond the VIC to area hotels, bed-and-breakfasts, convention centers, and community buildings (city halls and county courthouses) to ensure that visitors are exposed to cultural heritage information. Training may also be broadened to include front-desk personnel, waitstaff, taxi and trolley drivers, and other service providers. As turnover is frequent in the travel and tourism industry, hospitality training must be continuously planned and offered for optimal results. The choice of where the VIC is located, especially if in historic buildings, may help emphasize the important heritage of the area and add a unique character to the VIC experience. See the profile of the VIC of Lexington, Kentucky, at the end of this chapter for more information.

Figure 13.1 Participants enjoy a tour, Tulsa Foundation for Architecture—Tulsa, Oklahoma.

Beyond the VIC: The Resident as Host

The role of host and guest extends throughout the entire visit, beyond the potential entry point (at the VIC or front desk). Residents' attitudes toward and interaction with visitors can positively (or negatively) impact opinions about a community's hospitality culture. A visitor's experience is the sum of all the parts: the attractions, activities, accommodations, services, food, tours, transportation, weather, and people—the whole experience.[10]

The term "host–guest" describes the "hospitality involved in receiving and entertaining outsiders."[11] For cultural heritage tourism, hospitality must be reflective of the destination or host organization and is often delivered by residents as well as employees. With the desire for local immersion, the receptivity and engagement of residents are paramount to the delivery of high-quality cultural heritage tourism experiences. Smith advises that when individuals spend discretionary income for travel, they expect gracious and prompt service.[12]

To ensure that residents are positive contributors to the visitor experience, educational sessions and other informational forums may be necessary. Cultural heritage managers and planners can influence the quality and quantity of visitor interaction through a variety of resident engagement strategies:

- Offering residents the opportunity to critique new tours and programs before they are marketed to visitors
- Giving residents advance viewing or a window for prepurchasing tickets to blockbuster exhibits and special events

- Hosting "Lunch and Learn" educational forums for residents on special cultural heritage themes or topics
- Recruiting residents to serve as local ambassadors (This effort can be included as part of a community-wide hospitality training program, with special recognition for participants, such as "Ask Me" or "May I Help?" buttons worn by residents to assist visitors)
- Organizing cultural training programs on how to host international visitors, with insights into sensitivities, protocols, and other ways to respect different nationalities, religions, and cultures
- Speaking at annual chamber of commerce events, civic club gatherings, neighborhood association meetings, and other business, government, and industry events to discuss the impact of cultural heritage tourism on the city, community, and county as well as the important role of and benefit for residents in growth and sustainability.

As development and marketing of cultural heritage tourism is an ongoing effort, so is hospitality training and cultural engagement. Whether the effort is part of a city program (such as via the Community Development or Tourism and Ambassadorship office), designed and administered by the Convention and Visitors Bureau or chamber of commerce, or organized by cultural heritage institutions, resident engagement is vital to ensuring three things: (1) understanding the value of cultural heritage tourism to the community at large, (2) recognizing the important role that residents have in positively influencing visitor behavior (length of stay, spending, and decorum), and (3) ensuring (or exceeding) delivery of the destination's brand promise of exceptional experiences.

Figure 13.2 A positive, balanced relationship between host and guest is important to maintain for the benefit of both residents and visitors.

The Role of the Guest

As important as the resident is as "host" to the positive delivery of a cultural heritage experience, so is the behavior of the visitor as "guest." Marketing materials, especially directed in the planning phase, can help visitors understand whether the destination is a good match for their desired experience. For example, the Albuquerque Convention and Visitors Bureau provides instruction on "cultural etiquette" on its website and describes how to honor Native American culture and traditions.[13]

During the visit, the guest should be encouraged to act appropriately and responsibly. This behavior includes following rules and regulations (especially regarding safety, litter, parking, and noise). Accepting cultural norms set forth by either specific institutions, indigenous peoples, or government agencies is also respectful guest behavior.

The ecotourism segment of the industry, including the National Park Service, has excelled at offering instruction to visitors on how to be good stewards at natural sites. Other organizations, such as the Leave No Trace Center for Outdoor Ethics (see figure 13.3), provide guidelines for businesses and consumers.

Outdoor Ethics for Heritage Sites—The Leave No Trace Center for Outdoor Ethics

PLAN AHEAD AND PREPARE

- Know the rules and regulations for the area you'll visit.
- Check to be sure the site is open and find out if you need a permit.
- Plan to keep pets and pack animals restrained and away from sites.
- Visit in small groups. Assure sufficient leadership to supervise youth groups.

TRAVEL AND CAMP ON DURABLE SURFACES

- Durable surfaces include established trails and campsites, rock, gravel and dry grasses.
- Stay on designated roads and trails; soil disturbance can cause significant and irreversible impacts to heritage sites.
- Climbing, sitting, or walking on walls and other constructed features weakens them. Walls that are stressed may suddenly collapse.
- Avoid walking on artifacts and middens. Middens are trash dumps that are usually soft dark soil areas near heritage sites.
- Where allowed, camp at least 200 yards from heritage sites.

DISPOSE OF WASTE PROPERLY

- Pack it in, pack it out. Pack out all trash, leftover food, and litter.
- Never dig catholes for human waste disposal near heritage sites. Walk at least 200 yards from these sites.

LEAVE WHAT YOU FIND

- Artifacts and fossils left where they are help tell the story of the past. Rearranging them limits their scientific value and the experience of future visitors.
- It is illegal to dig, remove or collect artifacts and vertebrate fossils without a permit.

Figure 13.3 Outdoor Ethics for Heritage Sites—The Leave No Trace Center for Outdoor Ethics. Historic, archaeological and fossil sites are special places that tell the story of our past. These fragile, irreplaceable heritage resources may not be readily visible so be aware and practice Leave No Trace principles.

- Leave historic and prehistoric structures intact.
- Take photographs or make a drawing of the rock art or gravestones you visit. Touching, chalking and making rubbings and latex molds cause damage.

MINIMIZE CAMPFIRE IMPACTS

- Campfires cause lasting impacts. Use a lightweight stove for cooking.
- Where fires are permitted, use existing fire rings, a fire pan or build a mound fire.
- Collect only dead and downed wood that is clearly not from heritage sites. Collect wood and build fires at least 200 yards away from sites.

RESPECT WILDLIFE

- Never feed animals. It changes their natural behaviors and food left behind may alter the heritage site.
- Control pets at all times.

BE CONSIDERATE OF OTHER VISITORS

- Respect the past—Heritage sites hold clues to what life was like long ago.
- Educate others never to dig at sites or collect artifacts.
- Graffiti is vandalism—It damages rock art, ruins, cliff walls, trees and historic structures. Attempting to remove graffiti can cause further damage.
- Many Native Americans consider their ancestral lands sacred.

REPORT VANDALISM

If you see people vandalizing sites, report it as soon as possible by contacting the local law enforcement agency or land management office. Never confront or approach vandals or do anything to endanger your safety. From a distance, observe and report their physical description, activities, license plate numbers, time and location.

Sites on federal land are protected by the Archaeological Resources Protection Act. This law provides for prosecution, forfeiture, imprisonment and fines. Many states have similar laws.

For more information and materials:

1-800-332-4100 www.lnt.org

To report vandalism:

1-800-242-2772

AMERICA'S PRICELESS HERITAGE . . .

JOIN THE ADVENTURE, SHARE THE REPONSIBILITY

However, some visitors do not embrace the "guest in someone else's home" mentality when traveling due to either a lack of awareness or a disregard for local customs. Cultural heritage institutions, in particular, can help educate visitors on respectful engagement—especially at historic sites or during cultural festivals. Instruction on appropriate behavior at dark tourism locations (places of disaster or those identified with death and suffering, such as battlefields, slave markets or internment sites, graveyards, and cemeteries) or sacred places (churches, synagogues, mosques, and tribal ceremonial grounds) is particularly important not only for the respect of place and ancestry but also for the consideration of other visitors. Beyond standard etiquette, cultural heritage institutions and the community at large may want to help educate visitors on the importance of stewardship and respectful visitation. Instruction at historic and cultural sites and events may include:

- Understanding why shoes need to be removed at historic sites
- Communicating the importance of no-flash photography to avoid damage to artifacts, objects, textiles, or paintings (a conservation and protection policy)
- Disallowing photography or filming of any kind to respect the intellectual property rights and safety of artists (and also remove the glow of cell phones and cameras during concerts or performances)
- Asking visitors not to touch fragile buildings or sites or to stay on paths to avoid disruption at archaeological sites
- Requesting silence during religious ceremonies or at sacred sites
- Encouraging visitors to abide by all written policies and procedures for accessing historic, cultural, and natural sites so that future generations may also experience these special places.

Helping visitors understand the reasons behind restricted access or requests to modify behavior to preserve and protect authentic sites can lessen the perceived controls or discomfort. Sometimes, these restraints are also directed to visitor or resource safety, such as the limited use of selfie sticks at museums or outdoor areas.

Certain customs or behaviors may be considered offensive or unacceptable abroad. The Chinese and Thai governments have published "good behavior manuals" for their respective country travelers when going abroad in an effort to stem unruly behavior and provide instruction for these new markets of travelers on accepted protocols in other countries (including the United States).[14] TripAdvisor also provides an explanation of customs, habits, and etiquette for visiting the United States.[15] This instruction provides standard protocols for tipping, alcohol laws, and pets but also lists things to avoid (smoking, loud cell phone usage, and invasion of personal space) with additional advice on good hygiene, public transportation courtesy, dining etiquette, and gesturing. Helping visitors (especially individuals from other countries) feel welcome while educating them on acceptable local behavior is an important exercise to ensure a positive host–guest relationship.

Open and Accessible

The host–guest relationship is only one (although very important) component of delivering exceptional cultural heritage experiences. The sites, attractions, events, and other cultural heritage activities must be open the hours and days as published. Access should be inclusive and accepting for all audiences. Visitor-ready sites and attractions are obligated to deliver the marketed experience on the published schedule. This fundamental duty of hosting visitors is unwavering. If cultural heritage institutions do not meet this responsibility, the experience delivery fails.

Beyond opening doors and welcoming guests, the commitment to quality experience delivery expands to providing information in languages and formats desired by target markets. Translation of tour programs and exhibits goes a long way in delivering a quality experience for international visitors. Providing downloadable apps or materials for the hearing or sight impaired ensures that all visitors can participate in the educational experience. The availability of children's guides and instructional tools (coloring books or replicas to play with or hold) often enhances a family visit to a cultural heritage site. Designating an area for additional assistance—in the form of a satellite or mobile VIC—may encourage visitors to learn more about area attractions and activities, ultimately expanding their time and spending of money in the community.

> DMOs don't own the product, don't control what we are selling. Therefore, collaboration is essential to deliver on the brand promise. We need to think strategically about how to tell—and deliver—stories in a compelling way.
> —Tracey Wickersham, director of cultural tourism, Visit Seattle

Delivering the Full Authentic Experience

To satisfy the fourth stage of travel (experiencing) and achieve the fifth (sharing),[16] sites and destinations must knit together and deliver the desired visitor experiences. To achieve the maximum benefit for cultural heritage tourism, the collection of activities—from entry to departure—must resonate with the visitor. To meet the definition of cultural heritage tourism, the experience must also authentically represent the people and places of the past and present.

Experience delivery requires coordination and oversight. The process begins with partners from all experience components identifying how they contribute as a service provider. Representatives from public works and planning (agencies responsible for infrastructure), attractions, cuisine, retail, lodging, and resident clusters need to systematically determine how best to deliver the desired experiences. The inclusion of these six groups of representatives ensures an integrated approach to delivering the desired level of product, service, and hospitality. Ideally, each of these components of the authentic experience provides high-quality service and a product worthy of admission (or time), while ensuring local benefit.

The combination of these components, when enhanced by exceptional hospitality from local residents, results in visitors sharing positive stories and appealing images on social media or with friends and relatives. Industry partners must communicate about their offerings and cross-market—encouraging visitors to stop in to neighboring shops, restaurants, or attractions. Again, informed residents and VIC counselors can aid in the messaging by promoting local places of interest. Cultural heritage champions can ensure that local tourism industry partners are notified of upcoming activities and events. Keeping calendars current with up-to-date information on local websites and social media (such as Facebook pages for convention and visitors bureaus, chambers of commerce, planning offices, government agencies, cultural heritage institutions, and civic organizations) can also serve as resources for frontline personnel and visitors.

Experience delivery is a constant process that requires refreshing and enhancing to appeal to both repeat and new visitors. Deciphering when to expand hours or programs or to create new experiences requires investigation and analysis. Guarding against cultural exploitation,

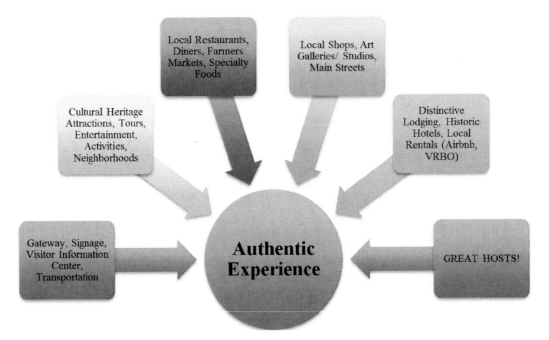

Figure 13.4 Putting the pieces together for a valued authentic experience.

Figure 13.5 Exterior, the Old Mill—Pigeon Forge, Tennessee.

museumization, and fake or staged authenticity also requires monitoring by planners and site managers. Throughout the life cycle of the destination or site, this delivery process requires balance and fluidity to respond to new demand and plan for new or enhanced experiences and to maintain a consistently high level of satisfaction for existing experiences. As evidenced in the profile at the end of this chapter, the Old Mill in Pigeon Forge, Tennessee, constantly refocuses on its heritage through the development of new products and programs.

In the quest to provide authentic experiences, planning and evaluation never end. Monitoring customer reviews and the delivery of experiences helps local cultural heritage tourism partners gauge satisfaction levels and identify areas for improvement. Whether checking TripAdvisor comments or conducting primary research in the form of exit surveys, destination and site managers should include ways to assess experience delivery. These strategies to measure impact and effectiveness are explored in detail in chapter 14.

Chapter Summary

Delivering exceptional cultural heritage tourism experiences requires a commitment to local engagement at all levels—from the visitor access points entering a destination or site throughout the delivery system, including where visitors tour, shop, dine, and sleep. For cultural heritage tourism to flourish in a sustainable way, each partner involved in offering the experience must commit to standards of excellence and authenticity. The importance of human interaction cannot be minimized in valued cultural heritage tourism experiences. Knowledgeable experts, informed guides, and engaging local residents all contribute to a positive atmosphere of hospitality. Respectful visitors interested in and appreciative of the cultural heritage and power of place are also integral to sustainability. Cultural heritage tourism relies on an overarching, integrated synergy to deliver the desired authentic experiences for ultimate visitor satisfaction and maximum positive impact.

* * * * *

Profile: A Historic Welcome VisitLEX
Lexington, Kentucky

http://www.visitlex.com/about/visitors-center

Prior to 1900, Victorian Square in downtown Lexington was a commercial complex with saloons, a cigar store, grocers, a hotel, a confectioner, an opera house with a restaurant to seat 600, and a collection of retail establishments selling everything from tobacco to stoves and riding apparel. During the next eight decades, the structures fell into disrepair. In 1983, renovation began on the 140,000-square-foot complex of sixteen buildings surrounding a central courtyard to create a downtown retail area. Encompassing almost an entire city block, the site is listed on the National Register of Historic Places. Building facades were left intact where possible, and interior renovations retained much of the decorative metal ceilings, along with the intricate tile work and ironwork found in halls and stairwells. Following $2.3 million in renovations, the Victorian Square Shoppes opened in 1985 with a mix of shopping, galleries, artist studios, restaurants, and bars.[7] One of the early tenants was Explorium of Lexington (the Children's Museum), which, since opening its doors in 1990, has hosted more than 1 million visitors.[8]

In 2012, the Lexington Convention and Visitors Bureau, now called VisitLEX, elected to locate its VIC on the first floor of historic Victorian Square, facing Triangle Park. A big blue horse on the awning marks the location of the VIC, conveniently located across from the Convention Center at a major intersection of Main and Broadway.

The renovated space (approximately 1,500 square feet) features a bourbon still and sniffing bar, a working barn door from Faraway Farms (home of racing greats Man O' War and War Admiral), and other local memorabilia to interpret the city's heritage. A Shaker chair, hat, and candle mold are on the wall near the Bluegrass History and Heritage section. A retail table is made from bourbon barrel staves and metal hoops. The staff work area is wrapped with Dry Stone Conservancy–built stone "fences" and topped with Kentucky River rock and a clear glass countertop. Five interactive screens share information about Lexington and the Bluegrass region. A life-size blue horse, fondly named "Big Lex," is strategically located at the front of the center for the perfect selfie shot. (Legend has it that a horse turned blue after grazing in the bluegrass pastures.)

In 2013 (its first full year of operation), the Lexington VIC saw 25,000 visitors—a 150 percent increase from the previous years at the location on Vine Street. Attendance continues to be strong with over 25,500 visitors in 2015. "The visitor center staff and I feel our location has played the biggest role in the incredible increase in traffic," said Julie Schickel, the Lexington VIC manager. She continued, "We believe we are assisting more meetings and convention attendees as well as leisure travelers because we are so much more visible and easily accessible."[9] VIC staff—a full-time manager and seven part-time and seven seasonal volunteers—include a retired teacher and retired tourism and business professionals. Staff training is continuous, as the goal is to be knowledgeable about area attractions, new restaurants, and new experiences. Visits to area attractions and local restaurants are scheduled on a regular basis for the VIC staff.

The VIC is open Monday through Friday from 9:00 a.m. to 5:00 p.m., Saturdays from 10:00 a.m. to 5:00 p.m., and Sundays in summer. Parking is available immediately in front of the VIC on Main Street; parking is also available on side streets and in the Victorian Square parking garage. VisitLEX has leased the property through 2017.

* * * * *

Profile: Walking Town—Tulsa Foundation for Architecture
Tulsa, Oklahoma

http://www.TulsaArchitecture.org

Early twentieth-century oil barons—including Skelly, Getty, and Phillips—committed to making Tulsa a cosmopolitan city by commissioning great urban architecture of the era. Tulsa's collection of art deco buildings rivals New York City's and Miami's in importance, but by the 1990s, many of these buildings were in disrepair and at risk of demolition. Recognizing the importance of saving these historic structures, the Tulsa Foundation for Architecture (TFA) was established in 1995 to lead preservation efforts and maintain an archive of historic building plans and drawings. This nonprofit organization is dedicated to helping to raise awareness, identify funds, obtain tax credits, save threatened structures, and guide restoration of architecturally significant structures, including the Philtower Building, the Mayo Hotel, the Mayo Building, the Atlas Life Building (now a Courtyard by Marriott), and others. The TFA has been the spark for revitalization efforts downtown and helped preserve the distinctive architectural heritage for the city, its visitors, and its residents.

Figure 13.6 Historic Tulsa—Tulsa, Oklahoma.

Figure 13.7 Historic Atlas Life Building, Tulsa Foundation for Architecture—Tulsa, Oklahoma.

"Our buildings are the tangible link between our collective past and where we are right now," said Amanda DeCort, executive director of the TFA. "We can tell a story, and the tour participants can see and touch the buildings. When we walk people around town and show them how our history relates to our architecture and how our architecture relates to how we live today, that's when we can really connect with people, and that's when people start to care."

The TFA regularly hosts guided tours of downtown buildings and districts, averaging 125 guests for its popular second-Saturday tours and up to 1,000 tour-goers for special events, representing a sizable increase in interest and attendance since the tour program's inception. Local residents and visitors alike participate in the tours. Hotel guests join frequently, and tours attract a broad range of participants—families, young couples, singles, and seniors. Participants purchase the tours online via the TFA's website. TFA membership provides early access to ticketed events. The Tulsa Underground tunnel tour weekend in August 2016 attracted 950 attendees. Custom tours of an hour or all day are also available for groups.

DeCort continued, "The tours program has exponentially expanded our reach into the community as an organization, and raising our profile locally gives us more access to regional and national groups and media. By the same token, when we build an appreciation of our city's architecture, that helps us promote Tulsa to visitors. We want everyone to love Tulsa as much as we do!"

* * * * *

The Old Mill
Pigeon Forge, Tennessee

http://www.old-mill.com

One of the oldest continuously operating mills in the country, the Old Mill earned listing on the National Register of Historic Places in 1975. The site is also listed on the Tennessee Civil War Trails. It's interesting that on the second floor of the mill was a Union knitting mill and on the third floor a hospital—in a Confederate state. No battles or skirmishes occurred in Pigeon Forge, but the mill played an important although secret role at the time. It is one of the most widely photographed and artist-painted mills in the country.

A true landmark in the area, the Old Mill was essential to everyday life. Not only did it provide a community gathering place, but its intended purpose was to grind the grains that were crucial for the settlers' day-to-day existence. It housed the first post office and produced electricity for the area up to the 1930s. Today, the Old Mill's giant waterwheel still harnesses the flow of the Little Pigeon River to power an antiquated yet reliable system of shafts, belts, and pulleys to grind gain, working to turn the 4,600-pound stones and grain elevators. Weighing one ton each, the massive flint granite stones, called French Buhrs, are only the second set ever used in the Old Mill's nearly 200-year history. When they're in action, the stones convert grain into about 1,000 pounds of product each day, six days a week. Resident millers then hand fill, weigh, and tie each bag of stone ground grain. The story of the Old Mill is shared during tours and special events, such as Heritage Day.

Today, the Old Mill is rooted in the same principles of quality and craftsmanship as it was a century ago and takes pride in how business units work together seamlessly. The grain from the mill is used in recipes at the Old Mill Restaurant as well as the bread at the Pottery House Café and

Figure 13.8 Miller at work, the Old Mill—Pigeon Forge, Tennessee.

Grille, the spirits at Old Forge Distillery, the Oatmeal Pie Cookies at the Old Mill Creamery, and so on. Expansion allows visitors the option to spend a full day in the Old Mill District.

"Whether you're in the Farmhouse Kitchen store or the Old Mill Restaurant, it still feels like the Old Mill to them because at the core we're providing a quality, down-home experience. Our menu at our Pottery House Café reads *if you go somewhere else to eat ask them if they bake their own bread, if they say yes, ask them if they grind their own grain, if they say yes, ask them if they make their own plates*," says Laurie Faulkner, marketing director. "We have visitors who take their annual family photo in front of the waterwheel every year and couples who come back to celebrate their anniversaries annually. People don't just visit the Old Mill; they make memories here," she continued.

The area's heritage is also being preserved through a variety of crafts that are practiced at the nearby shops of the Old Mill Square. Pigeon River Pottery has been home to pottery making for more than seventy years, using the same clay recipe that was once mixed at this site by horse-power. The Old Mill recently launched a new line of Heritage Preserves in its farmhouse kitchen, partnering with local farms in the area to make fresh jams and preserves. It's a large operation, with more than 400 staff, but the Old Mill hosts 1 million visitors annually. Visiting the Old Mill District has become a tradition for families.

Annually, the Old Mill hosts a free Heritage Festival for the community and visitors at large. While the event has seen steady growth, the commitment to quality is paramount as evidenced in the activities offered to families, the featured crafters, and the heritage honored. The Old Mill does see more traffic in its stores during the event, and that in turn creates an increase in revenue that day and beyond. But more, it creates a connection between what the Old Mill does and why it does it. And customers see that firsthand.

* * * * *

Notes

1. *Merriam-Webster's Collegiate Dictionary*, 11th ed. (Springfield, MA: Merriam-Webster, 2013).
2. Pearce, Philip L., *Journal of Tourism Studies* Vol. 15, no. 1 (2004). "The functions and planning of visitor centres in regional tourism," pp. 8–17.
3. Destination Marketing Association International, 2013 DMO Visitor Information Centers Study, p. 11.
4. Ibid.
5. Tena, O. and Raquel, G. (2014), *tourGUNE Journal of Tourism and Human Mobility*, issue 2 (2014): 10. The role of visitor information centers as an element of destination competitiveness in global markets-The Case of Bilbao.
6. "The Shopping Traveler," survey conducted by Travel Industry Association of America (now U.S. Travel Association) commissioned by Taubman Centers Inc. (2001), http://www.prnewswire.com/news-releases/taubman-centers-and-tia-release-first-ever-survey-on-us-shopping-and-travel-experience-82492677.html.
7. Commerce Lexington, Inc. "Bluegrass Advantage in the Visitor Industry" (May 2016), p. 2, http://www.locateinlexington.com/getattachment/SITE-SELECTION-SERVICES/Strategic-Targets/Visitor-Industries/Visitor-Industries-White-Paper-2016.pdf.aspx.
8. Explorium of Lexington, http://explorium.com/about/mission-statement-and-history.
9. "Lexington Visitors Center Greets Record Number of Visitors in 2013" (January 2014), http://bizlex.com/2014/01/lexington-visitors-center-greets-record-number-of-visitors-in-2013.
10. Transforming Communities through Tourism, p. 62. A Handbook for Community Tourism Champions based on Transforming Communities Through Tourism: A Workshop for Tourism Community Champions produced by Tourism Standards Consortium. http://linkbc.ca/sitefiles/85/files/TGTT.pdf
11. Smith V., "*Hosts and Guests* Revisited," *American Behavioral Scientist* 36, no. 2 (November 1992): 187–99; 1992 Sage Publications Inc. ABI/INFORMA Global p. 187.
12. Ibid.
13. Visit Albuquerque, "Cultural Etiquette," http://www.visitalbuquerque.org/albuquerque/culture-heritage/native-american/etiquette. This is the location for the Complete Cultural etiquette section.
14. *China's National Tourism Administration Guide to Civilized Tourism and Travel*, as reported in Gwynn Guildord, "Chinese Government Publishes Guide on How to Avoid Being a Terrible Tourist," *The Atlantic*, October 7, 2013, http://www.theatlantic.com/china/archive/2013/10/chinese-government-publishes-guide-on-how-to-avoid-being-a-terrible-tourist/280332.
15. TripAdvisor, "United States: Customs, Habits, and Etiquette," http://www.tripadvisor.com/Travel-g191-c3541/United-States:Customs.Habits.And.Etiquette.html .
16. Refer to Marketing Chapter 11 for section on Google's "Five Stages of Travel."

Chapter 14

Measuring the Impact of Cultural Heritage Tourism

Research is creating new knowledge.

—Neil Armstrong

Measurement and evaluation are critically important strategies for sustaining cultural heritage tourism. While this chapter focuses on the fifth step of sustainable cultural heritage tourism, the power of measurement lies in how research and analysis can help planners make more informed decisions at every stage of cultural heritage tourism. Each plan, program, promotion, or preservation strategy needs to include a metric that measures impact and return on investment.

One of the great lessons in measuring impact relies on understanding the definition of success and determining who evaluates (or judges) performance. Frequently, a defined vision offers the overarching measure of success for a destination, site, or organization. However, the interpretation of this vision may vary, depending on the stakeholder. As learned in chapter 5, different entities value or respond to different motivations. Business leaders and elected officials may define success in terms of jobs and economic impact. Destination marketing organizations (DMOs) favor increases in visitation by target audiences, positive brand recognition, and overnight stays. Cultural heritage organizations and managers of specific sites or attractions may appreciate and desire all these motivators but also relish the educational opportunity and potential to increase membership or stewardship. In addition to the tax relief afforded from spending by cultural heritage tourists, residents may find the increased level and diversity of activities as a catalyst for enhanced quality of life or as a motivator to attract new businesses. This chapter explores the various ways to measure impact and the evaluation process for any cultural heritage tourism plan, program, promotion, or product.

Defining Measurement

The key to evaluating impact relies first on having a foundation for comparison, followed by determination of the benchmarks to use for future comparison. These elements must be identified *before* implementation of any activity; otherwise, the analysis will be flawed. The foundation can often be found in the initial inventory or other baseline information gathered in the early stages of the planning process (see chapters 2, 4, and 6). The vision affords a benchmark for determining success; measuring how the activity, project, program, or district has helped realize any or all of the vision can prove powerful.

Cultural heritage tourism measurement differs from other, more traditional economic development evaluations due to the inclusion of two major stakeholders—the visitor and the cultural heritage community—in the research process. The visitor, as the external guest, is impacted by numerous conditions beyond the control of the host organization or destination. However, the visitor's decision to engage in activities and spend money and the visitor's satisfaction level are important factors to track in determining the growth and sustainability of any tourism program. The role of the cultural heritage institution and site manager as a host for events, activities, and programs is significant as well. Without understanding the host's desired benefits and metrics for success, a cultural heritage tourism program cannot be designed to fulfill expectations.

The PA Route 6 Alliance conducted a TripAdvisor campaign targeting the Canadian market from February to October 2014. The promotional cost of $15,401.90 was matched one to one by Brand USA. The PA Route 6 Alliance and participating partners received a total of 1.7 million impressions on the TripAdvisor.com website targeted at Canadians searching the Pennsylvania market. Each partner was required to have both the Brand USA and the PA Route 6 logo in its ads. The cost was less than .01 per impression and garnered .35 percent click-through rate (CTR); the industry standard at the time was .09 percent CTR. Canadian visitors to the PA Route 6 website increased by 2,002 visitors directly from TripAdvisor-Canada and overall increased from 2,013 visitors in 2013 to 4,074 visitors in 2014.

What key performance indicators are important to cultural heritage tourism? Typically, the desired outcomes derive from three interrelated impacts: economic, sociocultural, and environmental (see table 14.1):[1]

1. Economic
   - Spending—the revenue generated by visitors, preferably from outside the destination's boundaries or region (new money brought into the service area)
   - Tax revenue—the sales tax generated from the spending of visitors, often used on local programs and services, thereby creating tax relief to local residents
   - Demand for cultural heritage products—percent of repeat visitors and/or number of new visitors interested in cultural heritage products
   - Job creation—new or expanded jobs related to the availability of cultural heritage tourism programs, services, events, or products
   - Capital investment—the infusion of funding from either public or private sources for the expansion of existing or the development of new cultural heritage tourism products, events, or programs
2. Sociocultural
   - Services and amenities—the addition or expansion of local services and amenities available to support or attributed to cultural heritage tourism

Figure 14.1 TripAdvisor promotion with Brand USA for Canadian market to Pennsylvania—PA Route 6 Association, Pennsylvania.

- Community pride—increased awareness and appreciation for the availability of cultural heritage experiences, programs, activities, and products valued by both residents and visitors
- Media coverage—positive reporting about the destination and/or cultural heritage, contributing to brand recognition
- Local engagement—favorable public attitudes toward and participation in cultural heritage
- Local-oriented policy—incorporation and implementation of local ideas and leaders in cultural heritage development, marketing, and management; retention of local customs and language (such as placekeeping—recognition for distinct cultures, ethnic neighborhoods, and protection against homogenization and gentrification)
- Resident standard of living—increase in median household income and quality of life
3. Environmental
   - Preservation, restoration, conservation, and protection of historic, cultural, and natural resources

Table 14.1 *Key Performance Indicators (KPI) for Specific Cultural Heritage Tourism Categories*

Category/Segment	KPI	Additional Metrics
Main Street	Net new jobs (new jobs less loss of jobs)	Volunteer hours
	Net new businesses (businesses opening less businesses closing)	Attendance at downtown festivals
	Amount of public and private investment in physical improvements	Buildings sold
	Number of building rehabilitations	Business expansions
	Increase in property values	Facade improvements
Arts/cultural district	Net new jobs (new jobs less loss of jobs)	Number of events
	Net new businesses (businesses opening less businesses closing)	Retail sales
	Amount of public and private investment in physical improvements	Sales tax revenue
	Increase in property values	Attendance at events
	Return on investment to public sector	Brand recognition
Event/festival	Attendance	Attendance at other attractions
	Admission sales	Overnight stay
	Sales tax collected	Spending at other attractions, activities
	Number of vendors, exhibits, or partners (and revenue generated from fees and sponsorships)	Gross estimated sales of products (by vendors)
	Spending by nonlocals	Advertising effectiveness
New exhibit/program	Attendance	Motivation to visit
	Admission sales	Attendance at other attractions
	Retail sales of exhibit- and program-specific merchandise	Media coverage
	Sales tax collected	Memberships sold

- Stewardship of landscapes and aesthetics of place—design guidelines, building density, compatible in-fill, green space, noise and light ordinances, visual integrity, beautification, and landscape and tree ordinances
- Waste management systems—tourism solid waste disposal, recycling program, and ratio of tourism waste to local waste
- Traffic management—increased multimodal usage (bicycle and pedestrian-friendly paths) and traffic-calming strategies

Many of these impacts are featured in the Global Sustainable Tourism Council Criteria discussed in chapter 7. The measurement may yield an increase or a decrease in any of these impact categories.

As cultural heritage includes numerous subsets and categories, these definitions must also be considered when focusing on the measurement of a broader area (district, city or county, region, or state). Reviewing existing cultural heritage tourism reports or DMO market research may help identify the best definitions for use in data collection at individual sites and local destinations.

Developing a Measurement Strategy

After metrics and/or key performance indicators are established, planners and organizers can develop a measurement strategy. A measurement strategy begins with defining objectives and asking what questions need to be answered or problems solved. This first step is planned in tandem with the creation of the project or development process in order to build an effective, appropriate measurement methodology and schedule for the process.

Choosing the right research approach is often based on the type (both breadth and depth) of information required as well as the budget and time available to produce the research. There are two types of research; a quantitative (statistical) approach is typically more objective, whereas a qualitative (descriptive) approach is typically exploratory and/or is investigative in nature.[2] There are two sources for data: primary, where original research is conducted, and secondary, analyzing existing information to solve the problem or prove a hypothesis. If secondary data are to be used in the analysis, four questions about data drive the research design and process:

1. What data are needed? (to solve the problem or answer the desired questions)
2. Where are the data located? (specify location[s] of where to find the data)
3. How will the data be obtained? (are these public documents, or are permissions required for access and use)
4. How will the data be interpreted? (for statistical validity and reliability)[3]

Defining the research approach may dictate whether to hire a research professional to assist in the creation of the measurement tools and methodology. Just as hiring an outside planning consultant can be advantageous, the research expert can ensure that survey instruments minimize bias and that research is conducted at a statistically significant level.[4] One example of how visitor research helped transform the traditional house tour operation into a thriving attraction is the Alexander Ramsey house. Review the case study at the end of this chapter for more information.

Selecting the Right Measurement Tool

A measurement strategy may include several types of data collection over the course of a cultural heritage tourism plan, project, product, or program. Depending on the size and scale of what is to be measured and when, the process may be conducted in phases or use various research tools to obtain the desired information for analysis. Five common types of tourism research include the following:

1. **Visitor volume and profile data:** Determines the current number of visitors at a destination (volume). To obtain cultural heritage tourism data, the destination can ask what activities a visitor engaged in during his or her stay in the destination. By querying the tourist, additional demographic information may be obtained, such as where he or she lives (ZIP or postal code or origin city), age (traditionally asked by range), sex, race, education and income levels, marital status, and number in travel party (profile).
2. **Visitor expenditure data:** Determine how much the visitor (and his or her travel party, if available) spent in the destination. For cultural heritage tourism, the survey can ask specific questions about where money was spent and on what items. Several research methods can be used to collect these expenditure data:
    *   **Travel surveys**—either at the beginning of a trip (point of entry) to record anticipated expenditure and activities or at the end of a trip (exit) to recap spending and activities or via en route surveys (such as on a plane from one destination to another).
    *   **Household surveys**—conducted by mail, telephone, or personal interviews. Mail surveys are the slowest and have the lowest response rate but can be sent to a broader sample of visitors. Telephone calls are frequently used to conduct general tourism research, although the response rate is still low (due in part to telemarketers). Personal interviews cost the most but retain the highest volume of information and the greatest response rate. Online surveys are growing in popularity but do have bias (against anyone not owning a computer or e-mail address) and have low response rates unless incentives are offered and originate from a known address (to reduce spam).
3. **Potential customer surveys:** Designed to better understand the demographics, opinions, and behavior of desired target markets. Assembling focus groups comprised of representatives from the target markets or distributing a survey to these potential customers can obtain this information.
4. **Customer satisfaction surveys:** Often distributed at the end of a visit (at an attraction or hotel) as an "exit survey" or "intercept survey" to capture immediate impressions and opinions by guests. Destinations can also distribute customer satisfaction surveys electronically to former tourists to obtain feedback about experience satisfaction.
5. **Resident attitudinal surveys:** Identifying how residents feel about certain issues, activities, events, or plans can be captured in a survey distributed to a sample of residents. This type of survey can also be modified for specific host groups of the planning process (stakeholders, indigenous peoples, and cultural or heritage organizations). Asking opinions and gaining feedback is an important part of a transparent cultural heritage tourism planning process and to monitor progress or impacts on sustainability. Scheduling periodic attitudinal surveys (using some of the same questions from the initial planning questionnaire) can be informative for conducting change-over-time comparisons and analysis.

Research may be targeted for specific measurement of prior activities or to aid in the creation of new products or programming, especially if several phases of development are scheduled. For cultural heritage tourism, a site developer or destination planner may want to know the following:

- When lodging occupancy rates are lowest (the days of the week or the month of the year) to plan special promotions or packages or to develop new attractions, products, or activities
- The motivation for travel—how cultural heritage rates among other motivations (such as visiting friends and relatives)
- If and how the availability of cultural heritage impacted the decision to stay longer in the destination
- Experience satisfaction based on the availability of cultural heritage (delivery on the brand promise)
- How many cultural and heritage sites were visited or activities the travel party engaged in during their visit, comparing general leisure or business travelers to culturally or heritage-motivated travelers
- Expenditures (where, what, and how much), with both direct and indirect spending attributed to cultural heritage tourists
- Whether the tourist is planning to return and what would enhance future visits

These questions may scale above and beyond the traditional economic impact figures desired by government officials and destination marketers (see the section "Calculating Return on Investment" later in this chapter). Asking the right questions or defining the problems to solve at the start of the research process aids in the right data collection and analysis.

Conducting Surveys

Tourism impact studies are traditionally survey based. Survey creation begins with defining objectives, followed by conducting a feasibility assessment to determine whether the new primary research is plausible or necessary (or if there are other ways to obtain the desired information).

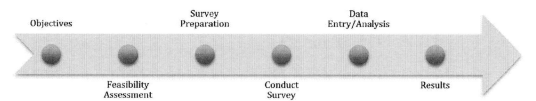

Figure 14.2 How to conduct a visitor survey.

Project management is important here to define local resources available or determine if outsourcing makes more sense. Figure 14.2 shows how to conduct a visitor survey.[5]

According to Young Strategies, one-third of the time expended on a research study is in methodology planning and survey writing.[6] Preparation includes determining the survey approach, writing the survey, designing the questionnaire, defining the sample size, preparing instructions to complete the questionnaire, and pretesting the questionnaire. Prior to conducting the survey, several factors should be considered: (1) where and when to conduct the survey, and (2) whether you will use interviewers and, if so, how you will manage them.

Tips on Designing Tourism Research Survey Instruments

- Use precise language. Stay away from jargon, acronyms, and abbreviations.
- Define the purpose of each question. Make sure the reader understands why it is being asked.
- Avoid negative and biased terms.
- Avoid double-barrel questions—which usually include the word "and." The respondent becomes unclear which of the two statements in the question he or she is answering.
- Make sure response categories are complete—add "NA," "Don't know," "No opinion," and so on.
- Ask, Can the respondent answer the question to determine if it is relevant or appropriate for the survey?
- Check for consistency of language; headers; names of activities, attractions, and sponsors; destination, and so on.
- Pretest the questionnaire to ensure that the questions are clear and delivers the desired type or level of answer.

Source: Scott Wayne, SW Associates, LLC (n.d.), http://www.sw-associates.net.

Database entry and analysis require time and organization. How data are defined and input will dictate both analysis and presentation. Several data input systems (including Excel and SPSS) exist to aid in the analysis process, and the choice and use will dictate the kind of analysis and graphing capabilities. Expert guidance may also be required to determine how to handle outliers (the answers that do not fit into an acceptable range and that may skew analysis). Keep the desired outcome and audience in mind when preparing an analysis so that a final report is easily created for sharing and distribution.

There are other ways to measure visitation, in particular, if a formal visitor survey is not feasible—especially if cost is a factor. Here are a few affordable ways to capture a snapshot of visitation to a site or destination:

- ZIP code surveys—ask hotels or bed-and-breakfasts, major attractions, and/or events to track this information to determine point of origin.
- Surveys on websites—poll visitors to your website or on social media about their motivations for travel and whether they are planning to visit (or have visited) or request e-mail addresses to follow up with more detailed surveys.
- Online surveys—use SurveyMonkey, Typeform, Google Forms, SurveyGizmo, Survata, or other online programs to create an e-survey, collect responses, and easily analyze data. Links can be shared in newsletters, sent to customer e-mail lists, or marketed via third parties (hotels, attractions, or DMOs).
- Guest books—record comments, size of party, and origin (ZIP codes and city, state, and country).

While these methods are typically not statistically valid and have a potential for bias, the information gathered can help inform what types of research should be considered and planned. A few more formal, comprehensive research methodologies are described below.

Calculating Return on Investment

Calculating return on investment (ROI) typically recognizes economic benefit and addresses not issues of overall effectiveness or societal benefit but, rather, the tangible financial gains or losses to government agencies or private investors. Where public funds are used, the ROI is created based on the governing agency's tax policy. Typically, the basic formula for calculating a state ROI is the following:

$$\frac{\text{(Increase in State Revenue} - \text{Initial State Investment)}}{\text{State Investment}}$$

This same model can be used to calculate the local government's ROI. When determining ROI, consider all benefits and costs related to the measurement subject. Direct travel benefits are the most obvious (employment, expenditures, travel-related payroll, and traveler-related taxes) but include indirect[7] and induced[8] benefits as well as psychological and developmental benefits (see table 14.2).

ROI for private or nongovernmental investment may use the same formula as government ROI calculation. Expenses related to the development of capital projects or hosting of programs and events must include both hard costs (contract labor, supplies, and land) and soft costs (volunteer hours and in-kind or donated goods and services). Without this complete snapshot of both benefits and costs, the calculated ROI may be skewed.

ROI is also a commonly employed measure of performance to evaluate state or local marketing campaigns. Many research firms compute the ROI for destinations to reflect the amount received by the community, city, or state for every dollar spent. However, not all research companies and destinations use the same methodology or include the same metrics for evaluation. For example,

Table 14.2 Direct, Indirect, Induced, and Intangible Benefits of Cultural Heritage Tourism (CHT)

Direct	Indirect	Induced/Intangible
• CHT jobs • CHT expenditures at hotels, restaurants, and attractions • CHT expenditures for transport and travel services • Traveler-generated payroll • Traveler-generated taxes	• Jobs cannot be exported • Generates need for new services • Reduces taxes paid by current households • Enhances local infrastructure • Diversifies economy • Attracts new businesses • Encourage entrepreneurship • Increases real estate values	• Direct and indirect spending by CHT organizations and employees • Increases community pride • Creates new events and festivals • Encourages historic preservation and resource conservation • Improves destination image • Enhances workforce skills

some calculations use advertising equivalency values (the cost of an ad placement of similar size) to represent the return on public relations activities. Other factors impacting ROI calculations include the following:

1. Whether incremental tax revenue due to advertising includes state tax, local tax, or both
2. Whether ROI measurements are based on long-term or short-term effects of advertising
3. Whether the investment portion considered in the analysis covers all costs associated with marketing and fulfillment, including salaries and office supplies, or only the cost of advertising[9]

Media costs (for advertising) are obvious for inclusion, but other costs—such as creative costs, printing costs, technical costs (such as website coding), management time costs, and sales costs—should also be factored as the investment required to execute a campaign.

Using Regional Multipliers

The Bureau of Economic Analysis of the U.S. Department of Commerce first provided regional input–output multipliers in the early 1970s as a tool for regional planners and developers. Today, researchers use multipliers produced by the Regional Input-Output Modeling System (RIMS II) for output, earnings, and employment. A users guide is available as a PDF at https://www.bea.gov/regional/pdf/rims/rimsii_user_guide.pdf for anyone who conducts or reviews economic impact studies.[10] Planners often use RIMS II to calculate the economic impact of a "final-demand change" on a regional economy. Final demand (final use) includes "purchases by customers outside the region; investment in new buildings, equipment, and software; purchases by government; and purchases by households." Final-demand change refers to the "change in the purchases of goods or services by final users."[11] Relative to cultural heritage tourism, planners often use RIMS II to report the economic impact of tourism spending, business investment, new development, or other large-scale, capital-intensive projects.

Another way to present the revenue generated from visitors is "tax relief" per household. The formula is as follows:

All Taxes Generated by Visitors ÷ Number of Households in the Jurisdiction =
Tax Savings per Household

Tax relief can also be presented as the amount that each household would have to pay annually if visitors did not pay local and state taxes.

Cataloging Motivations and Influence

Gaining consensus on what constitutes a "cultural" and/or "heritage" activity is important for consistent data collection, analysis, and comparison. Confirming the actual definition and language of each category among all researchers engaged in cultural heritage tourism is vital for accuracy and consistent analysis. This exact language is particularly necessary in quantitative research. Accurately capturing how the availability of these activities influences destination choice and trip planning, motivates visitation, serves as a catalyst for spending at other tourist attractions and activities, and/or increases length of stay is also important to define cultural heritage's importance to tourism impact and sustainability. This attribution is significant when focusing on behavioral or psychographic research with more qualitative findings to analyze. As Vizcaya

Figure 14.3 East side, Vizcaya Museum and Gardens—Miami, Florida.

Museum and Gardens prepared to celebrate its centennial, the organization set out to enhance engagement with area residents—especially their historic connection to the Vizcaya Village. To learn more about Vizcaya's planning for the future, read the profile at the end of this chapter.

Scheduling Consistent Data Collection

Ideally, cultural heritage tourism destinations and sites schedule data collection for primary research to monitor performance and satisfaction. This primary research may be conducted independently with partners (such as DMOs at the local, regional, or state level), as part of a comprehensive planning process, or through national organizations (such as the Visitors Count! tool by the American Association of State and Local History[17] or the Arts and Economic Prosperity Report produced by Americans for the Arts).[18]

Some research should be conducted annually; other research may need greater frequency—especially for seasonal operations. Table 14.3 provides a chart to help inform a research schedule for cultural heritage sites and destinations.

Where possible, data collection efforts should be coordinated with DMOs, cultural or business development districts, heritage areas, and other potential research partners to ensure that re-sources are leveraged, include consistent methodology (questions and categories of information requested), and have complementary schedules of collection. Tapping regional, state, and na-tional sources for schedules of planned research may provide additional opportunities to expand reach and comparison. National Tourism Week and National Preservation month (both in May) as well as Arts and Humanities Month (October) provide an excellent opportunity to communi-cate the impact of cultural heritage tourism locally, statewide, and nationally. The Washington State Department of Archaeology and Historic Preservation created a poster (see figure 14.4)

Table 14.3 Scheduling Market Research for Cultural Heritage Tourism (CHT)

Type of Research	When to Conduct	Frequency
Economic impact—CHT specific	After baseline has been established	Annually, if possible
Regional economic impact—CHT as part of the broader economic picture	As part of a comprehensive plan, outlook report, or other broader research effort	
CHT volume data	As benchmark against other general tourists	Annually, if possible, as part of DMO study
CHT tourism expenditures	As benchmark against other general tourists	Annually, if possible, as part of DMO study
Potential CHT customer survey	Prior to development or launch of new CHT product, programs, promotions, or events	
Resident attitudinal survey	To establish baseline of opinions and to determine issues or levels of (dis) satisfaction	Three to five years or following significant change
Individual site CHT visitation study	For general information	Quarterly (or seasonally)
Marketing return on investment	After major campaign or as part of annual advocacy report	Annually, before new budgets established—as part of legislative report
Business return on investment	After major investment or first year of new business	As required by investors
Event return on investment	After event occurs	Annually, for benchmarking
Customer satisfaction survey	After introducing new CHT product, programs, promotions, or events	

in honor of the fiftieth anniversary of the National Preservation Act. The statistics document the valuable contribution that historic preservation has made to the state, its residents, and its visitors.

Using Measurement Information

Too often, data are collected but not shared in a compelling way for key stakeholders to use and inform future decisions. Crafting research analysis in layman terms is vital to get attention and gain understanding. Data presented graphically are often easier to interpret as opposed to statistical presentation. Simply put, it's easier to follow a chart than it is to visualize a trend in a sea

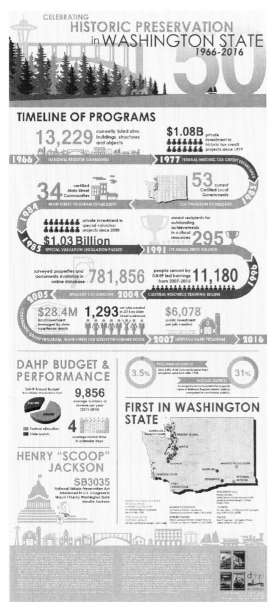

Figure 14.4 Preservation Month poster, Washington State Department of Archaeology and Historic Preservation—State of Washington.

of numbers.[19] Data need to be credible and reliable, but the delivery of data needs to help recipients understand the impact of the information—and what to do with this newfound knowledge. If visitation is down, sites and destinations can conduct further exploration as to what external factors may have contributed to the decline or ask what areas need improvement (or development). If residents start to grumble about tourism or growth, research can monitor these concerns and pinpoint strategies to specifically address these issues in future planning. If the ROI is high—for marketing or product development—planners may use this information to recruit other businesses and request additional funding for marketing. If events are growing exponentially, research can indicate whether prices can be raised without compromising integrity or impact—or perhaps devise ways to expand the event and thereby increase the days spent in the destination as well as attract more out-of-town visitors.

Chapter Summary

As with all these steps, the planning process must be carefully and deliberately thought through. Broadly consider the implications of all actions, at every phase of the planning process. And while the fifteen chapters in this book guide the five steps of a comprehensive and sustainable cultural heritage tourism program, the process is never finished. New stakeholders join the effort, market shifts occur, technological advances impact how information is delivered and received, and customer preferences change. Yet authenticity and sense of place remain high-water marks for all destinations and sites seeking to advance cultural heritage tourism. Without the quality and integrity of cultural, heritage, and natural resources, a place loses the very attributes that attract visitors and investors for asset-based economic development. Measuring and monitoring these impacts can ensure that cultural heritage tourism planners, site managers, and destination marketers stay on the course to sustainability—where tourism contributes to and values the culturally authentic and historically significant product.

* * * * *

Documenting Change—Alexander Ramsey House, Minnesota Historical Society St. Paul, Minnesota

http://www.sites.mnhs.org/historic-sites/alexander-ramsey-house

Built by Minnesota's first territorial governor, this Victorian-era home typifies many historic house museums. Filled with thousands of original family items and furnishings, the Minnesota Historical Society—owners and managers of the site—found attendance and admission sales lagging.

In 2011, the organization embarked on a new approach to refresh this and other sites in its collection to make them more relevant to today's visitor. Rope stanchions came down, removing both physical and interpretive barriers to tours. Programs explored new stories and focused on issues of importance or interest to broader and more diverse groups. Offering these programs at times when people wanted to visit—evenings and weekends—opened access to new audiences, particularly Millennials. A History Happy Hour is now scheduled every month for visitors to learn about a range of topics—from classic cocktails to Victorian spiritualism. A History Detectives Camp makes learning fun and interactive for younger populations. Varied programming trumps traditional hours of operation, where participants are encouraged to purchase tickets in advance. Preselling tickets helps increase revenue generation and anticipate staffing needs. Using social media to communicate upcoming events built a community of engaged customers.

Have these changes been successful? Very. Attendance has grown steadily each year from the baseline of 5,035 in 2011 (when the site was open only for the holiday season but had begun the redevelopment project) to 9,500 in 2013 to 13,132 in 2016. More important, perhaps, revenue almost doubled in five years—from $63,350 in 2011 to $124,123 in 2016. Special programs contributed almost half ($61,000) of the new revenue generated in 2016.

* * * * *

**Profile: Vizcaya Museum and Gardens
Miami, Florida**

http://www.vizcaya.org

Vizcaya Museum and Gardens, the South Florida estate of James Deering, vice president of International Harvester, receives 195,000 daytime visitors and a total of 231,000 visitors annually including programs and events. Visitation has doubled in the past decade, with an upward trend in all audience segments (children, adults, and seniors).[12] Currently, Vizcaya Museum and Gardens—a National Historic Landmark—receives 1.9 percent of the 15.4 million overnight visitors to Miami-Dade County and 2.9 percent of international visitation to the county.[13]

Perhaps one reason for the increase is that Vizcaya Museum and Gardens recognizes the importance of telling a story in native languages. In 2009, with the help of a grant from American Express and the Preserve America program and support from the Tomlinson Foundation, the museum produced a ninety-minute audio tour in English, Spanish, Portuguese, Haitian Creole, and French. While English remains the most popular language, followed by Spanish, this is the first permanent collection audio tour in Haitian Creole. Almost 12,000 visitors used the audio tour (in any language), either via their own earbuds or with headphones provided by the museum, in fiscal year 2014–2015. An independent evaluation of the audio tour determined a positive impact, with visitors connecting to the big idea of the museum's interpretive plan; 98 percent of audio users give it a "thumbs-up."

Figure 14.5 Library, Vizcaya Museum and Gardens—Miami, Florida.

Figure 14.6 Tea House, Vizcaya Museum and Gardens—Miami, Florida.

With a centennial anniversary in 2017, the communications and interpretation staff convened to discuss its vision of Vizcaya and define the public face for the next century:

> Vision: A Vizcaya that is recognized internationally for its cultural and historic significance, high-quality preservation, and dynamic visitor experience—inspiring broad participation in advancing the organization's mission.

While increasing attendance and economic impact is an important goal, so is engaging the local community and telling the story of Vizcaya, yesterday, today, and tomorrow. According to Charlotte Donn, Vizcaya's marketing and public affairs director, "We are focusing on a master plan for the restoration, development and integration of Vizcaya Village into the visitor experience. The Village is where people worked and lived to maintain the Deering household. It tells the story of agriculture and the service industry of the early days of Miami."[14] More than 1,000 workers—about 10 percent of Miami's population at the time—created Vizcaya. They came with varied skills—artists, designers, and craftsmen—from different origins (Italy, Colombia, Germany, Scotland, Ireland, Czechoslovakia, and the Bahamas).[15] "Our goals go beyond daily admissions. We seek to grow our local membership base and build relationships with the philanthropic community. Historic restoration is an intensive undertaking, and the support of our community is vital to our success. In recent years, we have developed a successful series of public programs, member events, and contemporary art exhibitions, all with the needs and wants of the local residents in mind," Dunn continued. Given that 37.5 percent of overnight visitors to Greater Miami and the Beaches stay with friends and relatives, focusing on continually educating the local population is a smart strategy—for both visitation and community engagement.[16]

Notes

1. UNESCO, "Towards a UNESCO Culture and Development Indicators Suite," http://www.unesco.org/fileadmin/MULTIMEDIA/HQ/CLT/creativity/pdf/culture_and_development_indicators/Dimension%203%20Heritage.pdf.
2. Atlas Qualitative Data Analysis, "Comparison of Qualitative and Quantitative Research," http://atlasti.com/quantitative-vs-qualitative-research.
3. Paul D. Leedy and Jeanne Ellis Ormrod, *Practical Research: Planning and Design*, 9th ed. (Edinburgh: Pearson Education, 2010), p.105.
4. "The probability that researchers use as their cutoff point is the significance level. A result that, based on this criterion, is deemed not to be due to chance is called statistically significant" (ibid., p. 279).
5. Arizona Department of Tourism, "How to Conduct a Visitor Survey" Toolkit (n.d.). https://tourism.az.gov/sites/default/files/documents/files/HowtoCreateavisitorSurvey_0.pdf
6. Written correspondence with Berkeley Young, Young Strategies, July 18, 2016.
7. Indirect effects concern intermediate consumption for the production of goods and services in the tourism sector. These are goods and services that tourism companies purchase from their suppliers, forming the tourism supply chain. Indirect effects can be particularly important for the production of local products. So-called frontline companies take the initial purchasing decisions that determine what visitors can consume. It is therefore important to encourage the tourism sector to procure locally produced goods and services in order to maximize the economic impact of tourism revenue in a country or region (François Vellas, "The Indirect Impact of Tourism: An Economic Impact," presented at the Third Meeting of T20 Tourism Ministers, Toulouse University, October 2011, 1.1.2, p. 4).
8. Induced effects concern expenditure by employees from wages paid by companies in direct contact with tourists. Induced effects also include the consumption of companies that have benefited directly or indirectly from initial expenditure in the tourism sector. An example of such induced effects would be purchases of consumer goods, such as clothing and electronics, by people employed in the hotel sector. For companies, this would be purchases of capital goods or expenditure related to the reinvestment of profits (ibid.).
9. A. Ahmend, "Measuring Return on Investment of Tourism Marketing—A Review of Sixteen State Tourism Offices" (December 2016), University of Minnesota Extension, Center for Community Vitality, p. 2.
10. Bureau of Economic Analysis, U.S. Department of Commerce, "RIMS II, an Essential Tool for Regional Developers and Planners" (December 2013), http://www.bea.gov.
11. Ibid., p. G-3.
12. Correspondence with Wendy Wolf, Vizcaya, July 6, 2016.
13. Greater Miami Convention and Visitors Bureau, "Greater Miami and the Beaches 2015 Visitor Industry Overview," data prepared by Ipsos Loyalty, pp. 20 and 22.
14. Correspondence with Charlotte Dunn, Vizcaya, June 30, 2016.
15. Documentary on Vizcaya produced by WPBT2, http://www.wpbt2.org/vizcaya.
16. Greater Miami Convention and Visitors Bureau, "Greater Miami and the Beaches 2015 Visitor Industry Overview," p. 11.
17. Visitors Count! is a research program customized to institutions to capture feedback from general visitors or visitors. The American Association for State and Local History offers this program to members for a nominal fee (http://tools.aaslh.org/visitors-count).
18. The Arts and Economic Prosperity Report documents the key role played by the nonprofit arts and culture industry and their audiences as a powerful advocacy tool for specific local communities. Americans for the Arts produces the report for individual arts organizations for a nominal fee (http://www.americansforthearts.org/by-program/reports-and-data/research-studies-publications/arts-economic-prosperity-iv).
19. Correspondence with Berkeley Young, Young Strategies, July 18, 2016.

Chapter 15

Cultural Heritage Tourism

Collaborating for Success and Sustainability

Being busy does not always mean real work. The object of all work is production or accomplishment and to either of these ends there must be forethought, system, planning, intelligence, and honest purpose, as well as perspiration. Seeming to do is not doing.

—Thomas A. Edison

As an economic development strategy, cultural heritage tourism has the potential to revitalize destinations and provide a financial base (through earned income, taxes, and other forms of revenue generation) for local organizations or governments. A recognized by-product that should not be overlooked is the potential for increased community pride—where residents value their cultural heritage and tout it to friends and family as well as visitors. However, one overarching premise of this book is the importance of collaboration. One of the greatest examples of the power of partnerships is the town of Ludington, Michigan. As the community and county profile attests (at the end of this chapter), community leaders work in tandem to achieve amazing results.

Whether an individual site seeks to increase its visitation or a destination wants to expand seasonality, partnership is key. Cultural heritage tourism relies on an interdependence of partners to deliver exceptional experiences. Yes, the burden of preserving or developing sites, interpreting stories, and offering compelling exhibits or entertainment venues often rests with the cultural heritage institutions. However, success and sustainability cannot be realized without the involvement and engagement of broader stakeholders—elected officials to recognize the value of cultural heritage; government agencies to provide oversight for quality management; the tourism industry to identify and market to target audiences; businesses to deliver desired places to shop, sleep, and eat; and, finally, residents for hospitality. A holistic, proactive approach to cultural heritage tourism yields the most positive outcomes.

Figure 15.1 Sculpture commemorates Ludington's agricultural heritage. The milk can symbolizes dairy farming, a sack of grain is leaning against the milk can, and a lug of cherries is in the foreground. Mason County borders the shore of Lake Michigan, and that climatic condition is conducive to growing fruit. The young woman has vegetables in her basket; vegetables in quality are produced here, too—Ludington, Michigan.

> Rural is different than urban. Rural has more heritage; urban often has more contemporary culture. Rural has moments of time that happened here. Urban includes traditional and contemporary culture, a tapestry of critical mass that is 'always on'—allowing for ongoing awareness, understanding, and opportunity for collaboration, partnerships, and integration.
> —Lisa Hasenbalg, senior director, arts and culture strategy, San Francisco Travel

The five sections of this book and the corresponding forms, sample documents, and best practices illustrate the comprehensive work and collaborative nature required to develop and sustain cultural heritage tourism. From understanding the visitor and determining local readiness to planning and setting policies, the cultural heritage tourism process relies on local input to determine the viability for various ventures. Local stakeholders again play an important role in ensuring that all desired outcomes are delivered through the creation of an aspirational vision.

Figure 15.2 The historic Etowah Train Depot has been converted to the Etowah Depot Museum—Etowah, Tennessee.

Developing a quality, authentic product is paramount to sustainability, as is telling your true story(s) in a compelling and relevant format. Essential—and often the lynchpin for growth—is funding your focus. Each site or destination must secure the necessary human and financial resources to develop, market, and deliver its cultural heritage tourism experiences with quality, integrity, and consistency. Marketing, of course, is central to getting the desired message to the target audience, whether through digital and social media or more traditional platforms. The importance of local awareness should not be overlooked, as the resident can be a knowledgeable and hospitable ambassador or a naysayer. Measuring the impact of each step is critical to ensuring a return on investment and the realization of desired outcomes. Sustainable programs build on success through maturity while staying true to mission or purpose. Effective organizations constantly evolve to meet the needs of stakeholders and visitors while the retaining integrity and quality of programs and interpretation. The Tennessee Overhill Heritage Association embodies success and sustainability in cultural heritage tourism, with creative programs, practical solutions, strong leadership, and constant engagement fostering unique collaborations. To learn more about the association's intent and its innovative approach to cultural heritage tourism development, marketing, and management, read the profile at the end of this chapter.

Chapter Summary

Ultimately, destinations and institutions must consider quality tourism management, especially when utilizing local assets. The policies and procedures required for quality experiences, good stewardship of cultural heritage resources, adequate infrastructure and to monitor impacts and carrying capacity are essential ingredients for public–private partnerships. Delivering the brand

Cultural Heritage Tourism

promise is the responsibility of all partners involved in cultural heritage tourism and is a constantly evolving process required to meet the needs of residents and resource managers. Applied holistically, the process attracts the type of visitor—a cultural heritage traveler—who tends to stay longer and spend more due to the availability of the site or the destination's authentic experiences. When stakeholders collaborate around a unified vision, the community can realize cultural heritage tourism's maximum potential—beyond the economic impact. A successful and sustainable cultural heritage tourism program affords the creation and availability of great attractions, activities, and hospitality that contribute to a distinctive sense of place while also preserving and protecting resources, increasing community pride, and enhancing quality of life of residents.

* * * * *

Profile: Ludington, Michigan

http://www.ludington.org

Earlier in this book, the story of how two women created a children's museum in a small coastal community demonstrated the potential of local-based initiatives. Sandcastles Children's Museum is only one facet of a community-wide cultural economic development strategy.

The success of Ludington, Michigan, in large part, stems from visionary leadership, dedicated citizens, and strong collaborations. The partnerships and the pursuit of big ideas galvanize investment, entrepreneurship, and sustained growth. Fund-raiser and community leader Dr. Bill Anderson (former director of the Michigan Department of History, Arts and Libraries) spearheads many of the development initiatives—from the Mason County Cultural Trails to the Port of Ludington Maritime Museum. Anderson says, "Although the Cultural Economic Development Task Force spearheads the initiative and its strategic plan gives direction and focus, the impact and synergy is generated by broad-based engagement.

"There are myriad examples that illustrate this dynamic: the Ludington Area Convention and Visitor's Bureau funds the OnCell technology platform, which allows visitors to hear the stories along cultural trails, West Shore Bank annually sponsors two blockbuster musical concerts in Waterfront Park, Sandcastles Children's Museum will be part of the Agricultural Trail given its emphasis on farm life, the Village of Fountain is creating a logging sculpture and will soon join the Lumber Heritage Trail, and the West Michigan Fair Association is part of the Agriculture, Sculpture, and Barn Quilt Trails," Anderson stated.

This author had the privilege of working with leaders of Ludington and Mason County to create their cultural economic development plan. Yet plans often sit on a shelf. Not here. The county embraced the concept of cultural heritage tourism to forge its path in asset-based economic development. The process set forth in motion a plethora of complementary projects to attract visitors and their spending, enhancing the quality of life of current and future residents. Several initiatives are worthy of a mention, especially as they leverage diverse stakeholders and partners.

The Mason County Sculpture Trail, initiated in 2001 on the banks of Lake Michigan and now one of four Cultural Trails (others include Lumber Heritage, Barn Quilt, and Agricultural), tells the story of community life and Ludington's history in bronze. Private contributions funded creation and placement of each of the sculptures. Artists from Norway, Florida, Ohio, Colorado, Utah, Indiana, and Michigan received commissions to cast the bronzes to interpret maritime history, agricultural heritage, early settlements, and law enforcement. Each sculpture includes appropriate landscaping to enhance its setting. For example, fruit trees surround the agricultural heritage sculpture, and a sculpture depicting an old stump inhabited by wildlife pays tribute to the coastal town's abundant natural assets. With a goal of extending the sculpture trail to communities throughout the county, the City of Ludington has raised $53,000 to help subsidize sculptures for the villages of Custer and Fountain and the city of Scottville.

The SS *Badger*, the well-known car ferry crossing Lake Michigan from Ludington to Manitowoc, Wisconsin, has survived numerous challenges ever since its maiden voyage in 1953. Throughout its history, it has adapted to meet these challenges, enhancing the coal-fired steam-powered system to retain ash without compromising the integrity of its historic propulsion system. In May 2016, the SS *Badger* received designation as a National Historic Landmark from the National Park Service of the U.S. Department of the Interior. The recognition hailed its excellent original design, the durability of its construction, and the dedication and perseverance of its ship and shore crew members serving as guardians for many generations. An important part of Ludington's history fondly remembered by vacationers of past and present, the SS *Badger* will continue to serve the lake transportation needs of passengers and shippers on Lake Michigan for years to come.

The $5.2 million renovation of the 1934 Coast Guard Station to the Port of Ludington Maritime Museum adds a new attraction to the downtown waterfront. The building, listed on the National Register of Historic Places, initially posed some challenges to the City of Ludington and its partner, the Mason County Historical Society, on transfer of ownership. Removal of lead-based paint and asbestos, along with structural repair due to water damage, resulted in costly delays. However, the Mason County Historical Society—having entered into a long-term concessionaire's agreement with the city to develop the museum—persevered to complete exterior historic restoration, interior modifications, and exhibit designs. The museum serves as an anchor to the Ludington Maritime Heritage Park, with two maritime sculptures and a restored historic fish market (donated by the Lake Michigan Carferry Service to the City of Ludington).

Downtown revitalization has generated both pedestrian traffic and retail sales. "During the last decade, we have seen a transition of thought and have begun the long process of supporting the cultural economy as a viable supplement to manufacturing. As a result, we now provide more sustainable and responsive options for locals than seasonal tourist businesses," said Heather Tykoski, community development director for the City of Ludington. She continued, "Creating a cultural economy is challenging, rewarding, with a continual process of change and adaptation. Not only must the community believe and support these efforts as viable economic engines, entrepreneurs must also trust in the community to support their efforts and investment." The popularity and national media notoriety of the Mitten Bar—a Millennial-owned bar featuring Michigan-only beers, wines, and spirits—highlights this increased support and engagement and spurred the opening of a sister establishment focused on whiskey and scotch called Barley and Rye. Several other retail venues showcasing handmade products have located downtown, adding to a total of thirty-five new businesses in the past two years. Established businesses also realized benefit from the added capacity and revitalization efforts, reporting all-time record sales in 2015.[1]

Perpendicular to Main Street, South James Street is also experiencing a revitalization of sorts. The City of Ludington, with support from state agencies, is helping new building owners repair historic structures for commercial use. Love Wines, a local boutique winery, opened in 2014, and Ludington Bay Brewing Company opened in the fall of 2016—adding to the area's burgeoning craft beer and wine scene that includes the Jamesport Brewing Company (Ludington's first brewpub) and the nanobrewery Starving Artist Brewing Company. Cops and Doughnuts,

Figure 15.3 The new $5.2 million Port of Ludington Maritime Museum opened in 2017 in the historic 1934 Coast Guard Station, listed on the National Register of Historic Places—Ludington, Michigan.

originally founded by several Clair, Michigan, police officers to help save a local bakery, recently expanded to Ludington to save the town's historic McDonald's bakery, in operation since 1898.

"One way I measure economic impact is to obtain the taxable value and tax revenue on all second homes owned by nonresidents," said Dr. Anderson. "These home owners could have built or purchased a second home anywhere but chose a location in Mason County. I believe the decision to locate here is due primarily to their perception of an appealing quality of life," he continued. Given that the total taxable value of this property is $393 million, or approximately 22 percent of the county's total tax base, this metric marks a huge success for the county. The tax base generates $18 million annually, further contributing to the economic vitality of the area—and demonstrates engagement of these residents in local initiatives.

Most part-time residents experience a destination first as a visitor. Ludington's tourism business is thriving, with record room rental income of $12.3 million recorded in 2015, representing a 25 percent increase compared to member lodging income in 2011. Ludington State Park, located seven miles from the city, attracts 800,000 annually and contributes heavily to the seasonal influx of visitors, boasting the most booked campground nights of any Michigan state park.

"Ludington offers visitors the whole package—cultural experiences set against the backdrop of a quaint community with miles of pristine Lake Michigan shoreline," said Kathy Maclean, executive director of the Ludington Area Convention and Visitors Bureau. "Whether visitors drive the Mason County Barn Quilt Trail for a fall color tour or take in a Ludington Mariners Old Time Baseball game, there is something for everyone, and in a beautiful setting."

With a new Sports Center on the horizon, a proposed Sport Fishing and Coast Guard Rescue Museum, the expanded sculpture trail, an enhanced and thriving downtown, and current attractions and annual festivals, Ludington and Mason County are poised to expand current visitation into an evergreen economy.

★ ★ ★ ★ ★

Tennessee Overhill Heritage Association
Southeastern Tennessee—Polk, Monroe, and McMinn Counties

http://www.tennesseeoverhill.com

Linda Caldwell's vocabulary never included the word "no." When applied to her community, the mere mention that something couldn't be done often resulted in a fervent desire to prove the naysayers wrong. As one of the original pilot areas for the National Trust Heritage Tourism Initiative in the early 1990s, Caldwell and the Tennessee Overhill Heritage Association (TOHA) faced numerous challenges but persevered to bring focus on the cultural and historic assets of a rich nature-based region. The boundaries of the pilot area matched the area where the Overhill Cherokee settlements once rested along the rivers in McMinn, Monroe, and Polk counties—thus the name Tennessee Overhill. TOHA recognized the value of the past and its relevance to communities—and visitors—today in its mission:

> To promote and preserve the natural and cultural resources of McMinn, Monroe, and Polk Counties through a cultural tourism program designed to increase visitation to the region, serve as an educational tool, act as a catalyst for economic development, and strengthen local capacity.

The entire southern half of the Cherokee National Forest, as well as two state parks, lies within the boundaries of the Tennessee Overhill. TOHA quickly realized that the U.S. Forest Service and other managers of public lands needed to be partners. TOHA also recognized the importance of marrying outdoor recreation with heritage and culture. Luckily, the leadership of two state parks and a national forest agreed.

Figure 15.4 The L&N Railroad excursions and rafting are two favored activities in the Tennessee Overhill Heritage Area—southeastern Tennessee.

Diverse partners contributed to TOHA's success. The organization worked with and tapped for its board or advisory board natural resource managers, archaeologists, historians, artists, planners, academia, and outfitters. Linda Caldwell's motto is "Know what you don't know, and figure out who knows it, and then get them to help you."

Beginning in 1990, monthly supper meetings of partners helped build trust and often found resolutions to collective problems. The team also mobilized to take advantage of opportunities. For example, collaborations became particularly important when the region prepared to host water sports on the Ocoee River for the 1996 Olympics. TOHA partnered with artists from the region and local communities to create a "Cultural Olympiad" and bring international attention to the region's artistic and cultural resources. A particularly instructive exhibit, *Roadside Signs, Expression of Place*, helped visitors better understand the local culture and how to appreciate the hospitality and assets in rural Tennessee.

TOHA became an independent 501(c)3 in 2003. Governed by a volunteer board, the organization has diversified its funding sources to include local government "dues," grants, donations, earned income, and partnerships. Principles and a step-by-step planning process gave TOHA a framework to look at a big picture but implement via small tasks. As Linda Caldwell says, "Rather than eating the whole elephant, we did it a teaspoon at a time." This effort netted the organization—and region—some huge successes, projects that probably wouldn't have happened without strong leadership, innovative ideas, collaborative partnerships, and, according to Caldwell, "a little bit of luck." Preservation, relevance, authenticity, and quality continue as guiding principles for the organization today. These standards are demonstrated through some of the organization's most successful projects.

Furs to Factories Heritage Trail: TOHA's first effort highlighted how the industrial revolution played out in the Tennessee Overhill. New exhibits at Overhill museums focused on specific historic occupations (fur trade, railroading, mining, timber extraction, textiles, and farming). Interpretive signage was installed at key points, and a free tour guide was published.

Niche Marketing: TOHA went to work identifying regional assets and niche markets that would be attracted to those assets. TOHA published the first agriculture trail brochure in Tennessee and followed it with a number of online and print fulfillment pieces aimed at other niche markets. Most recently, TOHA developed a brochure and map to guide people to waterfalls in the Tennessee Overhill.

Tennessee Overhill Legacy Project: In 1995, with help from the Tennessee Arts Commission, TOHA secured a grant from the National Endowment for the Arts to hire a folklorist for three years to inventory artists and artistic traditions in the region and develop public programs at local cultural facilities to showcase them. Approximately 500 local makers of knives, guns, and brooms and other traditional artists were identified. Bringing a cultural specialist on board at that time proved helpful, as the folklorist was charged with developing the Cultural Olympiad that took place as part of the 1996 Whitewater Slalom Races on the Ocoee River. TOHA's emphasis on traditional arts has not diminished. TOHA is currently in production of its third artist directory. In keeping with current technology, the directory is presented as part of the Tennessee Overhill website. Key components of the Tennessee Overhill Legacy Project include the following:

1. Forest Inspirations: TOHA expanded its efforts to document traditional arts and artists by contracting with folklorists for additional fieldwork. One such project aimed at identifying

art forms that relate to the Cherokee National Forest. TOHA was excited by what was uncovered and created an event that included exhibiting a broad range of artists—from painters to woodworkers to taxidermists. Additionally, demonstrations were held on fly tying, woodcarving, and turkey calling.

2. Celebrations of Home: One outgrowth of the Legacy Project was the development of public programs to highlight artists who created substantial bodies of works that were inspired by the Tennessee Overhill. The series was named "Celebrations of Home." The fabric art of Lora Creasman and George Scarbrough's poetry were successful components of the project.

3. Tennessee Overhill Traditional Performance Series (T-PAS): As TOHA grew in popularity, so did the number of festival and events in the region. Event organizers sought out local talent—musicians and artists—to perform at their festivals. As TOHA recognizes the importance of paying artists, TOHA formed an incentive program to encourage book-ing—and paying—local artists and musicians at events. Primary funding for T-PAS comes from the Tennessee Arts Commission. Local festivals contact TOHA, and TOHA suggests artists who perform traditional art forms from their inventory. The festival books the entertainers or artists, and TOHA gives them a check to pay local artists. The program, now in its twentieth year, has booked hundreds of artists at scores of festivals, providing greater awareness for the artists while strengthening the events.

Historic L&N "Old Line" Railroad: Perhaps one of the most monumental achievements in recent years is the preservation of a forty-seven-mile railroad built in 1890. CSX abandoned the line between Etowah and Copperhill in 2001 after freight business declined. TOHA formed the Old Line Railroad Coalition to save the line, and the group negotiated with CSX to purchase the railroad. The Cherokee National Forest and the Southeast Tennessee Development District provided technical assistance and interceded with CSX on the behalf of the community. The congressional delegation also lent support to the cause, as TOHA initiated the purchase pro-cess. Glenn Springs Holding Inc. loaned $1.6 million to TOHA to buy the railroad. To offset debt payment, administrative costs, and a $12,000 annual property tax to Polk County (more than the county's annual contribution to TOHA), the organization leases the line to TVRM for passenger train service and occasional freight operations.

Dubbed the "Hiwassee River Rail Adventure," ticket prices range from $55 for coach to $100 for first class, depending on the season. About 10,000 people ride the trains annually. Funding from the Tennessee Historical Commission supported a thorough historical survey of the line, resulting in nineteen miles being placed on the National Register of Historic Places. The National Register designation set in motion conversations with an adjacent landowner who owned property that included the view shed from the historic railroad loop, which is the highlight of the train ride. Additionally, the historic switchbacks were also located on the land-owner's property. An assortment of partners that included the Foothills Land Conservancy and private donors arranged for the property to be placed into a conservation easement, pro-tecting the historic switchbacks and view forever.

How the organization came to own a railroad shows TOHA's true commitment to and stewardship of the region. "Cultural heritage tourism is not just marketing," says Caldwell. "More importantly, cultural heritage tourism is about the preservation and management of resources for the long term so that assets can be used beyond marketing." Thanks to TOHA, southeastern Tennessee has preserved great cultural and natural assets for the en-joyment and education of visitors both now and in the future.

Figure 15.5 Englewood Textile Museum was part of the "Furs to Factory" Tour, TOHA's first thematic tour—Englewood, Tennessee.

Unicoi Turnpike Trail Project: As part of a nominated Millennial Trail Project, TOHA led the development of Tennessee's Unicoi Turnpike Trail, part of a three-state Cherokee Heritage Trail project that was managed by the North Carolina Arts Council. TOHA convened a resource team—including the state folklorist, U.S. Forest Service archaeologists and recreation planners, a National Park Service interpretive specialist, and representatives from the Eastern Band of Cherokee Indians—to assess proposed sites to be included on the trail. The Unicoi Turnpike was identified as one of the most significant Cherokee heritage resources in the project area. American Express awarded the trail project $10,000. The State Humanities Office provided support for research and a driving tour brochure on the section of the trail that runs from Murphy, North Carolina, to Vonore, Tennessee. U.S. Department of Agriculture Rural Development and the East Tennessee Foundation funded directional and orientation signs. The Cherokee National Forest preserved more than two miles of original roadbed for an interpretive hiking trail. Fort Armistead is a nationally significant historic site that sits along the Unicoi Turnpike Trail at Coker Creek, Tennessee. One outcome of the Unicoi Turnpike Trail Project was the increased awareness of the fort and its significance to American history. It was located on private land. The increased interest in the site by the Cherokee National Forest and community members resulted in federal funding that allowed the forest to purchase the site from the owner. Archaeological work continues on what has been described as "the most pristine military archeological site on the Trail of Tears in the nation."

Trail of Tears: Working on the Unicoi Turnpike Trail project raised people's curiosity as to the exact route taken by Cherokee citizens who were held at Fort Butler in Murphy, North Carolina, and transported through Monroe and McMinn counties to Fort Cass at Charleston, Tennessee, as part of the Trail of Tears in 1838. TOHA secured support from the National Park Service to work with archaeologists, the Cherokee National Forest, and local people whose families held stories of their removal. More than a year of research resulted in identifying two routes that were used and additional encampment sites. TOHA has plans to continue its partnership with both federal agencies to sign and interpret the route.

In November 2013, Caldwell handed the reins of TOHA over to Gerald D. Hodge Jr., a native of the region. The retired U.S. Army lieutenant colonel elected to move back to his homeland after tours of duty in Kansas, Kentucky, Georgia, Korea, Germany, Iraq, and Norfolk, Virginia, and, most recently, at the Pentagon.

"The Tennessee Overhill Heritage Association (TOHA) is at a mature but not complacent period in its life. The development of cultural tourism in the region took time and the investment of resources by local, state, federal, and private partners to begin to fully realize the vision of its charter members. TOHA is not just in a sustain phase of our existence, but we continue to find new and innovative ways to challenge ourselves in both our research, development of our niche markets, and the use of old and new technologies," said Hodge.

"I see two challenges that we face in cultural tourism. The first is a sense of place, and the other is complacency. We are at a place in our world history that brings little to the sense of place and especially to the Millennial generation. We currently have massive immigration into and migration with the United States. The society is more mobile than ever before. The multigenerational, extended family is weaker or nonexistent than ever before," shared Hodge. He continued, "All these factors erode the younger generation's socialization and appreciation of family, community, and regional history. In turn, this leads to complacency by our educators, governmental bodies at all levels, and society to be the guardians of our cultural and natural resources. We see it every day with the wasting of resources on development, the destruction of cultural landmarks, the attempts to close access to public lands, and the abject apathy at investing in our past to preserve it for the future generations. We may not be able make a gross course correction overnight, but we did not get into this predicament overnight either. It will take a continual nudge inside the wheelhouse of this big ship to put us back on course."

Note

1. Statistics provided by Kathy Maclean, Ludington Area Convention and Visitors Bureau, via e-mail (July 2016).

Resources and Reference Materials

Resources

Federal

Advisory Council on Historic Preservation (ACHP), http://www.preserveamerica.gov

Bureau of Land Management (BLM), http://www.blm.gov

Institute of Museum and Library Services (IMLS), http://www.imls.gov

National Endowment for the Arts (NEA), http://www.arts.gov

National Endowment for the Humanities (NEH), http://www.neh.gov

National Park Service (NPS), http://www.nps.gov

President's Committee on the Arts and the Humanities (PCAH), http://www.pcah.gov

U.S. Department of Agriculture, Forest Service (USFS), http://www.fs.fed.us

U.S. Department of Commerce, National Travel and Tourism Office, http://www.travel.trade.gov

National

American Alliance of Museums (AAM), http://www.aam-us.org

American Association for State and Local History (AASLH), http://www.aaslh.org

American Indian Alaska Native Tourism Association (AIANTA), http://www.aianta.org

American Bus Association (ABA), http://www.buses.org

American Institute for Conservation of Historic and Artistic Works (AIC), http://www.conservationus.og

American Planning Association (APA), http://www.planning.org

Americans for the Arts, http://www.artsusa.org

Association of African American Museums (AAAM), http://www.blackmuseums.org

Association for Living History, Farm and Agricultural Museums (ALHFAM), http://www.alhfam.org

Association for Preservation Technology International (APTI), http://www.apti.org

Destination Marketing Association International (DMAI), http://www.destinationmarketing.org

Federation for State Humanities Councils, http://www.statehumanities.org

The Foundation Center, http://www.foundationcenter.org

The Getty Conservation Institute, http://wwwgetty.edu

Land Trust Alliance, http://www.lta.org

National Alliance of Preservation Commissions, https://napcommissions.org

National Assembly of State Arts Agencies, http://www.nasaa-arts.org

National Association for Interpretation (NAI) http://www.interpnet.com

National Association of Tribal Historic Preservation Officers (NATHPO), http://www.nathpo.org

National Conference of State Historic Preservation Officers (NCSHPO), http://www.ncshpo.org

National Historical Publications and Records Commission (NHPRC), http://www.archives.gov

National Main Street Center (NMSC), http://www.mainstreet.org

National Tour Association (NTA), http://www.ntaonline.com

National Trust for Historic Preservation (NTHP), http://www.savingplaces.org

Preservation Action, http://www.preservationaction.org

Rails to Trails Conservancy, http://www.railstotrails.org

Scenic America, http://www.scenic.org

Society of American Travel Writers (SATW), http://www.satw.org

Travel and Tourism Research Association (TTRA), http://www.ttra.com

United States Tour Operators Association (USTOA), http://www.ustoa.com

U.S. Travel Association, http://www.ustravel.org

World Tourism Organization (UNWTO), http://www.unwto.org

World Travel and Tourism Council (WTTC), http://www.wttc.org

Reference Materials

Americans for the Arts/Destination Marketing Association International (DMAI). Toolkit for Community Marketing Organizations and Cultural-Heritage Organizations. http://www.destinationmarketing.org/sites/destinationmarketing.org/master/drupal/files/Toolkit_for_AFTA-DMAI.pdf.

American Planning Association Arts and Culture Briefing Papers (2011). http://www.planning.org/research/arts.

Canada's Federal-Provincial-Territorial Ministers of Culture and Heritage (FPT). "Cultural & Heritage Tourism—A Handbook for Community Champions" © 2012 produced by Bruce Whyte, Terryl Hood, and Brian P. White (eds.). ISBN 978-0-7726-6604-8.

Cities Institute. Cultural Planning Toolkit. Project of *Creating Cultural Opportunity in Sustainable Communities* (May 2007). T. Curson, G. Evans, J. Foord, and P. Shaw.

Failte Ireland (National Tourism Development Authority). A Tourism Toolkit for Ireland's Cultural Experiences, http://www.failteireland.ie/getmedia/d2be800f-afdd-4ee3-bf60-68375c0f49a4/FI-Culture-Tourism-Toolkit-with-Activated-Exercises.aspx.

Farm2U Collaborative Resource Center. Cultural Heritage Toolkit (Cultural Heritage as Community Development; Culinary Heritage Tourism; Cultural Heritage—Preserving, Sharing, Fundraising; Mining for Gold Capitalizing on Your Local Treasures—A Guide to Community Assessment and Engagement; Raising the Barn—Building Effective Teams in Your Community; Building Tourism in Your Community) http://farm2u.org/resource-center/toolkit.

Heritage Tourism Handbook: A How-to-Guide for Georgia, Georgia Department of Natural Resources/Historic Preservation Division. http://www.georgia.org/wp-content/uploads/2013/09/GA-Heritage-Tourism-Handbook.pdf.

Mayor of London. Cultural Tourism Toolkit (2015–2017). https://www.london.gov.uk/sites/default/files/london_cultural_tourism_toolkit.new_.pdf.

National Main Street Center and Project for Public Spaces collaborated for workshops on "Cultivating Place in Main Street Communities"—Free downloadable guide on how to plan a community-oriented market is available for free via http://www.pps.org/reference/main-street-guide-to-markets.

National Park Service Preservation Briefs, #32 Making Historic Properties Accessible by T. Jester and S. Park. http://www.nps.gov/tps/how-to-preserve/briefs/32-accessibility.htm.

Tourism Standards Consortium (TSC Western Canada). "Transforming Communities through Tourism"—A Handbook for Community Tourism Champions, produced by (n.d.) http://linkbc.ca/siteFiles/85/files/TCTT.pdf. Additional references available from www.bctorc.ca.

UNESCO World Heritage Sustainable Tourism Online Toolkit. http://whc.unesco.org/sustainabletourismtoolkit/sites/default/files/UNESCO%20toolkit%20PDFs%20guide%207C.pdf.

Glossary

Each industry and profession has its own glossary and jargon. This compilation[1] breaks down the barriers of language and provides definitions of common terms used in tourism, historic preservation, the arts, planning, research, and legislation. These terms are frequently used in cultural heritage tourism.

Accreditation A procedure to establish if a tourism business meets certain standards of management and operation.

Acquisition The act or process of acquiring fee title or interest other than fee title of real property (including acquisition of development rights or remainder interest).

Activity/activities In tourism statistics, the term "activities" represent the actions and behaviors of people in preparation for and during a trip in their capacity as consumers.

Affirmative maintenance A requirement in historic preservation ordinances that a building's structural components are maintained.

Aggregated data The result of transforming unit-level data into quantitative measures for a set of characteristics of a population.

Aggregation A process that transforms microdata into aggregate-level information by using an aggregation function, such as count, sum average, or standard deviation.

AIO variables Activities, interests, and opinions—used to measure and categorize customer lifestyles.

All-inclusive package A tour package in which most travel elements are purchased for a set price. Also called an "all-expense" package.

Alteration Any act or process that changes any portion of the exterior architectural appearance or exceptionally significant interiors of a building, structure, or object, including but not limited to the erection, construction, reconstruction, or removal of any exterior architectural features or interior architectural design of a structure; treatments such as sandblasting, water blasting, chemical cleaning, chemical stopping, or removal of any architectural feature but not including changes to the color of exterior paint.

Alumni tour A tour created for customers who have previously traveled with a tour operator. Also called a reunion tour.

Amenity package A cluster of special features, such as wine at dinner or bar credit, usually as a bonus or extra feature. Usually used to induce clients to book through a particular travel agency or organization.

Americans with Disabilities Act (ADA) A law prohibiting discrimination to persons with disabilities by requiring, among other things, that places generally open to the public, such as restaurants and hotels, be made accessible. Special rules apply to historic buildings and facilities.

Appraisal The process of determining the value and thus the disposition of archival records based on their current administrative, fiscal, and legal value; their evidential and informational value; their arrangement and condition; their intrinsic value; and their relationship to other records.

Archaeological Resources Protection Act The primary federal statute governing archaeological resources.

Archives (1) The noncurrent historical records of an organization or institution, preserved because of their enduring value. (2) The agency responsible for selecting, preserving, and making available records determined to have permanent or continuing value. (3) The building is which an archival repository is located.

Archivist One who is professionally trained for or whose primary duties consist of appraising, describing, referencing, and caring for archival records.

Arts exposure Refers to students visiting arts organizations and cultural organizations to see examples of the arts (such as via field trips) or performance demonstrations that may take place in a school setting. Generally, these are "one-time" or "short-term" arts opportunities for students.

Assets Something of value that will provide future benefit or utility or can be used to generate revenue; usually owned, so simply described as "things we own."

Attractions Items of specific interest to travelers, such as historic sites, natural wonders, cultural activities, or entertainment.

Average daily room rate The total guest room revenue for a given period divided by the number of rooms occupied for the same period.

Bed-and-breakfast Overnight accommodations, usually in a private home or boardinghouse, often with a full American-style or Continental breakfast included in one rate.

Benchmarking Process of comparing performance and activities among similar organizations either against an agreed standard or against those that are recognized as being among the best.

Benchmarks Points of reference—which may include standards, critical success factors, indicators, and metrics—against which things may be compared (to judge the quality or level of other, similar things).

Best practice Operational standards considered the most effective and efficient means of achieving desired outcomes.

Bias An effect that deprives a statistical result of representativeness by systematically distorting it, as distinct from a random error, which may distort on any one occasion but balances out on the average.

Block A number of rooms, seats, or space reserved in advance, usually by wholesalers, tour operators, meeting planners, or receptive operators who intend to sell them as components of tour packages or conventions.

Break-even point The point at which revenues and expenses are the same.

Break-even pricing Pricing a product based on a forecast of the break-even point and the cost of achieving the break-even point.

Building code Law setting forth minimum standards for the construction and use of buildings to protect the public health and safety.

Business plan An action plan that entrepreneurs draw up for the purpose of starting a business; a guide to running one's business.

Capacity management A process that seeks to ensure that organizations operate at optimum capacity while maintaining customer satisfaction levels.

Capital expenditure The cost of long-term assets, such as computer equipment, vehicles, and premises. Importantly, these are bought to be used over several years and not for resale.

Carrying capacity The amount of visitor activity that a site or destination can sustain.

Carrying-capacity analysis Originally, a term applied in ecology referring to the maximum number of animals of a given species that a particular habitat could support. In the context of tourism, it refers to the maximum number of tourists that a destination can support.

Casual research A form of marketing research that is used to test cause-and-effect relationships between a marketing program and customers.

Census The complete enumeration of a population or groups at a point in time with respect to well-defined characteristics, such as population, production, or traffic on particular roads.

Certificate of appropriateness A certificate issued by a preservation commission to indicate its approval of an application to alter, demolish, move, or add on to a protected resource.

Certification A process by which an independent agent verifies that the claims made by a product, service, and so on are valid. Many certification programs exist through which products meeting independent standards may use a label or logo to indicate that their claims have been verified.

Certified local government A city or town that has met specific standards enabling participation in certain National Historic Preservation Act programs.

Certified tour professional A designation conferred on tour professionals who have completed a prescribed course of academic study, professional service, tour employment, and evaluation requirements. The certified tour professional program is administered by the National Tour Association (Lexington, Kentucky) and is open to individuals employed in any segment of the tourism industry.

Certified travel counselor A designation attesting to professional competence as a travel agent. It is conferred on travel professionals with five or more years of industry experience who complete a two-year graduate-level travel management program administered by the Institute of Certified Travel Agents (Wellesley, Massachusetts).

Certified travel industry specialist A designation conferred on American Bus Association member company employees who successfully complete five correspondence courses—three required and two electives—and written evaluation of eight marketplace seminars.

Chain-ratio method A method for forecasting market demand by multiplying a base market figure by a series of consumption constraints.

Chamber of commerce A destination marketing organization that operates at the local level and is comprised of businesses, not all necessarily associated with the tourism industry.

Charrette A meeting that brings together experts to develop ideas on how to improve a cultural or historic resource. The outputs of their efforts are maps and designs that offer solutions to such issues as preservation, access and use, interpretation, and development.

Charter To hire the exclusive use of any aircraft, motorcoach, or other vehicle.

Charter service The transportation of preformed groups (organized by someone other than the carrier) that have the exclusive use of the vehicle.

Circle itinerary A travel-routing design that overnights in different locations and returns to the point of departure without retracing the travel route.

City tour A sightseeing trip through a city, usually lasting a half a day or a full day, during which a guide points out the city's highlights.

Closed-end question A question for which the answers are provided for the respondent, who chooses only from those answers.

Code of conduct Guidelines advising a tourism stakeholder, including tourists, on how to behave in a culturally and/or environmentally responsible manner.

Code of ethics, conduct, or practice Recommended practices based on a system of self-regulation intended to promote environmentally and/or socioculturally sustainable behavior.

Commission A percentage of a travel product's price that is returned to the distributor when the product is sold.

Commissionable tour A tour available through retail and wholesale travel agencies that provides for a payment of an agreed-on sales commission to the retailer or wholesale seller.

Comp policy Arrangements for free tickets, rooms, meals, and so on.

Competency of Bidder Clause 00900 Series A contract clause used to evaluate qualifications of restoration specialist firms for specific projects of the U.S. General Services Administration. Developed to improved quality of projects awarded by competitive budding. Contracts are awarded to the lowest competent bidder. Firms are required to submit proof (project photographs, descriptions, and references) of successful experience in the specialty. Technicians performing restoration specialty work are also evaluated to ensure that workers assigned to General Services Administration projects have the required skills.

Complimentaries (comps) Items provided free of charge, such as rooms, meals, tickets, airfare, gifts, and souvenirs, for promotional use or as part of a familiarization or research trip.

Comprehensive historic preservation planning The organization into a logical sequence of preservation information pertaining to identification, evaluation, registration, and treatment of historic properties and setting priorities for accomplishing preservation activities.

Comprehensive plan An official plan adopted by local governments that guides decision making over proposed public and private actions affecting community development.

Computerized reservation system An automated system used by travel agents that contains pricing, availability, and product descriptions for hotels, car rentals, cruises, and air transportation.

Conservation Can be broadly interpreted as action taken to protect and preserve natural and cultural heritage from harmful features of tourism, including pollution and overexploitation of resources.

Consolidator A person or company that forms groups to travel on air charters at group rates on scheduled flights to increase sales, earn override commissions, or reduce the possibility of tour cancellations.

Consumer (customer) The actual user of a product or service.

Consumer protection plan A plan offered by a company and/or an association that protects the customer's deposits and payments from loss in the event of company bankruptcy.

Consumption constraints Issues that limit the number of people in a market who will purchase a product.

Contributing structure A building or structure in historic district that generally has historic, architectural, cultural, or archaeological significance.

Convenience sample A collection of research subjects who are the easiest for the researcher to select.

Convention and visitors bureau (CVB) A nonprofit destination marketing organization that operates at the county or city level. A CVB typically encourages groups to hold meetings, conventions, and trade shows in its destination and also entices leisure travelers to visit. The primary functions of the CVB are research and planning; product development; marketing, promotion, and sales; community relations; and visitor relations. There are typically two types of CVBs: (1) membership based (where the CVB markets the destination at large but provides pay-to-play marketing opportunities for enhanced member benefits) and (2) nonmember based (where the CVB markets the entire destination; this is the more common model today).

Coop tour Selling a tour through a number of wholesalers, cooperatives, or other outlets in order to increase sales and reduce the possibility of tour cancellations.

Cooperative (coop) advertising An agreement between two parties to share the cost of placing an advertisement.

Costing The process of itemizing and calculating all the costs that the tour operator will pay on a given tour.

Criterion (pl. criteria) A standard on which a judgment or decision may be based; a characterizing mark or trait.

Crowdsourcing The process of leveraging an online community to assist in services, content, and ideas for your business.

Cultural artifacts and properties Objects manufactured, used, or modified by humans that express the particular characteristic of a people or peoples, including way of life, spiritual beliefs, or a collective sense of history.

Cultural authenticity Ensuring that the appropriate stories, spiritual beliefs, history, ceremony, and art are attributed to the relevant area.

Cultural district A specific geographical area in a city or town that has a concentration of cultural facilities, activities, and assets. It is a walkable, compact area that is easily identifiable to visitors and residents and serves as a center of cultural, artistic, and economic activity.

Cultural heritage The ways of living developed by a community and passed on from generation to generation, including customs, practices, places, objects, artistic expressions, and values. Cultural heritage encompasses material culture in the forms of objects, structures, sites, landscapes, and natural environment shaped by cultural practices and traditions over time as well as living (or expressive) culture as evidenced in forms such as music, crafts, performing arts, literature, oral tradition, and language. The emphasis is on cultural continuity from the past, through the present and into the future, with the recognition that culture is organic and evolving.

Custody The guardianship of records and manuscripts, which may include both physical possession (protective responsibility) and legal title (legal responsibility).

Custom tour A travel package created specifically for a preformed group or niche market.

Data Pieces of information that any particular situation gives to an observer.

Data collection The systematic process of gathering data for official statistics.

Data compilation Operations performed on data to derive new information according to a given set of rules.

Database A computerized, organized collection of individual customer information.

Day tour An escorted or unescorted tour that lasts less than twenty-four hours and usually departs and returns on the same day. *See also* Sightseeing tour.

Degradation Any decline in the quality of natural or cultural resources or the viability of ecosystems that is caused directly or indirectly by humans.

Demand generators Strategies and programs developed by destination marketing organizations and suppliers to generate destination demand. Examples include festivals, events, cultural tours, and consumer promotions.

Demographics Population measures, such as age, gender, income, education, race or ethnicity, religion, marital status, household size, and occupation.

Demolition by neglect The process of allowing a building to deteriorate to the point where demolition is necessary to protect public health and safety.

Descriptive research A form of marketing research that is used to provide detailed answers about customer markets.

Design guidelines The *Standards for Rehabilitation and Guidelines for Rehabilitating Historic Buildings* as adopted by the secretary of the U.S. Department of the Interior and other guidelines that may be adopted from time to time.

Designation The act of identifying historic structures and districts subject to regulation in historic preservation ordinances or other preservation laws.

Destination (main destination of a trip) The place visited that is central to the decision to take the trip. *See also* Purpose of a trip (main).

Destination alliance A destination marketing organization that operates as a for-profit association of select suppliers who form a paid-membership network to promote their services to travelers.

Destination management company A for-profit company that operates similar to a convention and visitors bureau by providing planning and execution services for the convention and meeting market.

Destination marketing organization (DMO) An organization that promotes a location (city, county, region, state, or country) as a travel destination.

Direct marketing Sales and marketing communication that features a direct interaction between a company and its customers without any distribution intermediaries.

Diversification The process of developing new products for new markets in order to achieve business growth.

Docent A tour guide who works free of charge at a museum.

Domestic tourism Comprises the activities of a resident visitor within the country of reference, either as part of a domestic tourism trip or as part of an outbound tourism trip.

Domestic tourism consumption The tourism consumption of a resident visitor within the economy of reference.

Domestic tourism expenditure The tourism expenditure of a resident visitor within the economy of reference.

Domestic tourism trip A trip with the main destination being within the country of residence of the visitor.

Domestic visitor As a visitor travels within his or her country of residence, he or she is a domestic visitor, and his or her activities are part of domestic tourism.

Due diligence Taking what is considered in law to be reasonable care.

Easement (preservation or conservation) A partial interest in property that can be transferred to a nonprofit organization or governmental entity by gift or sale to ensure the protection of a historic resource and/or land area in perpetuity.

Economic analysis Tourism generates, directly or indirectly, an increase in economic activity in the places visited (and beyond), mainly due to demand for goods and services that need to be produced and provided. In the economic analysis of tourism, one may distinguish between tourism's "economic contribution," which refers to the direct effect of tourism and is measureable by means of the Tourism Satellite Account, and tourism's "economic impact," which is a much broader concept encapsulating the direct, indirect, and induced effects of tourism and which must be estimated by applying models.

Economic hardship Extreme economic impact on individual property owner resulting from the application of a historic preservation law.

Economic impact study Research into the dollars generated by an industry and how these dollars impact the economy through direct spending and the indirect impact of additional job creation and generation of income and tax revenue. Economic impact studies aim to quantify economic benefits—that is, the net increase in the wealth of residents resulting from tourism, measured in monetary terms, over and above the levels that would prevail in its absence.

Educational tour A tour designed around an educational activity, such as studying art or learning about history.

Eligible property Property that meets the criteria for inclusion in the National Register of Historic Places but that is not formally listed.

Elite or academic culture The culture and knowledge taught officially through formal curricula and instruction, such as schools, colleges, museums, and conservatories, as opposed to folk culture or popular culture.

Eminent domain The right of government to take private property for a public purpose on payment of "just compensation."

Enabling law A law enacted by a state setting forth the legal parameters by which local governments may operate; the source of authority for enacting local preservation ordinances.

Environmental assessment or impact statement Document prepared by a state or federal agency to establish compliance with obligations under federal or state environmental protection laws to consider the impact of proposed actions on the environment, including historic resources.

Environmental scan The process of monitoring important forces in the business and political environment for trends and changes that may impact a company or industry segment.

Escorted group tour A group tour that features a tour director who travels with the group throughout the trip to provide sightseeing commentary and coordinate all group movement and activities.

Estimation Concerned with inference about the numerical value of unknown population values from incomplete data, such as a samples. If a single figure is calculated for each unknown parameter, the process is called "point estimation." If an interval is calculated within which the parameter is likely, in some sense, to lie, the process is called "interval estimation."

Executive Order 11593, "Protection and Enhancement of the Cultural Environment," 3 CFR 559 (May 13, 1971) Requires federal agencies to survey properties under their jurisdiction and nominate appropriate candidates to the National Register of Historic Places. Until surveys are completed and nominations made, each agency must ensure that no resources that may be eligible for the National Register are inadvertently damaged, destroyed, or transferred. Whenever possible and economically feasible, any properties transferred are to be used "in a manner compatible with preservation objectives." The order sets forth requirements for consultation and review of any federal actions affecting properties that might be found eligible for the National Register.

Exit survey A systematic program to collect information about the perceptions, behaviors, attitudes, or characteristics of the survey participants on the completion of a particular activity.

Exploratory research A form of marketing research that is used to obtain preliminary information and clues. It is most often used when the marketing problem is ambiguous.

Familiarization tour A free or reduced-rate trip offered to travel professionals and journalists to acquaint them with what a destination, attraction, or supplier has to offer.

Federal undertaking Any activity directly or indirectly using federal funds. Also, the sale, transfer, or delegation of responsibility for federal property to a nonfederal body.

Fly-and-drive tour A package tour for independent travelers that includes air travel and a rental car and sometimes other travel components.

Folk culture The culture and knowledge passed on over time informally by word of mouth, imitation, and observance in the context of daily life. Also known as traditional culture and folklife.

Forms of tourism There are three basic forms of tourism: domestic tourism, inbound tourism, and outbound tourism. These can be combined in various ways to derive the following additional forms of tourism: internal tourism, national tourism, and international tourism.

Free independent travel A custom-designed, prepaid travel package with many individualized arrangements. Such travel is unescorted and usually has no formal itinerary.

Fulfillment Servicing consumers and trade who request information as a result of advertising or promotional programs. Service often includes an 800 number, sales staff, and distribution of materials.

Gateway or gateway city A major airport, seaport, or rail or bus center through which tourists and travelers enter from outside the region. May also be the access point to a national park, national landmark, wildlife refuge, or other major attraction.

Gross value added of tourism industries The total gross value added of all establishments belonging to tourism industries regardless of whether all their output is provided to visitors and the degree of specialization of their production process.

Group independent travel Group travel in which individuals purchase a group package in which they will travel with others along a preset itinerary.

Group leader An individual who has been given the responsibility of coordinating tour and travel arrangements for a group. The group leader may act as a liaison to a tour operator or may develop a tour independently (and sometimes serve as the tour director).

Group rate A special discounted rate charged by suppliers to groups. Also called a tour rate.

Group tour A travel package for an assembly of travelers that have a common itinerary, travel date, and means of transportation. Group tours are usually prearranged and prepaid and include transportation, lodging, dining, and attraction admissions.

Guaranteed tour A tour guaranteed to operate unless canceled before an established cutoff date (usually sixty days prior to departure).

Guide or guide service A person or company qualified to conduct tours of specific localities or attractions.

Guided tour A local sightseeing trip conducted by a guide.

Guidelines Interpretive standards or criteria that are generally advisory in form.

Heritage area A place where natural, cultural, historic, or scenic resources present a distinct location arising from patterns of human activity.

Historic building preservation plan Computerized preservation planning document. It is less comprehensive than a historic structures report but provides general information for evaluating historic properties, ranking the historic or architectural significance of a building's spaces to determine appropriate treatment, and prioritizing and pricing the work needed.

Historic context Patterns or trends in history by which a specific occurrence, property, or site is understood and its meaning and significance within history or prehistory is made clear. Historic contexts are historical patterns that can be identified through consideration of the history of the property and the history of the surrounding area. Historic context may relate to an event or series of events, pattern of development, building form, architectural style, engineering technique, landscape, artistic value, use of materials, or methods of construction or be associated with the life of an important person. Also, the setting in which a historic element, site, structure, street, or district exists.

Historic district A defined geographical area that generally includes within its boundaries a significant concentration of properties linked by architectural style, historical development, or a past event.

Historic integrity The ability of a property to convey its significance; the retention of sufficient aspects of location, design, setting, workmanship, materials, feeling, or association for a property to convey its historic significance.

Historic preservation According to the National Historic Preservation Act, includes identification, evaluation, recordation, documentation, curation, acquisition, protection, management, rehabilitation, restoration, stabilization, maintenance, research, interpretation, conservation, and education and training regarding the foregoing activities or a combination of the foregoing activities.

Historic preservation team member Preservation consultant on an architecture and engineering design team. Members review designs and prepare submission material (project descriptions, photos, and special graphics) for Section 106 compliance. Design scopes of work identify the member discipline(s) required for a specific project. Examples include historical architect, architectural conservator, architectural historian, historical landscape architect, and art conservator.

Historic property A district, site, building, structure, or object significant in American history, architecture, engineering, archaeology, or culture at the national, state, regional, county, or local level.

Historic significance Determines why, where, and when a property is important. Historic significance is the importance of a property with regard to history, architecture, engineering, or the culture of a state, community, or nation. The key to determining whether the characteristics or associations of a property are significant is to consider the property within its historic context. Properties can be significant for their association or linkage to events or persons important in the past, as representatives of manmade expression of culture (design and construction) or technology, or for their ability to yield important information about history or prehistory.

Historic structures report Comprehensive reference documents providing long-term preservation guidance for historic property. Survey work involves both documentary research and in-depth on-site inspection. Reports typically include narratives on the property's history and construction, descriptions and photographs showing its original appearance and current conditions, original paint colors, materials conservation analysis, and masonry cleaning and mortar specifications for restoration work.

Historical value In appraisal, the value that documents the history of an organization. Sometimes referred to as archival, continuing, or enduring value. Secondary historical value does not document the history of an organization but does recognize a record containing information that is useful for conducting historical research.

Hosted group tour A group tour that features a representative (the host) of the tour operator, destination, or other tour provider, who interacts with the group for only a few hours a day to provide information and arrange for transportation. The host usually does not accompany the group as it travels.

Hotel occupancy tax (accommodation tax or lodging tax) A city or county tax added to the price of a hotel room or vacation or short-term rental property. Local funds are often designated for tourism marketing conducted by convention and visitors bureaus or destination marketing organizations; some funds may be allocated to support cultural heritage tourism product development.

Hub-and-spoke itinerary A travel routing design that uses a central destination as the departure and return point for day trips to outlying destinations and attractions.

Icon A facility or landmark that is visually synonymous with a destination.

Inbound operator A receptive operator that usually serves groups arriving from another country.

Incentive tour A trip offered as a prize, particularly to stimulate the productivity of employees or sales agents.

Inclusive tour A tour program that includes a variety of products and services for a single rate (airfare, accommodations, sightseeing, performances, and meals).

Independent tour A travel package in which a tour operator is involved only with the planning, marketing, and selling of the package but is not involved with the passengers while the tour is in progress. *See also* Free independent travel.

Indigenous communities Tribal peoples in independent countries whose social, cultural, and economic conditions distinguish them from other sections of the national community and whose status is regulated wholly or partially by their own customs or traditions or by special laws or regulations.

Indigenous peoples Usually considered to include cultural groups and their descendants who have a historical continuity or association with a given region or parts of a region and who currently inhabit or have formerly inhabited the region either before its subsequent colonization or annexation or alongside other cultural groups during the formation of a nation-state or independently or largely isolated from the influence of the claimed governance by a nation-state and who furthermore have maintained, at least in part, their distinct, linguistic, cultural, and social and organizational characteristics and in doing so remain differentiated in some degree from the surrounding populations and dominant culture of the nation-state. Also, people who are self-identified as indigenous and those recognized as such by other groups.

Intensive survey A systematic, detailed examination of an area designed to gather information about historic properties sufficient to evaluate them against predetermined criteria of significance within specific historic contexts.

Internal tourism Internal tourism comprises domestic tourism and (international) inbound tourism or the activities of resident and nonresident visitors within the country of reference as part of domestic or international tourism trips.

International visitor An international traveler qualifies as an international visitor with respect to the country of reference if (1) he or she is on a tourism trip and (2) he or she is a nonresident traveling in the country of reference or a resident traveling outside of it.

Interpretation Revealing the significance and meanings of natural, historic, and cultural phenomena to visitors, usually with the intent of providing a satisfying learning experience and encouraging more sustainable behavior.

Inventory A list of historic properties determined to meet specified criteria of significance.

Itinerary A list of a tour's schedule and major travel elements.

Keeper of the National Register An individual in the National Park Service responsible for the listing in and determination of eligibility of properties for inclusion in the National Register of Historic Places.

Key performance indicator (key success indicator) Quantifiable measurements, agreed to beforehand, that reflect the critical success factors of an organization. Such indicators reflect organizational goals.

Land trust A nonprofit organization engaged in the voluntary protection of land for the purpose of providing long-term stewardship of important resources, whether historical, archaeological, or environmental, through the acquisition of full or partial interests in property.

Land use A general term used to describe how land is or may be utilized or developed, whether for industrial, commercial, residential, or agricultural purposes or as open space.

Landmark A site or structure designated pursuant to a local preservation ordinance or other law that is worthy of preservation because of its particular historic, architectural, archaeological, or cultural significance.

Lien A claim or charge on property for payment of debt, obligation, or duty.

Limits of acceptable change Environmental indicators that can monitor changes over time as a consequence of tourism.

Living culture The activities or by-products of a particular group of people. It is to be distinguished from inert cultural artifacts, perhaps from a nondead tradition except as these artifacts are given new life by the descendants of the original practitioners. Living culture is also to be distinguished from the cultural forms learned from members of a community and staged by students or professional performers.

Locator map A map of an area or a city, showing locations of attractions and hotels.

Lodging Any establishment that provides shelter and overnight accommodations to travelers.

Management company A firm that owns several lodging properties.

Market All existing and potential customers for a product or service.

Market demand The amount of a specific product or service that may be purchased during a certain period of time in a particular geographic area.

Market forecast The realistic demand within a given time period for the products produced by all companies within a certain industry or product category.

Market segmentation The process of dividing a broad market into smaller, specific markets based on customer characteristics, buying power, and other variables.

Market share The measure of company sales versus total sales for a specific product category or industry.

Marketing mix The four P's of marketing traditionally focus on product, price, promotion, place (distribution).

Marketing plan A written report that details marketing objectives for a product or service and recommends strategies for achieving these objectives.

Marketing research The function that links the consumer, customer, and public to the marketer through the systematic gathering and analyzing of information.

Measurement Limiting the data of any phenomenon—substantial or insubstantial—so that those data may be interpreted and, ultimately, compared to a particular qualitative or quantitative standard.

Measurement error An error in reading, calculating, or recording numerical value.

Media Communications channels such as broadcast (radio and TV), print (newspapers, magazines, and direct mail), outdoor (billboards), and digital (Internet).

Meetings/conference tour A tour designed around a specific meeting or conference for the participants.

Meetings industry If a trip's main purpose is business or professional, it can be further subdivided into "attending meetings, conferences or congresses, trade fairs, and exhibitions" and "other business and professional purposes." The term "meetings industry" is preferred by the International Congress and Convention Association, Meeting Professionals International, and Reed Travel over the acronym MICE (Meetings, Incentives, Conferences, and Exhibitions) which does not recognize the industrial nature of such activities.

Memorandum of agreement Document executed by consulting parties pursuant to the Section 106 review process that sets forth terms for mitigating or eliminating adverse effects on historic properties resulting from agency action.

Metric Describes a quality and requires a measurement baseline.

Mission (sales) A promotional and sales trip coordinated by a state travel office, convention and visitors bureau, or key industry member to increase product awareness and sales and to enhance image. Target audiences may include tour operators, wholesalers, incentive travel planners, travel agents, meeting planners, convention and trade show managers, and media. Missions often cover several international or domestic destinations and include private- and public-sector participants. Mission components can include receptions, entertainment representatives of the destination, presentations, and prescheduled sales and media calls.

Mission statement The concise description of what an organization is, its purpose, and what it intends to accomplish.

Motorcoach A large, comfortable bus that can transport travelers and their luggage long distances.

Motorcoach tour A tour that features the motorcoach as the form of transportation to and from destinations.

Motorcoach tour operators Tour operators that own their own motorcoaches.

Multiday tour A travel package of two or more days. Most multiday tours are escorted, all-inclusive packages.

Mystery tour A journey to unpublicized destinations in which tour participants aren't told where they will be going until en route or on arrival.

National Environmental Policy Act The primary federal law requiring consideration of potential impacts of major federal actions on the environment, including historic and cultural resources.

National Historic Landmark Property included in the National Register of Historic Places that has been judged by the secretary of the interior to have "national significance in American history, archaeology, architecture, engineering, and culture."

National Historic Preservation Act of 1966, as amended, 80 Stat. 915, 16 U.S.C., 470 et seq. Enacted to protect federal historic/cultural property and promote the preservation of state-controlled and privately owned historic properties. The most important law governing the policies of federal agencies toward historic preservation. Section 101(a) authorizes the secretary of the interior to expand and maintain a National Register of Historic Places for cultural resources. Section 106 outlines specific actions required of federal agencies to protect cultural resources. An environmental impact assessment and environmental impact statement must consider the effects of a proposed federal undertaking on the resources. The act establishes the Advisory Council on Historic Preservation to comment on federal actions having an effect on cultural resources. Supplemented by Executive Order 11593 in 1971.

National Register Criteria The established criteria for evaluating the eligibility of properties for inclusion in the National Register of Historic Places.

National Register of Historic Places The official federal listing of projects properties. Includes structures of historic or architectural significance, archaeological sites, and sites of research value for the study of American cultural resources.

National tourism Comprises domestic tourism and outbound tourism, or the activities of resident visitors within and outside the country of reference, respectively, as part of either domestic or outbound tourism trips.

National tourism organization A federal government-level destination marketing organization that promotes the country as a travel destination.

Native American Graves and Protection and Repatriation Act A federal law providing for the repatriation of Native American human skeletal material and related sacred items and objects of cultural patrimony.

Natural heritage Natural features consisting of physical and biological formations of groups of such formations that are of outstanding universal value from the aesthetic or scientific point of view; geological and physiographical information and precisely delineated areas that constitute the habitat of threatened species of animals and plants of outstanding universal value from the point of view of science or conservation; natural sites or precisely delineated natural areas of outstanding universal value from the point of view of science, conservation, or natural beauty.

Net promoter score A customer loyalty metric based on the question, "On a scale of 0 to 10, how likely is it that you would recommend (our company, product, service, or destination) to a friend or colleague?" People who respond with a 9 or 10 are designated as "promoters" and those with a 7 or 8 as "detractors." The percentage of customers who are detractors is then subtracted from the percentage who are promoters to arrive at the company's or destination's score. Passives are ignored.

Net wholesale rate A rate, usually slightly lower than the wholesale rate, applicable to groups of individuals when a hotel is specifically mentioned in a tour brochure. Wholesale sellers of tours mark up the rate to cover distribution and promotion costs.

Niche market A highly specialized segment of the travel market, such as an affinity group with a unique special interest.

Occupancy The percentage of available rooms occupied for a given period. It is computed by dividing the number of rooms occupied for a period by the number of rooms available for the same period.

Off peak Slow booking periods for suppliers. Also called the low season.

On-site guide A tour guide who conducts tours of one or several hours' duration at a specific building, attraction, or site.

Open-ended question A question that allows the respondent to provide a free-response answer.

Open-jaw itinerary A travel routing design that departs from one location and returns to another. For example, travelers may fly into one city and depart from another.

Outcome Something that follows as a result (of an action) or consequence.

Output The goods and services produced by an establishment, (1) excluding the value of any goods and services used in an activity for which the establishment does not assume the risk of using the products in production and (2) excluding the value of goods and services consumed by the same establishment except for goods and services used for capital formation (fixed capital or changes in inventories) or own final consumption.

Pacing The scheduling of activities within an itinerary to make for a realistic operation and give a certain balance of travel time, sightseeing, events, and free time.

Packaged travel A package in combination of two or more types of tour components into a product that is produced, assembled, promoted, and sold as a package by a tour operator for an all-inclusive price.

Paid social media Refers to the use of social media for ad placement. The most common types of paid social media are native advertisements, such as Facebook ads, Twitter-promoted tweets, LinkedIn-sponsored updates, and YouTube-sponsored videos. Other forms of paid social media include traditional display ads on social networks and Twitter-promoted accounts.

Patronage program A program that rewards the customer for loyalty and repeat purchase, such as frequent-stay programs at hotels.

Placekeeping active care and maintenance of a place and its social fabric by the people who live and work there.

Placemaking multifaceted, community-based appoarch to redesigning and reinventing public space to maximize shared value and represent the physical, cultural, and social identities that define a place.

Peak season A destination's high season, when demand is strong.

Per capita costs Per-person costs.

Perceived value The ratio of perceived benefits to perceived price.

Pilot survey Tests the questionnaire (pertinence of the questions, understanding of the questions by those being interviewed, and duration of the interviews) and checks various potential sources for sampling and nonsampling errors (such as the place in which the surveys are carried out and method used, the identification of any omitted answers and the reason for the omission, problems of communicating in various languages, translation, the mechanics of data collection, and the organization of fieldwork).

Podcast A type of audio file available through the Internet, typically produced as a series that listeners subscribe to.

Popular culture Culture and knowledge passed on through mass media, such as the Internet, newspapers, radio, and television.

Positioning strategy The development of a clear, unique, and attractive impact for a company and/or product in the minds of target customers.

Pre- and posttrip tour An optional extension or side trip package before and/or after a meeting, gathering, or convention.

Preservation The act or process of applying measures necessary to sustain the existing form, integrity, and materials of a historic property. Work, including preliminary measures to protect and stabilize the property, generally focuses on the ongoing maintenance and repair of historic materials and features rather than extensive replacement and new construction. New exterior additions are not within the scope of this treatment; however, the limited and sensitive upgrading of mechanical, electrical, and plumbing systems and other code-required work to make properties functional is appropriate within a preservation project.

Preservation notebook A technical circular series initiated by the Historic Preservation Program of the U.S. General Services Administration/National Capital Region to promote innovation and quality in federal preservation projects. "Notebook" issues circulate prototype solutions and answer commonly asked questions relating to preservation project design, contracting, construction, and historic buildings management.

Press/publicity release A news article or feature story written by the subject of the story for delivery and potential placement in the media.

Press trips (media research trips or media familiarization tours) Organized trips for travel writers and broadcasters for the purpose of assisting them in developing stories about tourism destinations. Often, journalists travel independently though with the assistance of a state's office of tourism of a destination marketing organization.

Primary research The collection of data specifically to solve the marketing problem at hand.

Probability sample A sample selected by a method based on the theory of probability (random process) by a method involving knowledge of the likelihood of any unit being selected.

Promotion mix Promotion tools, including advertising, direct marketing, sales promotion, digital marketing, and public relations.

Promotional group tour A travel package composed of tour elements that match the specific needs and wants of niche customers who aren't part of an organized or preformed group.

Promotional partnership The combination of two or more companies to offer special incentives to customers.

Protected area Any area of land and/or sea dedicated to the conservation, protection, and maintenance of biodiversity and natural and cultural resources that is managed through legal or other means.

Provenance The office or agency of origin that created records that were created and received in the course of business.

Psychographics Measures of a person's lifestyle. *See also* AIO variables.

Public relations A management function that determines the attitudes and opinions of an organization's publics, identifies its policies with the interests of its publics, and formulates and executes a program of action to earn public understanding and goodwill.

Pull strategy A marketing approach that creates demand at the distributor level by providing resellers with an incentive to push (sell) a product to consumers.

Purpose of a trip (main) The purpose in the absence of which the trip would not have taken place. Classification of tourism trips according to the main purpose refers to nine categories: this typology allows the identification of different subsets of visitors (such as business visitors and transit visitors).

Qualitative research Involves looking at characteristics, or qualities, that cannot easily be reduced to numerical values.

Quantitative research Involves looking at amounts, or quantities, of one or more variable of interest.

Questionnaire A group or sequence of questions designed to elicit information on a subject or a sequence of subjects from a reporting unit or from another producer of official statistics.

Questionnaire design The design (text, order, and conditions for skipping) of the questions used to obtain the data needed for the survey.

Quota sample A research sample that involves forming groups based on certain characteristics. A random sample can then be selected from the quota segments.

Rack rate The published (brochure) rate for a travel component.

Reach The measure of how many people in a market will be exposed to a certain advertisement via a specific medium.

Receptive operator A local tour company that specializes in services for incoming visitors, often for tour operator groups.

Reconnaissance survey An examination of all or part of an area accomplished in sufficient detail to make generalizations about the types and distributions of historic properties that may be present.

Reconstruction The act or process of depicting, by means of new construction, the form, features, and detailing of a nonsurviving site, landscape, building, structure, or object for the purpose of replicating its appearance at a specific period of time and in its historic location.

Records management The application of management techniques to the creation, utilization, maintenance, retention, preservation, and disposition of records, undertaken to reduce costs and improve efficiency in record keeping. Includes management of filing and microfilming equipment and supplied; filing and information retrieval systems; files, correspondence, reports, and forms management; historical documentation; micrographics; systems applications; retention scheduling; and vital records protection.

Regional historic preservation officer An individual within Public Buildings Service responsible for compliance with federal preservation laws and regulations. Prime liaison to the Advisory Council on Historic Preservation and the State Historic Preservation Office.

Regulations Rules promulgated by an administrative agency that interpret and implement statutory requirements.

Rehabilitation The act or process of making possible a compatible use for a property through repair, alterations, and additions while preserving those portions or features that convey its historical, cultural, or architectural values.

Rehabilitation tax credit A 20 percent federal income tax credit on expenses for the substantial rehabilitation of historic properties.

Relationship marketing The process of building and nurturing ongoing, solid relationships with customers.

Research constraints Those issues, such as cost and timing, that will limit the scope of marketing research.

Research design A statement of proposed identification, documentation, investigation, or other treatment of a historic property that identifies the project's goals, methods and techniques, expected results, and the relationship of the expected results to other proposed activities or treatments.

Restoration The act or process of accurately depicting the form, features, and character of a property as it appeared at a particular period of time by means of the removal of features from other periods in its history and the reconstruction of missing features from the restoration period. The limited and sensitive upgrading of mechanical, electrical, and plumbing systems and other code-required work to make properties functional is appropriate within a restoration project.

Revolving fund A fund established by a public or nonprofit organization to purchase land or buildings or to make grants or loans to facilitate the preservation of historic resources.

Rightsizing Redevelopment of the community in response to prolonged job and population loss, housing vacancy, and abadonment of infrastructure.

Room rates The various rates used by lodging properties to price rooms. These include day rate (usually half the regular rate for a room used by a guest during the day up to 5:00 p.m.—sometimes called a use rate), flat rate (a specific room rate for a group agreed on by the hotel and group in advance), group rate (same as flat rate), net group rate (a wholesale rate for a group business to which an operator may add a markup if desired), net wholesale rate (a rate usually lower than the group rate and applicable to groups or individuals when a hotel is specifically mentioned in a tour brochure), and published rate (a full rate available to or advertised to the public—also called the rack rate).

Sales margin A term used by resellers to describe profit as a percentage of sales revenue.

Sales mission Where suppliers from one destination marketing organization travel together to another state or country for the purpose of collectively promoting travel to their area. Sales missions may include educational seminars for travel agents and tour operators.

Sales seminar An educational session in which travel agents, tour operators, tour wholesalers, or other members of the travel trade congregate to receive briefings about tourism destinations.

Same-day visitor (or excursionist) A visitor (domestic, inbound, or outbound) is classified as a tourist (or overnight visitor) if his or her trip includes an overnight stay. Otherwise, the visitor is classified as a same-day visitor (or excursionist).

Sample The portion of a population chosen to represent the population being studied for research.

Sample (historic properties) survey A survey of a representative sample of lands within a given area in order to generate or test predictions about the types and distributions of historic properties in the entire area.

Sample (market) survey A market research survey carried out using a sampling method.

Scheduled tour A tour that is set in a tour operator's regular schedule of tour departures and that is often sold to the general public. Also called a retail tour.

Search engine optimization The practice of increasing the "organic" visibility of a Web page in a search engine, such as Google. It refers to "free" tactics that enhance the search ranking of a page.

Secondary information Research data that were collected by another company or person and usually for a purpose that's different than the research objectives and tasks at hand.

Section 4(f) A provision in Department of Transportation Act that prohibits federal approval or funding of transportation projects that require "use" of any historic site unless (1) there is "no feasible and prudent alternative to the project" and (2) the project includes "all possible planning to minimize harm."

Section 106 A provision in National Historic Preservation Act that requires federal agencies to consider the effects of proposed undertakings on properties listed or eligible for listing in the National Register of Historic Places.

Shoulder season Those periods between the peak season and the off-season when destination demand is moderate.

Sightseeing tour Short excursions of usually a few hours that focus on sightseeing and/or attraction visits.

Simple random sample A sample that draws a group of respondents randomly from all members of the population.

Site plan A proposed plan for development submitted by the property owner for review by a planning board or other governmental entity that addresses issues such as the siting of structures, landscaping, pedestrian and vehicular access, lighting, signage, and other features.

Social media marketing The use of social media by marketers to increase brand awareness, identify key audiences, generate leads, and build meaningful relationships with customers.

Souvenir A product purchased by a tourist as a reminder of a holiday.

Spacial justice Strategic intentional process to organize human societies and influence social relations through geographically equitable distribution of resources, services, and access.

Special event tour A travel package that features major happenings, such as concerts or cultural events, as the reason for the journey.

Special permit A device allowing individual review and approval of a proposed development.

Split itinerary An itinerary in which part of the group does one thing while the other part does something else.

State historic preservation officer Under Section 106 of the National Historic Preservation Act, this person reviews all federal undertakings that may affect historic structures, sites, or archaeological artifacts. "Undertakings" range from building repair, alteration, and renovation projects to new construction, road building, or any other work that may directly or indirectly disturb cultural resources. Under Executive Order 11593, this person oversees federal agency compliance with the requirement to identify and protect historic resources by submitting nominations to the National Register of Historic Places and preparing preservation plans. Washington, D.C., functions as a state.

Step-on guide A tour guide who boards a motorcoach to give detailed, expert commentary about the city or area being visited.

Strategic plan A report that describes a company's, an organization's, or a destination's vision, mission statement, goals, objectives, and strategic actions.

Streetscape The distinguishing character of a particular street as created by its width, degree of curvature, paving materials, design of the street furniture, and forms of surrounding buildings.

Supplier The actual producer and seller of travel components.

Survey An investigation about the characteristics of a given population by means of collecting data from a sample of that population and estimating their characteristics through the systematic use of statistical methodology.

Sustainability The use of resources, in an environmentally responsible, socially fair, and economically viable manner, so that by meeting current usage needs, the possible use by future generations is not compromised.

Sustainable tourism Tourism envisaged as leading to the management of all resources in such a way that economic, social, and aesthetic needs can be filled while maintaining cultural integrity, essential ecological practices, biological diversity, and life support systems.

SWOT analysis A summary of a company's, an organization's, or a destination's strengths and weaknesses and the environmental opportunities and threats that will most influence it.

System of National Accounts An internationally agreed-on standard set of recommendations on how to compile measures of economic activity in accordance with strict accounting conventions based on economic principles. The recommendations are expressed in terms of a set of concepts, definitions, classifications, and accounting rules that make up the internationally agreed-on standard for measuring indicators of economic performance. The accounting framework for the system allows economic data to be compiled and presented in a format that is designed for purposes of economic analysis, decision making, and policymaking.

"Taking" of property The act of confiscating private property for governmental use through "eminent domain" or by regulatory action.

Target market The group of customers who will be the focus of a company's, an organization's, or a destination's marketing efforts.

Tariff (1) A fare or rate from a supplier; (2) a class or type of fair or rate; (3) a published list of fares or rates from a supplier; (4) an official publication compiling rates or fares and conditions of service.

Tax abatement A reduction, decrease, or diminution of taxes owed, often for a fixed period of time.

Tax assessment The formal determination of property value subject to tax.

Tax credit A dollar-for-dollar reduction on taxes owed.

Tax deduction A subtraction from income (rather than taxes) that lowers the amount on which taxes must be paid.

Tax exemption Immunity from an obligation to pay taxes, in whole or in part.

Tax freeze A "freezing" of the assessed value of property for a period of time.

Technical visit A tour designed for a special interest group, usually to visit a place of business with a common interest. The tour usually includes part business and part leisure and is customized for the group.

Theme tour A tour designed around a concept of specific interest to the tour participants, such as history or culture.

Tiered pricing When suppliers offer different prices to receptive operators, tour operators, and group leaders so that each party can earn a profit by marking up the supplier's price while still offering a fair price to customers.

Tour A prearranged, prepaid journey to one or more destinations that generally returns to the point of origin, is usually arranged with an itinerary of leisure activities, and includes at least two travel elements.

Tour guide A person qualified (and often certified) to conduct tours of specific locations or attractions. *See also* Docent, On-site guide, Step-on guide.

Tour manual A compendium of facts about a destination, tour procedures, forms, and other information that a tour operator gives to its tour directors.

Tour operator A person or company that contracts with suppliers to create and/or market a tour and/or subcontract their performance.

Tour order A voucher given to the purchaser of a tour package that identifies the tour, the seller, and the fact that the tour is prepaid. The purchaser then uses this form as proof of payment and receives vouchers for meals, porterage, transfers, entrance fees, and other expenses. *See also* Voucher.

Tour planner A person who researches destinations and suppliers, negotiates contracts, and creates itineraries for travel packages.

Tour series Multiple departures to the same destination throughout the year.

Tourism The business of providing marketing services and facilities for leisure travelers.

Tourism expenditure The amount paid for the acquisition of consumption goods and services, as well as valuables, for own use or to give away, for and during tourism trips. It includes expenditures by visitors themselves as well as expenses that are paid for and reimbursed by others.

Tourism industries Comprised of all establishments for which the principal activity is a tourism characteristic activity. Tourism industries (also referred to tourism activities) are the activities that typically product tourism characteristic products. The term "tourism industries" is synonymous with "tourism characteristic activities."

Tourism infrastructure Roads, railway lines, harbors, airport runways, water, electricity, other power supplies, sewage disposal systems, and other utilities to serve not only the local residents but also the tourist influx (suitable accommodation, restaurants, and passenger transport terminals form the superstructure of the region).

Tourism Satellite Account The Tourism Satellite Account is the second international standard on tourism statistics (Tourism Satellite Account: Recommended Methodological Framework 2008—TSA: RMF 2008) that has been developed in order to present economic data relative to tourism within a framework of internal and external consistency with the rest of the statistical system through its link to the System of National Accounts. It is the basic reconciliation framework of tourism statistics. As a statistical tool for the economic accounting of tourism, the Tourism Satellite Account can be seen as a set of ten summary tables, each with its underlying data and representing a different aspect of the economic data relative to tourism: inbound domestic tourism and outbound tourism expenditure, international tourism expenditure, production accounts of tourism industries, the gross value added and gross domestic product attributable to tourism demand, employment, investment, government consumption, and nonmonetary indicators.

Tracking survey A survey of customers before and after implementing a promotional campaign to assess changes in consumer behavior.

Transferable development right A technique allowing landowners to transfer the right to develop a specific parcel of land to another parcel.

Travel party Defined as visitors traveling together on a trip and whose expenditures are pooled.

Trip Refers to the travel by a person from the time of departure from his or her usual residence until he or she returns (round-trip). Trips taken by visitors are tourism trips.

Undertaking Federal agency actions requiring review under Section 106 of the National Historic Preservation Act.

User-generated content Media that have been created and published online by the users of a social or collaboration platform, typically for noncommercial purposes. User-generated content is one of the defining characteristics of social media.

Value The relationship between the benefits associated with a product or service and the costs of obtaining the product or service.

Value-based pricing Pricing a product based on buyer perceptions of value rather than actual product costs.

Variable costs Costs that change with sales or production levels.

Vernacular A regional form or adaptation of an architectural style.

Visit A trip is made up of visits to different places. The term "tourism visit" refers to a stay in a place visited during a tourism trip.

Visitor A visitor is a *traveler* taking a trip to a main destination outside his or her usual environment, for less than a year, for any main purpose (business, leisure, or other personal purpose) other than to be employed by a resident entity in the country or place visited. A visitor (domestic, inbound or outbound) is classified as a *tourist* (or overnight visitor) if his or her trip includes an overnight stay or as a same-day visitor (or excursionist) otherwise.

Voucher Documents that are exchanged for goods and services to substantiate payment that will be or already has been made.

Wholesale The sale of travel products through an intermediary in exchange for a commission or fee generally at reduced tariffs.

Word-of-mouth promotion Personal communication about a product or service from one customer to another.

World Heritage Area Land of cultural and/or natural significance inscribed on the World Heritage List.

World Heritage Site A site designated by UNESCO as being of special historical, cultural, or natural importance.

Yield management Calculating and analyzing the profits earned per customer.

Zoning The act of regulating the use of land and structures according to district. Laws generally specify allowable use for land, such as residential or commercial, and restrictions on development, such as minimum lot sizes, setback requirements, maximum height and bulk, and so on.

Note

1. Several sources were used to compile this glossary: UN World Tourism Organization (http://statistics. unwto.org/sites/all/files/docpdf/glossaryen.pdf); Global Sustainable Tourism Council, Global Development Research Center (http://www.gdrc.org/uem/eco-tour/t-glossary.html); National Park Service (https://www.nps.gov/history/local-law/arch_stnds_10.htm); General Services Association (www. gsa.gov/.../Preservation_Note_27_R2RI5I_0Z5RDZ-i34K-pR.doc); National Trust for Historic Preservation (http://www.preservationnation.org/information-center/law-and-policy/legal-resources/preservation-law-101/glossary-of-preservation-law-terms.html), Massachusetts Cultural Council, Texas Arts Council (http://www.arts.texas.gov/wp-content/uploads/2012/05/Cultural-Tourism-Glossary-of-Terms.pdf), HootSuite.com, and Paul D. Leedy and Jeanne Ellis Ormrod, *Practical Research: Planning and Design*, 9th ed. (Edinburgh: Pearson Education, 2010), pp. 21, 88, 94.

Acronyms and Abbreviations

AAA: Asian American Alliance or Automobile Association of America
AAM: American Alliance of Museums
AASLH: American Association for State and Local History
ABA: American Bus Association
ACE: Association of Cultural Executives
ACHP: Advisory Council on Historic Preservation
ADR: Average Daily Rate (for hotel room)
A/E: Architect/Engineering firm
AFM: American Federation of Musicians
AIANTA: American Indian Alaska Native Tourism Association
AIC: American Institute for Conservation of Historic and Artistic Works
AmJSA: American Journal of Science and Arts
APTI: Association for Preservation Technology International
BLM: Bureau of Land Management, U.S. Department of Interior
COA: Certificate of Appropriateness
CRS: Computerized Reservation System
CTC: Certified Travel Counselor
CTIS: Certified Travel Industry Specialist
CTP: Certified Tour Professional
CVB: Convention and Visitors Bureau
DCA: Department of Cultural Affairs
DMAI: Destination Marketing Association International
DMC: Destination Management Company
DMO: Destination Marketing Organization
F.I.T.: Free Independent Travel (usually international visitor)
G.I.T.: Group Independent Travel
GSTC: Global Sustainable Tourism Council
HBPP: Historic Building Preservation Plan
HOT: Hotel Occupancy Tax, a.k.a. Accommodation Tax, Lodging Tax
HSR: Historic Structures Report

KPI: Key Performance Indicator, a.k.a. Key Success Indicators
ICC: International Code Council
IMLS: Institute of Museum and Library Services
MOA: Memorandum of Agreement
MOU: Memorandum of Understanding
NASAA: National Assembly for State Arts Agencies
NATHPO: National Association of Tribal Historic Preservation Officers
NEA: National Endowment for the Arts
NEH: National Endowment for the Humanities
NEPA: National Environmental Policy Act
NGO: Nongovernmental Organization
NHA: National Heritage Area
NHL: National Historic Landmark
NHPA: National Historic Preservation Act of 1996
NPS: National Park Service
NPS: Net Promoter Score
NRHP: National Register of Historic Places
NTA: National Tour Association
NTHP: National Trust for Historic Preservation
NTO: National Tourism Organization
NTTO: National Travel and Tourism Office, International Trade Administration, U.S. Department
of Commerce
PA: Preservation Action
RevPAR: Revenue Per Available (Hotel) Room
RHPO: Regional Historic Preservation Officer
SATW: Society of American Travel Writers
SEO: Search Engine Optimization
SHPO: State Historic Preservation Office
SIA: Society of Architectural Historians
SMARTER: Specific, Measurable, Achievable, Relevant, Time-Bound, Evaluation, Reassess
SME(s): Small and Medium Enterprises
SWOT: Strengths, Weaknesses, Opportunities, Threats
TDR: Transferable Development Right
TSA: Tourism Satellite Account
UNESCO: United National Educational, Scientific, and Cultural Organization
VIC: Visitor Information Center
WHS: World Heritage Site
WTM: World Travel Market (London)
WTO: World Tourism Organization
WTTC: World Travel and Tourism Council

Index

Ludington, Michigan: 59, 63–64, 327, 328, 330–332
Lynch, Robert. L.: 144

Maclean, Kathy: 322
Main Street: 17, 30, 43, 46, 53, 61, 71, 94, 101, 102, 153, 165, 177, 178, 184, 221, 263, 283, 302, 312, 331
management: 2, 6, 9, 11, 14, 15, 38, 57, 111, 113, 115, 116, 125, 141, 142, 148, 169, 174, 176, 180, 193, 196, 227, 232, 253, 273–282, 311, 313, 318, 327, 329; brand, 252, 279; capacity, 112, 138; collections, 145, 182; interpretation, 194; project, 315; records, 357; regulations, 149; sustainable, 139, 150, 155–158; Tennessee Overhill Heritage Association, 335; visitor, 209; yield, 361
Mandala Research LLC: 7, 8
marketing plan: 11, 180, 229, 243, 244, 250, 252, 253, 257, 259, 260, 261
market segmentation: 246–247
McClimon, Timothy J.: Foreword
McCormick, Rosemary: 213
McKinsey & Company: 116
measurement: 9, 11, 57, 111, 175, 176, 180, 253, 309, 313–314, 317, 318, 320; Outline of a Cultural Heritage Tourism Plan, 138
media coverage: 125, 155, 311, 312
media relations: 247, 258–259, 266
Meeks, Stephanie: 37
memorandum of understanding (MOU): 81, 123, 136–137, 143
message: 28, 83, 167, 172, 177, 191, 280, 329; Global Sustainable Tourism Criteria, 157; interpretation, 193, 194, 195, 199, 200, 201; marketing, 243, 245, 247, 248, 249, 254, 255, 261; stakeholder engagement, 91, 98, 99, 100
metrics: 118, 125, 249, 252, 258, 310, 313, 317; Key Performance Indicators (KPIs), 312
Miami, Florida: 302, 319, 323–325
Michael, Vince: 141
microsite: 100
military tourism: 4, 17
millennials: 54, 55, 56, 61, 97, 198, 199, 247, 322
Minnesota Historical Society: 322
mission: 10, 17, 70, 112, 113, 119, 121, 122, 123, 170, 213, 221, 239, 270, 279, 329; Hotel de Paris Museum, 182; interpretation, 192, 193, 196; Iowa City, 204; Kansas City Public Library, 188; Mission San Juan Capistrano, 281, 286–290; Museum of African American History, 63, 65; Museum of Northern Arizona, 133–134; Outline of a Cultural Heritage Tourism Plan, 138; Rivers of Steel National Heritage Area, 126; Tenement Museum, 130–131; Tennessee Overhill Heritage

Association, 333; Virginia City, 223; Vizcaya Museum and Gardens, 324; ZORA! Festival, 101
Mission Preservation Foundation: 289
Mission San Juan Capistrano: 281, 287, 288
Mississippi Hills National Heritage Area: 196–198
Mitchell's Fine Chocolates: 218, 225
MMGY Global: 56
mobile tour: 202, 208
mobility: 34, 183, 278, 282, 293
Moore, Carole: 226
motivation: 6, 7, 36, 53, 58, 117, 191, 199, 244, 255, 246, 293, 309, 312, 315, 316, 318
Mount Vernon: 2, 204
murals: 32, 33, 100, 174; Paducah, 41, 42, 155
Museum of African American History: 56, 57, 61–63
Museum of Northern Arizona, The: 123, 133, 134
museums: 8, 17, 21, 23, 30, 32, 37, 38, 52, 53, 59, 60, 70, 92, 93, 112, 122, 129, 145, 165, 166, 167, 168, 169, 170, 171, 176, 178, 182, 191, 195, 204, 215, 219, 221, 265, 268, 298, 322, 334
music tourism: 4, 17–18, 165, 276

Nantucket Historical Association, The: 121
Napa Valley Tourism Improvement District: 221
National Association for Interpretation: 192, 193, 194
National Endowment for the Arts: 2, 20, 130, 135, 170, 187, 334
National Endowment for the Humanities: 130, 195
National Heritage Areas: 2, 53, 129, 170
National Historic Landmark: 64, 117, 122, 127, 129, 131, 169, 223, 323, 331
National Historic Preservation Act: 142
National Historic Trails: 178
National Main Street Center: 30
National Oceanic and Atmospheric Administration: 169
National Park Service: 34, 35, 63, 126, 132, 170, 192, 219, 296, 331, 337
National Recreation Trail: 71
National Register of Historic Places: 30, 53, 131, 146, 153, 169, 180, 186, 208, 289, 301, 305, 331, 332, 335
National Scenic Byways: 2, 71
National Society of the Colonial Dames of America: 180
National Tour Association: 257, 260
National Tourism Week: 319
National Travel and Tourism Office: 98
National Trust for Historic Preservation: 2, 3, 9, 13, 36, 37, 62, 63, 117, 132, 182, 215, 239, 281

Native American: 41, 60, 61, 133, 196, 197, 263, 296
Native Stone Scenic Byway: 72, 78–79

About the Author

Cheryl M. Hargrove, the National Trust for Historic Preservation's first director of heritage tourism, has consulted in all fifty states and more than ten countries to help destinations and organizations plan for, develop, and market authentic experiences for visitors and residents alike. Frequently tapped to speak at conferences and workshops, Hargrove draws on more than twenty-five years of experience in the industry. She holds a bachelor's degree from the University of Georgia, a master's degree in tourism administration from The George Washington University, and is an associate member of the Society of American Travel Writers.